The Rorschach: A Comprehensive System, in two volumes
by John E. Exner, Jr.
Theory and Practice in Behavior Therapy
by Aubrey J. Yates
Principles of Psychotherapy
by Irving B. Weiner
Psychoactive Drugs and Social Judgment: The(
edited by Kenneth Hammond and C. R. B. J(
Clinical Methods in Psychology
edited by Irving B. Weiner
Human Resources for Troubled Children
by Werner I. Halpern and Stanley Kissel
Hyperactivity
by Dorothea M. Ross and Sheila A. Ross
Heroin Addiction: Theory, Research and Treatment
by Jerome J. Platt and Christina Labate
Children's Rights and the Mental Health Profession
edited by Gerald P. Koocher
The Role of the Father in Child Development
edited by Michael E. Lamb
Handbook of Behavioral Assessment
edited by Anthony R. Ciminero, Karen S. Calhoun, and Henry E. Adams
Counseling and Psychotherapy: A Behavioral Approach
by E. Lakin Phillips
Dimensions of Personality
edited by Harvey London and John E. Exner, Jr.
The Mental Health Industry: A Cultural Phenomenon
by Peter A. Magaro, Robert Gripp, David McDowell, and Ivan W. Miller III
Nonverbal Communication: The State of the Art
by Robert G. Harper, Arthur N. Wiens, and Joseph D. Matarazzo
Alcoholism and Treatment
by David J. Armor, J. Michael Polich, and Harriet B. Stambul
A Biodevelopmental Approach to Clinical Child Psychology: Cognitive Controls and Cognitive Control Theory
by Sebastiano Santostefano
Handbook of Infant Development
edited by Joy D. Osofsky
Understanding the Rape Victim: A Synthesis of Research Findings
by Sedelle Katz and Mary Ann Mazur
Childhood Pathology and Later Adjustment: The Question of Prediction
by Loretta K. Cass and Carolyn B. Thomas
Intelligent Testing with the WISC-R
by Alan S. Kaufman
Adaptation in Schizophrenia: The Theory of Segmental Set
by David Shakow
Psychotherapy: An Eclectic Approach
by Sol L. Garfield
Handbook of Minimal Brain Dysfunctions
edited by Herbert E. Rie and Ellen D. Rie
Handbook of Behavioral Interventions: A Clinical Guide
edited by Alan Goldstein and Edna B. Foa
Art Psychotherapy
by Harriet Wadeson
Handbook of Adolescent Psychology
edited by Joseph Adelson
Psychotherapy Supervision: Theory, Research and Practice
edited by Allen K. Hess

Continued on back

DIAGNOSTIC UNDERSTANDING AND TREATMENT PLANNING

Diagnostic Understanding and Treatment Planning

The Elusive Connection

Edited by

Fred Shectman and William H. Smith
The Menninger Foundation
Topeka, Kansas

A WILEY-INTERSCIENCE PUBLICATION

JOHN WILEY & SONS

New York • Chichester • Brisbane • Toronto • Singapore

Library of Congress Cataloging in Publication Data:

Diagnostic understanding and treatment planning.

(Wiley series on personality processes)
"A Wiley-Interscience publication."
Includes index.
1. Psychology, Pathological—Diagnosis. 2. Psychodiagnostics. 3. Psychotherapy. I. Shectman, Fred,
1940–   . II. Smith, William H. (William Hugh),
1940–   . III. Menninger Foundation. IV. Series.
[DNLM: 1. Mental disorders—Diagnosis—Collected
works. 2. Mental disorders—Therapy—Collected works.
WM 141 D53665]

RC469.D5 1984   616.89′075   83-14583
ISBN 0-471-88779-X

Printed in the United States of America

10 9 8 7 6 5 4 3 2 1

To the Teachers, Students, and Patients Who Have Taught Us
and
To Our Families Who Have Sustained Us

Contributors

Jon G. Allen, Ph.D., Staff Psychologist, C. F. Menninger Memorial Hospital, The Menninger Foundation

Ann Appelbaum, M.D., Associate Clinical Professor of Psychiatry, Cornell Medical Center

Stephen A. Appelbaum, Ph.D., Professor, University of Missouri, Kansas City

George I. Athey, Ph.D., Staff Psychologist, C. F. Menninger Memorial Hospital, The Menninger Foundation

Mary S. Cerney, Ph.D., Staff Psychologist, C. F. Menninger Memorial Hospital, The Menninger Foundation

Doris Jane Chediak, M.S.W., Private Practice of Social Work, Oklahoma City, Oklahoma

Jorge de la Torre, M.D., Associate Professor of Psychiatry, Baylor College of Medicine

Philip S. Holzman, Ph.D., Professor of Psychology, Faculty of Arts and Sciences and Faculty of Medicine, Harvard University

Leonard Horwitz, Ph.D., Chief of Clinical Psychology, The Menninger Foundation

Martin Mayman, Ph.D., Professor of Psychology, University of Michigan

Karl A. Menninger, M.D., Chairman, Board of Trustees, The Menninger Foundation

Rowe L. Mortimer, Ph.D., Clinical Associate Professor, Oregon Graduate School of Professional Psychology

Paul W. Pruyser, Ph.D., Henry March Pfeifer Professor of Research and Education, The Menninger Foundation

Herbert J. Schlesinger, Ph.D., Professor of Psychiatry, University of Colorado School of Medicine

Fred Shectman, Ph.D., Director of Psychology, Adult Outpatient Department, The Menninger Foundation

Howard Shevrin, Ph.D., Professor of Psychology, Departments of Psychiatry and Psychology, University of Michigan

Sydney Smith, Ph.D., Dean for Academic and Professional Affairs, California School of Professional Psychology, San Diego

William H. Smith, Ph.D., Director of Postdoctoral Training in Clinical Psychology, The Menninger Foundation

Foreword

Interest in diagnosis among psychiatrists and psychologists has waxed and waned over the years with reasons having little to do with the possible utility of diagnosis for treatment. Psychiatry has only recently acquired a few specific treatments. For that matter, the very idea that diagnosis should have relevance for treatment in general is relatively new. Only recently have specific treatments become available to medicine. Until that time, and to a considerable extent today, diagnosing was largely in the service of taxonomy and at best served as a guide to expectation.

Kraepelin's description of dementia praecox and Bleuler's description of the schizophrenias give little assistance to treatment planning, nor were they intended to. On the other hand, Freud's distinctions between psychoneuroses and actual neuroses and between transference neuroses and narcissistic neuroses were made with implications in mind for treatment. But for the longest time the striving for diagnostic precision in medicine and psychiatry stemmed from one's scientific conscience rather than any practical interest.

The Menninger Clinic came into existence during the period of therapeutic nihilism when medicine had little to offer patients other than diagnosis and when the best treatment in psychiatry followed largely nonspecific hygienic principles. Psychoanalysis quite early became the dominant clinical and intellectual viewpoint at the Clinic and with it came the hope that accurate diagnosis could lead to more effective treatment.

Throughout these years Karl Menninger in his teaching and writing stressed careful case study and meticulous description of clinical phenomena. Case studies stressed both careful phenomenological recording and organizing historical information in terms of the personal meaning of events. Will Menninger adopted an approach to the treatment of hospitalized psychiatric patients based on psychoanalytic psychology which attempted to specify treatment based on a diagnostic understanding of the patient. He developed it further in the context of the programs of moral or milieu treatment already established at the Clinic.

In the 1940s the Nazi threat that led to World War II also had profound direct and indirect impact upon the Menninger Clinic. Many of the medical staff were drawn off into the armed forces, including Dr. Will, who became chief of psychiatry for the U.S. Army Medical Corps. Many dislocated European colleagues were invited to join the Clinic staff. One of the most important developments was the arrival of David Rapaport from Hungary via Osawatomie, Kansas. At the Menninger Clinic Rapaport began his monumental studies to demonstrate the psychodiagnostic value of a battery of psychological tests. He developed a systematic approach to the interpretation of test responses based on rationales for understanding the response process derived from cognitive psychology and from psychoanalysis. Rapaport and the successive generations of psychologists trained by him demonstrated the ability to detect significant psychopathology before it was clinically manifest and established testing as an important adjunct to the psychiatric diagnostic examination. Methods were refined to understand the cognitive, affective, and motoric functions of patients as these are organized by personality and distorted by psychopathology. The inquiry then broadened to include the relevance of refined diagnostic understanding for the treatment process.

The present volume is a collection of articles and chapters that has grown out of this tradition. They record the quest for the relevance of diagnostic understanding for the treatment process. As the subtitle indicates, the quest is not yet finished. To apply precise diagnostic understanding requires treatment methods of equal precision. In psychiatry these methods have been slow to come. In recent years more refined treatment approaches to patients with a variety of psychopathology and developmental disturbance have been proposed and are now actively being tested. The papers collected in this book provide an excellent introduction to the search for the elusive connection.

HERBERT J. SCHLESINGER, PH.D.

Series Preface

This series of books is addressed to behavioral scientists interested in the nature of human personality. Its scope should prove pertinent to personality theorists and researchers as well as to clinicians concerned with applying an understanding of personality processes to the amelioration of emotional difficulties in living. To this end, the series provides a scholarly integration of theoretical formulations, empirical data, and practical recommendations.

Six major aspects of studying and learning about human personality can be designated: personality theory, personality structure and dynamics, personality development, personality assessment, personality change, and personality adjustment. In exploring these aspects of personality, the books in the series discuss a number of distinct but related subject areas: the nature and implications of various theories of personality; personality characteristics that account for consistencies and variations in human behavior; the emergence of personality processes in children and adolescents; the use of interviewing and testing procedures to evaluate individual differences in personality; efforts to modify personality styles through psychotherapy, counseling, behavior therapy, and other methods of influence; and patterns of abnormal personality functioning that impair individual competence.

IRVING B. WEINER

University of Denver
Denver, Colorado

Preface

Professionals seeking to keep abreast of the mental health literature quickly confront a veritable explosion of theoretical viewpoints, treatment orientations, and techniques of intervention. Multiplicity rather than consistency rules the day, highlighting what has long been a problem: the difficulty in translating diagnostic understanding into meaningful and practical treatment planning. Many believe that too often the diligence expended in a diagnostic examination seems to contribute more to the bulk of a file than to the betterment of the patient's condition.

It is in response to such attitudes that we have collected these papers. All written by present or former staff psychologists at The Menninger Foundation, these articles reflect a tradition based on a set of principles and point of view about diagnosing and treating. However, our wish is not to pay homage or be self-congratulatory. Rather, we aim to illustrate the current utility of the heritage intrinsic in the selected articles, regardless of one's discipline affiliation or educational-work setting.

Nevertheless, we acknowledge that this volume holds special personal meanings for us as well. We were both professionally nourished by the ideas in the earlier papers, and the authors often presented such ideas to us directly during the course of our training. Other papers were written by colleagues, some by ourselves. So the volume is for us an attempt to share with others what has been so meaningful and useful to us, and in part is a way of expressing our gratitude to our teachers and colleagues.

This blend of professional and personal motives is aptly expressed in a lengthy Japanese classic, *Tale of Genji*. Prince Genji indicates that a man writes because of his "own experience of men and things, whether for good or for ill—not only what he has passed through himself, but events he has only witnessed or been told of—it has moved him to an emotion so passionate that he can no longer keep it shut up in his heart . . . he cannot bear to let it pass into oblivion. There must never come a time . . . when men do not know about it." As one of our colleagues, Sydney Smith, once observed to us, "What we can discover in Prince Genji's thought is a universal principle—that writing enables a man to transcend his time or his place and to affirm the worth of human knowledge, wisdom, and experience.''

This principle seems especially vital today when the kind of hard-won clinical understanding and way of looking at human nature which is embodied in the selected papers is in danger of being lost, for reasons alluded to above. As Prince Genji implies, a man writes mostly for himself, to satisfy something inside him. And so we edited this volume because it is important to us to publicly express what we stand for, what we are committed to, and what we believe in. Since these ideas and values are in jeopardy of perishing, it is all the more important for us to preserve them.

FRED SHECTMAN
WILLIAM H. SMITH

Topeka, Kansas
October 1983

Acknowledgments

This book derives in large part from the heritage and spirit transmitted across the years by successive generations of clinical psychologists at The Menninger Foundation. In fact, it is our hope that this volume itself will represent an extension of that tradition.

Thus we have been aided in this endeavor by many others in various ways. There are a few, however, whom we wish to single out for special thanks. Drs. Cotter Hirschberg, Leonard Horwitz, and Irwin Rosen were especially helpful in providing the time and technical assistance required for this project. Dr. Paul Pruyser was a frequent consultant, aiding us in organizing our ideas and giving form and substance to them. And Mrs. Virginia Eicholtz prepared the index with her characteristic thoroughness and dispatch.

And, of course, we are grateful to all those colleagues whose writing appears in this volume. Collectively, their work reflects a solidarity based on shared values. Principal among these values is a dedication to the painstaking understanding and care of patients based on a commitment to the value of the individual human being. And it is in that spirit that we offer this book to the reader.

F.S.
W.H.S.

Credits

The editors wish to express their gratitude for permission to reprint material from the following sources:

American Psychologist for "Conventional and Contemporary Approaches to Psychotherapy: Freud Meets Skinner, Janov, and Others," by Fred Shectman, Copyright 1977 by the American Psychological Association; and "Problems in Communicating Psychological Understanding: Why Won't They Listen to Me?!," by Fred Shectman, Copyright 1979 by the American Psychological Association.

Bulletin of the Menninger Clinic for "The Clinical Psychologist as a Diagnostic Consultant," by Jon G. Allen, Copyright 1981 by The Menninger Foundation; "Schizophrenic Thought Organization, Object Relations, and the Rorschach Test," by George Athey, Jr., Copyright 1974 by The Menninger Foundation; "Reflections on the Diagnostic Process by a Clinical Team," by Jorge de la Torre, Ann Appelbaum, Doris Jane Chediak, and William H. Smith, Copyright 1976 by The Menninger Foundation; "On Becoming a Hospitalized Psychiatric Patient," by Philip S. Holzman and Herbert J. Schlesinger, Copyright 1972 by The Menninger Foundation; "Group Psychotherapy for Borderline and Narcissistic Patients," by Leonard Horwitz, Copyright 1980 by The Menninger Foundation; "Language Pitfalls in Diagnostic Thought and Work," by Paul W. Pruyser and Karl Menninger, Copyright 1976 by The Menninger Foundation; "Diagnosis and Prescription for Psychotherapy," by Herbert J. Schlesinger, Copyright 1969 by The Menninger Foundation; "Interaction of Dynamic and Reality Factors in the Diagnostic Testing Interview," by Herbert J. Schlesinger, Copyright 1973 by The Menninger Foundation; "The Therapeutic Aspects of the Hospital Milieu: Prescribing an Activities Program," by Herbert J. Schlesinger and Philip S. Holzman, Copyright 1970 by The Menninger Foundation; "The Diagnostic Process in Psychiatric Evaluations," by Howard Shevrin and Fred Shectman, Copyright 1973 by The Menninger Foundation; "Psychological Testing and the Mind of the Tester," by Sydney Smith, Copyright 1976

Contents

PART ONE   CONCEPTUAL ISSUES AND APPROACHES
TO DIAGNOSING   1

1   The Diagnostic Process: Touchstone of Medicine's Values
    Paul W. Pruyser   5

2   The Diagnostic Process in Psychiatric Evaluations
    Howard Shevrin and Fred Shectman   18

3   Language Pitfalls in Diagnostic Thought and Work
    Paul W. Pruyser and Karl Menninger   55

4   Reflections on the Diagnostic Process by a Clinical Team
    Jorge de la Torre, Ann Appelbaum, Doris Jane Chediak,
    and William H. Smith   69

PART TWO   DIAGNOSTIC TESTING CONSIDERATIONS   83

5   Interaction of Dynamic and Reality Factors in the Diagnostic
    Testing Interview
    Herbert J. Schlesinger   87

6   The Masochistic Character as a Self-Saboteur (with Special
    Reference to Psychological Testing)
    Stephen A. Appelbaum   107

7   Early Memories and Character Structure
    Martin Mayman   122

8   Psychoanalytic Study of the Self-Organization with
Psychological Tests
Martin Mayman   141

9   Schizophrenic Thought Organization, Object Relations,
and the Rorschach Test
George Athey, Jr.   157

PART THREE   ISSUES IN THE COMMUNICATION OF
DIAGNOSTIC UNDERSTANDING   181

10   Psychological Testing and the Mind of the Tester
Sydney Smith   185

11   Problems in Communicating Psychological Understanding:
Why Won't They Listen to Me?!
Fred Shectman   191

12   Use of the Psychological Test Report in the Course of
Psychotherapy
Mary S. Cerney   209

13   The Clinical Psychologist as a Diagnostic Consultant
Jon G. Allen   220

14   Ethical, Social, and Professional Issues in Patients'
Access to Psychological Test Reports
William H. Smith   230

PART FOUR   DIAGNOSTIC UNDERSTANDING AND
TREATMENT IMPLICATIONS: FORGING THE CONNECTING
LINKS   237

Issues in Hospital Treatment   241

15   On Becoming a Hospitalized Psychiatric Patient
Philip S. Holzman and Herbert J. Schlesinger   243

16   The Therapeutic Aspects of the Hospital Milieu:
Prescribing an Activities Program
Herbert J. Schlesinger and Philip S. Holzman   264

17   An Approach to the Analysis of Activities: The Game of
     Chess
     William H. Smith   275

     Issues in Psychotherapy   283

18   Conventional and Contemporary Approaches to
     Psychotherapy: Freud Meets Skinner, Janov, and Others
     Fred Shectman   285

19   The Idealization of Insight
     Stephen A. Appelbaum   299

20   Parkinson's Law in Psychotherapy
     Stephen A. Appelbaum   328

21   Group Psychotherapy for Borderline and Narcissistic
     Patients
     Leonard Horwitz   338

22   Diagnosis and Prescription for Psychotherapy
     Herbert J. Schlesinger   355

23   The Use of the Psychological Test Report in Setting the
     Focus of Psychotherapy
     Rowe L. Mortimer and William H. Smith   364

EPILOGUE   371

INDEX   375

PART ONE

Conceptual Issues and Approaches to Diagnosing

The heritage of current diagnostic practice in the mental health field is classification (Campbell, 1981). Though phenomenologically descriptive, from a treatment standpoint such categorization has been relatively sterile. At most, such taxonomies aided in differentiating those disorders with good outcome from those with poor outcome. For example, Kraepelin's scheme included virtually no treatment implications, because disorders were viewed as fixed entities and thus expected to follow a predictable course. Only relatively recently, with the advent of psychodynamic thinking, has there been a shift away from such views of psychological disturbance as something static.

In keeping with such changing views, Menninger, Mayman, and Pruyser assert, "Diagnosis has gradually become a matter less of seeking to identify a classical picture and give it a name than of understanding the way in which an individual has been taken with a disability, partly self-imposed and partly externally brought about" (1963, p. 35). What they imply is a conceptual leap from diagnosis as classification to diagnosis based on an understanding of how and why the individual has succumbed. They also note that an understanding of just such factors means diagnosis in a new sense, one which is directly tied to treatment planning:

> It is diagnosis in the sense of understanding just how the patient is ill and how ill the patient is, how he became ill and how his illness serves him. From this knowledge one may draw logical conclusions regarding how changes might be brought about in or around the patient which would affect his illness. (p.7)

The first chapter in this section, by Paul W. Pruyser, illustrates just such a view of diagnosis. It thereby also serves to articulate a view of diagnosis which sets the tone for the following papers in this section. These chapters illustrate the essential components of such an orientation, including the importance of a "process approach," in which the patient is actively invited to participate in his or her own evolving examination. For Pruyser, diagnosing is thus a two-party interaction, in which the idea of a diagnostic partnership extends to diagnostic teamwork.

In fact, the papers in this section demonstrate how diagnosing need not make the patient into a dehumanized object of scrutiny nor simply pejoratively label or "pigeonhole" the patient. As such, these chapters constitute a response to recent objections that the very enterprise of diagnosis is authoritarian and impersonal: a violation of the patient's dignity at best and potentially stigmatizing and socially harmful at worse (for an extensive review of such criticisms and a reply to them, see Shectman, 1976).

In his lead chapter, Pruyser also addresses the humanistic values which can undergird or undermine the diagnostic process. He does not shrink from generating heat as he seeks to provide light. Thus, true to his belief in collaborative work, he raises the provocative idea that the ideal leader of the diagnostic team might be the patient!

Howard Shevrin and Fred Shectman, too, confront a host of controversial issues in diagnosis. In their discussion of such topics they explicitly fashion a method of diagnostic practice and illustrate its utility. Like Pruyser, they stress the importance of active patient involvement in the diagnostic enterprise. In fact, assessment of the willingness and resistance of the patient to participate in just such a mutual effort is a crucial part of the diagnostic task.

Moreover, Shevrin and Shectman do not view the patient's disturbance as a static entity which is localized in the patient alone. Instead, the key influences on the patient's functioning are potentially represented in the diagnostic interaction itself and can be assessed via the unfolding diagnostic process. Consequently, passive "fact-gathering" (e.g., history-taking) is discouraged as beside the point.

Such a way of thinking highlights the importance of the language used to convert patient complaints into issues which can focus the process. Indeed, language and diagnosis are closely intertwined. Language expresses the clinician's conceptual views about what is to be diagnosed, how, and why. As such, the language of diagnosis can reveal as much or more about the clinician as it can about the patient being diagnosed. As noted, early nomenclature classified in relatively static terms. A psychoanalytic approach brings with it several conceptual "languages" (Mayman, 1963). There is the language clinician and patient use to interact. In communicating with colleagues, however, the clinician may utilize a different "middle language" to formulate generalizations which are several steps removed from the language of the clinical hour. Finally, there is psychoanalytic metapsychology, which relies on "constructs" and is thus even more removed from the immediacy of the clinical encounter.

Over the years there has been considerable debate about the utility of such an abstract level of conceptualization and discourse (Gill, 1978; Pruyser, 1978). Roy Schafer has also expressed concern about the use of language in diagnostic and treatment work (1974). More recently, Schafer has proposed a new "action language" designed to close the gap between metatheory and clinical interaction (1976). At the heart of Schafer's thinking is a view of the patient as a doer, one ever engaged in some psychological activity.

Such ideas resonate well with the emphasis on the patient as active participant in the chapters by Pruyser, and Shevrin and Shectman. Schafer's close attention to language also fits with the serious role which Pruyser and Karl Menninger accord language in their contribution in this section. They analyze multiple diagnostic "languages" from various perspectives, e.g., nosology, classification, and treatment. They also enumerate the pitfalls leading to poor language use which reflects, and in turn promotes, poor thinking. Such thinking easily becomes reified and obscuring, if not misleading, and perhaps even detrimental. Moreover, all the while the enterprise of diagnosing may be confused (and blamed) for such language "disorders."

Distinguishing disorders from persons, Pruyser and Menninger submit that "an unpresumptuous 'person language' in the mother tongue is needed to define human predicaments." As such, the paper is a fine addition to (and example of) the rich collaboration between Pruyser and Menninger over the years in the service of a humanistic but disciplined point of view. Their chapter particularly demonstrates the difference which diagnostic practice can make.

In his opening chapter on the diagnostic process, Pruyser emphasizes the essential role of teamwork from the technical standpoint of distinct contributions by different disciplines. The final paper in this section by Jorge de la Torre, Ann Appelbaum, Doris Jane Chediak, and William H. Smith serves as an application of Pruyser's ideas, as well as others discussed in the other chapters in this section. The article pivots around an extended case example and illustrates how clinical hypotheses are formulated, tested, modified, and reapplied. The paper thus exemplifies a model for applying principles of diagnostic teamwork. Specifically, the authors view the unfolding and varied interactions with team members as a microcosm of the patient's general functioning and disorder. Consequently, the diagnostic process can set the stage for treatment by generating treatment planning which flows from the current diagnostic experience of the patient and team.

Each in its own way, the four chapters in this section demonstrate an underlying unity in their conceptual approach to diagnosis. This unity serves to organize, inform, and guide the diagnostic process by connecting it closely to the treatment that follows, in fact, helping to shape it. In particular, by recognizing and capitalizing on the similarities between the diagnostic and treatment situations, a "process approach" can yield a treatment-relevant understanding which the patient himself may recognize. The goal of mutual recognition makes the patient an integral part of the process and thereby can contribute to the patient's readiness to enter treatment by helping him be an active participant in understanding his difficulties and how treatment can be of help. Such a "diagnostic alliance" can thus become the forerunner of the "therapeutic alliance" in the treatment which follows.

REFERENCES

Campbell, R. J. The nosology of psychiatry. In S. Arieti & H. Brodie (Eds.), *American handbook of psychiatry*, 2nd ed., Vol. 7. New York: Basic Books, 1981, Chapter 32, pp. 649–771.

Gill, M. M. Metapsychology is irrelevant to psychoanalysis. In S. Smith (Ed.), *The human mind revisited*. New York: International Universities Press, 1978, pp. 349–368.

Mayman, M. Psychoanalytic study of the self-organization with psychological tests. *Proceedings of the Academic Assembly on Clinical Psychology*. Montreal: McGill University Press, 1963, pp. 97–117.

Menninger, K., Mayman, M., & Pruyser, P. *The vital balance*. New York: Viking Press, 1963.

Pruyser, P. "A child is being beaten": Metapsychology as the whipping boy. In S. Smith (Ed.), *The human mind revisited*. New York: International Universities Press, 1978, pp. 369–396.

Schafer, R. Talking to patients in psychotherapy. *Bulletin of The Menninger Clinic*, 1974, *38*, 503–515.

Schafer, R. *A new language for psychoanalysis*. New Haven: Yale University Press, 1976.

Shectman, F. Provocative issues in psychiatric diagnosis: A dialogue. *Bulletin of The Menninger Clinic*, 1976, *40*, 435–458.

Chapter 1

The Diagnostic Process:
Touchstone of Medicine's Values

PAUL W. PRUYSER

Worsened by healing
—Vergil, The Aeneid 12:46

The following episode recently came to my attention: A sixty-year-old married woman made a routine annual examination visit to her gynecologist's office, a group practice in which she had been a registered patient for many years. This time she was to be seen by a new partner, a man in his upper thirties. After having waited in the reception room for a considerable time, the patient was ushered by the nurse into an examination room and, after disrobing, positioned on the examination table. She had been lying there alone, in an awkward posture, for ten minutes, when the physician came in with the nurse. Leafing through the patient's chart, he said, "Well, ____ (grossly mispronouncing her first name) . . . let me see. . . . We had a little bleeding last time." The patient flared up with: "What? *We? I* had some bleeding. *You* didn't."

Common as this type of encounter appears to be, one can hardly imagine a more ludicrous or gruesome start for a doctor-patient relationship. The patient is first rendered supine, physically immobilized, and then insulted. The doctor takes it upon himself to address her by her first name, and that incorrectly; he does not really greet her, but falteringly reads her name from the chart; he disregards her matronly age; naively, he lets slip a "let me see," that dangerous giveaway of a profession always accused of voyeurism. And in his phraseology he identifies himself with the patient to the point of assuming her gender and

This work originally appeared as "The Diagnostic Process: Touchstone of Medicine's Values," in *Nourishing the Humanistic in Medicine*, William R. Rogers and David Barnard, editors. Published in 1979 by the University of Pittsburgh Press. Used by permission. © 1979 by Society for Health and Human Values.

sharing her symptom. What seems to be uppermost in his mind is not the person before him, but "the complaint"—a rubric that professionally, and in all likelihood habitually, prestructures his approach to and conversation with all his patients. Casting about for something under that rubric, he settles on last year's item, as charted. The implication is that he, the doctor, always wants a sign or symptom to legitimate a patient's presence in his office, even for periodic preventive check-ups! Everything else is subordinate to that rubric, in which his expertise is vested; and conceptual subordination spreads to become social subordination when, by using her first name, he puts the patient in the role of a little girl or an underling.

I want to use this brief initial phase of a visit to the gynecologist as a point of departure for some reflections about diagnosis. I take diagnosing as the heart of medicine, the single most important task of physicians and the most frequent functional activity in medical practice. Although it is true that some physicians, for example, surgeons, spend a great deal of time in specialized therapeutic interventions, many general practitioners, pediatricians, family physicians, and psychiatrists find the bulk of their work to consist of diagnostic explorations. They tease out and formulate problems, preliminary to writing prescriptions that initiate some therapeutic intervention. Much of the therapy is done by other parties, including impersonal, unseen drug action.

For my reflections I shall use a determinate vantage point: the precepts and body of knowledge that have accumulated in psychoanalysis, been more or less appropriated by dynamic psychiatry, and begun to hold clues for medicine in general. My contention is that psychoanalysis has most forthrightly raised some crucial questions about the diagnostic process and, in trying to answer these, provoked a cardinal shift in the whole *ethos* of diagnosing. To put this shift in a nutshell, anticipating the reflections that will form the bulk of this essay, psychoanalysis has changed diagnosing from a unilateral, often authoritarian, procedure in which a physician interrogates, inspects, palpates, and variously tests patients, and then pronounces "his" diagnosis (which is seen as the physician's professional and intellectual property), into a bilateral process in which patients, soliciting help from an expert, come to diagnose themselves. The diagnostic ethos has moved by some Copernican revolution from an *allogenic* to an *autogenic* center; *iatric* dominance has given way to the *patient's* initiative, and medical investigation has been restyled to maximize the patient's power for self-assessment.

Having summed up my contention thus decisively, I should enter the caveat that I am exposing a principle rather than describing a prevalent practice. Despite its anchorage in the humane tradition in medicine, the psychoanalytic principle goes so much against the grain of established views, habits, and prerogatives in the healing arts that there is a wide gap between the principle and the observable facts of practicing. Many psychiatrists fail to acknowledge the principle, find it noble but unworkable, or have great difficulty living up to it; and among psychoanalysts, backsliders are proportionately as numerous as in other high-minded movements. Nevertheless, the principle retains its revolutionary power and teaching value, and although its psychoanalytic origin is rarely acknowledged, it seems to be emulated implicitly today by quite diverse groups of health workers and consumers of medical science who find much to criticize in the prevailing ethos, style, and forms of health services. Many medical schools and hospitals are groping toward a change, not merely in curriculum and techniques, but in the very philosophy that should guide their enterprises; and if faculty or hospital staff members prove unwilling or slow to change, the students and "lower-echelon" health workers will exert relentless pressure, or face them with de facto alternatives of practice. Similarly millions of patients or prospective patients are demanding a change in medical attitudes, all groups arguing in one way or another for a much needed *humanizing* of medical practice, in which the patients' (and the doctors') dignity and modes of decision-making will be vouchsafed. Reflections on the spirit of health care are in the air, raising issues beyond those of medical ethics and forensics. That is why I am speaking of changes in the *ethos* of medicine, illuminated by thoughts on the diagnostic process.

WHO IS TO KNOW WHAT IN THE DIAGNOSTIC PROCESS?

Although medical diagnosing is typically seen as a two-party transaction, a great many disturbances in well-being are diagnosed by one party. After repeated instances of a burning sensation in the stomach, one says to oneself "heartburn" and buys antacids. A critical (but culturally and personally highly variable) point must be reached for simple self-assessment to give way to a desire for a two-party diagnostic transaction. In that transition, the ailing person assumes a new, provisional role—patienthood—for the time being, until he or she can be released from that role by cure, talked out of it by being denied the privilege, or hardened into it by chronicity, incurability, or further mishaps. Assuming patienthood is an ambiguous thing, conferring rights, duties, and exemptions from duties, and usually verified, certified, or legitimated by a second party, the physician, who is granted some influence over a third party, the relevant public, on the patient's behalf. In the patient's role, once assumed and certified, one must manifest two contrary series of convictions: on the one hand, there must be signals of impediment, pain, dysfunction, and so forth; on the other hand, there must be a desire for health, signs of betterment if possible, and at least some willingness to entertain contracting for certain interventions or ministrations that are not standard procedures in normal life.

In a medical two-party transaction, who makes the diagnosis and how is it formulated? The first answer is, of course, the doctor, in the vocabulary of the medical profession. Doctors are trained to know what to look for, what to ask, what tests to run, and to put the result of their searches and cogitations in a verbal formula commensurate with the nosology to which their profession subscribes. Apparently, the diagnostic formulation, although ostensibly made for the patient's benefit, is owed primarily to the physician and his or her colleagues, for there are arguments whether or not the diagnosis is to be shared with the patient, particularly when it has ominous prospects. As the phrase has it: "Should the doctor *tell* the patient he has cancer?" This phrase itself implies that at least some diagnoses are shrouded in professional secrecy. The formulation and its occasional secrecy also imply that the patient is not a full partner in the diagnostic process, but is in some sense only its subject, and that he or she is kept at bay while the doctor does the probing and thinking. To put it starkly: The diagnostician is the knower, the patient is an ignoramus; the diagnosis is written in the chart to which the patient has no access; and the diagnostician may or may not propound the ailment's name or description to the patient after the latter has offered himself or herself for inspection and study. It requires benevolent wisdom or art rather than science to decide whether sharing the diagnosis with the patient will have a soothing or scaring effect, and which of these is therapeutically desirable in a given case. In this sense, the diagnosis does not stand alone, but is caught up in curative efforts, in which indeed the whole diagnostic process may be embedded from the start. I will say more about the relation between therapy and diagnosis shortly.

I have described a prevalent model of medical transaction so as to tease out its underlying principle: that diagnosing is the doctor's duty and prerogative. I am not insinuating that these are acquired by medical usurpation; it may well be that both the duty and the prerogative have been granted to doctors by patients through centuries of evolving mores and legislation. My sole point is that, in this conception of diagnosis, the parties are unequal—the doctor's position elitist, the patient's role passive and submissive—and the diagnostic outcome is likely to be skewed by the selective attentions and inattentions of the diagnostician, particularly when she or he is a specialist in a particular branch of medicine.

A second answer to "Who makes the diagnosis?" is given by psychoanalysis. At its inception, psychoanalysis was practiced in a medical subculture suffused with diagnostic terms and labels that had arisen from nosological ignorance: hysteria, neurasthenia, psychasthenia, neurosis, and so on. At the end of the nineteenth century, these medical terms were only hapless words, pretentious ones to be sure, that stood for mysterious, poorly understood disorders that could be delimited only as vague clinical pictures, overlapping both with each other and with a few better-known disorders such as epilepsy and toxic states. Recognizing their scientific ignorance about these clinical pictures, Breuer and Freud took the poor diagnostic labels only as a starting point for a new kind of diagnostic process in which patients, speculatively held to be suffering from "reminiscences," were offered the opportunity for an astute self-assessment with the help of a mentor. Moreover, the crucial shift that Freud managed to introduce in the doctor-patient relation was for the doctor to abandon the authoritarian technique of hypnosis to become a good and sympathetic listener, and for the patient to abandon passivity and become the diagnostician (and by implication the nosologist) of his or her own case. By freely subscribing to a rule of ruthless honesty, the patient comes to discover the psychological rationale and psychohistorical origin of his or her symptoms or complaints and thereby to see alternative modes of problem-solving. And the diagnosis at which the patient arrives, after much soul-searching and interaction with the analyst, is not a nosological noun, such as "hysteria," but a personal or existential action phrase, such as: "When I seemed so cool on that occasion, I was really terrified by my mother's stern demand."

At this point, the reader may object that I am comparing apples and oranges. After all, physical symptoms and psychic complaints require very different approaches, stylized in the differences between "medical" and "psychiatric" diagnoses. The fact is, however, that in a doctor's office the distinction between physical and psychic is quite academic and can at best be made only at the end, not the beginning, of a diagnostic process. Thousands of general practitioners assert that between one-half and two-thirds of their patients come with unclassifiable complaints; many patients talk with psychiatrists about body dysfunctions; and pediatricians are frequently presented with phenomena that can at first be described only as undesirable conduct or behavior disorders. Sedatives, tranquilizers, and mood-altering drugs are widely prescribed in response to mere complaints that have not been properly diagnosed; this is paradoxical, for it means that precisely when doctors think "It's emotional," they decide to intervene physically by chemical action. If the practice of medicine yields any practical precepts, it is that in clinical situations the physical and the psychic are rarely distinguishable.

The psychoanalytic advice to the doctor is: "Don't rush to alter, except when life is acutely endangered. Don't take symptoms immediately away, for the patient probably needs them for the time being. The vaguer the complaint, the more likely are its adaptive value, its psychoeconomic utility, and its psychodynamic necessity." The psychoanalytic advice to the patient is: "I am not sure that you really want to be relieved right away, although you seem to say so. Try to understand why you have this symptom. Maybe you yourself can best figure out what brought it on and what makes it persist. It would be flippant to name your ailment, as if we knew what we were dealing with. Actually, you have to take the lead in making the diagnosis, and chances are that such a self-study will itself give you some relief."

These propositions round off to a very different diagnostic process, involving an ethos that advocates a diagnostic *partnership*. The doctor-patient relation in this partnership is egalitarian, not elitist or authoritarian. The patient can see in the doctor an expert who can provide counsel in the medical aspects of intended (and granted) self-explorations. Analogous to the designation of attorneys as "counselors at law," physicians may be seen as "counselors in medicine," assisting their patients in getting hold of their troubles and putting them in medical perspective. Humanistic values are thus being brought to bear upon diagnosis— that is, precisely at the point where the patient can reasonably make the greatest claim on assistance from the medical profession. For although the profession may not be able to offer a cure, or alleviation of suffering, it can always assist in teasing out what the trouble is.

FROM THE DIAGNOSTIC PARTNERSHIP TO DIAGNOSTIC TEAMWORK

Today, in hospitals, clinics, and certain types of group practice, the relationship between doctor and patient tends to be only one part—the center if one wishes— of a whole network of diagnostic relations. The patient's trouble is assessed by a diagnostic team comprising several disciplines whose members engage in their own transactions with the patient, eventually compiling their observations, test data, and interview material. It usually falls to the physician to head such a team, to draw inferences from the diverse data, and to formulate a diagnosis that is allegedly a synthesis of all team members' contributions to the diagnostic process. The social worker, the nurse, various laboratory technicians, consulting specialists, maybe a psychologist, a chaplain, or a physiotherapist, and of course the physician "in charge"—all have asked the patient some questions, assigned some task, or secured cooperation in some laboratory or testing procedure. In the course of these investigations, the patient visited different offices, was addressed in different vocabularies, met people of different moods and manners, and made some discerning observations about the efficacy of team functioning. When the studies have been completed, the patient sits beside the physician's desk to be informed about the diagnosis—if he or she is lucky. The patient is likely to have already received some provisional or definitive treatment and may even be ready to be discharged, without ever having heard a word about the diagnosis!

What I am trying to sketch is a "low" form of team diagnosis that is liable to repeat all the indignities, elitism, authoritarianism, and disregard for patients' right to understand their condition that we have found in some single doctor-patient relationships. Such a diagnostic team can add terrible feelings of being fragmented to patients' already sorry plight. They may feel poked at and analyzed into minutiae by so many people, each of whom begs questions by deferring to a rarely seen doctor, that they may despair of ever understanding anything about their ailments. They are glad to go home, possibly with the illness unchanged, but delivered from the nightmare of diagnostic investigations.

In reaction to this picture, we all seek to pride ourselves on being members of a superior diagnostic team. Our team consists of top-notch professionals, smoothly collaborating in a real team spirit, in which the patient is caught up, as if—be the metaphor permitted—infectiously. Still more humanely, we have organized our clinic or hospital to be like a little community in which the patients help each other to understand themselves, where by example and by conversation, or by guided group processes, they learn from each other to take hold of their condition and grasp something about the reasons behind their symptoms. Moreover, the team members frequently get together to discuss the patient at various stages of their studies, arriving in the end at a diagnosis based on group consensus. And the patient is at all steps fully informed! Even relatives are brought in for discussion and to prepare them for participation in the eventual treatment process.

Undeniably, these progressive features are large gains on the first model. There seems to be some partnership among team members, between each team member and the patient, and even among patients. But the trouble is that diagnostic teamwork cannot live by camaraderie and good spirits alone. If teams are justified by the adage that "two heads are better than one," their performance may amount to mere reduplicative busy work when these heads perceive, feel, think, act, and speak alike. The crucial rationale for a diagnostic team is that its members are *different* and maintain their differences, to give patients the benefit of studying themselves *from different vantage points*. Nor is the diagnostic team merely an organization in which labor is divided for greater efficiency and economy. The good diagnostic team is an interdisciplinary composite in which each member is a specialist maintaining her or his scientific, humanistic, and professional identity, in the conviction that only in this way can patients get hold of all the facets of their problems. The good team has autonomous members, who in turn help patients maintain their autonomy. It recognizes that most medical problems are complex, warranting study in diverse perspectives, each with its own integrity and its own power of resolution.

Interdisciplinary diagnostic teamwork requires many constraints imposed by scientific and humanistic value considerations. In the first place, team members must maintain a delicate balance between disciplinary specificity and dedication to a common goal. Each discipline is a unique perspective (backed by an identifiable combination of a particular basic science, applied science, and theory of technique) in which patients can be understood—or, more desirably, in which patients can come to understand themselves—with the help of an expert. Multiplicity of perspectives is the team's raison d'être. Ideally, this means collaboration of peers, not subordination to a hierarchy in which the disciplines (and their representatives) are ranked in order of alleged importance. It means deliberate maintenance of distinct language games, each germane to a particular discipline. The interdisciplinary team seeks to reach a higher-order synthesis of the compiled diagnostic contributions from the participating disciplines, a diagnosis that not only combines, but rounds off, all the vantage points that have been used.

Second, dedication to the team's common goal (which is explicitly more holistic than any particular discipline can manage to be) should include constraint on the drift toward accommodation to one discipline's dominance. The uniqueness of each perspective must be maintained, or it stops being a perspective. For instance, if a hospital social worker adopts too many medical concepts and accommodates outright to the prevailing medical language, his or her discipline loses its unique moorings and stops being a special vantage point. Its operation in the hospital becomes duplicative, redundant, or worse—a watered-down form of medicine. One profession is sold out to another profession, and the team deteriorates into a management device for the division of labor. And patients are sold short on the promise that their conditions warrant consideration in multiple perspectives; in the end, they will be regarded from only one vantage point.

Third, the interdisciplinary team I am describing requires constraint on answering the question of its leadership. Ideally, its leadership should fall to the profession or person having the greatest synthesizing power in describing and defining the patient's problems and finding workable avenues for intervention. If the diagnostic formulation is to rise above the bits and pieces of the contributing disciplines, synthetic judgment and great integrative capacity are required. Does any discipline have this to an acceptable degree? Does any profession specifically train its members to acquire these capacities? Which discipline can we trust to accomplish this without reverting to the pretentious queen's position of theology or philosophy in the Middle Ages?

Some professionals have answered these difficult questions by vesting their hope, not in any one discipline, but in the team as a whole which, under rotating leadership, strives for a group consensus. But committees are notorious for turning out camels from designs for a horse. Others have answered these questions by subordinating them, often tacitly, to the nature of the institution or organization in which the interdisciplinary team operates. In clinics and hospitals, the team leadership is given to medicine, often to one of its specialties. But can medical thinking transcend its own limits and partialities to do justice to the social, economic, psychological, cultural, existential, and life-situational vantage points in which the patient's predicaments are apprehended by various team members?

In the face of these critical rejoinders, one might toy with the thought that the ideal diagnostic team leader should be *the patient*. If, in each partial diagnostic study, patients were not merely asked to cooperate with or succumb to the various procedures of data-gathering and inference-making, but were fully engaged in self-diagnosis with the help of a particular expert, they themselves might be in the best position to arrive at a synthetic diagnostic formulation. Thought has to be given to the pace at which patients can assimilate diagnostic findings, which may well prove to be quite demanding. But that by itself would not detract from patients' unique suitability for making a diagnostic synthesis attuned to their own life situations. The expected rebuttal to this proposition is, of course, that most patients are too dumb, too illiterate, too invested in their symptoms, and generally too passive to achieve such a synthesis. It will be said that patients, in their perplexity over themselves, turned to the experts in the first place in order to get their answers. How would one dare turn the tables on them?

But this rebuttal is, as we all know today, full of open or subtle denigrations, celebrated in the terms *layman* and *patient*. The layman has always provided an occasion for professional oneupmanship, and not only in medicine. Competence is attributed to professionals, not laymen. The assumption of patienthood is widely seen as an admission of incompetence, helplessness, and weakness. But do these admissions of failure necessarily encroach on judgment? Should they be allowed to truncate the patient's dignity? Should they make the patient a subordinate subject of diagnostic investigations conducted and orchestrated by others? Where does reverence for the patient come in—not just politeness or civility—but reverence? Albert Schweitzer struggled with these questions, and even this towering figure failed to answer them satisfactorily, perhaps precisely because of his toweringness. The questions remain oppressively open, and that is what bespeaks their ethical import. They should not be shoved under the rug or decided by management theory. Nor should they be answered too glibly by sociological clichés which hold that only verbally gifted upper-middle-class patients would have the wherewithal to preside over their own diagnostic exploration, and that lower-class patients are incapable of such self-assessment. If we are concerned with the ethos of medical practice and medical education, these are the kinds of questions we must constantly press upon the mind of the profession's members, particularly the young ones who have not yet succumbed to the routines that feign to have settled them.

HUMANISTIC VALUES UNDERGIRDING
THE DIAGNOSTIC PROCESS

To become a professional implies much more than acquiring the knowledge and skill of one's chosen discipline, to accept peer review, and to uphold technical standards. It demands more than knowing and abiding by the profession's code of ethics which addresses—in the helping and caring professions—such issues as confidentiality, preservation of life, and loyalty to the Hippocratic oath. Whatever peers may demand, professional people in the helping disciplines must put themselves under steady scrutiny for improving the quality of their thoughts and activities, the quality of their interactions with their patients or clients, the quality of their professional and public utterances, the quality of their technical and extracurricular melioristic moves. Most of these self-scrutinies will have to be self-generated, for their subject matter bypasses laws or codes and is not greatly subject to sanctions. To use a psychoanalytic distinction, the "undergirding" values in the diagnostic process I am alluding to in this section have more to do with the professional person's ego ideal than with his or her superego.

For instance, in the helping professions and especially in medicine, thoroughness is a value—a virtue—to be emulated; thoroughness, not from fear of malpractice suits or from ambition to get the institution's top job, but from the humanistic conviction that the patient is entitled to the best, and that anything shoddy is an offense to the patient's and the physician's own dignity. Thoroughness within a collaborative diagnostic process also demands that diagnostic skill include interpersonal skill guaranteeing at all points the patient's human rights. If patients trust themselves to a professional helper, they have a right to that helper's best thoughts, best advice, best understanding. The professional promise to help, with or without fee, obtained in whatever economic system, permits no flippancy. The more we acknowledge that human problems of health and illness are typically complex (witness the inherent difficulties in defining health and illness), the more thorough and comprehensive should be our diagnostic reasoning. I say *reasoning*, not *procedures*, for multiple tests and special studies are sometimes only a foil for poorly directed thought and judgment. Within the limits of the profession and the patient's rights, no stone should be left unturned to foster the patient's (and the doctor's) understanding of the ailment, the condition, or the problem. The patient is worth the effort, and diligence and zest in one's work, now experienced as a collaborative task, are the physician's professional joie de vivre.

Helpers and carers today are the last bastion of respect for the individual in a society that tends more and more flagrantly to trample people underfoot in mass action and mass manipulation. Individuality and personhood are beleaguered from all sides by regimentation and bureaucracy, mass hysteria, and artificially induced low self-regard. The Renaissance made no bones about the grandeur of the individual, and the biblical psalmist considered man "a little lower than the angels." Who today dares echo such positive evaluations of personhood? It seems to me that one social function of professional helpers and carers is to nurture the tender plant of human dignity, and to do so pointedly in relation to all patients or clients if only by providing them with a haven—however limited in space and time—where privacy, tolerance, and reverence can be vividly experienced. This means that no diagnostician can lord it over a patient, and that one should be vigilant to the subtle pseudoprofessional arrogance that relegates the patient to the status of "only a layman." It means adopting a watchful attitude toward the misuses of one's professional language, avoiding inappropriate labeling of individuals by medical class terms such as a carcinoma case, an epileptic, a schizophrenic (not to speak of "schiz"), a mongoloid.

A third set of undergirding values in the diagnostic process centers on the diagnostician's scientific responsibility and identification with a profession and its advance. If one is to be a physician, a nurse, or a psychologist, one had better be a very good one, knowing the basic and applied sciences in and out, always updating, amplifying, correcting, or reworking the knowledge and skills acquired in the past. Although such strivings involve scientific curiosity and perfection of craftsmanship, they partake of a humanistic value orientation when one reflects on their obligatory ethical tenor. One *owes* these strivings to all parties concerned: to patients for their betterment, to the profession for its advancement, to the public which has given this profession a special status, with duties and privileges. And, we should not blush to say, to oneself as a person dedicated to competence and as a creature accepting the biblical challenge of having been made "a little lower than the angels."

Along with these positive values, to be emulated and practiced, there are some "unvalues" to be despised, some cultural or personal penchants to be consciously avoided. Some of these have already been mentioned in the preceding pages. They are more difficult to sum up because they are likely to be time- and culture-bound and imply a degree of corrective reactivity on the part of any professional worker, a watchful counteraction to besetting fads and fashions. Those who pride themselves on performing thorough diagnostic work know all too well that an antidiagnostic wave is sweeping the country, of diverse origin and with different impetus. Therapeutic furor may ride slipshod over diagnostic patience. Misuse of diagnostic labels (especially in psychiatry) and diagnostic procedures has caused disenchantment or negativism in many people—professionals as well as patients—regarding the uses of diagnosis. Militant diagnostic nihilism is sometimes only a mask for quackery. Belief in patent medicines is close to belief in panaceas, both of which render diagnosis spurious or superfluous. Zealous do-good-ness may foster irrationality and produce antiscientific attitudes. And so on. The main point I wish to make is that in the end, however thoughtful the origins of some of these antidiagnostic penchants may be, patients are sold short on the right to know and understand their predicament and are in addition more likely than ever to be manipulated by somebody's ill-considered activism. However complex the interactions between diagnosis and treatment may be (and they do intertwine and overlap), rationality as well as reverence for troubled people dictate that diagnosis comes before treatment, and that any prescription should logically evolve from diagnostic knowledge.

This bit of medical orthodoxy (literally "right belief") about the logical sequence of steps in the helping process is systematically undermined by some features in modern medicine itself, notably specialization and pharmacotherapy. To put it all too succinctly, when specialists are too numerous, too visible, and overrespectable, a view of the patient as a whole is harder to get. The remaining general practitioners become gatekeepers to the specialists, who are likely to view each patient from one vantage point in which knowledge is on the order of "more and more about less and less." Although I would hold, within the ethos I am considering, that patients are entitled to, if need be, the most specialized knowledge of and interventions in their troubles, I also hold that they should not be truncated from a holistic view of themselves, especially when their problems are complex. By virtue of their specialization, specialists have to leave out many alternative or complementary vantage points and have a hard time considering patients in their personhood, as the opening portion of this essay shows. To boot, in their role as gatekeepers to the specialists, the general practitioners run some risk of becoming triage agents toward patients, allocating them to certain rubrics, referring them to third parties, or "managing" a patient through a succession of referrals. Whatever the intention, such triage and referral work is likely to make patients feel fragmented and unable to gain a comprehensive view of their ailments or predicaments. They will feel sold short again, despite the minutiae of knowledge they may acquire from the specialists to whom they have been referred.

The advances in effective pharmacotherapy, much to be lauded per se, have at times fostered diagnostic sloth in physicians who are otherwise quite thoughtful. A case in point is the prescription of tranquilizers, not after careful diagnostic study, but on the basis of a presenting symptom taken at face value, such as anxiety or agitation. Such overeager symptom treatment can entail tragic results: At times, bereft people who would do well to go through the natural phases of mourning are chemically prohibited from using their natural resources for restoration by these potent, instant tension relievers. The epigraph to this essay alludes to the ever lurking possibility that hasty interventions may make patients worse. A symptom is not a freak happening; it is a determined process that is to be seen in the light of its origin, function, and purpose; in other words, it is to be diagnosed instead of being quickly eliminated. The temptation to do the latter is great when the means are so readily available; worse, the accumulation of such quick symptom removal sets up a dangerous adiagnostic or antidiagnostic backlash that the profession is bringing upon itself.

Finally, if we are identified with the diagnostic ethos whose premises I have sought to outline, we should be wary of conceptions and modes of speaking that threaten to have an opposite tenor. I for one am suspicious of the increasing use of terms such as "health delivery systems," "health maintenance organizations," and other applications of the systems concept to medicine by medical professionals themselves. (This unease on my part does not extend to the heuristic use of general systems theory in the basic sciences of medicine, which has an entirely different aim.) The prevalence of such phrases betrays a penchant for dealing with the problems of medicine in predominantly managerial terms. Borrowed from engineering, industry, political science, or administration, these words are hard to rhyme with the ethos I have stressed. If the individual, particularly the suffering individual, in our society is as beleaguered as I think, I have no hope for an eventual rescue through systems and organizations. On the contrary, we are in dire need of humanizing our existing systems and organizations, not of further bureaucratizing our few remaining persons. Helping and caring require some degree of spontaneity, some feeling of good will, some degree of intimacy, and an enormous respect for individual freedom—all intangibles that cannot be systematized. And just these intangibles, I think, are the deepest wellsprings of our professional ethos. They are the undergirding values of the diagnostic process.

Because of this intimate relation between values and diagnosis, I am tempted to propose a new test: Tell me how you diagnose, and I will tell you what kind of person and what manner of doctor you are.

Chapter 2

The Diagnostic Process
in Psychiatric Evaluations

HOWARD SHEVRIN AND FRED SHECTMAN

We propose, develop, and defend the following thesis on the nature of diagnosis: In the diagnosis of mental disorders the diagnostician, through the *medium of a personal relationship, elicits and observes* a range of *psychological functioning* which he considers *relevant on some theoretical grounds* for understanding the disorder so that he can make a *recommendation* which stands a good chance of being *acted on as a basis for dealing with the disorder.*

From our point of view, diagnosis is *not* the unsolicited observation of unselected functioning existing in a purely impersonal empirical realm unrelated to theoretical orientation and indifferent to outcome. Even those who claim to have no use for diagnosis must rely on it implicitly although in a highly attenuated and grossly limited way, usually ignoring one or another key term in our thesis. A correct diagnosis is a difficult and delicate matter to achieve because it rests on a number of achievements: the sensitivity with which the clinician has used himself in eliciting the functioning, the thoroughness with which he has observed it, his theoretical position and his grasp of that position, the astuteness with which he formulates a recommendation, and, last but not least, the preparation in the relationship with the patient for presenting the recommendation as well as the tact with which it is presented. No wonder good diagnosis is hard to come by. In a field in which concepts, theories, and treatment fads and fashions are a dime a dozen, it is surprising that in the large literature dealing with the diagnosis of various disorders, there are relatively few papers which deal with the theory and process of the diagnostic process itself.

This paper has two main purposes: (1) to make a contribution to the theory of diagnosis which will help pave the way for a widely shared clinical method, and (2) to assist the practitioner, no matter what his level of experience, to relate

Reprinted with permission from the *Bulletin of the Menninger Clinic*, 1973, Vol. 37, No. 5, pp. 451–494, © 1973 by The Menninger Foundation.

his techniques to some broader concept of diagnostic method which should enhance his clinical acumen. We will try to show that diagnosis *can* be conducted in a clear, empathic, and useful manner.

Before considering the nature of the diagnostic process, we will discuss a number of controversial issues in diagnosis.

CONTROVERSIAL ISSUES IN DIAGNOSIS

Diagnosis Is Overly Intellectual and Too Concerned with the Past

Much of the current spate of encounter and other experience-oriented groups represents a repudiation of diagnosis, if diagnosis is taken to include understanding. Indeed, it is this very use of the intellect to which many such groups object. One reviewer of the encounter movement has written, "Much of the activity . . . within sensitivity training . . . is a concerted effort to turn away from the emphasis on intellect . . . on mediation of any experience through reflection, and to push the participants toward a direct experience that is not thought about and is not analyzed" (Back 1972, pp. 207–08). The point this orientation seeks to make is that an overemphasis on reason stifles feeling and thereby bypasses the core of a person's experience. This movement seeks to redress this onesidedness by going to the other extreme and abandoning reason altogether.

We agree that a reliance on reason to the exclusion of feeling is undesirable. However, we feel that overemphasis on reason is not an inherent part of diagnosis but a poor diagnostic practice reminiscent of early psychoanalysis when it was thought that once the culprit in the unconscious causing the symptom was identified the patient would be cured. By seeming to force a choice between experiencing and understanding, encounter groups act as if to be rational prevents one from being a "feeling" person. This antiintellectual trend which is so evident today appears to confound use of the intellect for purposes of understanding with use of the intellect for purposes of defending against the emergence of feeling, and to discard both in the hope of getting rid of the latter. The critics may reply that the effort at understanding in itself spoils the experience, but that is a curious argument. For, if understanding broadens and deepens what we are, then it can only spoil what we do not want to have understood, e.g., something irrational. The situation is somewhat like the heavy smoker who reads that smoking may cause cancer—and who then decides to give up reading because that knowledge interferes with his enjoyment of smoking! At any rate, this present antiintellectual trend may account for the antagonism toward systematic diagnostic understanding as a first step in undertaking treatment.

Rogers (1951) anticipated this misuse of understanding and feared that in diagnosis the clinician would become overly intellectual and too concerned with sterile and impersonal theorizing, which could result in an impressive intellectual display by the diagnostician but be far removed from the patient and his experience. Indeed, an emphasis on intellectualizing about experiences could result in the patient becoming engrossed with what in the past may have brought about the maladjustment at the expense of what the patient is currently feeling and contending with. Again, we would agree that such an approach is poor, but it is not necessarily synonymous with a sound diagnostic approach.

Nevertheless, some clinicians regard diagnosis as primarily involving the gathering of much information about the past, with a view toward reconstructing it for explanatory purposes. Such a point of view could convince the clinician that what he hears and sees is unrelated to what is currently important. He would then focus less on the present and not see the past as "alive" in terms of what is currently going on in the patient. It is as if the patient possesses a fossilized past which the diagnostician is interested in describing as if it were a specimen. Only that past is important which continues as an active influence in the present. There is no mystery in this. The diagnostician is a scientist and a scientist is interested in explaining phenomena. Any phenomenon one observes has causes which must extend from the present into the past in an unbroken chain. As will be more fully discussed later, it is far easier to find the right track by going from the present to the past than by making a leap into the past and working one's way forward in time.

There are some clinicians who see their work as a contrast between the gathering of historical data on the one hand and a diagnostic-therapeutic process on the other. This contrast is worth thinking about, since it could be argued that anything going on between clinician and patient is part of the diagnostic process. It is more a matter of what form it takes, how helpful it is, and how aware we are of it. For example, the patient is not simply "retrieving" historical data from a computer memory bank, but is to some degree shaping his recall for present purposes. As such, these "data" are inflenced by all the forces at work in each of us when we remember the past, especially to whom we are telling it, for what reasons, and with what hopes, fears, etc. Moreover, identifying these forces as they are at work in the diagnostic process may tell us more about the patient than the historical "facts," for these present actions are the contemporary representatives or effects of significant past actions or causes. In short, it is the form the communication takes in the diagnostic process that is as important, perhaps even more significant, than the historical information which the communication contains. It is noteworthy that in some psychiatric case summaries it is traditional to devote only one portion to the "psychological examination," which is distinguished from "historical information" as if the two were separable. We stress these points because such seemingly slight shifts in conceptualizing the diagnostic process can lead to quite different ways of thinking about it and using it.

Diagnosis Is Inhumane, Harmful and Makes the Patient into a Passive Object

Rogers (1951) asserted:

> . . . the very process of psychological diagnosis places the locus of evalution so definitely in the expert that it may increase any dependent tendencies in the client, and cause him to feel that the responsibility for understanding and improving his situation lies in the hands of another. . . . There is a degree of loss of personhood as the individual acquires the belief that only the expert can accurately evaluate him, and that therefore the measure of his personal worth lies in the hands of another. The more he acquires this attitude, the further he would appear to be from any sound therapeutic outcome. . . [pp. 223–224].

Here the implication is that the diagnostician not only violates the integrity and dignity of the patient, but is positively harmful to him as well. This conception of diagnosis is an either/or approach: either the patient or the clinician. It allows no room for cooperative endeavor, as if to diagnose must mean that the clinician sets himself up as omniscient. Therefore, the patient must feel subservient and without self-esteem because he does not see all that the diagnostician does. It is as if the patient feels he will know nothing about himself unless he is the only one who knows all there is to know.

Rogers believes that the patient's self-confidence will be shaken by the realization that he cannot fully know himself—as if that will always be an undesirable outcome and therefore inhumane because it is painful. But is the surgeon inhumane because he causes pain and injury in operating in order to ultimately benefit the patient? Closer to home, most clinicians have had the experience of pointing out things which are painful to a patient but which are necessary for him to grapple with if the patient is eventually to improve. In fact, it has been suggested that for some patients confrontation of characteristic ways in which they defend themselves strengthens the ego (Kernberg, 1968).

The recent impact of behavior modification may be viewed as a more contemporary form of Rogers' fears that diagnosis results in dehumanizing the patient. On a symposium with Skinner, Rogers submitted:

> For the behaviorist, man is a machine, a complicated but nonetheless understandable machine, which we can learn to manipulate with greater and greater skill until he thinks the thoughts, moves in the directions, and behaves in the ways selected for him [Wann 1964, p. 129].

Because behavior modification can lead to an unwitting patient being harmfully manipulated by a controlling clinician, there is certainly cause for alarm. In principle, however, behavior modification need not be intrinsically harmful to the patient. It is easy to be critical of this method because its techniques may involve pain (e.g., aversive conditioning) or because its mechanistic approach may clash with ideas about the dignity of the patient. But the behavior modifier could well ask if it is any more dignified or humane to reject procedures which could be of potential value in relieving mental suffering. Moreover, fears about the patient being controlled seem less compelling when applied to nonhospitalized patients who choose to undergo behavior modification. It has been argued that, even under these conditions, control is all the more insidious because patients could be less aware of being so controlled. Yet many a clinician has wished he could better influence his patients—this inability in itself bearing witness to how resistant people are to being so easily controlled.

For us, then, the charge that behavior modification involves callous and frightening manipulation is directed more at a set of values than at scientific considerations. While those behavior modifiers (like Greenspoon and Gersten, 1967) who seek to use psychological testing to improve their effectiveness might be lauded for their attempts at using diagnosis, they might be scientifically faulted for their limited approach. In particular, they greatly underemphasize the importance of the relationship between the patient and the clinician and thereby minimize that aspect of our definition which stresses the ''medium of a personal relationship.'' But there is a growing body of evidence which suggests that elements of suggestion play a powerful role in behavior therapy (Klein, Dittmann, Parloff, and Gill, 1969), and that patients' feelings about their behavior therapists are more important in what brings about change than the particular modification techniques used (Ryan and Gizynski, 1971).

If the experience-oriented groups stress feeling over thought, their counterparts, the behavior modification advocates, strive for the role of super-scientists. They seek to rely primarily on a set of procedures which they boast are based on hard laboratory findings and unambiguous concepts implemented in an impersonal, ''scientific'' manner on a seemingly passive patient—''seemingly'' because, as cited, research reveals that a great deal is going on in the thoughts and feelings of the patient, however much it may be ignored. It is of further interest that even the relevance of hard experimental results and unambiguous theory has been challenged by one not unacquainted with behavior therapy. In a recent article on behavior therapy, London (1972) dismisses the behavior modifiers' stress on learning theory and hard science as a polemical device to gain entry into clinical work which has now outlived its usefulness. This is of some interest because London is in sympathy with the behavior therapy point of view. Certainly there is sufficient reason to take issue with both extremes—

the encounter group refrain that only feelings count, and the behavior therapists' insistence on the purity of a hard scientific approach.

Another factor which may turn the diagnostic process into an "active" diagnostician working on a "passive" patient is a tendency to try to get at the "problem" as directly as possible and thereby unwittingly bypass the active engagement of the patient in this cooperative enterprise. It is indeed difficult not to succumb to the patient's implicit (if not explicit) plea to do something, rather than to help him experience and understand what it is that troubles him. Some have attributed this tendency to a medical background:

> Fresh from medical-school training, where they [psychiatrists] have been taught to identify diseases, they come into psychiatry, where they see illness and hence expect to find diseases. . . . They seek, then, to rid the patient of this—his disease. They can scarcely wait to begin treating the patient and observing his "improvement" under their ministrations [Menninger, Mayman, and Pruyser 1963, p. 6].

But such an orientation need not be intrinsic to medical training. The good diagnostician in any specialty (from psychiatry to internal medicine to plumbing) must discover what is wrong or, more specifically, what functions are impaired. The best way to do this is to try to elicit these functions so that they can be observed and their malfunctioning demonstrated. The physician errs in dealing with psychological problems when he forgets that he must elicit and observe psychological *functioning* and not merely obtain an *account* of them. In diagnosing ulcers, a good physician will not rely on the patient's account of his symptoms but will make his own examination and will carry out his own laboratory procedures in order to determine what direct evidence there is for the presence of an ulcer. He will determine how the organs involved are functioning and whether the impairment of these functions can be accounted for by something like an ulcer. And over and above these considerations, which are part and parcel of all good diagnoses, there are specific psychological considerations the physician in any specialty should keep in mind. While it may be more humane for the surgeon to operate than not to, it is all the more humane to take the patient's feelings about the operation into account. Indeed, research has shown that dealing with these psychological factors will speed convalescence by shortening both the length of hospitalization and the amount of post-operative medication required by the patient (Egbert, Battit, Welch, and Batlett 1964). The diagnostic process can go amiss when a medical orientation is misapplied and attempts are made to circumvent the patient's functioning in favor of his "problem." The clinician does not have a "problem" to deal with; rather he has a person with a problem to deal with.

In short, we think it is important to guard against the tendency for the diagnostic enterprise to become: a) an exercise in nosological pigeonholing rather than an unfolding or evolving process; b) a static instead of an active involvement; c) an activity in which the clinician acts on a passive patient rather than a collaborative endeavor in which the patient is engaged.

To illustrate:

> A constricted, withholding man was evaluated by a resident whose major concern was how he could get at what the patient was concealing in order to discover his "problem." The supervisor suggested that the important point was how the patient had put the psychiatrist in a position which could lead to a tug of war; and that the major concern was what took place between the two in the office, not some "secrets." These observations would eventually yield more about the nature of the "secrets" than the patient could ever tell the psychiatrist directly.

> Another evaluation involved a man who had had a snowmobile accident which left him badly damaged, physically, neurologically, and psychologically. Reports had been sent by his doctor, his wife had been contacted, and arrangements for an inpatient evaluation had been made. It was only at a team meeting prior to the date the evaluation was to begin that it was revealed that no one had ever contacted the patient himself. Only then did it become clear that he had been treated as a passive participant—as someone we would do things to rather than actively engage in the evaluation. This key diagnostic issue told something about the way people react to the patient.

Diagnosis Has Detrimental Social-Political Implications

This concern is an outgrowth of the previous fear about the patient being controlled. Here the fear is extended beyond the individual patient to an apprehension concerning control by society at large, or at least by certain groups within society. Szasz, for example, has long feared that diagnosis could be used as a social-judgmental way of stigmatizing certain behaviors to sanction incarcerating in mental hospitals those people who manifest undesirable behavior (1961, 1966, 1970). In short, he argues that diagnosis can be used as a "justificatory rhetoric" to exclude systematically certain groups under the guise of their being regarded as mentally ill. To prove this point, he has called attention to an article published in 1851 by a psychiatrist who argued that behavior of the Negro slave which was unacceptable to his white master was due to mental illness and should be treated by punishment and further enslavement (1971). Commenting on this early abuse of diagnosis, Szasz asserts:

> By substituting involuntary mental patients for Negro slaves, institutional psychiatrists for white slave owners, and the rhetoric of mental health for that of white supremacy, we may learn a fresh lesson about the changing verbal patterns man

uses to justify exploiting and oppressing his fellow man, in the name of helping him [1971, p. 239].

Such concerns also bring to mind the Russians' use of "treatment centers" for its dissidents.

The point, then, is not that Szasz is right or wrong, for he might be either, depending upon the circumstances in a particular case, but by tarring all diagnoses with the same brush, he acts as if this misuse were built into diagnosis, rather than being an abuse of it. To do away with diagnosis because it can be misapplied is tantamount to abolishing surgery because some physicians perform unethical or unnecessary operations. Nevertheless, the point implicit in Szasz' criticism is that where there is no clear body of agreed upon and established scientific knowledge about what constitutes psychiatric disturbance and treatment, the way is open to abuses of the kind he notes. This observation holds true for the recent treatment fads which are justified on little more than the claim that "it has worked for my patients."

If one is concerned about diagnosis leading to social control, then what can be said for treatment itself? Certainly the potential for such control is much greater in treatment because of its length and the depth of personal relationship involved. Are we then to shy away from treating patients because the potential for social control exists? Neither Szasz nor Rogers spell out how the clinician provides the conditions under which the patient can grow and develop without at the same time being in a position to exercise some control by virtue of his special relationship with the patient. The issue which Szasz and Rogers struggle with is how to insure that in helping people to mental health we do not end by controlling them. Because this danger exists they see interventions as inherently harmful and want, in effect, to throw the baby out with the bathwater. For us, however, the answer is more a recognition that probably any human endeavor which creates conditions of psychological intimacy has the potential of being misused, and one must at all times guard against that danger by continual scrutiny of one's own and one's colleagues' professional behavior. Surely, the best way to guard against the imposition of deleterious control for nontreatment motives is to develop a sound body of knowledge which would provide a reasonably objective basis for treatment decisions: sometimes a person needs to be controlled for his sake and others, but when? Indeed, control in itself is not inherently bad. Society, for example, must exercise control via institutions or else chaos would ensue. An intellectually limited individual may need some "control" (a sheltered residential setting, for example) because of his inadequate capacities. Not to provide such control would be inhumane. The issue, then, concerns the control which the patient himself is capable of (self-control) and how that can best be fostered. The development and practice of diagnosis can lead to a reasonable answer to this and other questions.

Diagnosis as a Mere "Label" or an Invalid "Reification"

Dissatisfaction with diagnosis also arises because it is seen as "labeling" or "pigeonholing." Goolker (1956) makes this point explicit by asserting:

> The emphasis in descriptive psychiatry on diagnosis . . . used largely as a labeling device, has brought about a reactive trend in extramural psychiatry against rigid classification. In addition, the historical shift of emphasis to dynamics and understanding of the individual patient tended further to discourage formal diagnosis. In the twenties and early thirties one could often hear leaders in psychotherapy excoriate their colleagues for wasting time in diagnosis instead of studying the patient as an individual with problems [p. 364].

The last two statements are particularly interesting because they imply that diagnosis is inherently antithetical to "dynamics and understanding" and to "studying the patient as an individual with problems." This viewpoint implies that diagnosis must necessarily exclude these things because it can only be labeling!

Beck (1962) succinctly illustrates the tendency to equate diagnosis with labeling. He wonders about

> . . . the degree to which the psychiatrist depends on the diagnostic label in actual clinical decision-making. It could be argued, for instance, that the psychiatrist is seldom bound exclusively by the actual diagnosis (except, perhaps, in "organic cases") but bases his treatment recommendations on such characteristics as the severity or chronicity of the illness, the degree of impairment of reality testing and social effectiveness, the capacity for insight, and the motivation for health. Under such circumstances, he might simply regard the clinical diagnosis as an additional bit of information . . . which may support the therapeutic decisions made on the basis of other factors [p. 213].

It is evident that Beck distinguishes diagnosis from the other "characteristics" he mentions which can form the basis for treatment considerations. This is striking, because it is these other characteristics which are at the heart of the diagnostic enterprise and which form the basis for the unfolding of the diagnostic process—just as labeling itself plays a relatively small part in diagnosis.

Menninger *et al.* (1963) make a case for labeling, or naming, as being a necessary but not sufficient part of the diagnosis:

> Naming has long been a feature of diagnosis; giving a name to something implies an acquaintanceship with it. This can be very misleading; an acquaintanceship can be shallow or deep, and there is no easy way of telling which it is. Furthermore, giving a name to something implies a degree of mastery over it. . . . Medical

science has mastered many diseases not by giving them names but by coming to understand their nature [p. 36].

At another point they submit:

> . . . even more important than the treatment is skillful diagnosis. But this means diagnosis in a new sense, not the mere application of a label. It is not a search for a proper name by which one can refer to this affliction in this and other patients. It is diagnosis in the sense of understanding just how the patient is ill and how ill the patient is, how he became ill and how his illness serves him. From this knowledge one may draw logical conclusions regarding how changes might be brought about in or around the patient which would affect his illness [pp. 6–7].

Thus, the limited idea of diagnosis as labeling is a contrast to our conception of it as an assessment of individual functions leading to ways of using such an understanding to plan for treatment.

Closely related to dissatisfaction with diagnosis because it is used as labeling is the objection to diagnosis as invalid reification, which assumes that the label refers to one given entity. When diagnosis is regarded as this kind of reification, the argument often follows that because the patients placed in a given nosological category (e.g., schizophrenia) differ and manifest much intragroup variability, diagnosis is faulty and hence useless. This line of thought misses the very essence of diagnosis which is to determine ways in which each patient differs from the model or ideal type. These departures from the norm reflect the patient's individuality which can only be assessed in terms of specific psychological functions. As Alexander has noted, "What the therapist is primarily interested in is not the nosological classification of a person, not in what way he is similar to others but in what way he differs from them" (1956, p. 694). The point is that it is a misapplication of diagnosis to expect the patients' disturbances to fall neatly into classical nosological categories. This error is compounded by then objecting to diagnosis because such reifications of ideal types do not apply to each case and are thus invalid. This apparent lack of validity occurs because of a narrow and misleading conception of diagnosis. The fact is that individual disturbances do not correspond to ideal types in textbooks because only ideal types based on general principles appear in textbooks. Otherwise, the latter would be little more than endless catalogues or listings of individual variations of little use to the student who wants to understand a particular patient in terms of general principles and how his deviations particularize him. The "label" as such should serve as a beginning, not an end point in diagnosis—because once the broad nosological category is determined it then becomes crucial to delineate in what ways the particular patient fits and does not fit the abstract ideal type.

An opposite kind of error can also be made, i.e., stressing individuality to the point that it would not allow for principles which transcend the individual. Alexander (1956, p. 694) has asserted, "Psychoanalysis is the most individual type of treatment which medical science has ever produced. Each case is a unique problem. . . . Every person has his own potential formula of adjustment. . . . which takes cognizance not only of a given social environment but also of the uniqueness of every person." This view raises another problem: If we are all unique, in what way are we all human? And if we are all so unique, would it not be impossible to establish general principles of human nature and to learn and to be able to generalize? Would we not be totally ignorant of how to help each new patient if all previous ones were also unique?

One final objection regarding labeling involves the socially pejorative effect of diagnosing the patient, for example, as schizophrenic. Menninger *et al.* argue that, "The pragmatic point . . . hinges upon the effect that such labeling is apt to have upon those who might bring about improvement in the patient were they not deterred by the implications of the label. This means not only the physicians but his relatives and friends, the community at large, and even the patient himself" (1963, p. 46). But here, too, we are talking about diagnosis as equivalent to labels and thereby doing an injustice both to our patients and to the diagnostic endeavor, although certainly the diagnostician should take into account what effects certain terms have on people in formulating his recommendations.

When we become engaged in discussions over whether the patient is schizophrenic or not, we can mistakenly slip into pigeonholing or name calling. Even at best we would probably be approaching the task at too high a level of abstraction to be of value. In short, we need to define the issues in any case as more function oriented than label oriented.

The Unreliability of Diagnosis

Pasamanick, Dinitz, and Lefton (1959) state that, "Any number of studies have indicated that psychiatric diagnosis is at present so unreliable as to merit very serious question when classifying, treating and studying patient behavior and outcome" (p. 127). But is such unreliability a basis for doing away with diagnosis? Or is it not instead a reason for redoubling our efforts to refine diagnosis so as to make it more useful? Menninger *et al.* (1963) meet this issue squarely:

> We, the authors, vigorously oppose the view that treatment, other than first aid, should proceed before or without diagnosis. On the contrary, we feel that diagnosis is today more important than ever. The very fact that psychiatric designations have become so meaningless by conflicting usage makes it more rather than less necessary that we approach the specific problem of illness with a cautious, careful scrutiny and appraisal that has characterized the best medical science since the early days. It is still necessary to know in advance, to plan as logically as we can, what kind of interference with a human life we propose to make [p. 6].

Beck (1962) has critically examined a number of studies with an eye toward assessing the reliability of psychiatric diagnosis. He submits that nosology itself is but one of the factors which can increase variability. In particular, he points out that unreliability seems due to the varying degrees of training and experience of clinicians. Pasamanick *et al.* (1959) also respond to critics who object to diagnosis because of its unreliability. They emphasize that unreliability can be due to differences in psychiatrists' theoretical orientations. To help remedy this bias, they propose developing more objective criteria of classification.

There is another point to be made about theoretical orientation, observer bias, and unreliability. Theories are often based on different concepts about the same disturbance, due in part to the fact that diagnosticians look at different aspects of disturbance: what they look at depends upon the explanations they accept for these disturbances. Also, divergences which reduce reliability enter in because different interventions flow from these explanations. These interventions in themselves alter the functioning under observation and shape the feedback from what is observed and thereby change what is observed from then on. When a phobia is treated by desensitization, it is unlikely much will be learned about the personal meaning of the phobia. Thus, the behavior modifier need not encounter data which conflict with his understanding of the process. He need only say, "It works!"

This interdependence among observers, the understanding of functioning, and the effects of intervention based on this understanding constitute a reply to those who argue that since everything is bound to come out in treatment anyway, why bother with diagnosis separate from treatment. The point is that once explaining begins, interventions occur which modify what is subsequently observed. "Everything" does not emerge, for the unsolicited observation of unselected functioning clearly never occurs.

Diagnosis Is only Valuable if Treatment Is Available or if Treatment Choices Are Available

If no treatment is available, why diagnose? The answer is that diagnosis in itself can lead to eventual treatment discoveries by virtue of its use of investigation, experimentation and research. General paresis was differentiated (Coleman 1956) by the careful noting and describing of the symptom pattern by Bayle which led to its differentiation as a specific form of mental illness. Further diagnostic work by Esmarch and Jensen, Argyll Robertson, Krafft-Ebing, Schaudinn, Von Wassermann, and Plaut revealed that syphilis caused paresis and that the spirochaeta pallida caused syphilis. These findings then led to the development of diagnostic procedures for determining involvement of the central nervous system and for the presence of spirochaetes in the blood stream. It was not until a century after Bayle's description that Ehrlich and Wagner-Jauregg developed the first treatment for paresis. Sound diagnosis ultimately led to the identification of causes and to the development of a specific treatment.

Why diagnose if no treatment alternatives are available? Patterson (1948) assumes there are ". . . basic elements of maladjustment common to all mental disorder. . . . a common basic etiology. . ." (p. 157). He argues, "Since all maladjustment is similar in origin, diagnosis . . . is not essential to therapy. Similarly, knowledge of the content of the conflict involved is unessential as a prerequisite of therapy, since the technique of therapy does not depend on the nature or content of the conflict. . ." (p. 158). A unidimensional theory of disturbance gives rise to a unidimensional treatment, obviating the need for diagnosis. But would it not be helpful and humane to know in advance whether a patient can or cannot use the single treatment modality available? If a patient's "positive growth forces" are not strong enough to enable him to profit from this treatment, would it not save time, money, and energy to know that before beginning? For Patterson, those patients who are inaccessible to his treatment approach need to be excluded, at least until their positive growth forces reemerge; but would it not be helpful—indeed obligatory—to try to discover, diagnostically, why such forces are not available and how they might be mobilized? Finally, what of those patients for whom treatment has proven ineffective? Patterson offers no alternative treatments. But might not diagnosis help to develop new treatments which could be beneficial, as exemplified by the history of general paresis?

Diagnosis Is Based on Outmoded and Unworkable Machinery Built According to the Medical Model

Patterson (1948) takes issue with the idea that mental disorder can be understood in terms of a medical model. Linking the medical model to physical disease, he questions the applicability of that model to "mental disease." He argues that two different levels of functioning are involved, e.g., physical-chemical versus psychological-social. Moreover he submits that, ". . . while in physical medicine accurate differential etiological diagnosis is possible, leading to the selection of specific remedies, in the field of mental disease no such specific etiological diagnosis is possible, nor are there specific, discrete psychotherapies which have differential effects from which to choose" (pp. 155–156).

The medical approach to diagnosis is seen by Patterson as limited to identifying discrete entities like "diseases" and "pathogenic agents." His opinion appears to be that the medical model in psychiatry is used mainly to describe rather than to explain. A polarity is drawn between description and explanation; static versus active; Kraepelin, the father of descriptive psychiatry, versus Freud, the originator of dynamic psychiatry. Finally, because of the medical model's reliance on such things as "etiological factors" and "disease agents" it is seen as encouraging an emphasis on specific contents or information per se rather than on the patient-doctor relationship and what it can reveal.

More recently the application of the medical model to psychopathology has been attacked because of a presumed overemphasis on "intra-psychic" as opposed to "inter-personal" and "environmental" factors. The physician as psychiatrist looks for an "intra-psychic conflict" much as the internist looks for a "bug." The psychiatrist is thus blinded to events in the patient's life which may be of greater importance than the "psychic bug." Lastly, the medical model is criticized because it is seen as a weapon in the political warfare between physicians and other professionals, in particular, psychologists. Priority and status, according to this argument, are attributed to those who have society's sanction to "practice medicine" as if the medical model—a mode of clinical investigation—could be the property of any one group.

In our view, the "medical model" is an effort to apply scientific method to the study of mental and physical disorders. The underlying principles of the medical model, as in all science, are to observe, classify, explain and verify with the addition that the explanation often results in a treatment. Psychologists and other nonphysicians can recognize in the medical model another version of the scientific method applied to a particular range of phenomena. Because psychologists have a general scientific background they are in a good position to assess the ways in which the medical model as actually practiced approximates or diverges from the basic tenets of scientific method. In a certain sense, this is what we are undertaking in this paper.

In most of the objections to the medical model cited, especially Patterson's, a fundamental error is made: the particular findings or techniques of the method involved in the medical model are confused with the nature of the method itself. Because the medical model has resulted in findings which make sense in terms of a disease model or have led to the discovery of specific disease causing agents, some assume that this is all the medical model can bring to light. But a method may give rise to many techniques and to many findings. Astronomers look through an optic telescope themselves or they may place a photographic plate where their eye was and get a different kind of record. Both are techniques useful in exploiting the method of optic viewing of the heavens and give rise to different findings. There is no reason why the medical model as here discussed cannot be applied to interpersonal and environmental factors as easily as to intrapsychic factors.

We view diagnosis as a guide to understanding. We believe that a diagnostic point of view fosters a way of approaching clinical issues and conceptualizing them. As such, it uses the basic methods of science. Thorne states, "It is not desirable for psychologists to retrace the steps of generations of physicians and psychiatrists in discovering the principles of clinical science, or for physicians and psychiatrists to retrace the steps taken by modern psychology in applying the experimental method to the study of personality'' (1947, p. 159). In order to avoid the rediscovery of what is common knowledge to each of the professions, we need to integrate these apparently different approaches by realizing that the medical model can be used as an example of how the scientific model can be applied to clinical problems.

THE NATURE OF THE DIAGNOSTIC PROCESS

We are now ready to consider the nature of the diagnostic process and how it can best be practiced on the basis of the definition we offered in the introduction in which a number of key terms were emphasized. To clarify these key terms, we will consider them separately.

"... Through the Medium of a Personal Relationship. ..."

The psychodiagnostician often forgets that he is becoming acquainted with a person through a personal relationship no matter how transitory and tentative. If psychological functioning is to be elicited and observed, it can only be done in the context of one person responding to another with the psychological means at his disposal. When viewed in this way, it is clear that diagnosis does not begin when the patient arrives. It has started before, or he would not even be coming for help. And how it has started is related to how the patient has perceived his future relationship with the clinician. The clinician, then, is entering into an ongoing process which plays a role in shaping the patient's response to the diagnostic process even before the patient is seen. And it is just this perceived relationship which can greatly color what follows, as Holzman and Schlesinger (1972) have discussed in a paper dealing with ''beginnings.''

"Eliciting and Observing ... Psychological Functioning."

In order to elicit and observe psychological functioning the diagnostician must have a *method* so he can examine what he must understand. This is far from a simple matter and requires careful, explicit consideration. Different methods are possible which have their own special links to the diagnostician's frame of reference which can also be equally various. However, it is uncommon for method and theory to be linked explicitly in practice. Nevertheless, the need remains to trace through the relationship between method and theory so we can say that we understand what we are doing. An esoteric example far removed in content from our contemporary preoccupations may serve to clarify these issues. For a phrenologist, the diagnostic method would involve an examination of the skull. Very likely he would palpate the skull for bumps and protrusions and refer to a chart for the different size estimates and locations. He would then be ready to draw inferences about personality. The method is exquisitely simple, the links to theory a model of precision, and the technique to be mastered is straightforward. In this example one can neatly distinguish between the method (examination of the skull for bumps and protrusions) and the technique (palpating the skull). One could use another technique (X-rays) while still using the same method. However, the distinction between method and technique and the relationship between method and theory become blurred once we opt for intrinsically psychological approaches. It becomes hard to keep clearly separated in one's mind the assumptions we are making about psychological functioning from the way we hope to find out about them. A good example of this confusion is the conscious or unconscious resort to suggestion in which the clinician's ideas (his explanations or theories) are offered to the patient before the application of his method has advanced far enough to generate sufficient evidence for or against his ideas. Moreover, once the suggestion is conveyed it becomes a methodological impurity which distorts the new evidence gathered (e.g., the patient may provide the clinician now with positive evidence to please him, now with negative evidence to thwart him).

In a series of posthumously published lectures, Rapaport (1967) analyzed what he considered to be the assumptions the diagnostician makes when he asks another person to tell him his troubles. He refers to this exchange as the "clinical-historical method." He demonstrates that whoever undertakes to use the clinical-historical method in a consistent and reasonable way will be making a number of assumptions about what people are like. First, like all other scientists, the diagnostician assumes that phenomena, no matter how mysterious or baffling, are determined, and that a pattern of factors exist which, once known, will dispel the mystery. The phenomena in question are the patient's troubles, his account of them, his manner of telling about them, and his accompanying actions. Clearly the patient himself is baffled by his complaint; usually his efforts at dealing with his problems have proved ineffective or he would not have come for help. Phobias, uncontrollable rage attacks, somatic symptoms without physical cause, repetitive failures in significant life situations (work, marriage, school), hearing voices, seeing things, etc. are all experiences which do not "fit" with our usual expectations. They create *discontinuities* in the relatively ordered course of life.

Rapaport suggests that if we take seriously the fact that the "discontinuity" (e.g., a phobia) is "psychic" (a psychological experience, e.g., fear) then it is reasonable to assume that at least some causes for the discontinuity must also be psychic. Thus the broadly shared scientific assumption of determinism can be further specified to apply to the historical-clinical method in the form of *psychic determinism*. From this assumption it then follows that there are psychic factors of which the person is unaware or else he would be able to tell them to us and the "discontinuity" would vanish. *Unconscious psychic factors emerge as a necessary corollary of psychic determinism,* which in turn is derived from the broader scientific assumption of determinism. From this point of view, the psychodynamic frame of reference is an intrinsic part of the historical-clinical method no matter how explicit the clinician's recognition of it may be. Although no paraphernalia other than a couple of chairs in a room are necessary, sitting and talking to a person about his troubles implicates a number of significant ideas and assumptions about people and a method is being applied as surely as when a skull is being examined.

We should stress that in what we have said thus far we have not touched at all on specific theories about the *content* of the patient's complaints, e.g., the nature of symptom formation as in phobias, neurotic and psychotic disorders, etc. On these grounds there may be much disagreement. But despite these disagreements, we are proposing that anybody who sits down with a person to listen to his troubles with the express purpose of doing something about them must, as a minimum, make the assumptions we have discussed although he may ignore them and try to act as if they were not at work.

It is interesting to note that when four clinicians were asked by NIMH to spend a week observing how Wolpe and Lazarus, two pioneers in behavior therapy, actually conducted their clinical work, the group concluded that the behavior therapists involved themselves in their diagnostic sessions much as would psychodynamically-oriented clinicians:

> The popular notion of simplicity in behavior therapy covers not only treatment techniques but diagnostic procedures as well. Many people suppose that the therapist begins by clearly and systematically defining the patient's problems in terms of manageable hierarchies and then selects appropriate responses to be strengthened or weakened. We found little support for this conception of behavior therapy diagnosis in our observations. Indeed the selection of problems to be worked on often seemed quite arbitrary and inferential. We were frankly surprised to find the presenting symptomatic complaint was often side-stepped for what the therapist intuitively considered to be more basic issues. Most surprising to us, the basis for this selection seemed often to be what others would call dynamic considerations. The distinction between "secondary" (that is, the superficial) and "primary" (the more basic, underlying) was even made openly on occasion by behavior therapists: The words we have put in quotes are their terms. The literature, of course, gives no hint of this development [Klein, Dittmann, Parloff, and Gill 1969, p. 261].

The distinction between "secondary" and "primary" would be comparable to what we are referring to as the discovery of a discontinuity which is then followed by some effort to determine what underlying causes are at work which are not available to the patient.

Once we have clearly in mind the broad context defined as the clinical-historical method, then we can focus on some implications for technique, or on the specific manner in which a person's account of his difficulties is elicited. If we grant the assumption that discontinuities are likely to appear in the patient's account and that he cannot readily fill in these gaps for us, then in our technique we must act to clarify where these discontinuities exist and how much the patient himself is able to explain about them. Even before the patient tells his story, he conveys information and perhaps raises questions by his very presence, e.g., his gait, expression, choice of chair in the office, and posture. As his story unfolds, the clinician must work hard to avoid further diagnosing, that is, the way in which the patient tells why he comes cannot help but raise questions (his choice of words, degree of congruence between what he says and his mood, his attempt to make sense of and correct his troubles). And all this is considered in addition to the issues raised by the content of what the patient says, i.e., what he reveals and what he conceals—especially what inconsistencies stand out which highlight discontinuities in his psychic life. It is easy when a phobic patient himself recognizes the unreasonableness of his fear, but it is more difficult when the problem is one of subtle, recurrent patterns of self-defeating behavior, e.g., a college student fails in subjects when there is no reason to suspect intellectual limitations. In such a case one must listen with great care and elicit the kind of account which, like a puzzle falling into place, begins to outline in clearer and clearer detail the missing pieces. The clinician cannot choose to have such things be present or not, for the patient brings with him such issues as aspects of his problems and his personality makeup. The clinician can only choose whether he will pay attention to such issues or not. But once he seeks to help the patient understand himself, he cannot avoid being aware of incongruities which raise questions for him and, ultimately, for the patient as well. This is so because in treating the patient certain things need to be focused on or else the interaction becomes a random discussion with no issues being differentially weighted. From this standpoint, it is impossible not to note the things which puzzle, raise questions, and lead to tentative hypotheses which are explored with the patient.

The crux of the matter becomes, then, how explicit the clinician is in his observations and questions, how systematic he is in pursuing hypotheses which clarify and raise new questions, and at what point in his work with the patient he does this. Does he do it only after some not very well thought through interventions do not work leaving him and the patient dissatisfied? Or does he do it before formal treatment is undertaken—in fact, using his prior understanding to shape treatment? It is the latter way of thinking which Cameron (1953) had in mind when he regarded diagnosis as ". . . a design for action. This statement—that the diagnosis is a design for action—is simply part of the general statement that the question, 'What is it?', is always bound up with its twin question, 'What am I going to do about it?' " (pp. 33–34). As such, diagnosis generates a program for doing something "about it" which flows from answering the question, "What is it?"

The largest pitfall in diagnosis is for the diagnostician to "conduct an examination." If he does so, he forgets that he is interacting with another person to whom he very quickly begins to mean something and who begins to mean something to him. If, for example, the patient experiences the interviewer as a tough, intolerant person (perhaps because the patient tends to see all people in positions he considers to be prestigious and powerful in that way), then he may be uncooperative, withholding, and defiant. In fact, these observations may be the most meaningful diagnostically. From the point of view of the "examination," the "facts" are somehow assumed to be objective events, hard and immutable, which the patient can observe and report. As we noted earlier, there can be no observations without prior expectation and this applies to the patient with even greater force than to the scientist struggling to be objective. The interviewer must always be attuned as much to the patient's attitudes as to the events he describes, which, considering the purpose of the interview, may be even more relevant than the events themselves, for these attitudes are related to the critical ways in which the patient *functions* in a given situation. As we shall discuss at greater length later, it is precisely these modes of functioning in which we are especially interested.

To focus on the "facts," then, is to make the patient into a reporter or recorder and to ignore him as a person interacting with the interviewer. If the criticism of diagnosis made by Rogers has any validity, it is as applied to the diagnostic process as a fact-gathering enterprise which largely ignores the person and what he is doing at the time. But ignoring the person is not simply "antihumanistic"; mainly it is not doing the job of understanding the person and his difficulties with a view toward helping him. Often the neophyte physician treats the person with psychological complaints as if he were suffering from physical complaints and the physician simply elicits an account of them. The intuitive diagnostician in any specialty in which people are his concern is always aware of the influences we have been trying to describe. Nevertheless, it is only for the diagnostician of mental disorders that the very target of inquiry is the person and his psychological functioning. To conduct a history-taking inquiry is thus beside the point; nor will the attempt to counterbalance this with a "psychological examination" or "mental status" examination succeed in rectifying this error. These are still "examinations" in which the patient is placed in a passive, impersonal position of being the reporter, not of past events, but of his own current functioning.

We do not naively believe that patients eagerly enter into a diagnostic alliance. Most patients come for help or relief, not diagnosis, and tolerate the latter as a required preliminary step. But we do submit that the patient is often not given a chance to involve himself because he is seen as little more than a passive conveyor of information. What is missed is seeing the patient as someone whose very involvement allows for the necessary assessment of current functioning. In the interview the patient is revealing his psychological functioning when he is telling the examiner about his life; one need not change the task in order to observe his functioning.

". . . Eliciting and Observing *Psychological Functioning*. . . ."

The processes and states we infer from behavior are describable in terms of psychological functions: perceiving, feeling, wanting, judging, remembering, attending, concentrating, thinking, fantasizing, dreaming, acting, etc. We may conceive of these functions as making up the *form* of the mind. These are the processes which give the mind its shape, coherence, and order as well as its uniqueness of style and balance. This psychic form is not a static structure like the frame of a building; it is closer to the formal elements of music which are extended in time—fluid, repetitive, built up of complex simultaneities—many functions going on at the same time creating harmonious chords as well as discords. But as in music, or in any human undertaking, there is always a theme, or some content: what the functions are about. To change the analogy from music to mathematics, a function has to do with some variable or factor. Although we can think of addition as a mathematical function in the abstract, in any given case there is always something being added. Similarly, in any specific case we cannot imagine psychological functions without the particular ideas, impressions, impulses they operate with. Generally and most importantly, the content concerns relationships with people. If psychological functions provide the form, then personal relationships by-and-large provide the content of our minds. Thus, we speak of psychological functions as constituting *formal* properties, while personal relationships in general provide the main *content. Mental disorder can be defined as the disturbance of certain psychological functions bearing on specific personal relationships.*** Once we define mental disorder as the disturbance of psychic functioning dealing with personal relationships, then we can see more clearly why the diagnostician must pay careful attention to how the patient reacts to him, for it is the clinician's presence and purpose which *elicits* the patient's particular pattern of functioning with respect to that specific personal relationship. Only in this way can the diagnostician be reasonably sure that he is sampling

---

* It may seem that we are not offering a real distinction between psychological functioning and personal relationships since it could be argued that all psychological functioning has to do with personal relationships. This is not so. Experimental psychologists, for example, are concerned with depth perception which may have little "loading" for personal relationships. At the same time, there may be some seemingly emotionally neutral functioning (e.g., lining up a tilted rod in a frame, seeing a fixed source of light appearing to move) which may have significant relationships to how people function in their personal life and thus may be of help diagnostically. It is of further interest to note that some brain diseases may seriously affect psychological functioning while not affecting personal relationships as extensively. The converse of this, however, is not true. It is difficult to imagine a disturbance of personal relationships without a concomitant disturbance of psychological functioning.

actual functioning and not obtaining a pale account of a remembered event which he may mistakenly treat as a significant "fact." The "fact" is merely a particular content whose special form and significance is determined by the shape of the vessel into which it is poured.

". . . Relevant on Some Theoretical Grounds. . . ."

A useful diagnostic method requires a level of clinical formulation of issues which initially is only one or two inference steps removed from the observations themselves. A good theory and method well thought through and applied not only helps us understand things not otherwise understood but, perhaps even more important, throws into sharp relief those things which we do not understand and cannot deal with readily. It takes light to cast shadow. Whenever we are dealing with complex subject matter in which many factors are at work, we are confronted not only with describing many relationships but also with the task of assigning degrees of saliency or importance to these various relationships. Thus, Anna Freud has remarked in her *Studies on Developmental Profiles* (1965) that in any individual case we cannot be sure that a given factor, no matter how important it may appear from a theoretical standpoint, really was important in that particular individual's life. We may assume on theoretical grounds that an early, prolonged separation from the mother should have serious consequences and yet it may not because of other factors which one could only learn about through a thorough knowledge of the patient's life.

Earlier we cited a brief clinical example of a patient whose role in the evaluation was seemingly ignored by the team who were preoccupied with the patient's wife's great concern about the patient's physical and psychological difficulties. The patient had become a passive nonparticipant whose welfare was being looked after. How did it happen that even before the patient arrived he was already treated in a certain definite way? Was the family conspiring to do this? Was this the patient's way of exploiting his difficulties? Was it the staff's strictly "medical" reaction to a patient with clear physical complaints? One does not need to be a psychoanalyst to formulate these questions, yet without them one cannot begin to diagnose. These are questions quite different from asking whether or not this man is a passive-aggressive personality. This question places a bet against long odds, requiring a considerably longer chain of inference to be correct in the absence of any real evidence. Secondly, why should *this* possibility be selected and not others? It may very well be that the man is so physically debilitated that he literally cannot take an active part in his evaluation. The level of issue formulation closely related to the current situation should leave the door open to the possibility that the patient could turn out to be a passive-aggressive personality once he arrived on the scene and the diagnostic process could get underway.

Another illustration may further clarify this point.

A mother wrote the Diagnostic Service about her daughter, a 19-year-old girl previously diagnosed as retarded, who was now quite withdrawn and talking to an imaginary companion. There was a notable omission in the letter: the mother did not mention her husband's role, although the letter was articulate, quite detailed and conveyed a tragic sense of the agony this mother experienced in trying to live with a demented girl. One would have thought that she was widowed or divorced, although we knew from one brief mention that her husband worked for some local concern and that indeed there was a father involved. Why did the mother not refer to her husband's involvement with the same meaningfulness as she did her own? Did he remove himself from the house, unable to tolerate the emotional stress? Did the mother exclude him, thus creating a close bond with the daughter? Or was there tension between father and daughter which resulted in the father's retreat? (One of the team member's first response to these issues was to announce that we should call the mother and make sure the father came for the consultation. For him it was not a diagnostic issue but a call to action.) Actually, the husband arrived with the mother and the patient. We discovered he was the stepfather who had an especially warm and tender relationship with his stepdaughter. The mother's apparent exclusion of him appeared to make sense in terms of her own guilty dedication to her ill daughter for whom she accepted full responsibility—an attitude which had been a source of resistance to acting on previous recommendations that the daughter be placed in a vocational rehabilitation program and be trained for the kind of simple occupation she could master. This attitude was also one of the main resistances in the current evaluation. At the same time this maternal dedication could become a source of great support for a treatment program if it could be mobilized realistically.

We emphasize that the kind of reasoning just described remains close to observation and is relatively free of theoretical complexity. Nevertheless, the argument is guided by certain methodological assumptions, e.g., the absence of reference to the father is a "discontinuity" for which there must be a psychic cause. We hypothesized the cause to be the wife's need to join her own fate to her daughter's and thus overlook the valuable relationship the husband had with her daughter. There may have been other "deeper" causes having to do with her competition with her husband, her identification with her own mother, etc. In order to explore these hypotheses for confirmatory evidence, it would have been necessary to focus the evaluation more on the mother than on the daughter who was the patient. In clinical work explanatory economy can be defined as that extent of explanation necessary to deal with the problem at hand. This conception of explanation is far different from the scientific ideal of a complete explanation.

There is also another important theoretical construct included in our limited explanation—resistance, a clinical concept introduced to explain why any patient would pose difficulties in the way of achieving what he wants for himself in treatment. Clearly this mother wanted to cooperate in the treatment program for her daughter. She herself was sinking into physical exhaustion as a result of her efforts to be at her daughter's beck and call; yet whatever theatened to remove the daughter from the home she opposed. Her other daughters (two of whom had recently moved out of the home) attested to their mother's strong grip on the family. Here was another "discontinuity" which we could explain on the basis of some unconscious need to hold onto her destructive relationship to her sick daughter. In order for any recommendation to be accepted, this resistance would need to be moderated. The social worker, in joint interviews with the parents and the patient, was able to point out the pattern of previous rejections of treatment recommendations and the mother's current anxiety about any treatment which would take the patient away from home. There was no need to plumb for any deeper reasons other than to accept the mother's dedication to her daughter as a source of her resistance. An acceptable program was worked out.

The importance of what we shall call *middle level issues* can be schematized in the form of a diagnostic triangle whose height is a time line drawn from childhood to the present and whose base represents the many potentially influential factors at work in the patient since early in life (see Figure 1). The triangle itself represents the shape of an individual's character organization. The lines inside the triangle represent lines of progressive influence of certain given factors as they interact with life circumstances and shape character. Lines that stop short of the apex have ceased to be of current importance. The figure also represents how character itself is a slowly developing structure gradually achieving its final form and size (integration of many inner and outer influences). We can draw many other baselines at closer points in time thus creating new triangles smaller than the original but contained within it. One such triangle would represent the situation at the time the patient seeks help; its baseline would represent the current underlying forces, derivatives of the past, which are producing discontinuities in the patient's life. The apex of the triangle, C, stands for the current issue, or discontinuity of greatest importance, because it arises from the confluence of the major determining factors and thus provides a point of entry into assessing their strength and quality for diagnostic purposes.

But what if the wrong issue has been identified or no issue at all as in a strictly examinational or history-taking approach? (See Figures 2 and 3.) When the wrong issue is defined, C', and even if some of the currently influential forces are identified correctly (represented by a portion of baseline DE being included in triangle A'B'C') the entire conception of the personality will be wrong (represented by the obtuse triangle A'B'C' rather than isosceles triangle, ABC), the role of certain significant personality factors will be missed (represented by the dotted lines within the isosceles triangle cutting across triangle A'B'C' and not converging on C'), some critical current factors will be missed (represented by the portion of line DE not included in triangle A'B'C'), as well as some critical early factors (represented by line AA'), while hypotheses about

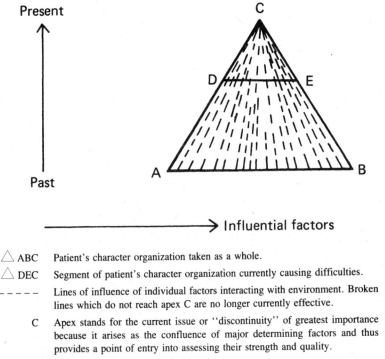

Present

Past

Influential factors

△ ABC   Patient's character organization taken as a whole.

△ DEC   Segment of patient's character organization currently causing difficulties.

- - - - -   Lines of influence of individual factors interacting with environment. Broken lines which do not reach apex C are no longer currently effective.

C   Apex stands for the current issue or "discontinuity" of greatest importance because it arises as the confluence of major determining factors and thus provides a point of entry into assessing their strength and quality.

Figure 1.   The diagnostic triangle

nonexisting factors will be added (represented by line BB′). The closer the misleading issue is to the real one, however, the more nearly will the emerging triangle approximate the correct one.

In a history-taking approach in which no attempt is made to define an issue, facts gathered from the patient's account will usually provide information about some underlying factors (represented by line DE′) which will generally lead to additional facts going back to childhood about some of the developmental forces. However, as the patient's account may be erroneous and distorted, some purported factors will be spurious and will lead to emphasizing as important various noninfluential recent and early factors (this is represented by the broken lines DD′ and AA′). But most important, the entire shape of the character organization is mistaken (represented by trapezoid D′E′B′A′) and most currently operative forces and their specific effect in the present are entirely lost (represented by nothing being at the level of the present).

Finally, a premature formulation of a character picture before any evidence

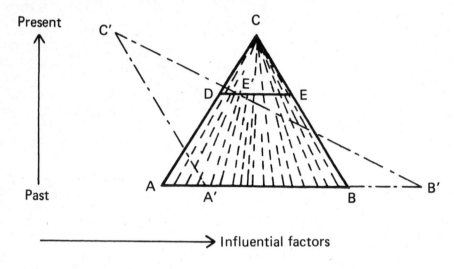

Present

↑

Past

⟶ Influential factors

△ A'B'C'   Erroneous conception of patient's character organization represented correctly by △ABC.

C'   Misleading current issue.

$\overline{DE'}$ Currently influential factors correctly identified in otherwise misleading diagnosis.

$\overline{E'E}$ Currently influential factors not correctly identified.

$\overline{AA'}$ Early influential factors not identified by incorrect diagnosis.

$\overline{BB'}$ Nonexistent early influential factors identified by incorrect diagnosis.

Figure 2.   A misleading issue is defined

has been assessed or issues defined (e.g., patient is a passive-aggressive personality) is simply a figment of the diagnostician's imagination and only with luck will it coincide with the actual personality. This needs no figural representation.

How do we "select" the right factors so that we are reasonably sure we are dealing with the main forces in a person? We know that the past must have some bearing on the present—a point at which significant past factors are currently active. It is finding that point of current activity which we believe to be crucially involved in the finding of the "middle level" issues of significance. Somehow subtly excluding her husband emotionally, like the mother in the last case, or engaging the psychiatrist in a stubborn battle over withholding information, like the patient cited previously, may be the critical behavior which is the current representative of a significant personal issue going back into the past. Issues of this kind permit the clinician to enter the right triangle by way of its apex in the

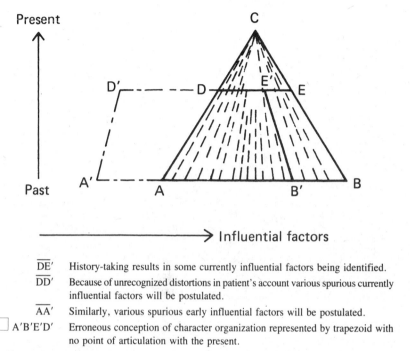

$\overline{DE'}$	History-taking results in some currently influential factors being identified.
$\overline{DD'}$	Because of unrecognized distortions in patient's account various spurious currently influential factors will be postulated.
$\overline{AA'}$	Similarly, various spurious early influential factors will be postulated.
A'B'E'D'	Erroneous conception of character organization represented by trapezoid with no point of articulation with the present.

Figure 3.   A history-taking approach

present. A "fact gathering" or "history-taking" approach would simply result in accumulating an assortment of descriptions of current and past events which would invite speculation as to how they fit together. These speculations would result in constructing any number of triangles, one of which may be the real one. But even if the diagnostician hits on the right triangle, it will be in the context of an intellectual exercise in which the patient has been either an informant or a scientific collaborator. Difficulties are likely to develop when the clinician undertakes to share his recommendations with the patient, for then the patient must be emotionally involved and actually struggling with the issues and not simply talking about them.

". . . A Recommendation Which Stands a Good Chance of Being Acted On as a Basis for Dealing with the Disorder. . . ."

Another example may serve to illustrate the use of the diagnostic triangle and, in particular, why the recommendation must be considered an intrinsic part of the diagnostic process.

The patient was a 47-year-old professional man with a long history of unsuccessful psychiatric treatment. In recent months he had quit work, retreated to his home, and complained of becoming increasingly depressed and worried about himself. When he first contacted the Diagnostic Service he seemed to be asking for hospitalization but then began an equivocating process of negotiation with the admissions officer over the phone which finally resulted in a "compromise": he would come for a three-day consultation and might permit himself to be tested. This first contact with the institution was already, it should be noted, in the context of a personal relationship—between the patient and the admissions officer—and already some interesting psychological functioning had been elicited and observed. It appeared that once a recommendation for doing something about his predicament emerged as likely, he became doubtful, raised questions about time, money, etc., and ended by rejecting the recommendation or asking for another with which the same process would take place until finally a minimal recommendation was accepted. The diagnostician who was going to see the patient began to wonder if this behavior might explain the failure of previous treatments about which he knew nothing at this point. He also wondered if this same problem would emerge as the major obstacle to working out a successful recommendation in the forthcoming consultation. At the same time this "resistance" would pose a significant diagnostic question: what lay behind this kind of behavior? When the patient is offered the help he appears to request he ends by seriously compromising it. The diagnostician had thus formulated a question at the apex of the diagnostic triangle which at the same time could provide the opening dialectic of the consultation; while raising this question with the patient the diagnostic process could be advanced and the ultimate acceptance of any recommendation made more likely.

In this example we can see how thoughts about the recommendation and its acceptance cannot be separated from the diagnostic process as a whole. In a history-taking approach, the recommendation finally offered to the patient must appear as a bit of psychiatric legerdemain: the facts are all registered, written on a pad, and somehow out of these diverse elements emerges a plan for action which the patient has not been made party to. But as our illustration shows, the very forces which cause resistance *within* the examination may result in resistance to the recommendation offered at the end of the examination. Our diagnostic understanding, in other words, should have clear implications with respect to the nature of the recommendation itself as well as to the manner in which it will be broached.

But what about the patient who needs to believe in a particular distortion in order to accept the recommendation, e.g., a patient who clings to the belief that the hospital staff members are omnipotent and will magically remake him stronger and better than before? What if he would flee from treatment if such a distortion were focused on? Is it not better to accept the fact that the patient needs to begin at that point and could be undercut if his belief were shaken too much? We would agree with these concerns but would add that the strength of the need for such a belief could be assessed, as could its potential for being modified. If tactful and sensitive inquiry revealed that the patient was too brittle to shift at that moment, then at least that diagnostic information would be available to those who would treat him.

Our point is that understanding must go on in the mind of the clinician and need not go on to the same extent in the mind of the patient—or at least not at the same level. But the greater the experience and understanding the patient has of his resistance to accepting the recommendation, the more likely will he be prepared to implement it.

TRACING AN OUTPATIENT EVALUATION: AN ILLUSTRATION OF THE DIAGNOSTIC PROCESS

At a preliminary meeting, the psychiatrist reported to his supervisor that a 34-year-old minister's wife had written complaining of having flashes of anger which she regarded as relatively unprovoked. Her husband had observed that his wife's expressions of anger had become more frequent and intense during the last few years; he saw them as paralleling her change from being timid to a much more forceful person over the course of their twelve-year marriage. He noted that she directed her anger at other men, rarely making him the overt target. The husband further reported that two years ago his wife had confessed to him that she had been frigid throughout the marriage. Although he had always wanted children she had always been against it. Nevertheless, in their letters they both stated that they got along well with each other.

On the basis of this information, the psychiatrist concluded: "On the surface, it doesn't look like a difficult diagnostic problem. Our recommendation will probably be for psychotherapy." At this point he expressed concern about the availability of psychotherapy because the couple resided in a small midwestern town. It was as if the diagnostic process had ended before the couple had arrived for an interview, with the focus already shifting from diagnosis to treatment! What could account for this? The answer seemed to be that the psychiatrist had unwittingly slipped into a history-taking approach, responding to the information as a set of facts which dictated a ready prescription. The supervisor, on the other hand, was thinking in terms of formulating issues which were closely tied to what the couple had reported. Specifically, the supervisor had noted two discontinuities in addition to the obvious precipitating complaint (unprovoked rage attacks): 1) although the wife had become increasingly angry, her anger was directed at men other than her husband; 2) although she had been frigid throughout the marriage, she had revealed this fact to the husband only two years ago.

The first middle-level issues to be formulated by the supervisor were: 1) why was the wife not angry at her husband, and 2) why did she hide her sexual problem for so long, and is even now less concerned about it than her husband?

The supervisor asked how the first issue could be raised with the couple. The psychiatrist responded, ''I don't think that will be difficult. You can do that very directly just by asking questions about tensions that have been present during the course of the marriage—dissatisfactions and frustrations she has had.'' The supervisor pointed out that by phrasing the question this way there would be a noteworthy shift in the diagnostic process toward the past and hence toward information collecting. To ask about past tensions is to ask about history. The patient might then recall an argument or two to illustrate that there had been some past tensions. Such an approach would obscure the current issue concerning why both spouses clearly present themselves as not having any problems between them. By making that the issue the diagnostician can work with the couple's present concerns. It would also draw their attention to the paradoxical fact that their relationship has not been affected by their serious difficulties—difficulties which should have caused dissatisfactions, e.g., the wife's frigidity and the fact that she withheld that information from her husband for ten years.

The assumption that discontinuities exist in a troubled person's course of behavior makes it possible to focus on what does not make sense. What follows is that some of the causes of such discontinuities are also psychic. Hence the need to formulate issues at a level which will allow for these causes to be understood. The way to understanding depends, in our view, on how the diagnostician elicits the patient's functioning, what these functions are, and what personal relationships are brought to light. For example, the supervisor noted that by posing the issue as suggested above, the psychiatrist could learn if the patient could step back and look at the paradox as well as learn something about the way she felt toward her husband. In this way the present status of functions such as reflectiveness, psychological-mindedness, etc., can be assessed as well as the nature of any possible conflict with her husband. By contrast a recollected history of marital discord may or may not be currently relevant.

Another factor which may have led the psychiatrist to foreclose prematurely on certain diagnostic issues is the tendency to assume that one potential hypothesis must be correct rather than to regard it as one of several possible alternatives. The psychiatrist assumed, for example, that the reason the couple did not mention the conflict between them was that they wanted to preserve a good appearance. Similarly, the psychiatrist assumed that the husband's reported recent depression was a response to his learning that his wife had been frigid all along. These hypotheses could have been correct, but by acting as if they were, certain diagnostic triangles were selected and others were eliminated—before they were ever explored!

Perhaps an example can clarify this. Suppose the clinician assessing the patient's symptomatic frigidity, her well-written letter with the absence of material suggesting a severe disturbance, had concluded that the wife had obtained a high level of psychological development and was probably suffering from hysteria rather than from an infantile personality or a potential psychotic reaction. The treatment of choice would then have been a form of expressive psychotherapy. The point is not so much that this way of thinking is wrong, but that such an approach could be misleading. That is, it could touch on several aspects of the wife's psychopathology and hit upon several diagnostic triangles but would run the risk of missing the important one. Or, it would start the evaluation at a point too far removed from the patient's current difficulties by arriving at an explanation before the patient had the opportunity of setting forth her problems in her own way. It would result in a situation like that schematically represented in Figure 3. To define the issue at the level of "hysteria" is too abstract and the clinician runs a risk of not being in tune with the patient. Thus, unless the frame of mind of the patient, the mood and spirit in which she comes to the evaluation is kept in mind, the clinician might select the incorrect triangle, and even if the correct one is selected, the patient can easily be bypassed unless the issues are formulated so as to allow both diagnostician and patient to enter the correct triangle at its apex in the present. In this way, the issues form a bridge between the patient and diagnostician which makes for their concurrent involvement and active participation.

The importance of formulating the issues close to the level of the clinical interaction, as a way of involving the patient and thereby sampling actual functioning, clearly emerged in the first team meeting. In the present case, both the first few clinical interviews and the psychological testing highlighted the wife's tendency to idealize her husband while venting her anger at others in positions of authority. How would this express itself in the course of the evaluation? Would she idealize the psychiatrist and try to comply with what she thought he wanted so as to support her idealization? Would she too readily agree with the treatment recommendation because of this idealization? Would a superficial compliance mask a deep-seated tendency to frustrate and defeat the treatment recommendation, just as she had frustrated her husband by keeping her frigidity a secret for ten years and by refusing to have children? Or would she respond to the psychiatrist as a relatively safe target for anger which would otherwise be directed at her husband? And, perhaps more precisely, under what conditions would she put the psychiatrist in each of these roles? Thus, by keeping in mind the different ways the patient tends to perceive and react, we are able to maximize the chances of entering the correct diagnostic triangle at the apex and of her entering it with us. Again, the avenue for entry is the assessment of the patient's functioning. For example, what are the limits of her reflectiveness, and what happens when her reflectiveness wanes? Under what conditions can the patient begin to see her predisposition to idealize, to frustrate, and to become angry?

As we mentioned before, the treatment recommendation should flow naturally from the diagnostic process. The middle-level issues should lead to the formulation of a treatment program. How the formulation is presented depends upon the nature of the relationship between clinician and patient. Ideally, then, the patient should become gradually aware of what is needed as a result of what has already taken place. If a history-taking approach has been employed, however, the diagnostician will be inclined to present the recommendation as another bit of information, similar to the information he has obtained from the patient. In the present case, the psychiatrist sought to convey a recommendation while overlooking the status of his relationship with the patient—as if the recommendation were only a neutral prescription to be accepted and acted upon. Based on the indications of some weakness in the patient's personality organization, the psychiatrist wanted to convey to her that she needed to have psychotherapy in a setting where hospitalization would be available in case she became as panicky and upset as she had before in her life. In so doing, however, he forgot to take into account at what point she was in her understanding of the evaluation, and what she was expecting from it. The supervisor anticipated that the psychiatrist's recommendation for "intensive treatment near a hospital" would come as a blow to the patient's self-esteem, because she feared placement in a mental hospital as she had previously indicated had happened to her sister. When the psychiatrist presented the recommendation to the patient, her anxiety over being seen as someone as sick as her sister was triggered, and she responded to the psychiatrist's factual statement with panic and tears, thinking he had said she needed long-term hospitalization.

It is precisely because the recommendation for treatment is part of the diagnostic process that its acceptance or rejection by the patient is influenced by the very conflicts and resistances which become evident as the clinician tries to understand the patient. If the clinician deals with the recommendation as a separate entity which comes after (and is separate from) the diagnostic process, he will be treating the patient as a completely rational person who acts only to help himself—as if he were suddenly freed of those interfering problems and resistances which made him seek help in the first place. We do not mean that it is the diagnostician's task to ensure the acceptance of the recommendation, as if his understanding of the patient were inherently incorrect if the rejection of the recommendation occurs. But we do mean that part of the diagnostic task is to subject the recommendation to the same kind of thought, understanding, and planning that is involved in thinking about the patient and his problems. The diagnostic process should bring about enough of a shift so that the patient can act on the recommendation. In fact, it is our belief that it is just this point which differentiates psychiatric diagnosis from other kinds of diagnosis. To our knowledge in no other diagnosis is it necessary for the diagnostic process itself to prepare the way for accepting the recommendation.

In our case example, the team in working to bring about a change to help the minister's wife accept the recommendation considered several pitfalls. First, she might too willingly accept the recommendation because of her idealization of the psychiatrist, but this acceptance would be suspect because it might mask an underlying obstinacy. Also, there existed the possibility of her seeing a psychiatrist closer to home until she and her husband could move to a community where long-term treatment would be available. The danger in such a plan was that she could develop a positive relationship with the local psychiatrist and believe that was all the help she needed. To counter that possibility, the team agreed that someone should provide an interim contact to facilitate implementation of the recommendation by not allowing another psychiatrist's relationship with the patient to be used as a substitute for more intensive treatment. In laying the groundwork for the shift towards a true acceptance of the recommendation, the team considered the value of drawing the patient's attention to her overreaction when the recommendation was first made. To ask her to be more reflective about her overreaction could serve several purposes. First, it would make for more diagnostic assessment, e.g., how psychologically-minded can she be? Will she get distraught again, or could she reflect on it now? More important, in terms of the shift that was desired, was the hope that she could learn something about why she resists; then presumably her fears would subside and her efforts to implement the recommendation would become stronger and more genuine. A clue to the nature of her fears was provided by her having heard the psychiatrist as recommending separation from her husband, i.e., that she would have to leave him in order to come to a city where treatment was available. The team hypothesized that the fear was a disguised wish to leave her husband altogether. If she saw treatment as raising that possibility or temptation, her anxiety-arousing wish for separation might become a major resistance to accepting the recommendation. This hypothesis could be tested by calling attention to her overreaction which could provide a starting point for helping her see how she could try to flee from her conflicts by rejecting the recommendation. The psychiatrist did discuss her upset with her, and she was able to look at her ambivalent feelings about her marriage. In so doing she appeared to take a big step toward the shift necessary to accept the recommendation.

As the evaluation drew to a close, it was evident that the couple had indeed shifted enough to begin seriously implementing the recommendation—with all its implications of pulling up stakes, moving to a new city, and continuing the painful process of self-understanding. And yet, even at the end, some of the anticipated issues seemed to surface. Not surprisingly, the wife's strong positive feelings for the psychiatrist were quite evident. In fact, the last thing she asked during the concluding hour was if the psychiatrist could be her therapist. He refused. He explained to the supervisor, "I wouldn't tell her this, but I am very reluctant to accept an evaluation patient as a treatment patient because my job is primarily selling treatment and doing an evaluation and it's a little hard to deliver the service and be the seller of it too.'' The final exchange between the patient and psychiatrist raises several issues. By seeing himself as a salesman rather than as a diagnostician, the psychiatrist regarded his role as incompatible with that of the therapist. Clearly, then, he felt that his task required him to step outside a therapeutic relationship. This is particularly striking in view of the often heard truism that diagnosis and treatment are two sides of the same coin, or that both are points along a continuum. In practice, however, and at the level where it counts—the clinical interaction—the psychiatrist felt compelled to act in a way which he regarded as compromising his future effectiveness as a therapist—as if he had contaminated himself. It is likely that this occurred because the psychiatrist saw himself as a persuader rather than as one who works with resistances, which, when understood, would allow for the necessary shift in the patient to take place. In short, his felt need to step outside a diagnostic framework reflects a particular attitude toward diagnostic work as something unsavory. This indeed may help explain its current unpopularity. This view of diagnosis as ''salesmanship'' echoes Rogers' objection that diagnosis involves doing something to the patient—especially controlling or influencing him, or at least treating him like an object.

By quickly denying the patient's request because of personal uneasiness, the psychiatrist perhaps foreclosed on other issues. For example, was the wife's acceptance of the recommendations tied to an implicit expectation that the idealized psychiatrist would himself treat her? Also, the team's understanding of her included an emphasis on her difficulty in tolerating separation. To what extent was her request an attempt to attenuate the impact of separation? We do not yet have the answers, but the point is that by stepping outside the diagnostic framework, the psychiatrist lost an opportunity for further diagnostic work directly bearing on the fate of his recommendation.

An important final point is that the team left the door open as to whether the wife was more infantile or more hysteric. Such high level abstractions were subordinated to framing middle-level issues which engaged the patient directly. This permitted the formulation and subsequent modification of hypotheses put forth to specify the conditions under which different kinds of reactions would take place based on an assessment of her psychological functioning. These reactions included psychological factors relevant to accepting the recommendation, an acceptance which in itself reflects a shift due to the diagnostic process.*

---

* Some six months later the following letter was received by the examining psychiatrist from a psychiatrist contacted by the patient and her husband:

   ''I was glad to talk to you last month about Mrs. — and her husband, Rev. —. They were in on March 9th, and we discussed at some length a possible psychotherapy program for both of them in the office, starting as you suggested, with frequent visits for Mrs. —.

CONCLUSIONS

Although we have necessarily focused our inquiry on the nature of the diagnostic process, we do not wish to leave the reader with the impression that we distinguish sharply between diagnosis and treatment. In fact, our approach requires that in order for a recommendation to be accepted some shift on the patient's part is necessary, that is, some change must take place, if only in the direction of acknowledging the nature and the extent of the disturbance. To the extent that change has taken place, we say that treatment has begun. Nevertheless, this recognition should not obscure the fact that the major task remains a diagnostic one: to understand the nature of the disturbance with a view toward recommending a treatment program which would hopefully provide the major vehicle for change. Similarly, we recognize that in treatment itself, diagnosis is always going on. The therapist should assess the patient's communication before making any intervention, otherwise he is simply playing a guessing game, although he may be reduced to guess-work when for whatever reason he fails to understand the patient. However, the main aim of treatment in contradistinction to diagnosis is to bring about change consistent with the goals shared by patient and therapist. It is a longer process than diagnosis and draws on a greater range of means and facilities. It is possible, nevertheless, to conceive of our definition of diagnosis as a general statement applicable to all circumstances in which understanding a patient's disturbance is linked to some effort to change it. From this standpoint, the diagnostic process as such would be one end point and treatment the other.

It is also worthwhile to draw attention to the fact that our definition of diagnosis in no way biases the diagnostic process in favor of purely intrapsychic or purely interpersonal methods of treatment or of diagnosis. In one illustration, we cited how the social worker helped the patient's mother deal with her unwillingness to let her daughter leave home; in another illustration we referred to work with the husband and wife although the wife was the one who originally presented herself as the patient. The good diagnostician, like any sound scientist, follows where the problem leads. We only insist that no matter where the problem may take him the diagnostician must be aware of his relationship to the patient and any other people involved; for it is through the medium of this relationship that

"Their attitude toward a psychotherapy program was good, and both of them expressed a feeling of considerable improvement, which apparently accompanied their experiences at Topeka. They have moved from — to — in order to be closer for this program."

The letter further illustrates that the evaluation had not ended when the couple and the team ended their meetings but continued in the minds and lives of the couple as a consequence of the psychological shift that had taken place. The letter confirmed the team's belief that a significant shift had taken place during the course of the evaluation and that the couple were making the necessary changes in their lives to accommodate long-term treatment. As a final note, we would add that the letter was received after the case was selected for this paper and the manuscript completed.

he can evaluate the psychological processes dealing with the significant personal relationships confronting him. Whenever and for whatever reasons the diagnostician ignores his impact on the situation, he is ignoring the only instrument on which he can rely. Ask a biologist to abandon his microscope or an astronomer his telescope and you would have a comparable handicap. The relevant phenomena can no longer be observed and thus escapes understanding. Unfortunately, in psychiatry, it is possible to note behavior even when the relationship is ignored, thus the diagnostician is seduced into believing that what he observes exists in some realm independent of his presence. It is this attitude which results in the history-taking, fact-gathering approach, as well as in the behavior therapist's belief that his impersonal techniques (as he defines them) are the effective change agents. He thus fails to see that the contract he makes with the patient before beginning the treatment process is already based on a personal relationship which has introduced factors well before techniques are applied. MacLeod (1947) referred many years ago to the stimulus error in experimental psychology which he defined as the psychologist's tendency to assume that what *he* considers the stimulus to be *must* be the stimulus for the subject. Experimenters are discovering that even for the laboratory subject the stimulus is not just the light in the box or the click in the ear but is also the experimenter himself and the experimental situation as a whole. How much more must this be the case when highly personal matters are at issue in a person suffering from emotional distress and in need of help.

There are certain research implications in the proposed diagnostic model. For one, the model calls for a classification of initial issues rather than for a classification of presenting complaints. There is a significant difference between issues and complaints. An issue is the diagnostician's initial hypothesis about the patient's disturbance which is in part based on the patient's complaint. On the other hand, the patient's complaint is his necessarily limited view of his distress. The patient may complain about being afraid; the diagnostician, however, wonders why, if he has been so afraid, he has delayed coming for help. The diagnostician tries to formulate the relevant discontinuity; the patient at best can only experience discontinuity implicitly and at worst may be totally oblivious to it. By classifying issues we thus can arrive at a taxonomy of hypotheses guiding our diagnostic work. Certain issues, or discontinuities, may appear often with respect to a given disorder. Research on this level would focus on the current impact of the disorder on the patient's life rather than on distant etiological factors, hazardous in view of our current state of knowledge, or on broad nosological categories, which are of little immediate practical value.

Once we have the beginnings of a classification system for initial issues or hypotheses then we can trace the relationship between such issues and the development of the diagnostic process, its success or failure as judged by the patient's acceptance of the recommendation and his readiness to act on it. As a prior step one might compare diagnostic efforts in which no issues were defined with those in which some were. Our anticipation would be that the latter diagnoses would be more successful than the former. Following this effort, research could then focus on relationships between different issues and outcome.

Finally, our approach calls for a good deal of attention to the actual *method* of diagnosis beyond the formulation of issues to the handling of the diagnostic relationship itself and the relationship to other methods, such as psychological tests. Recently Weiner (1972) has argued persuasively for the value of psychodiagnostic assessment based on tests in the course of which he dealt with some of the same criticisms leveled at the relevance of diagnosis considered in this paper. There is thus a significant convergence between the diagnostic use of the psychiatric interview and the diagnostic use of psychological tests which would be worthy of further exploration.

REFERENCES

Alexander, Franz: Psychoanalysis in Western Culture. *Amer. J. Psychiat.* 112: 692–99, 1956.

Back, K. W.: *Beyond Words: The Story of Sensitivity Training and the Encounter Movement*. New York: Russell Sage Foundation, 1972.

Beck, A. T.: Reliability of Psychiatric Diagnosis: I. A Critique of Systematic Studies. *Amer. J. Psychiat.* 119:210–16, 1962.

Cameron, D. E.: A Theory of Diagnosis. In *Current Problems in Psychiatric Diagnosis*, Paul Hoch and Joseph Zubin, eds. New York: Grune & Stratton, 1953, pp. 33–45.

Coleman, J. C.: *Abnormal Psychology and Modern Life*, Ed. 2. Chicago: Scott, Foresman and Co., 1956.

Egbert, L. D., et al.: Reduction of Postoperative Pain by Encouragement and Instruction of Patients: A Study of Doctor-Patient Rapport. *New Eng. J. Med.* 270:825–27, 1964.

Freud, Anna: *Normality and Pathology in Childhood: Assessments of Developments*. New York: International Universities Press, 1965.

Goolker, Paul: The Role of Diagnosis in Psychiatry. *J. Hillside Hosp.* 5:361–67, 1956.

Greenspoon, Joel and Gersten, C. D.: A New Look at Psychological Testing: Psychological Testing from the Standpoint of a Behaviorist. *Amer. Psychol.* 22:848–53, 1967.

Holzman, P. S. and Schlesinger, H. J.: On Becoming a Hospitalized Psychiatric Patient. *Bull. Menninger Clin.* 36:383–406, 1972.

Kernberg, Otto: The Treatment of Patients with Borderline Personality Organization. *Int. J. Psychoanal.* 49:600–19, 1968.

Klein, M. H., et al.: Behavior Therapy: Observations and Reflections. *J. Consult. Clin. Psychol.* 33:259–66, 1969.

London, Perry: The End of Ideology in Behavior Modification. *Amer. Psychol.* 27:913–20, 1972.

MacLeod, R. B.: The Phenomenological Approach to Social Psychology. *Psychol. Rev.* 54:193–210, 1947.

Menninger, Karl, Mayman, Martin and Pruyser, Paul: *The Vital Balance.* New York: Viking Press, 1963.

Pasamanick, Benjamin, Dinitz, Simon and Lefton, Mark: Psychiatric Orientation and Its Relation to Diagnosis and Treatment in a Mental Hospital. *Amer. J. Psychiat.* 116:127–32, 1959.

Patterson, C. H.: Is Psychotherapy Dependent Upon Diagnosis? *Amer. Psychol.* 3:155–59, 1948.

Rapaport, David (1944): The Scientific Methodology of Psychoanalysis. In *The Collected Papers of David Rapaport,* M. M. Gill, ed. New York: Basic Books, 1967, pp. 165–220.

Rogers, Carl: *Client Centered Therapy.* Boston: Houghton Mifflin, 1951.

Ryan, V. L. and Gizynski, M. N.: Behavior Therapy in Retrospect: Patients' Feelings about their Behavior Therapies. *J. Consult. Clin. Psychol.* 37:1–9, 1971.

Szasz, T. S.: *The Myth of Mental Illness.* New York: Hoeber-Harper, 1961.

————: The Psychiatric Classification of Behavior: A Strategy of Personal Constraint. In *The Classification of Behavior Disorders,* L. D. Eron, ed. Chicago: Aldine Publishing Co., 1966, pp. 123–70.

————: *The Manufacture of Madness: A Comparative Study of the Inquisition and the Mental Health Movement.* New York: Harper & Row, 1970.

————: The Sane Slave. *Amer. J. Psychother.* 25:228–39, 1971.

Thorne, F. C.: The Clinical Method in Science. *Amer. Psychol.* 2:159–66, 1947.

Wann, T. W., ed.: *Behaviorism and Phenomenology: Contrasting Bases for Modern Psychology.* Chicago: University of Chicago Press, 1964.

Weiner, I. B.: Does Psychodiagnosis Have a Future? *J. Pers. Assess.* 36:534–46, 1972.

The authors wish to express their appreciation to Dr. Ann Appelbaum, Director of the Diagnostic Service of the Menninger Foundation, for her support and for allowing them access to the rich store of clinical data from which they drew many of their illustrations, and to thank Drs. Lee Johnson and William Kearns for their cooperation. Mr. Arthur Mandelbaum, Dr. Sydney Smith and Dr. Jorge de la Torre read the paper and made useful comments. Discussions of the paper with the Menninger Foundation's clinical psychological staff, the Foundation's Diagnostic Service, and clinical members of the Psychology Department at the University of Michigan, were also very helpful.

Chapter 3

Language Pitfalls in Diagnostic Thought and Work

PAUL W. PRUYSER AND KARL MENNINGER

Long, long ago, a seriously disturbed person said of himself, "My name is Legion." Being possessed by multiple devils, his cure involved no less than a whole herd of swine who ran away with his ills, stampeded to their death, and left him behind in sober and sane simplicity. Legion have been the psychiatric patients in the history of mankind; legion also have been the names of their illnesses. Seventy pages of fine print in the appendix to *The Vital Balance* (Menninger *et al.* 1963) record the ever-changing list of these names, swelling and shrinking in number over the ages, alternating between sacred and vernacular designations, cheapening from scientific terms to household words, and sometimes regressing from clear descriptions to obfuscating prestige terms, in an astonishing juggler's act with language.

Today, Legion is no longer the name of the patients and their disorders. Despite the comeback of popular demonology and exorcism, the name has fallen into disuse. We propose, however, that the name Legion may be an apt designation of today's professional psychiatrist, alerting us to the fact that psychiatry is a multilingual enterprise. In this profession, expertise in word usage is of the utmost importance. Psychiatric work entails engagement in several distinct language games, each with its own syntax, grammar, and vocabulary. It also entails the responsibility of keeping these languages apart, differentiating them from each other, and using each one appropriately, commensurate with the purpose at hand.

Since one metaphor may easily lead to another by a process of associative drift, let us warn you that by the name *Legion* we are not alluding to the confusion of tongues alleged to exist *among* psychiatrists. We are not trying to describe the house of psychiatry as a Tower of Babel, whose workers stalled the enterprise of reaching to the sky because they could not communicate with each other. Our focus is on the confusion of tongues existing *within* each psychiatrist, on account

Reprinted with permission from the *Bulletin of the Menninger Clinic*, 1976, Vol. 40, No. 5, pp. 417–434, © 1976 by The Menninger Foundation.

of which he fails to have conceptual order and clarity of meanings within himself. We name him Legion in the sense that the course of his work, and its various contexts, force him to speak a multitude of languages which he often has difficulty in keeping apart. In a day's routine, the psychiatrist converses with a patient, consoles a distraught relative, jots down technical notes to himself, and composes reports for others to read. He hears reports from nurses, psychologists, social workers, and others. He reads laboratory data, conducts purposeful interviews, and makes telephone calls. He writes letters to judges, lawyers, and insurance companies. He fills out government forms, dictates process notes about his therapeutic work, uses the *Diagnostic and Statistical Manual of Mental Disorders* (DSM-II), receives consultations, and presumably goes home for dinner to engage with his family. All these activities and situations involve language—spoken, heard, written, or read—and that language is not one unitary system such as basic English or Esperanto. On the contrary, the psychiatrist speaks, hears, writes, and reads in a multiplicity of tongues, dialects, cants, argots, arcana, vernaculars, quasi-sacred phrases, languages of fact, conviction, or common sense, and at times abracadabra. To survey and comment on these various languages of the psychiatrist is the purpose of this presentation.

THE LANGUAGES OF A PSYCHIATRIST

What languages do we hear our man Legion speak? What language should he speak, or what languages might he learn to speak properly if he is to be a well-versed polyglot rather than a babbling Legion?

When one ponders these questions, several large language groupings come to mind. Psychiatry has long known four distinct language games: the language of nosology, the language of classification, the language of persons, and the language of therapeutic techniques. To be sure, the first two of these are often confused, so we will shortly set forth the differences. It is tempting to recognize from the start also a language of diagnosis, but we should withstand that temptation because diagnostic word usage is in fact most often an amalgam of the other four languages—a kind of supralanguage of the greatest artificiality. Anticipating some distinctions we shall make, we may say now that diagnostic language looms as the most problematic of all psychiatric languages, as the most haphazard linguistic artifact of the profession, as the most widely abused conflation of words, and the most manneristic form of psychiatric speech making. Let us first survey the four basic languages.

The Language of Nosology

Though often taken to be identical, nosology and classification are not the same thing. A system of classification is an exercise in taxonomy, guided by rules or

laws of grouping. The DSM-II is such a system. Nosology is the conceptualization of disease, yielding the material or entities that are subsequently to be
grouped. For instance, Bleuler's text (1911) on the schizophrenias is a nosological
work, not a classification.

Nosological language is a symbol system in the service of the science that
treats of diseases. Nosologists want to know what a disease is, and they regard
any particular disease within the context of some conceptual definition of disease
in general. The relation between the general and the particular raises profound
nosological questions, differently posed and answered in different epochs of
psychiatric history. For instance, when the general theory of humors prevailed,
particular diseases of humoral nature were formulated, e.g., Galen's melancholia.
When fevers assumed cardinal importance, particular mental disorders became
differentiated in terms of presence or absence of fever, e.g., Hippocrates's
phrenitis versus mania, and some deliriums of later writers. Prominence of sexual
pathology in the general theory led to the formulation of such specific diseases
as hysteria, satyriasis, the incubus of the Middle Ages and Renaissance, the
dysphrenia sexualis of Kahlbaum, and the various degeneracy conditions described as neurasthenia and psychasthenia. When it was believed that all mental
disorder was brain disease (e.g., Griesinger), the various clinical pictures were
seen as phases of one organic process or as distinguishable reaction types.

Thus, nosological ideas tend to derive from two very different sets of historical
determinants. The first set is composed of high-level conceptions of disease in
general which range from philosophical to empirical. They are saddled with a
heritage that includes on the one hand moral, religious, mythological, and de-
monological speculations; on the other hand, anatomical, endocrinological, neurological, psychological, or social extrapolations. The second set consists of
lower-level descriptions of distinguishable clinical conditions or courses of illness, amounting to word pictures saddled with a heritage of folklore (hysteria,
lycanthropy), arcana (hypochondriasis), names of people (Korsakoff syndrome),
age-specific descriptions (adjustment reaction of adolescence, senile dementia,
dementia praecox), and a large array of terms derived from presumed specific
agents (alcoholism), specific emotions (depression, mania), specific habits (certain behavior disturbances in children), specific developmental arrests (mental
deficiency), specific character structures (infantile personality), or specific social
nuisances (psychopathic personalities).

More often than not, nosologists have tried to keep the old words current
while changing their general or particular meanings by offering definitions of
their own. Some brave souls, such as Adolf Meyer, seeing the pitfalls of the
inherited nomenclature, tried to invent new words for subgroups of the clinical
pictures they wished to distinguish (e.g., parergasia, thymergasia) and added
words to denote their general conception of mental disorder (e.g., considering
all of them reaction types). As a result, nosological language is full of archaisms,

representing a plethora of hand-me-down words ill-suited to foster either a generic understanding of mental disorder or a clear grasp of any specific condition.

The Language of Classification

The language of classification is thoroughly confused by ambiguities about its use and application. The first noteworthy ambiguity pertains to what is to be classified, disorders or patients? Though the DSM-II purports to be an aid in the classification of disorders, its users frequently subvert it to a scheme for organizing patient statistics. Some patients have more than one disorder and would thus require multiple allocations to the entries in the classification system. Moreover, there is no generic rule, other than arbitrary, for ranking these patients' several disorders in terms of primary, secondary, tertiary, or subsequent orders of importance. Particularly when diagnoses are made to establish viable interventions, the therapeutic emphasis may be on a secondary or tertiary condition or symptom rather than the primary one.

A second important ambiguity in the language of psychiatric classification is due to the tension that exists between the conceptual generality of nosology and the clinical specificity of the individual case. A taxonomic system requires recognized constants that define each class at specified levels of abstraction. Though few scientific classification systems of complex entities have reached the degree of perfection of which the chemist's periodic table is the showcase, the entities of psychiatric taxonomy are notorious for their descriptive imprecision, and the scope of this taxonomy is notorious for the latitude granted to it in different eras. Galen recognized only a handful of disorders; Boissier de Sauvages formulated a dozen classes and hundreds of genera; and Neumann settled for only one disorder, to be called "insanity." Admittedly, psychiatry deals with many variables; therefore its classification schemes are more unwieldy than those of other disciplines which deal with fewer variables. But in all sciences the variables that count are abstracted from hordes of candidates most of which are rejected by a careful screening process. Obviously psychiatry has not yet been able to sort out the viable from the unproductive variables, and therefore its classification systems are beset by inconsistencies.

Thirdly, in psychiatry, no two cases of the alleged same disorder are alike to a firmly acceptable degree. Nor are the variables that differentiate one disorder or group of disorders from another taken from the same matrix of qualities. Some disorders are grouped as mood disorders (depression, mania), others are called adjustment reactions; some are ideational aberrations (paranoia, obsessional neurosis), others are limited functional failures of memory (dissociative reaction); some derive from a historical and quite holistic view of personality or character (borderline condition, narcissistic personality) hardly conducive to precise symptom descriptions, others take their cue from a circumscribed habit (alcoholism, fetishism) or a "special symptom" as the DSM-II calls it, such as enuresis or a speech defect. It is clear that not all of these units are just symptoms. It is also clear that if one would like to strive to focus on the symptoms in each category, the word *symptom* teeters between quite different levels of abstraction and precision. And even if one would like to devise a classification system consisting entirely of symptom descriptions, one will still have to reckon with the fact that phenotypical similarity may mask genotypical diversity and, its obverse, that genotypical sameness may be expressed in phenotypical differences.

The language of classification is further compromised and muddled by the fact that it functions as a meeting ground between two very different enterprises. On the one hand it is to serve the nosologists whose task is to conceptualize mental disorders with the greatest possible refinement including the symptoms, course, and etiology of each; on the other hand it is to serve the statisticians whose task is to spot clusters of correlations that confirm or contradict the various "packages" that any given classification contains. Nosologists are, or should be, interested in a precise and clear nomenclature by which mental disorders can be properly named without ambiguity. Statisticians are more likely to be attuned to the overlap of variables between one condition and another, however these are named, on the basis of a great many countings of a great many items—the latter of bewildering diversity. And the clinician is interested in lucid pictures he can match with the salient features of not a disorder or a person but a disordered person!

The Language of Persons

We are now ready to recognize the psychiatrist's third language, the person language he adopts in his clinical work. To put it sharply, and in terms of our previous emphasis on classification, the DSM-II, as all its forebears, is to be used expressly for classifying mental disorders—not patients! The classification scheme is a nosological tool, not an idiom in which to describe patients— apparently a hard lesson to learn. No less a psychiatric luminary than Bleuler objected to the term *dementia praecox* on linguistic grounds, deploring that it could not be turned into a label for the individual patient! Since one cannot speak of *a dementia praecox*, Bleuler sought a term with grammatical flexibility and concocted *schizophrenia* which enables one to speak of *a schizophrenic* and permits adjectival use as well. But that is precisely what should not be allowed, not only on humanitarian grounds but because technically no man or woman is identical with his or her disorder. And such naming is particularly inapt when the disorder itself is as yet only a symptom cluster of unexplained etiology, for many psychiatric patients are free from symptoms for greater or lesser stretches of time. Apart from objections to pejorative labeling that dehumanizes the patient or leads to social ostracism, the point here is that the kind of naming which Bleuler sought to make possible by linguistic means is actually a false labeling.

And this issue is not solved by subsequently inventing qualifying phrases such as *in remission*. When a person is designated as *a* hysteric, or *a* schizophrenic, in remission, logic demands that he be dead or has become a nonperson. What may be in remission is his symptoms on the basis of which a disorder was inferred in the first place and by which the patient is seen as afflicted. Only a disorder or a symptom can be in remission, not the person.

Person language, in psychiatry as anywhere else, is ordinary English (at least for American and British practitioners). Given the high proportion of foreign medical graduates in American psychiatry, it is perhaps not so surprising that ordinary English is so rarely used in the psychiatric description of persons. Foreign-born psychiatrists may find it easier to adopt scientific argot than to learn the subtleties of as complex and idiomatic a language as English, particularly when ease is coupled with the prestige attached to the use of technical terminology. For those not foreign born, ordinary English may seem too unscientific, too common, too easily accessible to laymen, which could—God forbid—include the patients themselves.

And yet, any psychiatrist worth his salt interviews his patients in ordinary English and hears the same language in return—barring occasional jibberish or word salad spoken by severely disturbed patients. His raw data are in this common, unpretentious language. He could and should describe his patients in the same tongue, if only to be able to share his reports with the patients themselves (were he curious and caring enough to seek the patients' verification of his reports) so as to engage with them in an open therapeutic contracting. But, alas, the moment we dictate our reports we seem to spurn good descriptive English in favor of conceptual phrases of a quasi-nosological order, or adapted from the classification system. Many patients are described not as sad, tearful, somber, or downhearted, but right away as *depressed*. Other patients are immediately dubbed *paranoid* when we are only justified in describing their attitude as suspicious or guarded. Instead of calling attention to flamboyant verbiage, histrionic manners, or abruptly changing moods, we take recourse to the term *hysterical*. In lieu of noting and recording the presence of certain rituals, we say *obsessive-compulsive*; a fearful attitude is rendered as *phobic*; a mannerism is labeled *catatonic*. All these words are nosological terms, i.e., adjectives describing a quality of some conceptualized disorder, or classification words. They are adjectival adaptations of listed nouns; they are neither descriptions of the persons before us nor faithful renditions of observed symptoms; they are premature attempts at classification that pigeonhole the person before he or she is faithfully portrayed. These words are clichés loading our reports with the categorizing contents of our own minds. The diagnosis is still to be made, but in recording the history and the psychological examination we have already used categorical words that make verification difficult and thwart communication.

We will have more to say about the language of persons at a later point, but be it noted here that considerable purification of the psychiatrist's mind is needed before he can master this difficult tongue.

The Language of Therapeutic Technique

The fourth psychiatric language in daily use is the language of therapy and therapeutic techniques. Patients tend to be sized up and described according to the interviewer's therapeutic orientation. Psychoanalytic case reports abound with words like *transference*, *associating*, *resistance*, *verbalizing*, *affect organization*, and *acting out*. Psychopharmacological persuasions come through in *bi-polar depression*, *dyskinetic*, and details of family trees. Milieu-oriented hospital psychiatric reports dwell on how the patient does in *structured* versus *unstructured* situations and how he reacts to father or mother figures; they specify his *object relations* and pay much attention to *reality contact* and *fantasy formation*. Neuropsychiatric reports speak of *syndromes*, particularly of the temporal lobe and limbic structures, and dwell on *confusion*, *amnesia*, or *epileptic phenomena*, minutely describing their status or fluctuations and how these are influenced by stressful events, all with an eye on therapeutic alteration of *thresholds*. Custodial hospital reports abound with old-fashioned nosological terms, highly categorical and mostly serving triage functions. Advocates of group therapies lard their assessments with *splitting*, *identification*, *loyalty*, and *role*. Transactional analysts adopt the verbiage of family roles; Gestalt therapists focus on *self*, *speaking out*, and *masking*. And so on. There is an enormous impact of therapy-derived words on the assessment process and what passes for diagnostic descriptions of patients.

The point is not whether this practice is good or bad—we ourselves would argue that scientific data are always a function of the perspective in which they are spotted and formulated. What we wish to indicate here is that the therapeutic perspective entails a special language game which should not be confused with other forms of psychiatric language. All too often the language of therapeutic orientation intrudes upon the language of evaluative description, and eventually upon the language of diagnosis, making them selective or partial at best, and badly skewed, if not muddled, at worst.

The Language of Diagnosis: Official Hodgepodge

Thus far, we have tried to show in a few broad strokes that psychiatry has recourse not to one but to several professional languages and that, in this sense, the name of the psychiatrist could well be Legion. We have also illustrated a prevailing occupational hazard in psychiatry, namely that of unwittingly speaking several languages at the same time, which amounts to a professional paraphasia. Thought and language always interact. Poor thinking leads to poor language use, and faulty habits of speech muddy the clarity of thought. Mere words can feign the existence of entities, and patent phenomena are overlooked when language habits disallow their recognition.

Even when our cautionary remarks in the preceding sections are heeded to the point that we would at least know clearly which language we were speaking at any given moment, we are still running against a formidable barricade in our linguistic housecleaning efforts. Ahead of us looms the spectre of psychiatric diagnosis, a veritable monster of linguistic abuse and obfuscation.

Perhaps the worst feature of diagnostic language is the great artificiality of its form and scope: It consists of a kind of telegraphic speech, highly abbreviated and condensed; typically, it has no verbs, as if to imply that it recognizes no action or process; it consists largely of nouns, noun phrases, and adjectives. While it purports to designate a condition, e.g., alcoholism or hysteria, all too often word choice freezes this condition into a fixed state, stripped of its dynamics, tensions, and process character. Thus, it conjures up entities which the imagination of the user elaborates in some fashion. For diagnostic language does not abbreviate by merely shortening a phrase or by contracting words (e.g., KS for Kansas), but by substituting abstractions and their invented names for a multitude of descriptions (which, as we have seen, are typically far from pure descriptions) and observations (which are often theoretically inspired) via an inference process that may vary from logical step-by-step induction and deduction to an aesthetic, visionary recognition of some mental picture that "matches" an unreflected assortment of phenomena.

A second feature of diagnostic language is that its word-treasure consists of a prescribed nomenclature, which is not just a finite universe of terms but a very small table of permissable words guided by narrow rules for combination and not allowed to grow. While other languages expand, differentiate, and become more versatile, diagnostic language is kept fixed, static, and uniform—whether for good or bad reasons. Due to its narrow bandwidth, it is a language that puts the user before a forced choice situation. The phenomena have to be made to fit the nomenclature, in contrast to ordinary speech and other forms of scientific language which are constantly being adapted to the phenomena and concepts that emerge. The user of a diagnostic manual is not given an opportunity to create the most astute formulation of his patient's conditions or problems, but he is asked to allocate (from *locare*—to place) and assign (i.e., to mark) in order to find the "proper place" for the patient's condition within a list or table. Note that the allocation pertains to the condition, not to the patient! Indeed, to bridge the gap between the condition and the patient, medical parlance takes recourse to the word *case* (from the Latin *casus*—instance). The allocation means, "This case (particular happening) is an instance of such and such (known) condition or illness." The patient himself is not "a case," but his affliction is reasoned to be an instance of a small number of more or less circumscribed conditions earmarked by official names. Again, we are exposing these features of diagnostic language not necessarily to decry them, but to record their peculiarity so as to warn the user of diagnostic terms of their pitfalls. Diagnostic nomenclature is a very odd language form serving a very circumscribed purpose. It is an artificial language game operating in a narrow circle.

A third point of note is that diagnostic language is a compound of diverse conceptions and levels of abstraction. A set of colored blocks of the same shape and size can be sorted according to color differences; each color becomes a rubric. A set of colored blocks of different shapes and sizes can be sorted according to three classes of rubrics: color, shape, size. Of these *color* and *size* contain continuous rubrics allowing measurement, and *shape* contains discontinuous rubrics with only a limited number of forms that allow no transitions. No one would hold that such simple sorting by means of clear variables is possible with mental disorders or medical disease. But the diagnostic categories of psychiatry are very remote indeed from any respectable model; they are an extreme conflation of such diverse groups of variables that one wonders whether they form any coherent order and can be dignified by the word *system*. Some entries exist by virtue of etiological considerations. Others are explicitly based on the course of the disorder and register an outlook. Still others are squarely based on symptoms or symptom clusters. Etiological groups, moreover, are not of the same order but stem from very diverse etiological theories or visions; symptom groups range from the clear and obvious act of "episodic excessive drinking (of alcohol)" to the fuzziness of "asthenic personality disorder." Behind these very diverse categories lie wholly different language games: Some have to do with brain states; others with psychodynamics; still others with character, adaptation, or social fitness. In some classes, there are allusions to distinctions between acute and chronic states; in others, something is implied about the reversibility or irreversibility of the disorder.

A fourth peculiarity of official diagnostic language is the ambiguity of the recognized genera. For instance, there is a genus *neuroses* and a genus *psychoses*—the latter conditioned by the phrase "not attributed to physical conditions listed previously." How are these genera conceived? Are neuroses and psychoses meant to be seen as continuous in some fashion, e.g., as roughly similar to respectively "mild" and "severe" disorders? If so, what does one do with the currently fashionable syndrome *Borderline State, Condition*, or *Schizophrenia* (for which DSM-II has no entry) when that condition (if it is a circumscribed one) is widely seen as attributable to "personality disorder"? And, indeed, where does the latter fit, if any continuity between classes is assumed? Is there or is there not some hierarchical conception that matches the biological distinctions between class, genus, and species, and puts these factors at discrete levels of abstraction? Or is the diagnostic table only a list, more or less fortuitously assembled in the face of the pragmatic complaints that come the psychiatrist's way, with today different from yesterday, and tomorrow different again? Do geographic locale and cultural milieu play some role in making the list what it is today? Is the list equally useful to private practitioners, military psychiatrists, penological institutions, and the Veterans Administration? Does it address the needs of psychoanalysts as well as state hospitals? If not, there must be something wrong with its over-arching principles and its hierarchical ordering—implicit or explicit. Small wonder, then, that each newly proposed diagnostic classification or nomenclature has its friends and foes, and that even its friends feel its use as a kind of professional onus that one has to put up with for the sake of conformity. And no wonder, also, that the language of official diagnosis becomes quickly misused as a kind of fraternity argot, or is perverted into an all-purpose idiom behind which one can hide ignorance or malcontent, particularly when its use adds a little prestige or feigned power.

An extremely important fifth feature of diagnostic language, which it shares with the technical languages of some other disciplines but has graver consequences, is the vulgarization of terms—that nasty process by which technical terms slowly move into the popular domain and lose the qualifications originally put upon their use becoming, in every sense of the word, cheapened. Journalists blithely write of Southeast Asian politics as "schizophrenic." Admirers of R. D. Laing use the same word almost as a term of praise and approval for gifted eccentrics venerated as luminaries. In literature, orderly persons are designated as "compulsives." Hapless compounds of some of our words are made at cocktail parties, such as *egomania*. The Hitlers, Stalins, and Quislings of this world, and indeed Freud himself, are constantly being diagnosed by literati who have never conducted a single psychiatric interview and are unfamiliar with the options in our diagnostic list but love some of our prestigious words. Yesterday it was (take your choice!) bad, or nice, to spot some neurotic traits in public personalities or in members of our social circle; today the epithets must be in the range of the psychoses to have some titillating effect; tomorrow the class of personality disorders will probably be in fashion. Homosexuality has been lifted from the diagnostic manual entirely and is now merely a designation of taste or style. In view of this vulgarization or popularization, one is tempted to quip, "Good riddance!" More temperately, one might say that psychiatry has lost its diagnostic language, which, deplorable as it is, may also be a marvelous opportunity for inventing a new one that will better serve its purpose. We recommend plain English as a viable alternative for the jargon that the public has run away with. Neo-Greek or Neo-Latin is no longer appropriate for designating the disorders which our patients present, if only because they are rarely so packaged that they stand out clearly from all the other features in these persons' lives or circumstances.

With all the frailties, oddities, and artificialities besetting diagnostic language, the psychiatrist is advised to pay heed to its rarefied status and withstand the temptation to use these terms outside the narrow circle of their applicability, if at all!

OTHER LANGUAGE PITFALLS IN PSYCHIATRY

Though psychiatrists, professionally vowed to be sticklers for words, should be pedagogues of language behavior, they are of course not immune to the twisting or perverting of language that is the common bane of mankind. Speech is an overdetermined function beset by special influences from the id, the superego, the ego-ideal, and the audience, and often poorly managed by the ego.

Upon reading psychiatric reports, one is struck by a number of tendencies which for many writers have become habits. One is to turn an act or a process into a state by word manipulation, e.g., the apt word *relation* is changed into the inapt word *relationship*. Another bad habit is overprecision that becomes ponderous redundancy, e.g., *ego defense* for *defense*. Poor theoretical grounding leads to the misuse of *acting out* for *enacting* or *making manifest in behavior*. Moralization comes through in such words as *perversion*, *psychopathic*, *inadequate personality*, *infantile personality*, and *character disorder*. Outright accusatory expressions are *castrating female*, *passive father*, *penis envy*, and *schizophrenogenic mother*. All too many psychiatric words have inapt space connotation: *borderline personality*, *underlying*, *ego boundaries*, *splitting*, *facade*. Words for the functions of conscience always stress its proscriptive side in general terms, i.e., *strict* or *demanding*, and rarely address its prescriptive aspect, as if to imply that conscience is only a damper rather than an organizer of behavior. Some word usage is tendentious: *compulsive* for *orderly*, *depressed* for *sad*.

Grossly inadequate use is made in many psychiatric reports of the words *appearing* and *seeming*. Misuse of these terms allows the writer to have definite opinions but to soften these in his presentation as well as to have no opinion but to give the impression of having one. Reports abound in "the patient seems to . . . ," "it seems that . . . ," "the patient appears to be . . . ," and "it appears that . . ."—all used interchangeably. *Appearing* is definite; it refers to something becoming clear and visible. But, in the mind of some users, it becomes associated with appearance, in the sense of mere semblance. *To seem* is less definite than *to appear*. The word *seem* implies that a particular beholder has as yet only an impression and is aware of his own subjectivity. Profuse use of these weasel words in psychiatric reports indicates that the writer equivocates between objectivity and subjectivity, between fantasy and reality, or between impressions and facts, pleading with the reader that he be allowed to have his cake and eat it. The psychiatrist who overloads his reports with such weasel words shows that he is under some strain to force his observations into the mold of some diagnostic category, building up a plausible case for the eventual diagnostic allocation he will make. Or else he has already put the patient intuitively into some pigeonhole (which may prove to be correct) and is now proceeding to see the patient from that nosological angle so as to achieve a good fit. These are some of the vagaries of allocating, fitting, and matching that the use of diagnostic nomenclature imposes, much to the discredit of the profession.

DIAGNOSIS AND THE DIFFERENCE IT MAKES

Much of the preceding exposition and criticism of psychiatric language(s) could induce one to adopt an antidiagnostic attitude or to advocate an adiagnostic position. This notion is far from our intention. We believe that diagnosis is not only a necessary psychiatric activity, but by far the most important single *raison d'être* for psychiatry as a profession. Members of many different professions as well as laymen have much to offer in alleviating the plight of the mentally ill, the emotionally disturbed, the psychologically disorganized, and—in the broadest sense—those who have difficulty in coping with the stresses and strains of life. Many interventions are possible and indeed are offered by a veritable army of eager workers. But unfortunately many interventions are made available and tried out without the least concern for their fitness to the condition to which they are being applied.

Many treatments are available on a self-referral basis, without prior diagnostic assessment and without explicit prescription. How much better use could be made of these treatments if some expert were available to match a defined condition with a judiciously chosen remedy by way of a logical and specific prescription! It is our belief that whatever psychiatrists may now wish to do or come to do in the future, their single most useful and desirable function lies in making diagnostic assessments that can be understood by diverse therapists and formulating prescriptions that map out specific therapeutic strategies and modalities.

Inherent in this proposition is the whole issue of specificity both of mental disorder and of therapy. The theory and practice of drug therapy highlights extremes on both sides of this issue. Not long ago when tranquilizers arrived, they were thought to apply very broadly to a great variety of mental disorders as a palliative for their commonest symptom: anxiety. They were widely prescribed for conditions that were not probed and differentiated, indeed hardly diagnosed at all, in the belief that anxiety, as the vaguest common denominator, could be lessened. To many prescribers diagnosis was not really needed since neither specificity of disorder nor specificity of remedy was deemed relevant. Today, however, for the use of a drug such as Lithium the greatest acumen is required in diagnosing the specific syndrome of bipolar depression, and even the prevailing phase thereof, in order to formulate a precise dosage. Thus, in psychopharmacology, we have moved in a few decades from general to specific treatment, with an increasing demand for precise diagnostic work and minutely calibrated prescription.

Many psychiatric conditions lie somewhere between the two extremes of generality and specificity. So do the therapies. If the psychiatrist's diagnostic ability is to be singled out as his professional forte and his most useful asset from a social point of view, everything will hinge on his articulateness in formulating a clear, pointed, and useful diagnostic summary of the condition presented by the patient, so that it can and will lead to a well-considered prescription which is not merely pragmatic or opportunistic but follows logically from his understanding of the patient's malady or problem.

What kind of language is required for such an endeavor? It seems to us, first, that diagnosing by merely naming the disorder will not do, if only because the currently officially listed disorders cover too wide a range from the specific to the general and from definite to vague formulations. Moreover, the patient's presenting complaints and symptoms are often so complex or unique that trying to fit them to the extant list may lead to their falsification. But perhaps more importantly, in the present state of psychiatric science, the naming of disorders in terms of the standard nomenclature gives insufficient clues to treatment. A language must be found that summarily describes the patient's disorder in such a way that many would-be helpers and adjudicators are informed by the condition and can be helped to calculate its impact.

Secondly, if diagnosing is to make a difference, as this conference holds, it will have to evolve into the science and art of prescribing. Here we have to face the fact that the semblance of unity and systematization present in psychiatric nosology, though still only a semblance, contrasts favorably with the rampant eclecticism and fierce disunity of psychiatric therapeutics. To put it more crassly, much psychiatric treatment, even after thoughtful diagnosis, is ad hoc, opportunistic, pragmatic, or overly and sometimes solely determined by what the would-be therapist knows or likes to do. At its best, there are volumes on various therapies and organized schools in which various therapists are educated, but we lack a unitary, comprehensive theory of psychiatric treatment. Even the most prestigious general psychiatric handbooks contain only separate chapters on selective modes of treatment, presented staccato, each being a forum for a special point of view and unrelated to one another. It is not surprising, therefore, that engagement in one therapy or another is often not instigated by a prescription, for knowledgeable prescribing should be undergirded by a comprehensive theory of therapeutics. The science and art of prescribing are perched between and atop two large intellectual enterprises: diagnosis (including nosology, taxonomy, and nomenclature) and therapeutics (including all remedies, particular approaches, and a theory of intervention and change).

Given his army of diagnostic and therapeutic specialists, the psychiatrist is somewhat in the position of a broker between various parties—patients, relatives, referral persons and agencies, institutions of various kinds, and many other caretakers and therapists. If his technical jargon pleases one of these parties, it is sure to displease others; if some understand his formulations, surely others do not; if his diagnoses instigate hope in some, they lead to despair or callousness in others. Brokerage requires skill, particularly in communication.

Shall the psychiatrist therefore become a wizard in languages, skillfully switching from one language to the other as he addresses his various parties to give each one his due? Unfortunately, his professional life does not allow him to be available to all relevant parties at once, like an interpreter at the United Nations. Yes, his situation does call for linguistic versatility and the skill of a polyglot, at times, to use the language that is appropriate to the situation. But his situations are so diverse, his actual and potential audiences so many, that it would be much better if he adopted from the start and maintained throughout his work the one language most likely to be understood by the largest diversity of people and the least likely to be misunderstood by anyone—the mother tongue. For psychiatric purposes, the mother tongue is the most viable professional instrument of communication. It is to be used deftly, tersely, clearly, and with precision. As the old Hebrew preacher put it: "Let thy speech be short, comprehending much in a few words" (Ecclesiasticus 32:8 [Apocrypha]). Or as Hemingway (1947) put it three thousand years later: "The first and most important thing of all . . . is to strip language clean, to lay it bare down to the bone" (p. 983).

After all, Legion was healed only after he stopped twisting words, and after the swine had taken his obscure utterances away with them to their graves.

REFERENCES

American Psychiatric Association: *Diagnostic and Statistical Manual of Mental Disorders*, Second Edition. Washington, D.C.: Author, 1968.

Bleuler, Eugen (1911): *Dementia Praecox or the Group of Schizophrenias*, Joseph Zinken, tr. New York: International Universities Press, 1950.

Hemingway, Ernest: Quoted from *Paris Was Our Mistress* by Samuel Putnam (New York: Viking Press, 1947) in *Familiar Quotations*, Ed. 13, by John Bartlett. Boston: Little, Brown, 1955.

Menninger, Karl *et al.*: *The Vital Balance*. New York: Viking Press, 1963.

Chapter 4

Reflections on
the Diagnostic Process
by a Clinical Team

JORGE DE LA TORRE, ANN APPELBAUM, DORIS JANE CHEDIAK,
AND WILLIAM H. SMITH

In the Menninger tradition, the diagnostic process is not seen as an activity to be accomplished with maximum expediency, nor is the diagnostic team organized to give comfort to its individual members. Diagnosis is, rather, seen as a serious, exacting, exciting, and often rewarding and frequently courageous enterprise. The team is careful not to slip into sterile or fanciful abstractions, but is always geared to one final product: improvement of the patient's condition.

In such a framework of tradition and practice, the psychiatric team participants are not substitutes for the functions of an ideal physician. Its members are skilled practitioners in their own right with original contributions to make to the diagnosis and treatment of psychiatric patients. In the general enthusiasm for psychiatric teams that arose in hospitals during the past decade, some of the principles and aims of multidisciplinary work may have become obscured. We would like to discuss these principles from the vantage point of the practitioners. Although the composition of a team varies according to its specific aim (frequently it will include nurses, activity therapists, psychiatric aides, teachers, or speech therapists), because of the time limit for this presentation we have confined ourselves to three distinct practitioners: a psychiatrist (Ann Appelbaum), a clinical psychologist (William Smith), and a psychiatric social worker (Doris Jane Chediak).

Clinical practice has given us strong convictions regarding the importance of a multidimensional view of a patient's functioning. Different perspectives with different observations and inferences yield several partial views of the patient which, when superimposed, give depth to the diagnostic image. All diagnostic

Reprinted with permission from the *Bulletin of the Menninger Clinic*, 1976, Vol. 40, No. 5, pp. 479–496, © 1976 by The Menninger Foundation.

work, moreover, has a longitudinal dimension representing the patient's history and a cross-sectional one representing the here and now that emerges during the examinations. If the diagnostic team is to operate as one articulate whole, functional cohesiveness with autonomy of units that share a common goal becomes necessary. The prerequisites for such a team include:

1. *Professional particularity*: Each member is to have a conviction about the worth of his professional work achieved through the maturation derived from training in his discipline. The opposite of professional particularity is professional diffusion, in which all members of the team try to be "accessory psychiatrists."

2. *Autonomy of diagnostic skills and tools*: Each member must feel comfortable and secure in using those particular skills and tools he knows best in such a way as to avoid competitive duplication.

3. *Role differentiation*: Each member must have a given position toward the diagnostic task, one member focusing on the intrapsychic functioning of the patient, others being particularly alert to the interpersonal or intrafamilial functioning, etc. The opposite of role differentiation is role homogenization.

4. *Ability to disagree*: Team members must maintain a climate of professional inquiry rather than slip into a stereotyped hierarchy leading to fearful acquiescence.

5. *Mutual respect*: This qualitative factor is based on regard for individual competence, with reciprocal opportunities to evaluate each other's contributions, instead of idealizing one member on the basis of his professional background.

6. *Group congruence*: The team upholds a coincidence in purposes that sustains rewarding working relationships; it resists malignant group dynamics.

7. *A common theoretical frame of reference*: This stance allows the team to pursue in depth certain inferences. Without such a frame of reference the team's work may be annulled by the disparity of theoretical premises.

8. *Supportive administrative structure*: Without administrative support all the previous *desiderata* become inoperative. The best clinical team will be rendered ineffectual if the administrative structure in which it operates does not take agreeable notice of its work, provide the necessary support, coordinate the work, make available the time, etc.

In order to reflect on the diagnostic process as we conduct it in our daily work,* we have chosen a particular patient with whom we worked to demonstrate

---

* A diagnostic evaluation of daily interviews with a psychiatrist while the patient's relative is seen by a psychiatric social worker. In addition, a full battery of psychological testing, physical and neurological examination, and laboratory and X-ray tests are also conducted. The whole process typically lasts between one and two weeks.

how clinical team members, representing different disciplines, actually engage each other. The case is not striking or unusual; on the contrary, it comes close to what most clinicians encounter in their practice. That, we feel, is precisely its didactic strength.

THE TEAM PSYCHIATRIST

At the beginning of the presentation, we hinted at the rewards of diagnostic team work. This case is somewhat exceptional in that the patient, Sally F., offered a spontaneous, grateful, and complimentary follow-up. A few weeks after her return home from her diagnostic evaluation, she wrote the following letter:

Dear Doctor:

I've been getting along very well since I got home two weeks ago. . . . I haven't felt nervous or depressed at all. I'm still having headaches, but I haven't had any severe ones and the ones I have had have been controlled pretty well by the medicine you gave me. Everything seems to be better. . . . My husband joined the church the Sunday after we got home, and for the first time religion plays a significant part in our lives. Believe me, it helps. I have already found a good part-time job which I will start next week. I bought a new sewing machine that will do almost anything, and I'm increasing my church participation and Bible study. Those things, with all I have been doing in spite of the headaches, should keep me busy enough that I won't have time to think about emotional things. Thank you again for what all of you did for my husband and me. I feel the trip was very profitable to both of us. I'll appreciate what you can do in helping to arrange for the further treatment you suggested for me here at home.

When the woman who wrote the letter first corresponded with us, she was so desperate after twelve years of a disabling illness that she wanted to move to Topeka from a distant state and put herself entirely in our hands. Her initial letter was a clear, well-organized account of unremitting daily headaches, punctuated with periods of severe anxiety, depression, fatigue, and emotional strain. She started each day by taking three or four Darvon capsules which she repeated every four hours with Bufferin in between. In the late afternoon she would rest and take Codeine without ever being relieved entirely of her pain. She had consulted many physicians. Ten years before she wrote to us she underwent an extensive neurological work-up including bilateral carotid angiograms and a spinal fluid examination which disclosed no neurological disturbance. At that time out-patient psychiatric treatment had been attempted for about six months followed by six weeks of hospitalization and electroshock treatment. But her condition remained unchanged.

During the ensuing decade, various tranquilizers in various dosages were tried. She had a thorough examination at the Mayo Clinic, where the headaches were attributed to muscle spasm and underlying emotional conflicts. By the time she contacted us, she was having excruciating, continuous headaches and thought she was losing her mind. She was taking 200 mg. of Mellaril daily to which she had added 200 mg. of Sinequan, in addition to Elavil, Dalmane, Premarin, thyroid, and iron.

In response to this woman's request for help, we asked that she and her husband participate with a diagnostic team in a two-week study of the problem. In advance of their coming to Topeka, we asked each of them to fill out a packet of self-administered tests, a task requiring about two hours of concentrated independent effort. We also asked them to contact the physicians who had previously treated Mrs. F. for their reports. The message conveyed by these requirements is a significant one: "A group of us will set aside two weeks to work intensively with you; but at the same time we expect you to work intensively with us. You are not just a sick person who will 'go through the clinic' like a piece of faulty merchandise on a conveyor belt, but rather you and your family will be active participants in a search for understanding." We set a tone of serious dedication, telling the patient and her husband that business and family life must be interrupted for a period of total devotion to unraveling the problem. In this case, as in many others, the impact of this preliminary phase of the study was such as to bring about a decrease of symptoms, a response which reflects in part hopefulness, and in part a shift of focus from suffering to working.

Before the patient arrived, the diagnostic team assembled for a brief conference to study the self-administered tests and other data. As one might imagine, the psychiatrist felt dubious about being able to help this chronically ill woman, the intractability of whose symptoms might represent, among other things, a wish to control and defeat those who wish to help her. Perhaps the unusual clarity and articulateness of her initial letter reflected a struggle to contain an impending disorganization. If so, the study might upset her balance, and lead to referral for hospitalization—and these people were of modest means and probably could not afford a long and costly hospital treatment. Indeed they were making a considerable financial sacrifice to come to Topeka for this outpatient examination. Would the psychiatrist's work make this sacrifice worthwhile? Would this psychiatrist prove to be as impotent as all her previous doctors had been? The team consultant helped make these trepidations explicit, so the team members could support one another in facing the challenge and the possible disappointments that lay ahead.

A solitary psychiatrist, functioning without the emotional and intellectual nourishment of a sentient group, would find it hard to contain, tolerate, and examine the human pain being brought for diagnostic study, and to deal with feelings of anticipatory discouragement and self-doubt. Such feelings are mitigated in the kind of diagnostic study described here by the knowledge that the task is a time-limited one. It is easier to sustain attitudes of alertness, optimism, and concern—just as it is easier to be brave in the face of physical pain—when an end-point is established in advance.

The diagnostic study began on a Monday morning. The psychiatrist and the social worker met with the patient and her husband for an hour to define the problem, clarify the expectations of the clients about the study, and outline the procedure. Over the next two days the psychiatrist met twice with the patient, and the social worker met twice with the husband. Meanwhile four hours of psychological testing were scheduled. A complete physical examination, a neurological examination, and a full battery of laboratory tests were carried out.

On the third day of the study, the psychologist, social worker, and psychiatrist met with the team consultant to compare notes. The psychiatrist felt frustrated and inadequate: In the interviews, the patient had expressed high expectations of being cured and a willingness to do anything asked of her, while at the same time she demonstrated her distrust of the psychiatrist and her doubt that she could be helped. When the psychiatrist invited the patient to reflect upon possible connections between these attitudes, events of the past, and current symptoms, she talked endlessly about how unbearable her headaches had made her life. She listed the famous doctors and clinics she had consulted and the variety of treatment regimens she had undertaken without benefit. She spoke with evident satisfaction of how she had come to be "her own doctor" by learning to combine different medications so as to get better results than any of her physicians had been able to produce.

The psychologist shed light on the difficulties the psychiatrist was experiencing: He had found in this highly intelligent woman difficulties in attention and concentration against which she struggled by maintaining an appearance of composed detachment. The testing had uncovered her propensity for delusional reasoning, and her difficulty in distinguishing between inner and outer aspects of reality. She was nearly overwhelmed by anxiety and depression to the point of experiencing depersonalization (which was what she meant by "losing her mind"). Her doubts about the psychiatrist's capacity to help her represented her deep feelings of helplessness and needfulness, which made her experience others as also helpless, immobilized, and unresponsive. Meanwhile the social worker had found the husband psychologically naive but genuinely interested in his wife, committed to her welfare, and able to keep his own balance in the midst of the great frustrations in his marriage. Putting all this information together, the team developed a working hypothesis: The psychiatrist's effort to move Mrs. F. toward insight had made the patient feel psychologically endangered. What she needed from the psychiatrist was a more accepting and supportive attitude and help in organizing her thoughts and sorting out her confusion.

In the ensuing eight hours with the psychiatrist, Mrs. F. rapidly responded to the more supportive atmosphere of the interviews by gradually becoming more tolerant of her inner experiences, putting her introspection at the service of improving her condition rather than of contending with her doctor. By the end of the first week she had discontinued all her tranquilizing medications, contenting herself with an analgesic which sufficed to keep the headaches within tolerable limits. A therapeutic alliance was beginning to emerge.

The team met for the second time at the end of a two-week period. The task now was to crystallize the plans that had been forming in the minds of the patient, her husband, and the team members as the work had been going on. Team members agreed that this woman was struggling with a concealed psychotic disturbance whose dynamics were reflected in the acceleration of her thought processes, in her disorganized thinking, her poor ego boundaries, and her experiences of depersonalization. Despite the nature of the illness, its chronicity, and her characteristic defensive efforts of manic denial, projection, and somatization, she had shown important assets that included high intelligence, a capacity to reflect psychologically and to be objective about herself and others. The basic strength of her relationship with her husband would stand her in good stead. The patient and her husband were ready to accept a recommendation for individual supportive psychotherapy for the wife, with periodic participation of the husband designed to help the two of them improve their capacity to talk with each other and to explore ways of having a more gratifying sexual relationship. Triavil, an antidepressant, antipsychotic medication, was prescribed, along with a mild analgesic. She was encouraged to refrain from taking other medication except as prescribed by the therapist to whom she would be referred. In a final meeting with the psychiatrist, the social worker, and her husband, the patient was advised to obtain a part-time job and stick to it even if she went through periods of depression and headaches, and to expand her life by participating in church activities and community volunteer work. The letter we received from her a few weeks after she returned home indicates how promptly and fully this woman translated all of these suggestions into action.

This patient is unique, but the method is typical: Team diagnostic work of this sort is one of a variety of diagnostic processes in use at the Menninger Foundation. The decision whether to resort to a formal one- or two-week study, or to do a more conventional consultation, in which the psychiatrist requests various additional studies in the course of the examination as the need arises, is a complicated one. We try to thread our way between the twin dangers of overdiagnosis and underdiagnosis, involving no more people and procedures than necessary—and no less. When a problem is clearly a complex one, and when the ultimate treatment decision may be as weighty as referral for extensive hospital treatment or psychoanalysis, we are likely to plan an extensive study from the beginning. For people who are unsure about whether they need help, or whose financial resources are limited, or who can be seen from preliminary data to be in need of crisis intervention, family therapy, or brief psychotherapy, we begin with a consultation designed either to explore the person's motivation, or to help with the best referral he can afford, or to serve as a beginning for brief psychotherapy.

The kind of study done with Mrs. F. and her husband has special advantages when the problem is severe and chronic and is producing a disruption of family life. Spending a week or two away from home in an unfamiliar setting often facilitates the renunciation of long-standing symptoms such as drug dependency or pathological marital interactions, since the symptomatic behavior is now detached from a thousand daily habit patterns with which the symptoms had become entangled. This brief respite from familiar pain and failure often is a first indication to a person that he can indeed help himself rather than remain a victim or an inflicter of chronic suffering. The emphasis on the patient helping himself is important because the time-limited work with the team minimizes dependent transference reactions both by diffusing these among the members of the team and by keeping in focus from the beginning the fact that an indefinite dependence upon the psychiatrist is not a possibility. At the end of the study, attachments are severed, goodbyes are said (often sad ones on both sides), and a new phase begins.

The work of a psychiatrist is often lonely, and periodic involvement in such a piece of team work—especially when successful—infuses new energy into a depleted clinician's system. Last but not least, the different team members also learn from one another.

THE TEAM SOCIAL WORKER

Patients who present themselves at the Menninger Foundation for a diagnostic study in most instances are accompanied by family members who are concerned about the patient and his problems. Since the stability of family life depends on the delicate emotional balance and gratifying interaction of its members, the upsetting behavior of one member often makes it difficult, if not impossible, for the family to contain the problems or to find solutions to them. Therefore, it becomes important to study the family as well as the patient during the diagnostic process.

There are two basic reasons for involving the family at the beginning of the diagnostic process:

1. Family members contribute a great deal of essential information which can enhance our understanding of the patient and help us pinpoint the relationship between the individual's problems and the family's problems.
2. In turn, an effective diagnostic process enriches the family's understand-

ing of the problem and makes it more possible for the family to work together in finding appropriate solutions.

In working with families, our overall goals are:

1. To obtain a detailed history of the family and of the presenting symptomatology as the family experiences it;
2. To assess the marital and family dynamics, noting strengths in relationships as well as pathological interactions;
3. To clarify the reality factors which influence what the family can or cannot do to help the patient;
4. To determine the reasons and the extent to which the family should be involved in further treatment; and
5. To convey to the family as well as to the patient our diagnostic impressions and recommendations.

To accomplish these objectives, we begin the diagnostic process with an initial interview in which the psychiatrist and social worker meet with the patient and the family to discuss the presenting problems and to clarify expectations of the examination. Afterward, individual interviews are scheduled to obtain pertinent history and to allow the individual members ample time to discuss their concerns. Additional joint interviews can be helpful and are often necessary to assess the nature of the family interaction and to test ways of modifying communication and/or relationship patterns. At the end of the diagnostic process, the psychiatrist and social worker again meet with the patient and the family to convey impressions and recommendations and to discuss issues which need further clarification.

In the case of Mrs. F., it was clear from the preadmission material that there had been an abrupt change in the marital relationship and thus a marital assessment was indicated. Her husband, who had been a heavy drinker for twenty years, gave up his drinking when she threatened him with divorce. Not only did he successfully give up his drinking, but his behavior reflected his wish to make changes conducive to a more gratifying marriage. While on the surface Mrs. F. seemed to welcome such a change, in reality it caused her to become painfully aware of her loneliness and her inability to have a close relationship with anyone.

Her family history gave us further understanding of her other conflictual relationships. An only child, she had lost her father by divorce and desertion and her mother because of mental illness and institutionalization. She had been unable to have children through miscarriages and had lost her first husband through divorce. She thought she had lost her second husband when his business demands and his drinking problem isolated him from her. However, when she challenged this loss by threatening divorce, she discovered instead a concerned husband who was willing to make personal changes in an effort to preserve and rebuild the marital relationship. In the context of this relationship change, Mrs. F. became aware of her emotional limitations and sought a different kind of personal evaluation for herself and her husband. At the same time her husband began to reflect on his increasing dissatisfaction with the marriage. He realized that both his drinking problem and his wife's constant headaches were largely responsible for their gradually deteriorating social and sexual activities. Although he was not particularly psychologically minded, he was eager to talk about concrete problems, especially sexual difficulties. During the interviews, no attempt was made to uncover with him the historical origin of the sexual problems, but he was receptive to what we might call "bibliotherapy": At the suggestion of the social worker he read and discussed several pertinent books which helped him clarify further some of his own concerns and to share these with his wife.

Diagnostically, the chronicity of Mrs. F.'s symptoms, her traumatic early history, and years of pathological marital interaction indicated a fairly severe emotional problem. On the other hand, her numerous achievements, her receptivity to change, and the growing evidence of an increasing healthier bond with her husband pointed to a more favorable prognosis. Through our detailed discussion at the first team meeting, it became clear that the couple showed potential for a closer and more mutually gratifying relationship which could foster growth in the marriage and help make continued psychological treatment more fruitful.

As this case illustrates, one of the primary goals of the team members is to understand the nature of intrapsychic conflict. A special task of the social worker is to assess the interplay between intrapsychic conflict and family conflict. In this regard, effective communication among team members is crucial. Once the significant data are gathered, there should be either enough internal consistency or enough contradictions among various reports to plan further diagnostic strategy. Often, joint interviews with the patient and various family members become useful to test out initial diagnostic leads and to clarify further the most appropriate treatment intervention for the patient and the family.

THE TEAM PSYCHOLOGIST

When a psychologist does psychological testing, he often does it at the request of another professional, frequently a psychiatrist, in order to answer some question that the referring clinician has about a patient. The psychologist may have little information about the patient other than the diagnostic question at hand, and may have no personal contact with his referral source. The psychologist may then see the patient and carry out testing which enables him to answer the referral question, as *he* understands it, and to *his* own satisfaction. A written report—with thanks for the referral if done on a private practice basis, or with a brief conversation or meeting if part of an institutional arrangement—may be the only communication *from* the psychologist, the psychiatrist then using what he has obtained in the way of new or confirmatory knowledge in his diagnostic or treatment role with the patient.

Some elements of this model are similar to the requests a physician makes for X rays or laboratory studies. Some elements are like that of an internist asking for a consultation by a surgeon, or a speech pathologist getting an opinion from an audiologist. Working in teams, that is, bringing the benefit of multiple perspectives to bear in diagnostic and treatment efforts, can take many forms. Ideally, however, the members of a team should have some particular expertise in the work being carried out, and the structural arrangements should allow each member to make his optimal contribution.

What working arrangements or structures enable a psychologist to contribute optimally when his role is to administer psychological tests? As an integral part of a diagnostic team, a psychologist can first bring his expertise to bear in the formulation of diagnostic questions to be answered. The psychologist's expertise does not reside within the tests themselves, but in the sensitivity and knowledge he acquires through training and experience, and he can assess what contribution testing can likely make to the problem at hand. In some cases, testing may be judged unnecessary when the data available through other sources are sufficient to meet the clinical needs. Ideally, the kind and amount of testing performed should be tailored to the presenting situation, though sometimes a test report is useful later for other purposes. For example, testing originally geared toward assessing a patient's suitability for an expressive psychotherapy might later be used by the therapist to anticipate likely transference paradigms, regressive potential around certain conflict areas, impulse-defense configurations, and so on. Another special point arises when the testing is relied on by colleagues who need support for their observations for reasons of inexperience, lack of confidence, or some form of legal necessity.

Decisions about how the testing should be focused may also grow out of the early test impressions of the psychologist or observations by others on the team. In the case of Mrs. F., the presenting situation dictated a full test battery, since she had never had a comprehensive study and the questions raised at the outset were varied and complex: How can we understand the patient's chronic symptoms on a psychological basis—can we rule out organic factors? In what sort of characterological context does her symptom exist? Are there significant masochistic leanings? Is she a help-rejecting complainer? Does the high degree of organization and clarity in her initial communication with us reflect strength that could be mobilized in the service of change, or hyperalertness in the service of controlling others which could be difficult to work with? With this history of chronic symptoms, will we find resources for responding to psychotherapy? Is more serious disturbance being held tenuously in abeyance?

At the time of the midweek team meeting, two testing sessions had been conducted and it was clear that the patient was struggling mightily to control serious thought disturbance. Her rather bland and detached manner stood in marked contrast to serious inner turmoil, with depression and anxiety accompanying a sense of helplessness, pessimism, and guilt. Alerting the team to the patient's real though not apparent distress, and the potential she had for disorganization and perhaps even suicide, led to changes in the psychiatrist's approach to the patient. This possibility of communication with other team members while an evaluation is in progress is another valuable element of good teamwork. With this patient, testing done and reported following the psychiatric interviews would not have been as useful; testing directed toward circumscribed questions (Is there organic damage? What is the patient's suicide potential?) might not have elicited other important findings: significant intellectual strengths which she could bring to bear on tasks in spite of some encroachment by thought disturbance, and an ability to improve her performance with time and encouragement. These findings suggested a better prognosis than had earlier been judged possible, and proved to be correct, at least from what follow-up we have available.

THE TEAM CONSULTANT

The efficacy of teamwork is further enhanced by an additional member—the team consultant—whose function is crucial in facilitating smooth teamwork. The consultant helps team members recognize their interdependence, the limitations of their partial views, and the need to synthesize these views for the sake of understanding the patient better. Clinical team members must share with their colleagues their knowledge, ignorance, confusion, or frustrations if they are to discover solutions to clinical problems. Such self-exposure is not to be frowned upon as denoting incompetency or insecurity, but should be seen as a mark of professional honesty and maturity.

In our setting, the consultant to a team never sees the patient except indirectly through the eyes of the team members. In this way he maintains a higher degree of objectivity, since he is not subjected to the patient's direct impact on him or prejudiced with preconceived, favorite clinical impressions that are likely to develop were he to interview the patient himself. He remains equidistant from the various team members as the diagnostic mosaic emerges, at first shapelessly, with different pieces of information and different levels of inferences closely juxtaposed.

Because of the position he occupies vis-à-vis the team members, and because of his being invested with a great deal of authority by the members who also hold high expectations of his performance, he is cast in the position of a leader. As one might expect, such a situation is likely to stir up infantile emotions, jealousies, and rivalries among the participants, each wanting to have the greater share of the leader's admiration and attention, or striving to compete with him for supremacy. However, if properly channeled and put to work for the patient's benefit, these dynamics can produce a more accurate and deeper understanding of the patient.

Since the type of examination we are describing fosters the rapid development of intense relationships through daily contact with the patient and his family, it is not surprising that irrational attitudes might propel the team to wish for premature closure, avoidance of painful areas, or rejection of conflicting views in the complicated group process that develops from the team members' interactions. The team consultant is in a position to understand and disentangle such interactions when they become an impediment to the diagnostic objective.

In the case of Mrs. F., when the team met for the first time a week before her arrival, anticipations were mixed. On the one hand, the clarity of the patient's initial request was perceived by some as being "controlling" since obviously she knew what she wanted and was determined to get it. The severity and chronicity of her symptoms made the team feel unenthusiastic about the diagnostic task; they anticipated an unrewarding patient who unconsciously would try to prove the team members impotent as helpers. Her psychopathology was well grasped, as was the fragility of her ego. However, her assets were not perceived with equal clarity, nor spelled out with much conviction. So, with that sense of skepticism, the team began its work. The consultant from the beginning, as he continued to do throughout all the meetings, had to define and redefine the primary task to which the group should address itself: a comprehensive understanding of the patient which could lead to solid recommendations for her improvement and predictions about her response. Indeed, the more a consultant helps the group to see its task clearly and stick to it, the less danger there is of the team being ruled and disrupted by unconscious basic assumptions. As tensions increase and surpass the optimal level necessary for a productive and useful working relationship, the effectiveness of the teamwork might be threatened seriously. Then the consultant must sustain the team members and deal with the anxiety engendered by the frustrations they experience.

In the case of Mrs. F., when the team convened after two days of work, the data available did not appear to gel. The psychiatrist felt she had little impact on Mrs. F. since the patient continued to be testy and suspicious of the psychiatrist's professional credentials. The patient resisted the psychiatrist's efforts to diminish the large amount of medication she was taking. The social worker reported that the husband was a psychologically unsophisticated man, though he appeared interested in the patient's welfare and seemed willing to make sacrifices for her. The psychologist pointed out the patient's easily triggered delusional potential, the evident thought disorder, and the rigidity of her defenses. The psychological tests provided more evidence than was available to any other team member of the patient's capacity to stick to a task, to respond well to structure, and to use her intellectual functions without disturbance from her anxiety. The picture of a woman who had the capacity to think clearly, to organize her thoughts properly, and to communicate informatively was a contrast to the earlier image of a "very sick" patient. The consultant, focusing on the apparent lack of continuity between these two impressions, helped bring together the material that had first appeared to fit poorly, and helped integrate the different inferences drawn from discrepant observations.

It became apparent that the resoluteness of this woman, if properly channeled, could become a definite asset in successfully implementing some treatment recommendations. What previously seemed to be a controlling stance now appeared to be the way she protected herself from inner disorganization that threatened her when situations were not clearly spelled out and her anxiety rose to unmanageable levels.

The psychiatrist, who had been nondirective in her initial contact, remaining rather neutral and inviting the patient to reflect in an open-ended style, now began to question the usefulness of this technique. It became clear that a more supportive and structured type of interview, capitalizing on the patient's assets and making them explicit to her, would be more useful. If this change in approach was in the right direction, then the patient's subsequent attitude and behavior should confirm it, just as an interpretation in a psycho-therapeutic hour is confirmed or invalidated by the subsequent material that emerges. When the patient's behavior is kept in the center of all diagnostic discussions, then the danger of formulating interesting but speculative or irrelevant hypotheses is minimized.

We should remember that up to this point the psychiatrist had not been able to persuade Mrs. F. to reduce her medication. It was still an open question as to how much of the behavior we had examined was clouded by the effects of Mrs. F.'s mixture of medications. Her willingness to reduce the use of drugs would become the gauge for measuring her needs to exert control and appear self-sufficient as opposed to her capacity for cooperation and self-reflection. When the psychiatrist changed her interviewing approach, the patient first agreed to diminish her medication and then she discontinued it almost entirely. She became more spontaneous and was able to develop a genuine therapeutic alliance with the psychiatrist.

It was the consultant's task to point out to the team members that all of the feelings they had initially experienced—the hopelessness, unclarity, and frustration about not having a definite direction—reflected Mrs. F.'s own views about her own life. Frequently the same polarizations that the patient experiences in relating to his internal objects are reflected in the reactions of the team members who find themselves unconsciously allied with one aspect or another of the patient's conflicts. Strong group countertransferences can emerge early in the contact with any patient and, if the team understands these factors, they can work with them to gain a different understanding of the patient's functioning and thus attain a conviction about the value and effectiveness of the team itself.

A diagnostic assessment, as conducted by this team, is a complete process with a beginning, a middle, and an end phase. The team consultant has to provide the monitoring function that relates the work of the diagnostic team to the different phases of the process. The end phase is of particular importance, for in that period the team's recommendations are discussed with the patient. Note that they are discussed, not given to a passive recipient. The patient, who has been active in the diagnostic process from the beginning, continues to be an active participant as the end approaches, suggesting and evaluating the treatment alternatives. As timekeeper of the process, the consultant reminds the team of the importance of making time available for working through the treatment recommendations.

SUMMARY

Working in teams, that is, bringing the work of various disciplines together—testing, interviews, social casework, as well as whatever physical studies may be indicated—provides a more accurate and complete picture of the patient than any one of them alone. None of them is the criterion by which the others are measured; none has an inside track on the truth. Mutual respect for the skill of individual team members and for the validity and importance of each point of view is a prerequisite for good teamwork. Integrating data which are virtually identical from these various disciplines is sometimes hard in itself, but to assimilate and organize information from interviews, tests, history, accounts by relatives, school and work records, etc., requires a high degree of conceptual and integrative skill. Apparent contradictions must be reconciled, views must be fit together like pieces of a puzzle, and understanding of a unique individual must emerge. For such teamwork, good communication is essential. If team members are unable to find a common language, the team which could be a tower of strength may become a Tower of Babel. To accomplish their goal of optimal service to patients, team members must be convinced about the worth of their own contribution, trust and rely on the special skills of others on the team, and work toward effective communication.

The kind of diagnostic work we have described is sophisticated, intense, demanding, and expensive. But as this presentation makes clear, for Mrs. F., who had been branded for many years with the label of chronic psychosis, it was a careful diagnosis that made the difference.

PART TWO

Diagnostic Testing Considerations

Contemporary approaches to psychological testing have a long and complicated history. Scientific efforts at psychological assessment are roughly 100 years old, if the work of Francis Galton on individual differences is accepted as the starting point (McReynolds, 1981). Subsequent development of mental testing and then personality measurement progressed in the early part of this century, providing tools for the developing profession of clinical psychology (Allison, Blatt, & Zimet, 1968). Initially the defining function of the profession, psychological testing remained a central task well into the 1960s (Holt, 1967), but more recently it has suffered some weakening in its prestige as a valued skill and service (Korchin and Schuldberg, 1981). The reasons for such a decline have been enumerated and analyzed by Holt (1967), Rosenwald (1963), and Weiner (1972), among others. All of these writers conclude that the practice and usefulness of diagnostic testing is still alive, if only moderately well, and that when apropriately used, psychological tests can be potent clinical instruments.

What, then, are appropriate uses? Put differently, there are different approaches to psychological testing, not only with respect to the tests used, but with regard to the guiding theories and conceptual approaches as well. The papers in this section illustrate a view of testing anchored in a particular historical and clinical context with certain guiding values and attitudes. It is not "diagnostic" in the sense of identifying a disease entity or even attaching a label, and not "testing" in the sense of determining quantitative values comparable to laboratory analysis. With the encouragement of Drs. Karl and Will Menninger in the context of their humanistic and dynamic orientation, David Rapaport began a systematic approach to the assessment of personality which proved to be as clinically useful as it was theoretically sound. His development of inference-making strategies which linked the content of test responses, their properties that can be scored, the specific verbalizations of the person, and his or her test behavior inspired generations of clinical psychologists to study his disciplined, yet creative, ideas about personality organization and psychopathology. A long list of students, colleagues, and successors at the Menninger Foundation and elsewhere—Roy Schafer, Robert Holt, George Klein, Martin Mayman, Paul Pruyser, Herbert Schlesinger, Philip Holzman, and Stephen Appelbaum, to name only a few—were stimulated by Rapaport's teachings, and added their own perspectives to the challenging and exciting work on assessment. From the earlier emphasis on impulse-defense configurations and the vicissitudes of thought organization, to the contemporary focus on self-experience and relationship dispositions, diagnostic testing at the Menninger Foundation has remained a lively and intellectually vigorous activity, one respected and relied upon by all the mental health disciplines in day-to-day clinical work.

The chapters in this section grow out of and reflect this particular tradition. The first chapter, by Herbert J. Schlesinger, addresses one important, but far from obvious, consideration in the testing situation. In contrast to a purely psychometric approach to assessment, diagnostic testing may be viewed as a dynamically significant event between two persons. Pointing to the similarities with interviewing and even psychotherapy, Schlesinger shows how the interpersonal context of the testing powerfully influences the patient's reactions and responses. Focusing especially on themes common to beginnings, he illustrates how a sensitive awareness of patients' hopes, fears, and assumptions not only facilitates the testing, but serves as additional data for diagnostic understanding.

Stephen A. Appelbaum also highlights the importance of the patient-examiner relationship in his illustration of how patients with significant masochistic strivings play out their needs to be criticized, punished, or humiliated in their behavior with the tester, as well as in the test responses themselves. Alerting us to this easily overlooked factor in psychopathology and in treatment impasse or failure, Appelbaum's clear descriptions will prompt many clinicians to reconsider past and current cases in a new light, and sharpen our ability to detect and deal with this phenomenon in the future.

Using systematic review of patients' early memories as a testing technique, Martin Mayman points to the rich data the manifest content provides when viewed thematically, as one might regard dreams, fantasies, or TAT stories. Key conflicts, relationship dispositions, and life strategies are revealed through this intriguing medium. Not at all an attempt at genetic reconstruction of an actual past, this approach yields timely and treatment-relevant data in a language useful to both therapist and patient. Mayman's analysis of the memories is based on a highly sophisticated blending of drive psychology, ego psychology, and object relations theory which shows clearly that these theoretical points of view are just that: vantage points from which data can be viewed, ultimately in an integrated, clinically useful way.

In the following "self-organization" chapter, Mayman continues his effort at theoretical integration in relating ego structures to self-experience and identity. He argues for clear distinction between three different levels of language, focusing on the clinical usefulness of the "middle language," the one between metapsychology and our actual dialogue with patients. Again using the early memory technique, he demonstrates how a diagnostic view which captures the patient's various and conflicting ego states and self-experiences equips the therapist with concepts and language that directly orient and guide the treatment process.

A resurgence of interest in psychotherapy with schizophrenic patients has followed some disenchantment with the long-range effects of neuroleptic drugs. It is not news that drugs do not "cure" schizophrenia, but concern is growing that while drugs may clearly promote symptom remission, they may actually impede social adjustment and personality growth, as well as carry risks of dangerous side effects (Mosher and Meltzer, 1980; Karon and Vandenbos, 1981; Schooler and Spohn, 1982). Hence, diagnostic information and concepts which can assist psychotherapists in their efforts with these most disturbed and disturbing patients take on renewed importance. In his chapter on thought disorder and object relations, George Athey, Jr., uses Rorschach data to show how troublesome developments in the treatment situation can be understood through the link between thought disorder and interpersonal experiences. He demonstrates how the schizophrenic patient's thoughts as organized on the Rorschach Test parallel the way he experiences object relations in the transference during psychotherapy. Using Athey's concept of a continuum of thought disorder, therapists can better understand how they are being experienced by the patient and gear their therapeutic strategies and interventions accordingly.

The chapters in this section richly demonstrate the potential utility of diagnostic testing in treatment planning and implementation. Ensuring the treatment relevance of such testing is the compatibility between the procedures, concepts, and focus of the testing on one hand, and those of the psychotherapist on the other. Diagnostic testing done with treatment considerations clearly in mind differs substantially from that done for research, screening, or the attaching of a diagnostic "label." From determining what form treatment should take, to guiding its conduct and even evaluating its outcome, carefully done diagnostic testing can be a staunch ally for the clinician.

REFERENCES

Allison, J., Blatt, S. J., & Zimet, C. N. *The interpretation of psychological tests.* New York: Harper and Row, 1968.

Holt, R. R. Diagnostic testing: Present status and future prospects. *Journal of Nervous and Mental Disease*, 1967, *144*, 444–465.

Karon, B., & Vandenbos, G. *The psychotherapy of schizophrenia.* New York: Jason Aronson, 1981.

Korchin, S. J., & Schuldberg, D. The future of clinical assessment. *American Psychologist*, 1981, *36*, 1147–1158.

McReynolds, P. *Advances in psychological assessment*. New York: Jossey-Bass, 1981.

Mosher, L., & Meltzer, H. Drugs and psychosocial treatment. *Schizophrenia Bulletin*, 1980, *6*, 8–9.

Rosenwald, G. C. Psychodiagnostics and its discontents. *Psychiatry*, 1963, *26*, 222–240.

Schooler, C., & Spohn, H. Social dysfunction and treatment failure in schizophrenia. *Schizophrenia Bulletin*, 1982, *8*, 85–98.

Weiner, I. B. Does psychodiagnosis have a future? *Journal of Personality Assessment*, 1972, *36*, 534–546.

Chapter 5

Interaction of Dynamic and Reality Factors in the Diagnostic Testing Interview

HERBERT J. SCHLESINGER

I

It is a truism that all clinical work takes place in an interpersonal context, a statement rivaled in banality only by that academic pretender—"the organism is a whole." But, banalities and truisms have a way of being neglected. No longer disputed in principle they may be blithely disregarded in practice. I believe that interpersonal factors are least likely to be ignored when the clinician's explicit purpose with the patient is to engage in psychotherapy. Then such terms as interpersonal climate, resistance, transference and countertransference seem to "belong." These words are most often used as if they could apply only to the explicit psychotherapy situation. Occasionally, one can even observe that the same clinician who as a psychotherapist shows keen awareness of these interpersonal factors will, when he is doing a diagnostic interview, or doing diagnostic testing, or supervising a junior colleague, behave as if unaware of them or, at any rate, as if he would not be comfortable to give explicit recognition to them.

I hope to demonstrate through argument and example that it is possible and desirable to equip oneself with a single set of clinical principles that would be usable in all of these and in other kinds of clinical interactions.

In order to reduce my task to manageable size I shall impose several limitations. First, I shall confine myself for the most part to beginning interactions, first hours of relatively brief patient contacts. I impose this restriction because

Reprinted with permission from the *Bulletin of the Menninger Clinic*, 1973, Vol. 37, No. 5, pp. 495–517, © 1973 by The Menninger Foundation.

first hours of any sort are highly important in any clinical relationship, are technically demanding and allow certain essentials of interpersonal process to be seen in clearest relief because they are unmuddied by previous contacts. Second, I shall use as a paradigm of the beginning clinical interaction the first session of a clinical psychologist testing a patient in a psychiatric setting using the "team" approach. This paradigm implies that the tester has only a portion of the responsibility for the patient's psychiatric examination. He is not expected to take a clinical or social history or to work with the patient's spouse or relatives. Under other conditions of practice the principles governing the interaction would be the same even though the clinician might be carrying several functions. Thus, while I will deal most explicitly with the first few minutes of an opening interaction, I will discuss beginnings in general. And what can be said about the beginning interaction in this special context is, I believe, broadly valid for different kinds of clinical contacts and other phases of clinical relationships.

If all the kinds of clinical interaction are in principle the same, how can we account for the differences in appearance among them? The resolution of this paradox is that the apparent differences among the variety of clinical interactions are the result of differences in their short-term goals; short-term because the ultimate goal of all clinical interactions is therapeutic, the welfare of the patient, his restoration to health. But in the short range, differences in intent and practice are more apparent. The social worker wants to obtain a social history, the psychiatrist to examine his patient, obtain a clinical history and begin a treatment relationship, the clinical psychologist to administer a battery of tests in order to assist in the overall psychological examination.

The narrow or immediate purpose of the psychologist as diagnostician is, then, put crassly, to get his testing done. But testing can be done in any number of ways. Some psychologists feel that the ultimate value they serve is "scientific objectivity" and to this end they discipline themselves to test in an emotionally aseptic way. For such a psychologist the relationship with the testee may be viewed as a possible contaminant of the "pure" testing situation and he therefore attempts to conduct himself with the patient so as to minimize personal interaction. In this way he hopes that the patient's responses will be only to the test materials and not at all to himself. But it does not take a great deal of clinical sophistication to realize that what is ignored does not necessarily go away. The tester who seeks to efface himself in the testing situation may serve as a potent stimulus to the patient and may influence the test responses he gets far more than he realizes. At the opposite pole, perhaps, is the psychologist who is really a therapist at heart and who may even resent that the blots and blocks stand between himself and the patient. He uses the testing simply as an excuse to "get to know the patient." Often it seems he bases his report on "clinical impressions" gained in the course of testing, ignoring the tests entirely or perhaps only when they conflict with his "clinical intuition."

I sketch these polar attitudes not to draw a line down the middle and call it the "golden mean" but rather because I hope to show that both extreme attitudes, as dynamic psychology has often taught us, have much more in common with each other than the apparent gross differences between them would seem to suggest. Neither respects the tests nor the clinical interaction in which they are embedded. Our "scientific tester" forgets the truism that the meaning of any test response, or response of any kind for that matter, depends upon the context in which it occurs. Clinicians, no less than experimentalists, fall into the error of assuming that what the subject or patient responds to is necessarily what the experimenter or clinician has defined as the stimulus. On the other hand, the psychologist who *pretends* to test is in the difficult position of trying to engage a patient in an activity in which he himself does not believe in order to accomplish something he does not believe he should be doing. This is an unenviable handicap for the would-be helper to overcome. But having destroyed these two straw men, what can I offer as an alternative?

The alternative is based upon the proposition that the psychologist who tests for a team whose general orientation is the treatment of patients within the general model of psychotherapy (i.e., including hospital treatment that employs psychotherapeutic principles) has several responsibilities. His specific function is to test and thus contribute to the team's understanding of the case. But he must test in such a way that through his contact with the patient the therapeutic ideology of the team is also transmitted. An implication of this position is that the psychologist ought to test in such a way that he could later without embarrassment become the psychotherapist of the patient. Thus, both in order to fulfill his responsibilities to his colleagues and to the patient, the psychologist must strive to understand the context in which the patient's test responses are given.

This last, apparently simple, statement deserves some elaboration, for it implies a point of view toward testing that ought to be made more explicit. The psychologist has several sources of information open to him when he conducts the kind of standardized interview we call diagnostic testing. First of all, as in any other clinical interview, he has the patient's *behavior* in the testing situation, the manner in which the patient interacts with him and the way in which this interaction changes as the testing progresses to the end of their relationship. Second, the tester has the *content* of the patient's test responses, including the patterning among those responses as well as the patient's reactions to his own responses. Third, the tester has the *formal aspects* of the tests, the scores and their interrelationships. The psychologist's task is to attune himself to these several sources of information and to integrate the data from each of them. He must not ignore one source in favor of another but rather must see each source as having its own inner consistencies and its own relationships, however complicated, with the other levels of observation. Much of the art of psychological testing consists of the sensitive shifting of attention from one to another of these areas, making and checking inferences during the course of testing itself.

Thus the tester is not merely a detached observer of the patient but an active participant in the testing situation. He cannot avoid being a participant though he can avoid knowing about it. Even if he were to employ "objective" tests in an aseptic manner, for instance, having a clerk distribute MMPI's to a group of patients, I would remind him that each patient is doing this task *for someone* and has in his mind some image of that person and some idea about his purposes, an image and idea that condition his test responses in one way or another. Thus, the tester, present or not, is necessarily a part of the context in which the test response is obtained. Moreover, the tester who is present is an active and changing part of that context as the testing proceeds.

For this reason it is vital that the psychologist try to understand the way in which he contributes directly, or through the patient's perceptions of him, to the patient's test responses. The psychologist could subscribe to this view of his place in the interaction simply by keeping his third ear and third eye upon the vicissitudes of the relationship as he runs through the list of explicit test stimuli with the patient. Probably many skilled clinicians regard themselves as testing in this fashion, *passively* observing the tester-patient relationship while actively manipulating the test stimuli.

Passive and active as applied to the testing situation are much too global terms. How shall we describe, for instance, the tester's behavior in the Rorschach Test? He instructs the patient about how to take the test (active), hands the patient a Rorschach card (active), waits expectantly while the patient explores the blot and responds to it (passive) and, finally, inquires into the determinants of a response or other aspects of it that are not clear to him (active). It is clear that neither the terms passive nor active fully describe the tester in his explicit testing behavior. He is passive or active as he needs be to serve his purpose of understanding the patient's test responses. I suggest that the same point of view should prevail in regard to the tester's purpose of understanding the relationship he has with the patient. He should not be passive in the relationship on principle but rather passive or active* as these modes of behavior serve his purpose of understanding or diagnosing the state of affairs in the relationship. Thus, we could say that for a participant-observer to diagnose his situation he must understand the ways in which his participation changes the relationship. He understands by participating and by observing the results of his participation. This model is exactly analogous to the position of the physicist who cannot observe or measure in the subatomic world without significantly altering the object of his observation.

---

* Passive and active are also misleading terms in this usage by confusing activity and busyness. The silent and expectant observer is not only actively watching in the testing process, he is also a highly active influence upon the patient.

It is no more than a restatement of this general idea to say that in order for the diagnostic tester to understand (diagnose) the relationship with the patient he must attempt to change that relationship. The psychotherapist does this too when he attempts to treat the patient. He, too, attempts to understand the patient and the relationship. His successive hypotheses, communicated to the patient, both advance their joint understanding and change the relationship. This facilitation of change through communicated understanding amounts to the treatment process. Thus, one can view the interaction between the patient and clinician as a *diagnostic process* or a *treatment process* depending upon one's purpose in making the discrimination. We treat through efforts at understanding and understand through observing the results of our efforts to treat, i.e., to change the situation. Diagnosis and treatment, therefore, are not different *kinds* of activities but are simply two points of view toward a clinical process. They are complementary points of view, neither complete without the other.

II

Thus far, we have pursued our investigation of the testing situation as if only the tester were involved. While this conception may be understandable from the point of view of supplying needed emphasis to the tester's role, no treatment of the subject would be complete without a description of the other participant-observer, the patient. What is the patient up to while the tester is going through his complicated, three-pronged investigation? In what follows I hope to make plausible the idea that the patient is very similarly engaged. He, too, is immersed in a process that can be fairly called diagnostic, for he, too, is trying to figure out what the test instructions *really* mean and what the tester *really* wants and *really* thinks of him. He, too, is trying to change things, i.e., to treat the clinician—to get him to see things the way the patient does, to alter the situation to make it serve the purposes for which he came. In short, the patient and tester can be viewed as participating in a mutual diagnostic and treatment process (and one could substitute here for tester the terms therapist, psychiatric examiner, or social worker). Both the tester and the patient begin each not knowing the other, each not knowing what the situation will hold for him, and each attempting through the application of intuitive gifts and learned skills to find out about the other and to change the situation to serve better the purposes each has in engaging the other.

Some improper inferences could be drawn from the similarities I have been sketching between the testing process and the psychotherapy process. I am not inviting the tester to throw away his blocks and blots to engage in some free-wheeling "therapeutizing" of the patient. Far from it. The tester's efforts at treatment in the testing situation, that is, his efforts at understanding and changing the relationship with the patient, must be guided by the choice of an appropriate goal (in this way it is like any other treatment process). The appropriate treatment goal for the tester in the testing situation is to try to bring about a sense of mutual purpose with the patient so that the patient can become involved in the testing situation in a way that furthers the overall treatment process—in a way that enhances the patient's awareness that he and the tester are engaged jointly in a diagnostic process and that the patient's purposes will best be served by involving himself fully in that process. The goal, in other words, is to make the "testing alliance" an optimal one.

Simple as it seems, this appropriate treatment goal for the testing situation is often ignored or bypassed. Many a patient submits to testing because his doctor wants him to, or because he feels he has no choice in the matter, or because he is too used to complying with authority to permit himself to voice the fears and resentments he has about it.

In discussing this same idea as it applies to psychotherapy, I have somewhat whimsically compared the relationships of the patient and the clinician to the players of a chess game. I do not mean the ordinary kind of chess game with which psychotherapy has often been compared, for that comparison is not particularly apt. There is after all no analogy in psychotherapy to most of the defining characteristics of ordinary chess. What in psychotherapy compares with the set of well-defined chessmen of equal potential in the hands of each player? What, for that matter, is analogous to the *sine qua non* of any competitive game, the desire of each *opponent* to defeat the other?

Imagine if you will two players—notice I do not say opponents, though they may in the course of the game become such—seated across a rectangular but poorly articulated playing surface (it might even be a desk) which clearly provides for a large, but finite number of different kinds of moves. Let us equip each player with an indefinite number of pieces that he may expose or keep hidden. Some of these look familiar, having been used in other two-person games, but they are of unknown value at the outset of this game. Let us structure the game with a rule, but a nonbinding one that has no more force than a suggestion, that each of them move whichever pieces seem appropriate, usually moving alternately. Lastly, we must define a purpose for the game. Like any game, ours can have a number of purposes for the participants, at the very least, for instance, providing an occasion to get together. But more narrowly, the first purpose of each of our players is to discover what pieces the other player has, what value they have *for him*, what personal and self-binding rules govern his moving of these pieces, and also to discover what are the other player's several purposes in playing—purposes which each player, at the beginning of the game, may not even be aware he has.

I think this kind of fanciful "inverse chess" bears a much closer structural resemblance to the usual beginning clinical interaction than does ordinary chess. Can our two players moving tentatively, each striving to know the other, each wondering whether the other is playing the same game as himself, get together to play the same game?

I have described this "inverse chess game" of the clinical interaction as if it were a "fair" game, as if both parties were equally skilled and equally knowledgeable about playing it. Fortunately for our overall goals the tester is clearly at a tactical advantage. He knows better how beginners usually play the game and has had the experience of playing it with many others. He knows, too, the significance of certain kinds of gambits that patients are likely to use. He also knows better what his own stake in the game is and he understands his own and the patient's legitimate expectations—what the patient is likely to want and need of him. That is, he knows in a much more explicit way than the patient about the emotional experience of entering a new relationship in which one needs something from a prestigious person to whom one attributes the power to grant or deny one's request, to give or withhold relief from pain. So, fortunately, except for those patients who have been to many therapists and defeated many diagnosticians before, most of the skill is on the clinician's side. But to even things up a bit, most of the freedom of movement is on the patient's side—after all the clinician cannot get up and say, "I've had enough of this foolishness," and leave.

How can the clinician make use of his tactical advantage to further his general and specific professional purposes with the patient? His experience in doing psychotherapy should serve him well here. He has learned there are a few maxims that are better to heed than to ignore. These are worded so generally that it is hard to make use of them unless one knows a great deal about psychotherapy. Some of these are: One should begin with the patient where he is; in the interpretive process one generally should work from the surface downward; anxiety, or other affect should be dealt with before the defense against the impulse, and the defense against the impulse before the impulse itself; one should respect the metaphor in which the patient's communications are couched. There is also the general advice that the therapist should be tactful—advice that has implications for "dosage" and phrasing of interventions—respecting the patient's need to maintain his pride, perhaps through allowing him to hold onto certain rationalizations for his behavior. Lastly, he should allow the patient to participate as much as he can in the process, to discover for himself rather than being informed by the therapist. These maxims apply to all clinical interactions, not just to psychotherapy.

To return to the metaphoric chess game, let us examine some of the self-imposed "rules" that guide the patient's moves. I have mentioned that the patient has certain legitimate expectations of the tester. These stem from the patient's knowledge that the tester is a "doctor" of some sort, he has had professional training, he works with the psychiatrist who sent the patient to him, and he must communicate with the psychiatrist about the patient.

The patient also is burdened by a great number of nonlegitimate expectations that influence his moves. The very word "test," whether psychological or otherwise, conjures up images in most people's minds of quizzes or examinations, of being forced to compete, of being found wanting or stupid, and being shamed before others. These images become assimilated to memories and fantasies about school situations, clinical laboratory tests and X-rays. For not a small number of patients they raise such questions as, "Maybe they think I'm crazy," or "Maybe my doctor doesn't believe me," or "Maybe he doesn't know what to do with me." The varieties of unrealistic attitudes toward testing are too many to list here. I think it is a conservative understatement to suggest that for nobody is testing simply a neutral experience. It is for most, if not all, an anxiety-arousing situation and the anxieties aroused in it are experienced and dealt with in the patient's idiosyncratic ways and conditioned by the patient's overt and covert understanding and misunderstanding about the nature of the testing situation.

A third set of factors I have not yet mentioned specifically, although they have been implied in my comments about the tester and his professional identity. One might say that the patient has a number of legitimate expectations of which at the outset he is unaware or uncertain. For where he sees medical or psychiatric authority and where he fears moral condemnation or objective verification of his own fears of inadequacy, he is actually entitled to sympathetic and humane care, to that comfort and relief that the experience of being understood by another human being can bring. Further, where he can expect his illness to be labeled and then told what to do about it, to be the passive field of operation for the tester and the therapist to do their work, the patient actually has the right to participate fully in his own diagnosis and treatment. After all, it is to the patient coming to know *himself* better, not just our coming to understand him, that we are all dedicated.

Looking at the other side of the chess board, the tester also has some legitimate expectations of the patient. Not the least of these is that he will pay his bill and abide by whatever other administrative arrangements have been established for the orderly running of the clinic. The patient is also expected to some minimal extent to want (or at least to recognize that he needs) the sort of service the clinic offers. The forms in which this expectation (usually called "motivation") can be met satisfactorily (i.e., in an operationally sufficient way) by the patient are many and various. Occasionally, and especially during the examination phase of treatment, it may seem as if the patient has no desire at all for what the clinic has to offer and is present only under duress. But it is well to remember that even among patients who *do* want what they believe the clinic has to offer, that is, relief through some means, most come to testing only because they are required to. Thus, uncertainty about wanting or needing what the *tester* has to offer, and tending to see him and his tests as obstacles in the way of getting what *they* "really" want appear often enough as circumscribed issues even among patients who ostensibly "want treatment."

The tester, like the patient, may legitimately expect that the patient will treat him with respect. But "respect" is an ambiguous word. I do not mean the kind of "sirring" or exaggerated deference that the word could imply and that some patients adopt, but rather an appreciation of the tester for what he is and for what he hopes to do for the patient. This sort of attitude, if it is achieved at all, is generally achieved during the course of testing and is rarely present at the outset.

But, in addition to these legitimate expectations of the tester, there is a variety of unrealistic feelings and attitudes he may have about himself, his work and patients, that may affect his relationships with his patients. I have already alluded to some of these—there are testers who prefer to see themselves as scientists engaged in a sterile and meticulous examination of a laboratory animal, as it were. Some testers see themselves as detectives committed to finding "the truth" regardless of the patient's wishes. There are others who would rather not be testing at all, seeing the process as cold and mechanical, and would rather be treating patients and especially "curing" them. Also, the set of more or less universal experiences with quizzes, examinations, etc., that I described as conditioning patients' attitudes toward tests are shared by many testers as well. At least some psychologists feel, more or less consciously, that testing is an assault on the person, an intrusion into privacy, a kind of license to peek where one has no business looking, or a kind of "brain surgery" or "brainwashing"—that testing is necessarily a traumatic experience that they are forced to perpetrate on patients. We can expect that, just as with patients, such attitudes will be accompanied by lesser or greater amounts of anxiety or guilt, the expression and control of which may take different forms in the testing situation.

To summarize these considerations briefly: We can see that both the patient and the tester display a layering of attitudes ranging from social class and role expectations to frank transference and countertransference reactions that shapes the relationship between the tester and the patient and which, in turn, provides the context in which the patient's test responses must be understood. But does this say more than that the tester-patient relationship is important and so it is important to gain rapport? Most courses in testing give some attention to achieving "rapport," defined usually as a "good relationship" with the patient in which the patient is willing to be "cooperative" (more exactly "submissive"). The adjectives most often associated with rapport as it is usually described are "warm, kind, understanding, friendly, sympathetic," in short, an idyllic state of affairs that only the hardened misanthrope could carp at. But of course there is no need to inveigh against warm relationships as such with or without tests, but only with the wrong implication that there is some uniform emotional state toward which all patients and all relationships ought to be guided. The achievement of rapport, understood as such a uniform state, is as much a pursuit of a will-o'-the-wisp as the search for "morale" expressed in terms of specific "good" feelings or attitudes quite apart from the persons and situations involved.

But I would hold up a kind of optimum toward which the tester (and patient) could strive. This optimum might better be described as "genuineness," a state in which each can relate himself to the other as he really is. I am not advocating a return to nature here, for relating oneself to a patient genuinely—not ingenuously—within one's professional role is not at all a state of nature but is rather a work of art. One must know one's self and one's stimulus value for others exceedingly well before one can expect to achieve genuineness in this sense. The situation is similar for the patient who most often will have to be helped considerably to disentangle himself from the web of misconceptions he has that prevents him from presenting himself *genuinely as a patient*.

The problem of beginning the testing relationship has also been approached in other ways. In some settings it is customary to use a brief and relatively innocuous test (one whose data are not vital to the examination) as an "icebreaker"—I assume as a way of demonstrating that "testing isn't so bad." Alternatively, the diagnostic tester may open by interrogating the patient so that a "face sheet" can be filled out. Or, a brief history may even be taken. Under these latter procedures, the tester begins not by testing or dealing with the issues in the patient's mind about testing, but by asking for biosocial or clinical data. It is perhaps needless to say, in view of the foregoing arguments, that to use a test or a face sheet in this way serves merely to avoid the problem about beginning with the patient. The usual "face sheet information" might better be obtained from the referring doctor. If the information must be obtained from the patient himself, or if the tester is also responsible for obtaining a clinical history, it would be far better to obtain it after the patient's feelings about beginning have been explored. Then the patient might better understand the relevance of the historical or clinical details to the clinical relationship at hand. He might also have reason, stemming from the developing relationship itself, to want to offer personal information rather than merely submitting to the assumed authority of the tester to require answers to personal questions.

All these considerations are clearly relevant enough to psychotherapy or relationships that extend over a longer time than testing, but are they really important in the conduct of a short-term, task-oriented contact? There is no simple answer to this question for the answer must depend on one's purposes in testing. I dare say that far more testing has been done ignoring these principles than observing them. But to justify ignoring them one would have to hold that short-term relationships are intrinsically different from long-term ones, that in testing the only value that matters is getting the tests completed, that the context of the patient's responses do not matter, and that it is unimportant how the patient feels or thinks about his participation.

This last point of view toward testing and also toward other brief contacts, such as consultants' interviews, is all too prevalent. It implicitly assumes that one is dealing not with a patient, a person, but with a task or a problem. Anyone who has ever been in the patient's seat will know the difference. Such an attitude, which may be associated with either polite manners or with crude ones, can only persist when supported by the circumstance that the clinician will not have to face that patient again—that someone else, the patient's own doctor, for instance, will straighten out the difficulties caused by these hit-and-run tactics. Thus, I believe it is not merely desirable to take these considerations into account when testing, it is absolutely crucial to testing done within a clinical or therapeutic context.

III

The following paragraphs describe the interaction between a psychologist and his patient around the issue of obtaining some useful test results. The account is simply quoted as it was submitted to a seminar on the tester-patient interaction:

A twenty-nine-year-old physician doing his military service is married and has a daughter three years old and a son a year old. Last March while watching a TV program he had an abrupt pain in his chest and left arm which he took to be a heart attack. A physician was called and the possibility of a heart attack was ruled out. The pain has persisted off and on since its onset and he has been on relatively constant medication. In addition he has had several series of neurological tests both here and at his military base. The findings of the neurological examinations have not been consistent—some indicate a possibility of organic involvement, others indicate no organic basis for his complaint. He has also had psychological and psychiatric examinations at two different hospitals. During this time he periodically has been preoccupied with thoughts of suicide and feelings that the world is falling apart. He has been easily angered and depressed at times. During the initial case conference it was suggested that we be alert for signs of organicity and for a thought disorder, especially any indications of somatic delusions.

After introducing myself to the patient in the waiting room, I asked him to follow me to my office. Without speaking he sat in the chair which I pointed out. I explained that I was going to give him some psychological tests, and he interrupted rather abruptly to say he had already had a sizable number of psychological tests only two months ago and wondered what would be the use of repeating them. He pointed out that the tests were in his folder, or at least should be, and that if I would look there, I would find what I wanted to know. I said I had read the report and that we would start by giving him the Wechsler test which according to the report had not been administered. He said the Wechsler had been given to him at the last hospital, that I could get the report, and there was absolutely no reason to repeat the test. I took down the name and office to send for the report and indicated we might find it desirable to repeat the Wechsler even though he had taken it recently. He said, ''Well, all right, but it won't be original and there certainly must be some practice effect.'' I then presented him with the Word Association Test and asked him if he were acquainted with it. He said he had never taken it but he knew that the main idea was for the person to give a spontaneous response to the stimulus word. I experienced some sense of relief in finally getting to the test, feeling that I had got myself into a position where I had tried to justify the test on the basis of its novelty to the patient. I also had a distinct feeling that I was being sized up more by him than vice versa.

He took the Word Association Test seriously and paid close attention to the job. When I arrived at the recall section, he seemed surprised that he was not through. He said, ''You never know what a psychologist is going to pull next.'' He explained that in taking the Draw-a-Person test previously, he had finished one drawing and was then asked to draw the other sex. He seemed to imply that there is something underhanded about this technique and that he knew that I as a psychologist was up to the old tricks. On the inquiry to the Word Association Test I explained that I wanted to see if I could understand the connections between the stimulus word and his responses. I read off the stimulus word and his response, inquiring on the ones that seemed puzzling. He quickly caught on and when he thought I would inquire, he would quickly give his explanation of the association before I could say anything. In this way he not only controlled the inquiry, but told me what he wanted me to know. For instance, when I did not inquire about his response to the word ''suicide,'' and started to read off the following stimulus word, he interrupted and explained his response to the word, his feelings about suicide, and gave some details of how he asked his wife to take the gun out of the house during one of his periods of suicidal preoccupation so he would not kill himself. Several times I inquired on words which he had not anticipated, and he seemed a little surprised and maybe even resentful about it.

The Bender-Gestalt test was given next, and as I produced the cards he said, with a trace of exasperation, that he had taken this test before. I indicated I knew he had but I would like to do it again and I would follow a somewhat different procedure. I felt myself trying to justify the readministration to him by virtue of the new procedure. He settled down to taking the test in a sort of resigned way, executed the designs first from memory after a five second exposure and then by copying. I was impressed by the speed and the slashing bold lines he used to execute the drawings and yet retain the form. He made no attempt to conceal his distaste for the job and had a disgusted look on his face as he did the drawings.

On the Object Sorting Test he noted that the cigarette's tobacco was dried out and had crumbled out of the cigarette. He observed that it might be a good idea to get a new one. I didn't say anything in response but I had the memory of army officers who would, during inspections, give commands by way of suggestion.

At the beginning of the second day of testing I explained I had called and expected the Wechsler-Bellevue test but that it hadn't arrived yet and we would do the Rorschach today. As if warning me it would be useless, he said he would not be able to give anything original but just "automatic learned responses." I said that was all right but we would do it anyway and wondered what he thought of the test. He explained that he had taken it as a "guinea pig" for a psychology student eight years ago while he was in college and had enjoyed it very much the first time. Then two months ago, at the hospital, he had taken it again and had been surprised how many of the responses were the same as the first time even though there was an eight year interval between administrations. He had not seen nearly as much the second administration as he had the first and was sure he would find the third administration quite boring with nothing new to it. He started on the Rorschach as if it were a wearisome chore, and as if to make the point that it was a dreary piece of business, he said to Card III, "And again, here is the inevitable red butterfly," and on other cards mentioned how he was seeing the same responses as he had seen in previous administrations. On Card V he noted with mild surprise that the bird heads were new to him, but when asked if he had seen any other new responses he said no. On the inquiry he proved that he was an old hand at being a Rorschach subject and quickly reeled off the inquiry with little or no questioning from me. To the first card of the Rorschach he mentioned that I could expect him to have trouble with the TAT. He said he would not be able to do it honestly because he had such "definite stories" to the cards which he was sure he would remember. He had had a "strong reaction" to the pictures, had written down a story almost immediately upon seeing them and had finished the test in no time at all. I told him that was all right but we would have some pictures which would be different from the TAT cards he had seen before. The prospect of some novel cards did not seem to arouse his interest and he dropped the discussion of the TAT.

After finishing the Rorschach I brought up the matter of appointments to complete the testing next week. He said that it really did not make much difference to him when the appointments were—any time would be equally inconvenient for him. It was hard for him to rearrange his hours at work at the Base. I set an hour for the appointment; he said it was all right, said goodbye and left the office.

How can we understand this interaction? Clearly it was an uncomfortable situation for the tester to work with a patient who was manifestly unhappy about being tested. Still it seems obvious that if the tester had insisted the patient would have taken all of the tests in such a way that a report could be written— a report that would probably stress the patient's resistiveness and his poor motivation for seeing his problems in psychological terms. Would this conclusion be justified? Is there any reason to wish that the interaction might have gone differently quite aside from the matter of making it more pleasant for the participants?

Notice that the very first exchange between the patient and tester consists of a statement by the tester that he is going to administer some psychological tests. To this not unanticipated news the patient instantly takes exception, offering as the reason for his objections that he has already been through this procedure and that the tester could find out about it if he would only take the trouble. Let us put ourselves in the tester's shoes for a moment. He is obviously taken aback by the patient's stand—he seems not to have been expecting any resistance. He takes the patient's objection literally and tries to get around it and avoid further objections by proposing a test which he thinks the patient does not know. This initial interchange raises several questions. Why is the patient so vehement in his objections? Can it be that he has more in mind than he is saying? And, on the other side, why is the tester so ready to yield to the patient's objection? Does he feel he has to justify his tests to the patient on the basis of their novelty?

We might wonder why the tester was so surprised by the patient's stand. After all, knowing no more than the tester has reported to us in his process note, there would have been good reason to anticipate difficulty of some sort. Recall:

1. The patient has tried to get help for his problems at least twice previously that we know about and has had psychiatric examinations including tests on these two occasions. Presumably the help he sought was not forth-coming or he would not be here with us now.

2. His illness had a dramatic onset in the form of a severe somatic symptom which the patient himself misdiagnosed. The tester knows that the patient is not satisfied that "it is all in his head," as being referred for testing might imply his psychiatrist thinks.

3. The tester himself is not the person to whom the patient came but is rather someone to whom the patient was referred to satisfy, not the patient's felt need, but his doctor's.

4. Even if he were a long-suffering sort, which he is not, we might anticipate that the prospect of a third go-around with psychological tests would be met with less than enthusiasm.

5. The tester knows that the patient is himself a physician, and that some physicians, like other professional workers in our field, have difficulties in allowing themselves to be patients.

These few things, which were known at the outset, help make sense out of some of his negative feelings about testing and the form in which the feelings are expressed. But that is not all we know about the patient. There are other things we can surmise which do not necessarily lead to the behavior we are examining. For instance: (1) We know the patient is suffering and is eager enough to be helped to have persisted in the face of two previous disappointments. (2)

Having taken the trouble to come to a private clinic, with the expense this entails, he might expect a great deal from us. (3) Yet, having been disappointed in the past, he might experience a growing sense of concern that we, too, might disappoint him. (4) He may feel that coming to a psychiatric clinic, before he himself is convinced that his difficulties are psychological, may overcommit him to a psychiatric approach to them. (5) There is also the possibility, about which the process notes are not informative, that the patient, who is himself a physician, may have some reservations about being examined by a nonphysician of approximately his own age or a little younger.

In addition to these imponderables, we do know for certain that the patient was tested twice before and that his experiences in being tested are going to influence the way he takes the tests now. Also since he has been through our educational system, we can presume that he has the usual background of experience with tests and the attitudes toward taking tests that go with this experience. In addition, he will have developed certain attitudes toward examining patients and being examined that go with being a physician. Knowing or suspecting these things about our patient, how might we have used them and toward what end in the testing situation? Clearly, merely getting the patient to take the tests was not a problem. We saw that the patient would put up with them in spite of his objections. With a little more pressure probably the tester could even have persuaded him to take the disputed Wechsler.

What should the tester want to accomplish with any patient during the first few minutes? He is about to engage the patient in that kind of standardized interview we call testing. Does he not need to know "where the patient is"? What are the patient's initial attitudes toward this process? Does he see any relationship between what he is about to do and his desire for help with his difficulties? How does he conceive of the process he is about to enter? Assuming the patient's initial attitudes toward the testing leave something to be desired, what would it take to enable the patient to achieve a more optimal attitude? Note again, I do not mean by this last point that the patient should take the tests suffused by a warm glow, but rather that he should take them, if possible, feeling that they serve his own purposes, even if only in some indirect way. Again, to the extent this goal is possible, he should participate in this study of himself not as a guinea pig or as a passive respondent but as an active partner. In this connection, I believe that some of the most valuable information to be gained from testing comes from the patient's reactions to his own responses, reactions that are more likely to be given spontaneously and fully if the atmosphere in the testing situation encourages the patient's free participation. When the patient is invited to share in his own diagnostic study, it is possible additionally to see to what extent he can think about his own behavior in psychological terms.

The question might be raised if attending to all of these considerations does not take a lot of time, perhaps more time than is usually available to the busy diagnostician. I do not think it is a matter of how much time, but rather how the time available to prepare the patient for testing is used.

One might ask, should not the referring psychiatrist "prepare" the patient for testing and if he does so, would it not alleviate much of the problem for the diagnostic tester. Of course the psychiatrist should prepare his patient for testing just as for an encounter with any consultant or for a laboratory examination. Preparing a patient is an art in itself, but it is the art of the referring professional (and unfortunately it is an art rarely cultivated). Whether the patient is prepared effectively or not in no way relieves the diagnostic tester of his own professional responsibility to help the patient make maximum use of the services he offers. He must assure himself that he has done all he can to help the patient take the tests under optimum conditions just as he must assume responsibility for the entire diagnostic testing process. No one else can assume this responsibility for him, and no one can relieve him of it. However well-prepared by the referring professional, the patient will still have anxiety about being tested, the tester will still be a stranger, and the patient and examiner will still have to work out the kind of testing relationship they are going to have.

IV

These last points are central to the core issue in diagnostic testing. The main purpose of a diagnostic study is to improve the accuracy of clinical prediction, specifically prediction about the patient's probable response to possible treatment situations. For this purpose, the following questions could be asked: How does the patient react when threatened with anxiety arousing material? How psychologically-minded is he? Can he accept and use the help of a therapist to understand and master threatening material? Such questions, which are highly relevant to the prescription of psychotherapy, can be answered with greater confidence the closer in structure and atmosphere the diagnostic situation is to the psychotherapy situation to which the prediction is to be made. In other words, the ability to establish a "testing alliance" is predictive of the ability to establish a "therapeutic alliance." The processes through which these alliances are established are sufficiently similar that the skillful diagnostic tester can furnish much useful information to those responsible for prescribing psychotherapy and to the future psychotherapist.

But the tester in the example given did little to help the patient or the other members of his team in these ways. He was placed immediately on the defensive by the patient's attacks and tried to evade further contact and conflict with him by accepting his formulation of the situation. The patient's initial objections were acceded to and the attitudes implicit in them were left unexplored. The patient was left to stew in whatever feelings and fantasies he brought with him.

Clearly this examiner chose to ignore the resistance, or rather to evade it, rather than deal with it directly. By failing to help.his patient with the resistance, he effectively confirmed him in it. The relationship as described in the note hardly seemed to change in its quality from beginning to end.* I think it fair to say that a major reason for. the lack of change was that the examiner did not help the patient explore his resistance about beginning because he was not willing to engage in the process himself.

What kept the tester from acting on the knowledge he had available to him? We cannot explore here the psychodynamics of this tester, about which we know very little in any case, but we can begin our attempt at understanding with the observation that he seemed quite insecure in his role. From his statements in the process notes and from the others he made in discussing them, we learn that the tester thought he and the patient were in a struggle with one another from the first and that he was particularly concerned about not getting involved in a discussion about the adequacy or inadequacy of previous examinations of the patient or the merits of the tests themselves. In short, he was so concerned with not being trapped by the patient that he wanted to take refuge in ''let's get to the tests'' as quickly as possible. We could further suppose the patient's objections to being tested, which were couched in terms of the futility of a third round of tests, seemed so cogent to the tester that he was unable to see past them and hence was unable to help the patient with whatever latent content they might have had.

I would suggest that the major technical fault in what the tester did and did not do was his failure to see that the patient's objections to testing could also be expressing in a kind of metaphor other objections that he could not or would not at that moment state. I do not intend to deny that there was substance to the patient's objections as he voiced them. It clearly is a nuisance to be tested repeatedly within a brief period of time, and one could reasonably doubt the utility of this testing. But the patient's vehemence seems rather more than the situation calls for. To look at it from another side: as a physician himself he would hardly expect to go to a reputable clinic with his problem, especially with a history of therapeutic failure, and not be examined thoroughly. He would have every reason to want the clinic to conduct its own examination and not skimp on anything it thought necessary. There seems to me, therefore, ample reason to suggest that he is exploiting the fortuitous circumstance that he has been tested before to provide a rational cloak for attitudes and feelings which might seem less ''reasonable'' either to himself or to others.

---

* Some change is actually discernible as the testing proceeds; the patient tries to do well and also uses his knowledge of the test procedures to accommodate himself to the tester's unspoken wishes. Clearly, the patient is not governed solely by unwillingness to participate, but displays behavior from which a number of consonant and conflicting motives and character traits can be inferred.

V

At this point critical discussion of clinical material usually ends. It is far easier to point out what is wrong with an interaction than to correct it. Yet, it might be instructive to show the application of the point of view set forth here by re-creating the opening as it might have gone. The reader should understand that the result is a fiction, though a plausible one, and that the apparently smooth progression, while demonstrating one possible course of the beginning interaction, raises many more questions than it settles.

With these caveats, let me turn hindsight to foresight and equip our tester with the fruits of our analysis of his work. How might he have applied this understanding? Let me imagine how the process notes might have gone:

After introducing myself to the patient in the waiting room, I asked him to follow me to my office. Without speaking he sat in the chair I pointed to. I noted that he seemed tense, that his expression was rather grim, and that he glanced all about him as he came into my office. I asked him if his doctor had told him what this appointment was for. With a grimace he said he had told his doctor that he had already had psychological tests—twice! I nodded and said that I guessed he didn't see much sense in taking them a third time. For a second he tensed up as if he were going to explode and then in a few moments he visibly relaxed and said bitterly that it seemed like an expensive waste of time. After a few moments of silence, during which he seemed drawn into himself, I added, "And you've been looked at psychologically twice before and it hasn't helped." He responded with some bitterness, but even more sadly, that it wasn't just the psychologicals—nothing has helped. I nodded and after a moment said that I guessed that that was what led him to come to this clinic. He seemed to start to agree and then took it back by saying that the cardiologists couldn't find anything and said that it was all in his head. I added quickly, "But you're not convinced of that." Again he was silent for a moment as he seemed to struggle with himself. Then he said, "I don't know what to think . . . something is terribly wrong with me . . . sometimes I'm sure it's my heart . . . and I'm afraid. . . ." He seemed to break off here and I just echoed his last words, "You're afraid." He shook his head as if to say he couldn't or wouldn't go into that now, and added sadly, "But anyway I've had all these tests." He slumped in his chair. After a brief pause, I added, "And you don't have much confidence that doing them again would help you get an answer." He gave a quick shrug and a snort, saying that the kids who gave them didn't know very much. He then looked at me and said, "Even if I've taken them twice before do you still think you can get something new out of them?" I reflected a moment and said, "Perhaps—would you like to try?" He shrugged as if to say both I'm here and what have I got to lose.

I then talked to him a bit about the tests, noting that he was aware that there were practice effects, but if he would let himself take them so that his answers would represent how he was today and yet at the same time feel free to comment on his recollections of the previous times as well as anything else that seemed of interest to him in his experience of taking the tests, then I thought there was a good chance they would be useful. He nodded in agreement and we began the testing.

I shall not try to fantasy how the interaction during the rest of the testing might have gone. But I think with such a beginning the patient might have grown to be a more active participant in the diagnostic testing. While further challenges to the testing or other expressions of anxiety might have ensued, he might have grown to trust the examiner sufficiently (perhaps on the Word Association Test) to be able to say that what he was afraid of was "going crazy" and that he would rather be dead than insane; better his heart should be diseased than his brain. As his defensiveness lessened, he himself might have been able to observe that his thinking gets "fuzzy" when he gets anxious. Perhaps he even would have been able to identify for the examiner some of the things that make him anxious.

This fictional reconstruction of the interaction was intended to show what is common knowledge in most walks of life, that what a patient (a person!) is willing to tell and experience with the tester depends on the nature of the tester-patient relationship. The main fault to be found with the testing as it was originally conducted was that by failing to help the patient with his resistances about taking the tests, the tester allowed the adversary relationship of the beginning to persist and thus deprived himself (and the patient) of the data from the developing interaction itself that might have provided an opportunity to answer a number of vital questions about the treatability of the patient. The tester still has his scores and test responses from which to make inferences about treatability, but the inferences from these data are less direct and it is far from certain that they were unaffected by the unrelieved defensiveness of the patient.

I would not like this fictional reconstruction to leave the impression that the mere use of one or another opening phrase would have made all the difference. Rather it is the examiner's understanding of the clinical process, his knowledge of the patient, and his own observations that enable him to help the patient enter the testing situation in a way that makes it likely that he can gain maximum benefit from it. Neither would I like to leave the impression that this patient inevitably would have begun by complaining about the nuisance of repeated testing. I listed a number of issues through which the patient could well have expressed his anxiety and his doubts, and any of them or others would have served. In short, I do not think it possible, or at least not useful, for the examiner to develop a repertoire of "openings" or gambits in the manner of a chess master, but rather to rely on his knowledge of his tests, his clinical skill, and his intuitive and empathic understanding.

VI

A complete discussion of the tester-patient relationship would focus not only on the beginning of the interaction, but would cover issues that arise during the course of testing and characteristics of the ending of the process. But each of these topics, and there are other important ones as well, would deserve far more space than is available in the compass of this paper. Even the discussion of beginning might have been skewed by focusing on a single case example of a patient manifesting a particular kind of difficulty. It might be worth mentioning, at least to indicate the range of the problem, that some of the most difficult patients to test adequately are those who are manifestly "easy," those who are so defensive that they conceal their reservations and offer compliance and submission rather than true engagement and full cooperation.

Nevertheless, this paper will have served its purpose if it has succeeded in calling attention to the importance of understanding the patient and developing an optimal working relationship in which test responses are given both for the diagnostic task, defined narrowly, and for the larger therapeutic purpose for which diagnostic studies are undertaken.

Chapter 6

The Masochistic Character as a Self-Saboteur (with Special Reference to Psychological Testing)

STEPHEN A. APPELBAUM

I

Here are three familiar vignettes of clinical misfortune. (1) A patient's ego functioning is, in important respects, efficient and intact, but his behavior nonetheless acquires from skilled diagnosticians such categorizations as "schizophrenic," "psychotic," "disorganized." (2) A patient is presented at a diagnostic conference where usually reflective and controlled staff members find themselves using words as epithets to describe him—"spoiled," "infantile," "demanding"—the net impression being that the patient has created an unfriendly environment for himself where none existed before. (3) A patient is treated in psychotherapy by a trained therapist and is rewarded sporadically with apparently successful periods, but as time passes goals thought to be accessible by patient and therapist, and originally suggested by a diagnostic team, fail to materialize.

Such situations would be easy to understand if the patients were obviously uncooperative or unable to control their self-destructive impulses. But these situations may occur even in an atmosphere of apparent cooperation and ostensible mutuality of purpose. The paradox becomes less puzzling if one views these events as the successful fruition of the patient's goals, often kept secret from himself and others through the perversity that what he seeks, contrary to his avowed hopes, is the unnecessary elicitation of discomfort and self-defeat. This often overlooked feature of the patient shows itself from the start, during diagnostic examinations, in consistent and recognizable ways which I shall describe.

Reprinted with permission from the *Journal of Projective Techniques*, 1963, Vol. 27, No. 1, pp. 35–46, © 1963 by the Society for Projective Techniques, Inc.

These patients resemble those referred to as moral masochists, disorders of character which Freud (1924) distinguished from masochistic sexual perversion, and also from the biologically rooted impulses of feminine masochism. The term is used here as a convenient shorthand, referring only to the unnecessary elicitation of discomfort and self-defeat, regardless of the particular role this pattern may play in any of the dynamic and genetic explanations which have been noted, such as condition for sexual pleasure (Freud, 1919), need for punishment (Freud, 1924), acceptance of lesser evil to avoid a greater one (Reik, 1941), reinstatement of early unpleasant relationships (Berliner, 1947), restoring omnipotence through controlling others' responses (Eidelberg, 1934), ego defense (Menaker, 1953), and adaptation (Brenman, 1952).

Painful and self-defeating consequences of behavior are not unique to masochistic patients, but are common to the maladaptive patterns of all psychiatric patients. A meaningful distinction can be made, however, in terms of differing goals. Psychiatric patients for whom masochism is not a prominent problem are unable to permit or bring about pleasure and success because of fears and inhibitions, or through inefficient ego functions. Patients for whom masochism is a prominent problem seem in the grip of pressures to engineer and prolong travail, and to thwart situations which hold promise of change. How well they succeed in being misdiagnosed is pointed out by Brenner (1959): ''. . . the syndrome which is called masochistic character or moral masochism is difficult to separate diagnostically from a variety of other pathological conditions.'' How well these patients succeed in being made uncomfortable is attested to by Schafer (1954): ''The masochistic patient provocatively defines the entire situation [the psychological testing relationship] as one of torture and disappointment.''

One may ask how such patients know what to do to bring upon themselves such misfortune without at the same time making it obvious that they are up to no good for themselves. Presumably they have become adept at being misunderstood which, in a diagnostic context, means being misdiagnosed. Since they are usually ignorant of the technical criteria for diagnostic formulations, one can only surmise that at varying levels of awareness they know or fantasy the kinds of behaviors which will gain the requisite ends. It does not take much psychological sophistication, for example, to sense that self-centeredness and rule-breaking will earn dislike and impatience, whether one has heard of the term ''narcissistic character disorder'' or not. And surely patients can be at least tacitly aware that acting unpredictably and giving vent to ordinarily inhibited ideas is likely to make them appear ''crazy.'' Being mentally ill, despite recent strides toward social tolerance, is among the most humiliating ways of being viewed, and the consequences which may be anticipated even by the layman resemble, at least on the surface, what masochistic people characteristically attempt to bring about. Treatment of severely disturbed patients involves being *put in* a mental hospital (with loss of human, sometimes civil rights) having things done to them (such as restraints, cold wet sheet packs) and being *subjected* to treatments which are, or seem, *painful,* and which *violate* physical and psychological integrity (such as psychosurgery, electric shock, or insulin coma therapy). Fantasies which patients may have about these procedures need not be true, of course. And treatments which appear innocent of these connotations, such as "talking therapies," can be seen similarly by the patient. But it seems plausible that procedures used with severely disorganized patients are more easily interpreted by masochistic people in ways consistent with their secret goals and expectations.*

Clearly, if accurate predictions and recommendations are to be made with such patients, it devolves upon the diagnostician to recognize masochistic motives and to assess the means and effectiveness with which these determine behavior. Theoretically this ought to be difficult. Self-subversion, after all, flies in the face of common sense, and often such people, the better to screen these tendencies, may create an impressive surface presentation of a genuine need and desire for relief. Further, many writers believe masochistic tendencies can be found in all of us. Freud (1924) and Reik (1941) agree that a need for punishment can in itself be considered a masochistic phenomena, and since a "need for punishment . . . is invariably a part of normal super-ego functioning . . . some degree of masochism is ubiquitous" (Brenner, 1959). According to Loewenstein (1957) and others, masochism has its normal developmental prototype in the child's enjoyment of being frightened, warned, and tossed about. Helene Deutsch (1944) has pointed out adaptive aspects of feminine masochism in making bearable menstruation, childbirth, and the narcissistic blows of being a woman. Nonetheless, it has been my experience that many patients with pathologically strong masochistic trends act in distinctive ways during diagnostic procedures. This occurs even with those patients whose clinical histories do not show other indicators such as polysurgery or accident proneness.†

A number of attributes of diagnostic examinations, especially psychological

---

* A question of thought disorder or psychosis did come up for consideration in the examinations of all of the twelve patients in the series discussed here. Such a question is not uncommon, especially when examiners have had little opportunity to get beyond introductory data or early interviews; but with other patients in the population from which these cases were drawn, it is by no means universal. Seven of the patients were finally understood not to have a fundamental ego weakness; three were thought to be capable of occasional brief lapses into disorganization of ego functions, and one was labelled "hysterical psychosis." Even with the few patients who did show some ego weakness, it was, nevertheless, important to weigh the extent to which the masochistic elements seemed to add to the severity of the symptomatic behavior.

† Data were gathered from a series of cases which seemed to form a pattern among patients tested by the author in his capacity as Staff Psychologist of The C. F. Menninger Hospital, and, previously, the Adult Outpatient Department of The Menninger Foundation. Inferences drawn here were validated by confirmatory information from other members of the psychiatric team and by the patients' subsequent course in the hospital and during psychotherapy. Of 115 patients tested during a two-

testing, offer special opportunities to turn the optimal evaluation process—a cooperative endeavor toward mutual understanding—into a sado-masochistic encounter. Testing in our culture connotes punishment or reward; it can be construed as a way of checking on whether one has done what he is supposed to, whether one is "good" or adequate. Psychological tests are designed to discover things about the patient of which even he may be unaware, or perhaps only enough aware to be frightened of facing them. The tests are often relatively unfamiliar, and necessarily administered with a minimum of explanation as to their explicit purpose, or how best to proceed in complying with the examiner's demands. He takes down the patient's responses verbatim, uses a stop watch, maintains control over what is to be done and in what order, and, from the look of it, is learning things which the patient can only guess. Though the patient gives much, he gets back little in the way of direct explanations of his responses.

By way of the ambiguity and symbolic values of the test materials the patient finds himself involved with ordinarily hidden or inhibited levels of awareness. This quick access to preconscious and unconscious contents results in the novelty that strangers may share much intimacy quickly but for a short while. Some patients make use of this as people do with strangers on a train, feeling free to respond without undue worry since they are soon to take leave of their confidant. But the masochistic character can easily view the situation as one where he invests himself unilaterally, and is "rejected" as soon as he has been made use of.

The tester, on the other hand, is engaged in a task which exploits strong tendencies within himself, which, if not well controlled and channeled into adaptive purposes, can play into the masochistic needs of the patient. Schafer (1954) writes, " . . . however free [the tester's] work may be from the vicissitudes of unconscious personal conflict and primitive conceptions the autonomy or the freedom is always *relative*." Schafer details various roles into which testers may fall—voyeuristic, autocratic, oracular, saintly—each of which makes use of the patient to gratify the tester. While all these relationships can be used sadistically, the specifically sadistic tendencies of the tester are offered the opportunity to dig at the "faults" of others, label these pejoratively, and assault the patient's ways of maintaining equilibrium through prying into their effectiveness or pointing up their inefficiency—all under the cloak of helping.

The following case illustrations can be construed in various ways since all behavior is multi-determined, and test responses are often condensations of many

year period, ten per cent, all women, displayed to a major degree behaviors described here and were understood, in the light of the total diagnostic-therapeutic process, as having masochism as an important component of their character. There may, of course, be many people with similar covert goals who do not behave as these patients did. The behavior of male masochists, for instance, may be quite different. (One male who shared with this group many of these characteristics was a homosexual involved in a long-standing sadomasochistic partnership.)

aspects of the individual. The examiner decides on the most salient meanings of responses, for his purposes at a particular point in the examination, one way being to assess their function in the interpersonal relationship of the testing situation. Especially with patients such as those described here, one of whose hallmarks is their unique interpersonal goals, *why* a particular response is chosen at a particular moment is at least as useful a source of information as *what* the response is and *how* it is delivered. The following responses were selected as primarily indicative of masochism because each was one of a number of similar responses made by that patient, because of the behavior which accompanied the response, and because of the "fit" with the total context. It is likely that these criteria do not exhaust the various means, preconscious and subtle, by which inferences are made and convince the examiner that the patient's masochistic tendencies are influencing his response process.

II

Although having something done to them is an important feature, these patients paradoxically often give an impression of activity, dominance, and initiative. At times they seem less examinees than salesmen, less workers than impresarios. They enact a play, featuring themselves in unflattering roles and attempt to convince the tester that these are true-to-life stories. Reik calls the striving quality Flight Forward, and the histrionic display, the Demonstrative Feature. He distinguishes the latter from exhibitionism by noting that the exhibitionist-narcissist displays his good qualities, the masochist his bad ones: "It is striking indeed that so many masochists are not ashamed of their weaknesses and bad qualities but boast of them." (1941)

Stupidity is a frequently played role, no doubt encouraged by the right-wrong aspects of the tests. Some examples: "I hate to have my un-intelligence come out; I am the most uneducated person in the world." "Isn't that terrible, I forget so easily, it's pitiful." One patient followed her correct answer to the question, how many pints make a quart, by saying, "I can't cook, can barely get a meal on the table, I've been trying to learn to cook bread for ten years." Another patient evaluated herself as she went along: "I'm skirting around it, I do that quite often," "That's no explanation," "I doubt if I am right." After the usual instructions to the Thematic Apperception Test about making up the plot of a story, one patient redefined the task as a demand for sophisticated psychological analysis and complained she couldn't make up stories because, "I'm not too familiar with psychiatric terms."

Means of self-disparagement for reasons other than fancied intellectual deficiency are usual also. After seeing a vagina on the Rorschach Test, a patient said, "I'm beginning to feel perverted." When asked to define the word "belfry," several patients, after giving a scorable answer, laughingly added "bats in the belfry," referring to themselves. Other patients made references to aging, either in terms of a time when they were functioning better, which stood in sharp contrast to the way they were at present; or as having done a poor job all their life and now being too old to make up for it. The obvious inference of "depression" seemed to the examiner inadequate to explain the vigorous, accusatory, even triumphant manner with which these remarks were made.

All self-disparagement is to some extent humiliating. But these patients frequently and dramatically arrange to humiliate themselves through offering sexual references which serve to embarrass and shame them. Especially with a male examiner these remarks and responses, offered gratuitously by women, seem ways of stripping away the veils of modesty and social appropriateness with which women are usually protected. The superficially plausible explanation which they sometimes offer, that the testing procedure requires them to tell everything they think or see, not only is inaccurate (except for the Rorschach Test) but begs the question why they select from many possible responses and behaviors so many of this particular kind. Frequently, they give responses on the Rorschach Test having to do with menstruation and sexual parts, with an unusual amount of attention to detail: "Part of the penis you usually don't see," "uterus with menstrual discharge," "vagina with lips and vulva." After seeing "blood," one patient added, "That's because I am menstruating." Another patient volunteered a description of her menopause, "with my breasts hurting." During a test of recalling numbers read to her, a patient complained, "These cause me to have rectal spasms."

Some of the stimulus words on the Word Association Test are explicitly sexual, and most patients are momentarily embarrassed by them. Many patients attempt to neutralize the traumatic effect through various means such as blocking, defining the stimulus word, or repeating it. Masochistic patients, however, latch onto the words as opportunities. To *masturbation* one patient gave the association, "terrible" and "fine," * then explained that she used to think masturbation was terrible but now practiced it and thought it was fine. Another responded with "playing with one's self," then went on to tell how much experience she had, since her divorce, with masturbation of herself and men. A third patient responded to *breast* with "birds," and *nipple* with "buttons," explaining these were special words her husband used. Another of this patient's associations to *breast* was "target," meaning that her breasts provided a target for her husband. In responding to the question, "Why should we keep away from bad company?" a patient gave a full-credit answer then went on to tell of her recent sexual promiscuity. This same patient, when asked, "Why does the state require a

* Multiple word associations were gathered by an additional trial with the instruction to give the first word which comes to mind which is different from the previous one. (Applebaum, 1960)

license in order to be married?'' claimed she could not answer because, "I have a mental block caused by having to control sexual urges I now feel."

Other roles which are consistently enacted are those of the chronically rejected, the poor unfortunate, the martyr, and the apologist. In arranging pictures to tell a story, usually seen as a man embarrassed because it might appear to others that he was embracing a woman, one patient, instead, made the interpretation that he was humiliated because his partner was cold to him. In response to the examiner's changing his vocal delivery while spacing evenly digits to be recalled, a patient became disturbed because the unnatural evenness in his voice reminded her of her stern husband and father, and, suddenly, he seemed to be rejecting her like all the rest of them. The apologist appears less to be observing social amenities than using them as means of calling attention to real or fancied transgressions: "I hope you don't think I am obstinate." "I don't mean to be difficult." "I'm sorry I'm taking so much time." These patients, in fact, were not obstinate, difficult, or especially time-consuming except by virtue of their protracted self-criticism. As Schafer (1954) noted, some patients seem almost apologetic at being alive. When leaving the office, such a patient said, "Thank you for being so patient with me." Earlier, in response to her request, when test directions were repeated, she thanked the examiner profusely as if unaccustomed to being granted such "favors."

Some patients who present themselves as perennially jinxed seem resigned to chronic misfortune: "I have a knack for doing things the hard way." "I am always tempted to talk about my troubles." In answer to the question, "What would you do if you found an envelope in the street that was sealed, addressed, and had a new stamp?" one patient replied in a martyred fashion, "*I* would probably go out of my way and return it to the sender." Another, when asked why shoes are made of leather, meant to say "durable," but instead said "endurable."

Two patients supplied vignettes eloquent of the tenaciousness with which they pursue their ends. One, who wept copiously throughout the testing and complained bitterly of how trying and irrelevant the tests seemed at this difficult time in her life, was offered the option of ending the tests. But she insisted that we continue to the end. Another burst into tears upon seeing a Thematic Apperception Test picture which reminded her of the happy home that she was being denied. The examiner took the picture from her and placed it face down on a pile of already completed test cards, but she took it back and weepingly insisted on continuing with it. Other patients might have behaved in these ways out of a sense of duty or challenge, but these patients seemed clearly bent upon their portrayals of suffering and were not to be denied opportunities to play them to the hilt.

While behaviors demonstrating these roles complicate and lengthen the administration of the tests, and thus can be annoying, these patients engage in a number of behaviors which seem clearly to have a principal aim of making the tester angry. Reik (1941) calls this tendency the Provocative Factor, understood as the patient's sadism in the service of bringing onto himself the sadism of another. One clue as to when the examiner is being used in this way is his feelings toward the patient;* but in addition, the following trends would seem helpful alerting signs. Some patients exacerbate the technical difficulties of test administration by talking too fast or too much for the tester to take down responses verbatim: "The more I talk the more you have to write, I better not talk so much, you ought to learn shorthand." Or they make the examiner wait, with pen poised, as they dole out responses. Several patients showed unwonted hearing difficulties. With one of these the examiner repeated the same words she claimed to have failed to hear, but at a lower tone, yet she heard them. At least some of these patients seem at least partly aware of what they are doing: "I am giving you a hard time and myself as well." "You have the patience of Job, don't you? How do you stand it?" Another trend is to criticize the tests and the examiner: "It seems so damned silly to be sitting here and putting these things together." "I'm sure it is all significant" (sarcastically). With reference to the Rorschach: "Who dreamed these up? I wouldn't put orange with pink. These poor animals, wouldn't they be insulted if they could see how badly drawn they are." In response to inquiry into their responses: "That's for you to find out." "Don't you know anatomy?"

A prominent strategy is to cast the tester in the role of a harsh, critical inquisitor. A ubiquitous sign of this is the use of the phrase, "If *you* want . . ." One patient misheard my question, as to whether she had momentarily forgotten a piece of information or never knew it, as, "Didn't you ever learn anything?" Other comments: "Do I *have* to do this?" "Why can't you give me a pencil and paper?" "You are pinning me down!" "You sure make it hard, don't you?" "Maybe you're getting something out of this; I'm not."

When dual IQs are computed, one score standing for what the patient achieves and the other for an estimate of his capacity, the disparity between them may be due to self-defeating tendencies. The following examples illustrate ways which would lead the examiner to make this inference. On tests involving the manipulation of materials under time pressure, a frequent finding was "accidental" destruction of correctly arranged pieces. Arranging blocks to form a design provided an especially clear opportunity to observe self-defeating tendencies, as the major learning necessary to perform the task usually takes place before the routine moves which finish the problem. Thus, some of these patients characteristically manage the difficult step of discovering the principle, then inexplicably flounder during the repetitious implementation of it, either losing time

---

* Of course testers can be out of patience for reasons other than provocation on the part of the patient, and must learn to tell the difference.

credit or leaving an apparently careless error which deprives them of any credit at all. One such patient commented, "I guess I make things more complicated than they need be; I hurt myself by not taking care of myself." Other patients gave up on tasks which, upon urging, they demonstrated they could do, refused my invitation to guess, and failed easy items though able to perform more difficult ones of the same kind.

The interpersonal paradigm to which these patients respond is characterized by something done to a weaker person by a stronger one: a model which often finds its way into the diagnostic process in choice of words and explicit imagery: "The pride her husband had *over* her," "*subjected to* continuing his lessons," and "being whipped in a card game." One patient defined the testing as an opportunity for the examiner to practice on her "as a guinea pig." Another said, "If you want me to stand on my head, I'll be glad to." Thematic Apperception Test stories included such remarks as, "He has no choice but to be submissive to this action taken upon him." "He'll have this fellow doing everything he wants him to, he's told what to do, when to do it, and how to do it—no will of his own, like a puppet on a string." One patient said that she felt forced to be a beautiful manikin; her role in life was to smile and please others. Another said, "A woman is a poor-me object, her function is to love; the man needs it, he must be served."

The picturesqueness and exaggeration in these remarks bear out Waelder's (1936) point that masochistic fantasies are not a representation of femininity but a caricature of it. Brenner (1959) suggests that "masochistic fantasies and practices of adults reflect the small child's sadomasochistic theories and fantasies of what happens between men and women in sexual intercourse." There is much about masochism of the not-real, the theatrical, the dissembling, what Loewenstein (1957) refers to as the "playful or make-believe character underlying the masochistic devices . . ." The role-playing of masochism resembles wit as well. For both provide a vehicle for covert expression of hostility which at the same time lends itself to a style of relating one's self interpersonally, and both require a partner. The following story told to a Thematic Apperception Test card which often elicits information as to how a patient may relate himself to a helping figure, seems to capture all of these elements: dissembling, provocation, sadism, masochism, a mixture of pain and pleasure, and being one-up on another; all of it calculated to be self-defeating. "If I give the story I want to tell, the first one that came to mind, you'll say I am bitter against doctors, and I'm not." When the examiner did not respond to this sally, she continued, "I'm going to lie here and keep a straight face while a doctor tries to hypnotize me. But I know I'll do as in times past. I get tickled. This man is trying to make a fool out of me. Rather than be made a fool of I'll laugh just at the time he thinks he's got me under." In the psychotherapy of one such patient it has been possible to help her gain perspective on her character pattern by pointing out its dissembling aspect. As the buried aims emerge, and the play-acting properties of the masochistic role become clear, what seemed at first tragedy later took on an air of ludicrousness. And a streak of humor is not uncommon amidst the protestations of despair in masochistic patients, a phenomenon noted by many (Dooley, 1941; Reik, 1941; Loewenstein, 1957). In these patients humor was largely self-directed and bitter. In describing her Thematic Apperception Test stories one patient commented "Me and Shakespeare, I have to pat myself on the back, for the rest of the time I am destroying myself. I'm not a masochist but I certainly ask to be hurt." Another patient volunteered, after seeing a donkey on the Rorschach Test, "Maybe it's because I am making such an ass of myself." While crying, a patient said, "I am the wailing wall." Still another patient said, "I used to tell stories about myself, I'm the butt of my own stories, the one asset I had—I was a buffoon."

An important clue to masochism is available to the examiner when he finds an appropriate opportunity to compliment or otherwise reassure or support the patient. While he expects gratitude and the patient's relief, he feels instead strangely rebuffed, as if he had committed a *faux pas*. One patient with a potentially Very Superior IQ was asked who the President of the United States was and gave the wrong answer, saying, "That's my answer right or wrong." Later, the question was repeated, and she gave the right answer. In the ensuing discussion of how it was that she had at first given the wrong answer, the examiner asked if she felt she was hiding her light under a bushel. This provoked a flurry of excited protestations that she really did not know much of anything, and, in fact, wanted him to tell her test answers. Another patient replied to the question, "In what way are praise and punishment the same?" by saying, "Praise can often be painful to take." Whether praise in itself is painful, or whether the patients are made anxious by the threat to their masochistic equilibrium posed by a compliment, at times it does seem true, as in the joke, that the most sadistic thing one can do to a masochist is to be kind.

Thematic content of the Rorschach Test responses of masochistic patients has been fully detailed by Schafer (1954). One major test finding among the group reported upon here was the ubiquity of the word "hurt." When asked, "Why should we keep away from bad company?" a patient replied, "They will hurt us." On the Word Association Test this word is not uncommon, especially in response to such stimulus words as *cut* and *bite,* but it seemed to appear more often with these patients than one ordinarily expects, both on these stimulus words and others where it is ordinarily not found: *fire*-"hurt," *breast*-"hurt," *gun*-"hurt," *hospital*-"hurt," along with such other associations as *man*-"cruel," *love*-"murder," and *fight*-"beat" (physically). Another prominent finding was the particular choice of words used in defining vocabulary words. *Flout* was defined as "whip," "flog," and "clout—sort of a derogatory thing"; *chattel* as "slave," *amanuensis* as "emanicipate," *affliction* as "curse." Luborsky *et al.* report a masochistic patient who defined "traduce" as "the opposite of like a reprimand, I don't mean reprimand, I mean condemning" (1955). It seems that such prepotent words press for expression at any available opportunity. After finishing her responses to a Rorschach Test card, one patient said, "I guess I've about torn that apart," while another, in telling a Thematic Apperception Test story, used the phrase, "Grief that is soul-tearing."

Another prominent theme is a fusion of pain and pleasure: one patient described the loss of her father as "sweet-sorrow." In the Thematic Apperception Test story of this patient a man is made to tease a woman while ostensibly being tender. In a systematic test of early memories (Mayman), given to several of these patients, one of them ran pain and pleasure together in a single breath: "When I was vaccinated it hurt terribly; I was very comfortable sitting on cushions and looking out a car window." Another response on this early memories test supported Freud's (1919) observation in "A Child Is Being Beaten" that a typically feminine masochistic fantasy is of the brother being beaten by the father: "Daddy used to whip my younger brother. I used to go to my room and shake my fists. I thought it was so terrible. He never did it to me. I'm sure he didn't hurt him badly, but it sounded awful."

III

The case of Miss K., a 35-year-old woman, illustrates some of the difficulties in the diagnosis, treatment, and management of patients who appear as she did on tests. The test report of the protocol quoted in part below, written in 1947, suggested an "incipient schizophrenic process" beneath a surface picture of obsessional ruminations and doubt, along with fearfulness, lability, and phobias. With present nosological sophistication and increased understanding of thought disorder as revealed on tests, it is doubtful that an inference of schizophrenia, even latent schizophrenia, would be made from these tests. Indeed, the same psychologist re-checked the tests only five years later and was himself critical of these inferences. When the patient was retested ten years later, another psychologist questioned the conclusion of a schizophrenic process, and noted that the evidence previously thought to be suggestive of thought disorder issued from masochism rather than failing ego functions. The patient was diagnosed as "borderline psychotic" by several psychiatrists.

Miss K. had a psychoanalysis of seven years which terminated by mutual agreement. Three years later, or ten years after the first testing, she was re-examined. Since the end of the analysis, she had maintained a steady campaign to have the analyst see her again, claiming she was not at all improved and wanting to know why this was so, and challenging what she alleged to have been promises made by him that she would recover. After some counseling hours, which he warned would preclude further analysis with him, it seemed that more analysis would be necessary, and the patient was encouraged to do this work with one of several other suggested analysts. She visited these and other psychiatrists, but instead of attempting to benefit from these contacts she played one off against the other, all the while indulging in increasingly dramatic sexual and alcoholic escapades which she advertised among the various therapists. One of the psychiatrists reported, "Her desire has been to continue treatment with Dr. F. (the original analyst) on her own terms, and every one of her contacts with psychiatrists after Dr. F. discharged her was utilized only as an indirect way of forcing Dr. F. to take her back into therapy." After an extensive reevaluation by a psychiatric team, during which the psychologist remarked, "Present tests show remarkably little change from the previous ones," the patient was hospitalized. Treatment was marked by the major symptomatic behavior of, in the words of her hospital doctor, being "a very demanding unhappy, miserable woman who was constantly crying, threatening her hospital doctor with suicide . . . " At one point, although the patient was trained to do work remunerative of money and prestige, she chose to work in a department store for only one hundred dollars per month, remaining at this job six months despite encouragement to improve her lot. With gradual symptomatic improvement and imminent discharge from hospital supervision to independent living and formal psychotherapy, the patient decided to leave the city. For a long time after, she had not followed through on the recommendations that she maintain her own residence, support herself, and secure psychotherapy. The following examples of her test behavior and responses are from the first testing.

One measure of the patient's orientation toward vigorous interpersonal engagement, Reik's Flight Forward, is the filling in of the time between responses with comments, often with personal references and direct involvement of the examiner (more of which are cited below in other connections). Note her remarks, "Do all these asides go in?" "Do you have to put that down too?" "There's your answer, I guess," and "Let's not put that word in." Dramatizing an unlovely picture of herself, Reik's Demonstrative Feature, may be seen in the following:

(a) Self-Critical—On the Rorschach Test she said, "That's a poor explanation, I don't have much imagination I guess, I can't see anything else." On a timed subtest of the Wechsler-Bellevue her comment was, "moron level, it took so long." During the inquiry to the Word Association Test she remarked, gratuitously, "I consider myself a poor dancer."

(b) Humiliation—After arranging pictures, as people usually do, to tell a story of a man usually seen as walking off with a girl, she commented, "Just a plain old pick-up." To another story usually seen as a man sitting close to a bust which looked like a woman, she told of a man who was rejected by real women, "only a dummy to *operate* on." Her response to the Word Association Test stimulus word *breast* was, "I hate to say it . . . me." During the inquiry into this response she said,

"Probably I was thinking of me there. I am conscious . . . I am breast conscious, so much so that I don't like to hear the word. In fact, I avoid it." Her response to the stimulus word *drink* was "me." Her response to *penis* was, "Oh gosh, I'll spell that word . . . this is embarrassing . . . ejaculate." Her response to *suicide* was "me." To *vagina* she said, "Uh . . . uh*. . . I don't know what you call it. I'm thinking of a little pan that a nurse uses, a vaginal douche." To *dance* she said, "I thought of 'stand.' I don't know if that makes me a wallflower." During the inquiry to *masturbation* she said, "Well I've heard that eighty-five percent of the population does or has, and I am included in that."

She evidently fantasied the tester as a demanding and sadistic inquisitor. On the Rorschach Test she said, "I think I'm making myself see some of these things. It might flit through my mind. Well, that's what *you* want," and she sighed with the tone of resigning herself to being victimized. On the Wechsler-Bellevue she interjected, "Oh, you got me scared now," and, "There's *your* answer I guess." (Italics added.) Sadistic themes, and a choice of words which seemed dictated by sadistic fantasy, were prominent. On Rorschach Card II she saw, "Traffic accidents, pools of blood." On Card IV she saw, "A gorilla with no head, *throw* rug," (Italics added) and "an evil looking man, a devil, a harsh cruel man." Her understanding of "habeas corpus" was, "Guarantees protection to someone who was taken into custody? Can't have his head chopped off without due process of the law." She defined an armory as "a building; reserves meet in time of peace to perfect themselves for the next war . . . guns lying around." She defined guillotine as "instrument of death, a couple of knives come together and do the work on the neck." On the Word Association Test to the stimulus word *bite* she said, "kick" and elaborated in the inquiry, "Well it seems a little strong, but I was thinking of a real knock-down-fight in which I'd be biting, a dirty fight, both biting and kicking." In explaining her association "torso" to *trunk* she was asked whether she had a visual image at the time of responding. Her reply was "Yes, well I thought . . . you might have the idea that I was going to go out and saw someone in half and stuff them in a trunk. I sort of got the idea of a headline about a trunk murder. I don't know why I said that. Perhaps because I thought that someone would chop me up. Perhaps because I have thought in my hotel room here that someone might creep in and snatch me out and chop me into little pieces and stuff me into a trunk." This lurid response is an example of the kind of response which, if looked at solely from the point of view of its content, could, as was done in the first testing, be taken as a sign of severe ego disorgnization.

In contrast to most of her test productions, Miss K. was sufficiently humorous for the first tester to record that she got him to laugh. After responding with "breast" to *suck* she said, "I'll do a little sucking on a cigarette now." After responding to the stimulus word *mouth* with "smoke," she laughed and added "kiss . . . I'm not so kiss conscious, I don't think." A comment in the test report was, "Her depression alternates with facetiousness."

Notice her concern with the power aspects of relationships, and her assumption of the yielding position in them as implied by the following responses. She defined the word *affliction* as "It is imposed, not imposed, let's not put that word in—it has come to a person." In defining *chattel* she said, "An object or a person held in subjugation by someone or something." And she defined *proselyte* as "to consent."

On a test of repeating a series of digits which depends in large measure on concentration, she called attention to the way she was handicapping herself in attending to her cigarette at the same time she was supposed to be trying to learn the digits. After giving up on an arithmetic problem, she said, "Oh, I am not even figuring. Must we finish it? I have no idea how to start." When it later became clear that she was able to do this problem, she said, "I thought there was some super-deluxe way of getting it, by algebra or something." Her response to the question about what she would do if she were lost in a forest in the daytime implied her covert recognition of how she fails to exploit her capacities. *"Theoretically* I'd look for the sun." In defining "plural" she said, "Two of something." The tester asked her if plural meant just two, and her reply was "No . . . yes . . . why did you ask me that?" Thus she refused the tester's help and retained her incorrect answer. In other contexts this behavior could be interpreted differently, for example, as suspiciousness. Here, there was little else on the tests to support that inference, and much to support the inferences of provocativeness and refusal to be helped.

Miss K. may have unwittingly been telling a great deal about herself as she summed up the testing experience this way: "I was expecting I'd be embarrassed on some of these; I was looking forward to being embarrassed."

SUMMARY

A number of female patients seem to have as their covert goals being misunderstood and being made uncomfortable. This feature, which poses special obstacles to successful treatment, is often overlooked, although clues to self-sabotage are apparent from the start in the consistent and recognizable ways with which such patients respond to diagnostic procedures, especially psychological tests. These characteristic behaviors are described, with illustrative case material.

REFERENCES

Appelbaum, S. A. The word association test expanded. *Bull. Menninger Clin.*, 1960, *24*, 258–264.

Berliner, B. On some psychodynamics of masochism. *Psychoanal. Quart.*, 1947, *16*, 459–471.

Brenman, M. On being teased; and the problem of "moral masochism." *The Psychoanalytic Study of the Child,* 1952, *7,* 264–285. New York: Int'l. Univ. Press, 1952.

Brenner, C. The masochistic character: genesis and treatment. *J. Am. Psychoanal. Assoc.,* 1959, *7,* 197–226.

Deutsch, H. *The Psychology of Women,* 1. New York: Grune and Stratton, 1944.

Dooley, L. The relation of humor to masochism. *Psychoanal. Rev.,* 1941, *28,* 37–46.

Eidelberg, L. A contribution to the study of masochism (1934). In *Studies in Psychoanalysis.* Int'l. Univ. Press, 1952, 31–40.

Freud, S. A child is being beaten (1919). In *Standard Edition of the Complete Psychological Works of Sigmund Freud.* Vol. 17. London: Hogarth Press, 1955, 177–204.

Freud, S. The economic problem of masochism (1924). In *Standard Edition of the Complete Psychological Works of Sigmund Freud.* Vol. 19, London: Hogarth Press, 1961, 157–170.

Loewenstein, R. M. Psychoanalytic theory of masochism. *J. Am. Psychoanal. Assoc.,* 1957, *5,* 197–234.

Luborsky, L., Siegal, R. S., and Gross, G. Neurotic depression and masochism. In *Clinical Studies of Personality.* New York: Harper and Bros., 1955.

Mayman, M. Early memories and abandoned ego states. (unpublished manuscript.)

Menaker, E. Masochism—a defense reaction of the ego. *Psychoanal. Quart.,* 1953, *22,* 205–220.

Reik, T. *Masochism in Modern Man.* New York: Grove Press, 1941.

Schafer, R. *Psychoanalytic Interpretation in Rorschach Testing.* New York: Grune and Stratton, 1954.

Waelder, R. The principal of multiple function: observations on over-determination. *Psychoanal. Quart.,* 1936, *5,* 45–62.

For their invaluable help I am grateful to Drs. Martin Mayman, Herbert J. Schlesinger, and Richard S. Siegal.

Chapter 7

Early Memories and Character Structure

MARTIN MAYMAN

It has been traditional among psychoanalytically trained clinicians to look upon dreams and early memories as suspect clinical data. Psychoanalysis has repeatedly demonstrated that what seems manifest in dreams and memories may be illusory rather than real, contrived rather than true. Surface and depth are discontinuous, appearance and reality are not one, and the ways in which one experiences his world are unconsciously calculated to hide far more than they reveal. Freud several times went out of his way to caution psychoanalysts not to fall prey to the seductive meanings apparent in the manifest content of experiences, because such surface meanings will only divert attention from the more valid unconscious meanings of those same events. In the interest of finding his way back to the unconscious dream thoughts that are masked by the manifest dream content, Freud insisted that dreams be analyzed only by the psychoanalytic method, that is, the gathering of free associations and the unraveling of dream distortions.

His demonstration of the "concealing" or "screen" function of memories, perception and dreams (Freud, 1899, 1901) was one of the most important of Freud's clinical discoveries in that period of the history of psychoanalysis when the dynamic unconscious was being uncovered by painstaking analytic work. The "screen" metaphor has been a productive one in clinical psychoanalysis not only to describe screen memories, but also screen affects (Lewin, 1950), the dream screen (Lewin, 1946), screen defenses, screen hunger, and screen identity (Greenson, 1958).

However, with the advent of psychoanalytic ego psychology, and in its wake projective testing and the projective hypothesis, the screen function of con-

Reprinted with permission from the *Journal of Projective Techniques and Personality Assessment*, 1968, Vol. 32, No. 4, pp. 303–316, © 1968 by the Society for Projective Techniques and Personality Assessment, Inc.

sciousness came to take on a double meaning. Perceptions, fantasies, random thoughts which served the ego's countercathectic purposes, were seen to carry traces of the unconscious contents they were intended to mask. Like any good disguise, surface appearance represents a skillful blend of the camouflaging design and the images one wishes to hide.

In the fifty years which have elapsed from the time when psychoanalysis was largely an id-psychology, we have come to see that the distrust of manifest content is appropriate only in the context of an id-psychology. Today it is as important to the psychoanalyst to know about the ego, its designs, its ways of maintaining repression, as it is to know about that which is repressed. And, just as the latent content of conscious thought processes reveals much about the vicissitudes of the id, the manifest contents of these experiences reveal much about the workings of the ego.

One can find an abundance of evidence in recent psychoanalytic writings on dreams to support this claim (Babcock, 1966; Beck and Ward, 1961; Erikson, 1954; Noble, 1951; Richardson and Moore, 1963; Roth, 1958; Saul, 1940; Sheppard, 1963). Similar findings with childhood "screen" memories are fewer in number but promise to parallel in every respect the successful use of manifest dream content in identifying important trends of the personality (Eisenstein and Ryerson, 1951; Mayman, 1959; Mayman and Faris, 1960; Langs, 1965; Saul, Snyder, and Sheppard, 1956). The strongest such assertion was made by Saul, Snyder, and Sheppard (1956):

> Earliest memories are absolutely specific, distinctive and characteristic for each individual; moreover, they reveal, probably more clearly than any other single psychological datum, the central core of each person's psychodynamics, his chief motivations, form of neurosis, and emotional problem. This is the empirical, observable fact. . . . Because of their nature, earliest memories have a diagnostic and prognostic significance equal to that of the first dream of an analysis. They provide a clue to habitual emotional attitudes which are still operative and so illumine in advance the therapeutic problem, how these patterns will emerge, and how they will have correspondences in the analysand's life and in the transference.

I shall review here neither this body of literature on manifest content of dreams and memories, nor will I present any new research data. Nonetheless, I hope to make a convincing case for a set of working hypotheses about early memories which have proved productive to myself and my students in our clinical practice. I hope to be able to show that early memories are not autobiographical truths, nor even "memories" in the strictest sense of this term, but largely retrospective inventions developed to express psychological truths rather than objective truths about a person's life; that early memories are expressions of important fantasies around which a person's character-structure is organized; that early memories are selected (unconsciously) by a person to conform with and confirm ingrained images of himself and others; and that the themes which bind together the *dramatis personae* of a person's early memories define nuclear relationship-patterns which are likely to repeat themselves isomorphically in a wide range of other life situations. In short, I propose that a person's adult character structure is organized around object-relational themes which intrude projectively into the structure and content of his early memories, just as they occur repetitively in his relations with significant persons in his life. Consequently, one may sift the stories a person tells about himself and extract those intrusive interpersonal themes which define that person's enduring view of himself and his enduring expectations of others.

Though Alfred Adler is generally credited with the discovery that early memories are allegorical representations of a person's life style (Ansbacher, 1947), it was actually Freud (1910) who first introduced this idea in one of his papers on screen memories which provides us with the most suggestive rationale for this way of viewing early memories. In analyzing Leonardo da Vinci's earliest memory of a vulture swooping in out of the sky and perching on his bed, Freud argued that this was not a real memory, but a fantasy, "a fantasy which Leonardo formed at a later date and transposed to childhood."

> . . . This is often the way in which childhood memories originate. . . . They are not fixed at the moment of being experiences and afterwards repeated, but are only elicited at a later age when childhood is already past. In the process they are altered and falsified, and are put into the service of later trends so that, generally speaking, they cannot be sharply distinguished from fantasies. . . . Their nature is perhaps best illustrated by a comparison with the way in which the writing of history originated among the peoples of antiquity. As long as a nation was small and weak it gave no thought to the writing of its history. Men tilled the soil of their land, fought for their existence against their neighbours, and tried to gain territory from them and to acquire wealth. It was an age of heroes, not of historians. Then came another age, an age of reflection: men felt themselves to be rich and powerful, and now felt a need to learn where they had come from and how they had developed. Historical writing, which had already begun to keep a continuous record of the present, now also cast a glance back to the past, gathered traditions and legends, interpreted the traces of antiquity that survived in customs and usages, and in this way created a history of the past. It was inevitable that this early history should have been an expression of present beliefs and wishes rather than a true picture of the past; for many things had been dropped from the nation's memory, while others were distorted, and some remains of the past were given a wrong interpretation in order to fit in with contemporary ideas. Moreover people's motive for writing history was not objective curiosity but a desire to influence their contemporaries, to encourage and inspire them, or to hold a mirror up before them. A man's conscious memory of the events of his maturity is in every way comparable to the first kind of historical writing (which was a chronicle of current events); while the memories that he has of his childhood correspond, as far as their origins and

reliability are concerned, to the history of a nation's earliest days, which was compiled later and for tendentious reasons.*

My own data on early memories confirm in every respect this succinct summary of their nature by Freud. I had occasion a few years ago to collect early memories from a group of ten, eleven, and twelve-year-old children. The twelve-year-olds gave stories about themselves much like one hears from adults. Some of the ten-year-olds on the other hand didn't seem to understand what I meant by "early memories." They didn't seem to be far enough along in the process of consolidating a stable identity with its fixed past and predictable future to be able to tell me some of the personal myths out of which they would later construct their past.†

I had the opportunity to get a glimpse of this process of early memory formation in the recollections of one nine-year-old child, a sober, diffident, subdued boy, who was obviously depressed. When asked for his earliest memory, he told me, without hesitation, "I remember when I was born." Undaunted, I pushed on and established that, as usual, the memory was recalled in the form of a visual image of a particular scene. I asked him to tell me specifically what he saw in this image of his own birth. He pictured a scene, the nursery of a hospital delivery ward. He saw it as if he were looking in through the large glass window. There were rows upon rows of bassinets, each with its own little newborn baby. One of those was himself, he didn't know which. As he told the story, one was struck by the apartness of these children; there were no adults present; nothing was going on; and all of them were separated off from the viewer by a glass screen. He himself was identityless, anonymous, in an impersonal world devoid of familiar human values. It is hard to convey here the pathetic way in which he conveyed this image. There was a brief pause, and he then volunteered another memory of himself as a newborn baby. He was lying on a table, and could see himself "all red and wrinkled up like an old man." The equation of birth with the shrivelling up of old age accentuated the sadness of the first "memory" he had told.

* This is a provocative view of the purpose of writing history. We sometimes laugh at countries which rewrite their history books to fit with major political trends. But this only does openly what history books in all countries do tacitly without quite realizing it. A prime purpose of writing history, at least history as taught in grade schools, is to instil in children an ideology, to give them a common set of myths to live by, to choose for them the kinds of heroes with whom to identify, and to embody in the legends of their culture the values on which their group identity rests. It is therefore entirely appropriate, or at least understandable, that the American view of the American Revolution, for example, be quite different from the English view. The history of the revolution for Americans is a very selective report of what happened, in order to establish for Americans as a group one of the important landmarks in the development of their group identity.

† This preliminary finding will soon be put to more careful test, to determine whether the introduction of a historical dimension in one's self-definition does indeed occur at that point in life which marks the end of childhood and the beginning of adolescence.

This boy was convinced that these were his earliest memories. This is how life started for him. I suspected from the mood and content of these two stories what their source may have been, and asked him whether there had been any birth in the family in the last few years. Sure enough, a sister was born the year before. He was eight at the time. Until her arrival he had been an only child. We can conjecture what may well have happened to this boy a year before, when his special position in the family was disrupted and would never again be the same. From his appearance at the time he was tested, one would suspect that his reaction to the parents' sudden, inexplicable interruption of interest in him was to withdraw and nurse his wound in silence. But he surely listened intently to the talk about the new baby and the hospital. Perhaps he asked about the newborn baby, its looks, its whereabouts. Perhaps he was even taken up for a glimpse into the maternity ward despite the rules against this. Surely he spent a good deal of time thinking of the new baby, the fuss being made over her, and wondering about his own birth. His mood of desolate aloneness left its indelible mark on the images and fantasies he formed of his own birth. It remained only for him to attach to these images the feelings that they were *real* experiences and they were his *own* experiences for them to become "early memories." These images, these so-called early memories, became cards of identity, and served to represent for him the psychological truth which had become the dominant theme of his life. His depressive isolation seemed well on the way to becoming a fixed affect-state and the nucleus for the premature consolidation of a depressive character structure.

It is likely that most early memory formation follows much the same course, that from hearing about or thinking about an event, to visualizing that event in one's mind's eye, and finally to investing that image with a feeling of actuality and of "me-ness" which makes it seem to be a real *memory* rather than a mere fantasy. Once that last step is taken, it is difficult for most people to believe subsequently that their own early memories really derive from stories, or images, or fantasies as much as they do from fragments of real experiences. One takes his early memories for granted, and is inclined to balk at the suggestion that they never really happened to him the way he remembers them happening, if indeed, they ever really happened at all. That special feeling which identifies early memories as both familiar and real is, nonetheless, no more than a feeling, and as Federn (1952), Claparede (1911), and others have shown, it suffers the same vicissitudes as do other feeling states. The feelings of familiarity, of actuality and of me-ness are displaceable, for example, as we know from déjà vu experiences. We less often recognize that the displacement is a two-way process, and that events invested with these feeling-qualities can suddenly be divested of them, as in *jamais vu* and other estrangement experiences (some of which can be artificially induced, as for example, in satiation experiments). Images and fantasies are far more often personalized into early memories than early memories are *de*personalized into ego-alien images. But the latter process does occur. I had occasion once to test a young woman with total amnesia. She had no memory at all for anything prior to the morning of her arrival on the bus a few days before in this strange town. Since she could remember no early memories nor anything else about herself, I asked her to make up stories which *might* be early memories, stories she could imagine telling me *if* and when she remembered who she was. She entered into the spirit of this game with enthusiasm and no little imagination, I thought. She told stories about her early years in an orphanage, her brother, her parents (whom she thought of as alive despite the fact that she was in an orphanage). All of this was recounted with frequent disclaimers of, "Isn't this wild!" and I confess, it did seem pretty fanciful to me. A week later, when she recovered her memory, we learned that these stories which she thought she had made up out of whole cloth were true and corresponded closely to her non-amnesic early memories. During the two-week period of her amnesia, however, she could call up these images of herself only after dissociating them from any feelings of actuality or "me-ness." She could think of these events only by convincing herself they had never actually occurred.

These are, I admit, unusual examples. How valid is it to say of virtually all early memories that they are artifacts, visual fragments drawn from personal anecdotes, fantasies, photographs, and bits of real experience, transformed into "memories" by investiture with that special feeling-quality which distinguishes real from hypothetical events? It is, in fact, possible to demonstrate that virtually all early memories, which are so blithely taken for granted, could not have been experienced in the form in which they are remembered. One need only carry out a fairly simple inquiry. If one asks whether the memory occurs as a scene one imagines visually, the answer is almost always yes. If one then asks whether the informant appears as one of the figures in that scene, one learns that in more than half of all early memories the person *sees* himself as a little child as if he, the child, were another person and he, the observer, were looking on from some point away from the center of action. Moreover, the scene is often viewed from above, or from outside a window looking in, or from some other equally unlikely or impossible vantage point. One can imagine the event in that way, but surely the scene was never experienced that way in actuality. The memory is of a *reconstruction* of a real or a fantasied event rather than the re-experiencing of a *living* event. Even in those less common memories where the person says he *feels* himself to be present, and sees the scene as if from where he was standing at the time, one need only ask him from what eye-level he sees the people and things around him and how large they appear, to determine once again that he does not experience that scene as he would have at the age when the event is said to have occurred; he visualizes the setting as it would appear to him at an older age, or perhaps even as he would now view them as an adult.

There *are* some rare early memories in which an event *is* relived rather than merely recollected or reconstructed. Emma Plank (1953) has collected a number of these from autobiographical accounts of creative men; all are reminiscent of Proust's remembrances of things past. Their contrast with the garden variety form of early memory is easily demonstrated. Some years ago a writer who was gathering material for a popular article on the nature of memory recalled his own earliest memory. This went back to a year and a half or two years of age, and was of himself being carried and sung to by his grandfather. It was a highly cathected memory, but nonetheless one in which he experienced it as the detached observer looking on. He *saw* himself rather than *felt* himself in the arms of his grandfather. Suddenly, the memory changed. The visual image gave way to a wealth of other impressions. He could recall what he felt like as that child, the sensation of being carried, even the smell of the grandfather and the sound of the grandfather's voice humming the melody of that song. It was a fleeting moment, but in that moment the usual, more familiar, more detached memory reverted to its original form and became a living recall of that event.*

If we are moved by such considerations to take the most extreme position regarding early memories, we would come to view all early memories not as autobiographical, factual reports, but rather as "personal myths" (Kris, 1956a; 1956b), that is, as inventions which may have little or no relevance to actual events but great relevance to the personal themes which affect the way a person experiences events. Given this assumption, we are free to analyze early memories as projected fantasies, much as we now analyze TAT themes. Not infrequently, I have found the thematic analysis of a patient's early memories one of the more useful sources of information about his relationship predispositions—his capacity for forming object-relationships, the psychosexual level at which he is prone to define his object-relationships, and some of the major transference resistances he is likely to introduce into his treatment. In the little time which remains for this presentation I shall limit myself to a few brief illustrations.

These two earliest memories were told by an adolescent girl:†

> I had a little white kitten that I had found and was taking care of. Mother wouldn't let me keep the cat in at night. I remember this very cold night, it was snowy and icy outside. I begged her to let the cat stay in but she didn't even listen to me. The next morning when I woke up and looked out the window, the cat's guts and blood were all over the street. It had been run over during the night.

* The difference in quantity and in emotional impact which distinguishes these two radically different forms of early memory has a direct bearing on the theory and practice of psychotherapy. Some intellectualizing patients work hard at "remembering," but limit their recollections largely to more or less affectless pictorial reconstructions, and maintain in that way an effective resistance against emotional confrontations they are not yet prepared to face. Freud (1914, 1938) discussed this issue at length in two important papers on psychoanalytic technique.

† Some of the biographical data in each of the case examples used below have been altered to insure anonymity, but I have tried to leave the essential features of the patient's life, symptomatology and character structure undistorted.

Another time I came home sick from school. I had such an awful pain in my stomach, I was doubled over and couldn't stand up. It hurt me so badly I thought I was going to die. She just laughed at me and kept telling me it served me right for eating all that candy when she told me not to.

There were no representations of a good mother in her set of twelve early memories.* In fact, all of the really early memories of mother had been wholly blotted out; both of these memories were placed at 7 or 8 years of age. This girl's almost nightmarish inversion of the more normal image of mother; her feeling that she was at the mercy of a woman who was less like a mother than she was like a fairy-tale version of the evil witch or the cruel step-mother; and, by implication, the girl's enduring sense of impotent rage at this mother who makes such a mockery of the nurturant care the girl so much craved, all imply severe pathology in the expectancies she carries with her into any and all potentially nurturant relationships. These and her other early memories are representative samples of an inner world in which she experiences object-ties as empty, predatory and cold-blooded.

The presenting symptom in this case was murder. The girl had killed her mother by feeding her poison, and watched her die writhing in pain, laughing at her mother all the while, just as the mother allegedly laughed at her in her earliest memory. The kitten memory was reported after sentence had been passed, during the initial intake interviews at the state hospital where she had been confined. The stomach-ache memory was not recalled until two and a half years later, after two years of psychotherapy.

The next two memories were told by a 20-year-old boy during an intake evaluation prior to his hospitalization.

Don't know how old I was. It was at the age when they have these little toilet seats they fit on toilets for kids that would fall in otherwise. And . . . I go to the bathroom. Instead of putting the toilet seat on, my mother held me up. I was feeling scared about it, afraid I was going to fall in.

Another that sticks in my memory—My brothers and I were playing in the basement. They were going to play I was the bad guy and they were going to punish me by shoving me in the furnace. I sat on the cement floor. They were

* I've made a point of eliciting early memories much like one does TAT stories, i.e., not in freely ranging, free-association fashion but as a set of stories one is prepared to tell about himself in childhood. I regularly ask for and record verbatim the earliest memory; the next earliest memory; the earliest memory of mother; the next earliest memory of mother; the earliest of father; the next earliest of father; the happiest earliest memory: the unhappiest; and stories the family tell about the subject as a child, whether or not he himself remembers the incidents. When time permits I ask too for the "most striking" or "most special" early memory; the one in which the subject felt most fully himself; for an early memory that brings back the feeling of anger; of snugness; of fear; of thrill or excitement; and the feeling of shame or guilt.

going to scoop me with a shovel. It hurt quite a bit, pinching. And I started to cry and the game broke up.

This was how the patient experienced himself in two self-projections onto the screen of his memory. The faint allusions to such primal dangers as being sucked up into a gaping hole, or thrown into the jaws of a furnace showed how natural it was for him to view events in essentially oral-incorporative terms. Equally striking, and consistent with such incorporative relationship paradigms, is the inertness, the passivity with which he lets himself be victimized, and his clinging dependence on others to rescue him from pain or threats. Every aspect of his memories suggests a limpness in the face of adversity which did not bode well for success of the treatment.

This young man was brought to the hospital by his parents who were growing tired of supporting him psychologically, economically, and socially. He was a confirmed narcotics addict, had never worked except for a few odd jobs in unknown jazz combos. There had been some petty bad-check writing, which his parents made good for him. He had drifted into an impulsive marriage with a chronologically immature and psychologically infantile girl, whom he moved into the parental home after the marriage. He indulged in grandiosely unrealistic fantasies about his prospects, while at the same time his actions created in others the impression of ineffectualness, weakness, and worthlessness which called to mind the veiled parallels he drew in his early memories between himself and a lump of feces or a shovelful of dirt. His treatment was marked by pathological lying, all directed at denying his impotence to cope with any of the exigencies of life. He soon induced his indulgent parents to rescue him from the discomforts of treatment, as they had rescued him from previous difficulties when he cried out convincingly enough for help.

It is of parenthetic interest to note the similarity between this earliest memory and the earliest memories of three patients of Martin's (1959), all three reported memories of being held over a body of water and feeling terrified that they would be dropped. The implicit fear of losing control and being innundated was far from groundless. All three needed to be hospitalized in the course of treatment, two for schizophrenic episodes, and the third to help him control his drinking, his bad check writing and his fear of becoming psychotic. As with my patient, self-representations which depict the ego as helplessly vulnerable in the face of primal threats to survival, proved to be prognostic of severe ego weakness.

The themes around which people build their retrospectively convincing views of life as they lived it, run the gamut from such archaic themes to some quite mature forms of object relation. A distribution of themes implicit in early memories, collected more or less randomly from normal, neurotic, borderline and psychotic subjects, is summarized in Table 1, and illustrates the variety of "oral," "anal," "phallic," and "genital" self-representations and object-representations which commonly appear in early memories. The psychosexual terms are meant to designate developmental phases from which the relationship paradigm is drawn, rather than to refer to the more narrowly instinctual meanings of these terms as used in a psychoanalytic id-psychology. As used here these terms define a multiplicity of different ego-states, each organized around a distinctive affect and self-experience, and made up of a definitive need, a need-appropriate object-relationship and self-representation, and phase-appropriate conflicts, defenses and compromise formations, and ego-competencies. Implicit in an ego-state may be oral, anal, or phallic impulses but these impulses become accessible to the ego (and to the therapist of a patient) not in id-terms as raw impulses, but by way of ego derivatives including, most importantly, such ego-states (Mayman, 1963). Implicit in all the ''oral'' themes listed in Table 1 may be a primal hunger for nurturant supplies, an oral hunger which was once experienced by the person in its most archaically literal sense, but the primal oral wish appears in the memory only in its derivative form, as the product of an ego which itself carries the imprint of prior life experiences. Early memories organized around the oral-paradigm depict what the informant's ego and superego have made of the primal wish, rather than that wish itself. Whether the themes express oral optimism and the sense of basic trust, or oral misanthropy and mistrust, they refer to derivative states, adaptive or defensive positions taken by the person toward the still salient, still unfulfilled oral need.

Table 1A.   Prototypical Interpersonal Themes in Early Memories*

I.   ''Oral'' Configurations

    1.   Themes of basic mistrust:

        a.   Danger of personal extinction by abandonment, starvation, suffocation, being swallowed; sense of engulfing evil and impending doom. (Reminiscent of M. Klein's ''paranoid position.'')

Oral Pessimism

        b.   Bleak, empty aloneness; anaclitic depression; themes of getting lost, being sent away from home more or less permanently, death of parents; themes of traumatic separation and of depression verging on despair. (Reminiscent of Melanie Klein's ''depressive position.'')

    2.   Deprivation or insufficient supplies of attention, food or love: oral pessimism, dissatisfaction, bitter resentment, sense of unfulfillment (rather than of despair as in I.1.).

        a.   Temporary separation from others: parents are off by themselves and not aware of the child; child is sent off to school or to other relatives; feeling left out of some adult activities; all of which give rise to a poignant sense of not belonging.

        b.   Other themes of deprivation: insufficient supplies of comfort, reassurance, love, attention, care or food; dissatisfied with one's lot.

        c.   Loss of some treasured object.

* Early memories can be ''scored'' by using the notational schema employed in this table.

Table 1A. *(Continued)*

      d. Suffering an unpleasant or dangerous illness.

    3. Aggressive reactions to deprivation or frustration: demanding or grasping needed supplies rather than merely yearning for them as in I.2.

      a. Suffused with impotent rage.

      b. Greedy hunger for what one does not have: taking and holding onto, appropriating by snatching away, grasping, or biting.

      c. Resentment—and/or malicious treatment of—younger sibling.

      d. Meets with punishment, criticism or "accidental" injury as a direct consequence of oral-aggressive behavior.

    4. Gratification themes: sense of snugness, security, basic trust, expectation of fulfillment; sense of personal worth; availability of external comforts and supports.

Oral Optimism

      a. Snug pleasures of sleep, bed, breast, bath, food, or physical closeness.

      b. Comforting care during an illness.

      c. Close comforting attentive presence of mother or mother surrogate. (Father may fill this role at times.)

      d. Receiving gifts as proof of love with ensuing sense of warmth, belonging, and fulfillment.

      e. Being helped by an adult to learn to look after oneself, e.g., being taught one's name and address, how to tie one's shoes.

    5. Gratification themes with a reversal of roles so that one becomes the giver rather than the recipient of nurturant care.

      a. Taking the nurturing parent role toward a younger sib, pet, friend or sick parent.

II. "Anal" Configurations: Self-Differentiating Relationship Paradigms

    1. Retentiveness: willful stubbornness, defiance, passive-aggressive noncompliance.

Passive Agressive

      a. Withholding from adults; sulking.

      b. Defiance by refusal to comply with adult's requests—including food fads, refusal to eat, refusal to go to bed.

      c. Passive aggressive "inability" to produce what is asked for or expected by adults.

    *add [p.] if: Meets with punishment, ridicule, or attack upon one's self-esteem by a superego-figure due to one's retentive behavior.

    2. Expulsiveness: hurting self or others by dirtying them or treating them like dirt.

Hurting Self

      a. Insufficient sphincter control (usually with memory of shame, guilt or punishment); other forms of being dirtied or feeling oneself to be unclean.

* A "p." (punishment) "score" is added to a previous score when an activity meets with some form of injury, narcissistic hurt, or punishment.

132

b. Being the object of vilification; being treated by other "like shit."

Hurting
Others

c. Defiance by vilification, spitting, demeaning others, throwing things (especially rocks, dirt or mud); treating others "like dirt" or extruding others by pushing them away or keeping them at a distance.

*add [p.] if: Meets with punishment, ridicule, or other injury to one's self-esteem due to one's extrusive-aggressive behavior.

3. Sublimations or reaction formations:

a. Doing what one is supposed to do, avoiding conflicts with coercive parents.

b. Attention to cleanliness, cleaning up, being clean.

c. Preoccupation with one's own or another's possessions, with emphasis on quantity, orderliness and ownership.

III. "Phallic-Intrusive" and "Phallic-Locomotor" Configurations: Pleasure in Mastery; Pleasure in Proofs of One's Prowess, Strength or Competence

1. Active forms:

a. Expressing initiative, independence or eager curiosity; going off on one's own, wandering away to explore one's surroundings.

b. Boisterous play usually with peers; vigorous activity including physical attack; mischievously teasing play.

c. Active use of "phallic-locomotor" conveyance, with emphasis on the vehicles which carry one to adventures and new places; riding a bicycle, riding a horse, going on a trip. (Being taken for a drive should be listed as III. 2b.)

d. Competitive games: enjoyment of competition, pleasure in conquest, insistence on asserting one's dominance over people or impersonal obstacles (to be distinguished from the "greedy hunger" of I.3b.). Proving one is not inferior—being as good as someone else.

e. Identification with father; admiring father and wanting to be like him, to use his tools like him, to fix things as he does.

f. Setting fires and enjoying the ensuing excitement.

*add [p.] if: Any of these activities culminate in physical injury, narcissistic insult or physical punishment.

2. Passive forms:

a. Passively watching large moving vehicles or other wondrous objects; watching fires (but not setting them); watching the feats of others.

b. Being taken for a ride by an adult.

c. Being teased, being tossed about playfully by an adult, or carried by father in horse-and-rider play.

     d. Admiration and envy of phallic objects of others (symbolic or real); disappointment and unfavorable comparison with one's own phallic object or prowess; yearning to do as well as one's ego-models.

  *add [p.] if: Any of these activities culminate in injury, narcissistic insult, or punishment.

   3. Being the object of a phallic-aggressive assault.

     a. Being knocked down and overpowered by brute strength; fantasy of being whipped or beaten.

     b. Fear of dangerous, brutish creatures (including ghosts and bogey-men).

     c. Being shy, timid, fearful of exercising initiative.

     d. Themes of physicial injury: actual injury to the genitals, symbolic castration themes.

     e. Being hurt physically by a doctor; tonsil or other operation on body members.

IV. "Phallic-sexual" Configurations: Activities which are Frankly Sexual or Veiled but Recognizably Sexual in Nature.

   1. Intrusive forms: moving outward to make contact with sexual object.

     a. Playful, sexually-tinged curiosity or exhibitionism; sex play or secretive, sexually-tinged play with peers; interested examination of the sex organs of others but only as a "passive bystander."

     b. Proud or excited self-display, usually sublimated in dancing, singing or performing in some other manner before an audience of potential admirers. The accent here is on *doing* something to win favor, not *standing* by, *waiting* or *expecting* to be admired as in IV. 2b.

     c. Shame or embarrassment rather than pleasure following intrusive self-display.

  *add [p.] if: Intrusive sexual activity leads to physical injury, narcissistic insult, or physical punishment.

   2. Inceptive forms: trying to excite a sexually desired object to make a frank or veiled sexual approach.

     a. Being fetchingly coy, seductive; trying to make oneself attractive and endearing; teasing others in a sexually provocative manner.

     b. Pleasure in one's appearance; attention to pretty clothes, attractive grooming; pleasure in being looked at, noticed, admired or photographed.

     c. Shame or embarrassment rather than pleasure following inceptive self-display

  *add [p.] if: Inceptive sexual activity leads to physical injury, narcissistic insult, or physical punishment.

* A "p." (punishment) "score" is added to a previous score when an activity meets with some form of injury, narcissistic hurt, or punishment.

V. "Oedipal" Configurations: Competitive Striving to Win Favor With a Love-Object

    1. Male relationship patterns:

Hostile
Competitive

      a. Jealousy or rivalry (with father or a sibling) for the affection of mother or a mother surrogate; interest in mother's doings with another male.

      b. Failure to win mother's love, often accompanied by self-blame for one's personal inadequacy.

      c. Resentment or fear of the father as an overt or tacit rival for mother's love.

      d. Conflict between parents in which the child sides with the mother and rejects the father; angry at father for hurting mother.

Positive
Harmonious

      e. Denial of Oedipal conflict by stress on the warm, harmonious relationships with both mother and father.

      f. Doing things with mother which are pleasureful and exciting, with the father tacitly excluded.

      g. Pleasure in bringing mother a phallic gift.

    2. Female relationship patterns:

Hostile
Competitive

      a. Jealousy or rivalry with mother or a sibling for the affection of father or a father surrogate; interest in father's doings with another female.

      b. Resentment or fear of mother as an avowed or tacit rival for father's love.

      c. Failure to win father's love, with accompanying sense of personal inadequacy.

      d. Conflict between parents in which the child sides with father and rejects the mother.

Positive
Harmonious

      e. Denial of Oedipal conflict by stressing the warm, harmonious, non-competitive aspects of one's relationship with mother in the family triangle.

      f. Doing exciting or pleasureful things with father, with mother tacitly excluded.

      g. Interest in having a baby as mother did; or receiving some symbolically equivalent phallic gift from father; interest in pregnancy and childbirth.

      h. Playing house, playing with dolls, dressing up in mother's clothes, or in some other way doing as mother does.

VI. "Latency" Configurations: More Sublimated Peer-Group Activities

    1. Productivity and positive self-esteem.

      a. Socialization with peers; group play with well-differentiated roles.

      b. Industriousness, learning to do things, constructing and planning with others in a common endeavor.

      c. Turning manipulative skills to creative accomplishment.

Table 1A. *(Continued)*

    2. Inferiority:

        a. Withdrawal from, isolation in, or rejection by one's peer group.

Table IB. Clinically Meaningful Aspects of The Analysis of a Set of Early Recollections

Relationship Paradigms

1. To what extent does one represent himself as living in lonely isolation? In close interaction with others? How wide a range of relationships comes spontaneously to mind? To what extent do mother, father, other family members, and friends, "people" the patient's intrapsychic world?

2. What forms of relatedness seem most congenial, most ego-syntonic, easiest to maintain?

3. What is the quality and intensity of feeling implicit in these relationships? What is the "level" of relationship—impersonal? anaclitic? imitative? mutual?

4. Is there evidence of particular psychosexual paradigms serving as models for interpersonal relationships? Evidence of preferred psychosexual positions to escape from other more dangerous positions?

Coping Style

5. Does the patient represent himself as active or as passive in his relationships? If active, how? compliant? courageous? venturesome? defiant? autonomous? assertive? self-sufficient? If passive, what form of passivity? timid? self-abasing? compliant? limp? "feeling" and "watching," rather than "doing?"

Self-structure

6. Where is a person's "self-feeling" most fully invested? In which modalities of experience? sensual? kinaesthetic? affective? introspective? extroceptive? What forms of activity does the person readily invest himself in, and in which can he not invest himself?

7. What kinds of life-experiences seem ego-syntonic and which, by exclusion, ego-alien? Which qualities of experience remain split off from the self? Which threaten to disorganize the sense of self (i.e., are not only estranged but bring on some depersonalization)?

Imagoes

8. What are the principal representations of mother, father, and self? What is the principal representation of the self in relation to others? In what roles are the significant-others cast?

9. Are there traces of multiple or conflicting representations of significant-others and of oneself?

10. Which self-representations seem to have been encouraged or fostered by the parents? Which seem to have been incorporated into the ego-ideal?

136

Table IB.   *(Continued)*

Defense Modes

11. To what extent do "primal" or archaic memories occur?

12. To what extent is there a masochistic fixation upon fears, disappointments, dangers, injuries, pain, or illness?

13. How much repression do we encounter? To what extent does the patient feel himself cut off from his infantile origins, i.e., early sources of pleasure and early object-ties? How vague or nebulous are the memories? How selective is the memory process?

14. What defenses other than repression appear in the way in which the story is told? isolation? reaction-formation? projection? denial?

15. To what extent are memories phobic? depressive? self-punitive? counter-phobic? withdrawn? conflict-avoidant? shallow? self-preoccupied? warm and human?

A fairly typical example of the paradigmatic value of early memories for the diagnostic analysis of character structure are the earliest memories told by a forty-five year old, childless, married woman who had decided to seek psychiatric help when spells of tiredness, lassitude and incipient depression grew increasingly incapacitating at home and at work.* She had spent most of her life, and most of her energies in a career as a rehabilitation worker in a hospital for crippled children. She had been a key figure in developing a professional organization of rehabilitation workers in her state, and was still one of its leading lights. At eighteen, she married a pleasant, passive, unambitious man who neither encouraged nor interfered with her professional activities. They remained childless and the patient worked throughout her marriage.

Two paragraphs from her psychological test report describe some of the patient's emotional state and character structure at the time she came for examination.

Depression is as prominent in this patient's test performance as it is clinically, but even when the patient was at her worst, she did not seem to give in to her depressed feelings. Rather, she criticized herself for every failure, corrected her mistakes and insisted that she would have to do better. . . .

Her compulsiveness was even more impressive when as testing went on the depression receded. The emphasis on making demands upon herself, the unwillingness to tolerate any weakness or failure in herself, and the inability to allow herself to express or even to experience angry feelings took clearer and clearer shape. What-

---

* This example is drawn from a previous report of these same data and was discussed at greater length in that paper (Mayman, 1963), which is not easily accessible to most readers. [Ed. Note: ch. 8, this Volume]

ever happened she tried to brush off, or at least isolate off any resentful feelings she may have had. Severe reaction formations against her angry feelings were integrated into a self-image (and ego ideal) of a person whose life is spent in the service of others in an austere world of stern duties, values and standards. It seems clear that her ego has become thoroughly fused with a severe, uncompromising superego.

Her earliest memories fit well the austere, highly principled and stoically long-suffering way of life which characterized this woman at the time she presented herself for treatment. Her very earliest memory tells of being unjustly coerced, threatened and then punished by father, who wanted her to confess to something she hadn't done; she stoically and with stubborn adherence to principle accepted all of the punishment rather than tamper with the truth. Another memory describes her being forced to eat when she didn't want to. Still another told of her being disappointed one time at her father's failure to get for her one of the noisemakers that other children in the neighborhood had for Halloween: She added, "I was disappointed, but of course I couldn't show it."

Such themes of willful stubbornness or defiance, as if to make the tacit assertion, "This is me; I challenge you to budge me; I myself now define the limits of my autonomy," are typical form-variants of the "anal" paradigm. Other anal memories, representing other anal relationship paradigms, revolve around themes of retentiveness; themes in which one besmirches (or is himself besmirched) with words or other forms of vilification; themes of harmony and of order.

These self- and object-representations stand in striking contrast to phallic-intrusive, phallic-exhibitionistic and phallic-locomotor themes which some people choose as the most convincing vehicles for their retrospective self-definition. They call to mind activities in which the body, especially the striped muscles, is used assertively for conquest, mastery or the display of physical or sexual authority. Such themes generally allude to the pleasures of, or the fear of, making a self-assertive intrusive impact on one's surroundings. In such themes one ventures forth or takes a chance, even if this means meeting the world head-on. Not infrequently such themes appear in inverted form and depict the fearful consequences of venturing too far, or challenging too recklessly.

Illustrative of this phallic level of self-definition are a set of memories told by a man whose work, relations with other men, and attitude toward his wife was that of a very masculinely competent person. He came for treatment, however, because of sexual impotence. As is so common in people like this, his early memories consist largely of allusions to phallic prowess and mastery, phallic-locomotor competence, phallic-intrusive impulses, and phallic-aggressive threats. This man's memories alluded in one way or another to his wish to be as powerful as his father, his fear of the father's violent masculinity, his fear of phallic women, and his reminder to himself that aggressive, masculine assertiveness could lead to fearful consequences, like damage to his body or even attacks which could kill. These themes were wholly consistent with the man's life style and consistent also with his form of psychopathology.

The time has come to sum up. I have tried to call attention to a development in the proliferating science of projective methods which takes as its point of departure the discovery that the manifest content of a person's early memories convey more than the term "screen memory" would imply. Like the manifest content of dreams and other conscious thought processes, early memories provide a potentially rich source of data from which to infer defensive and adaptive choices made by the ego as it seeks to come to terms with powerful internal and external demands. Early memories may be analyzed as if they were fantasied representations of self and others, rather than as factual accounts of a few scattered events in a person's life. Clinicians stand to learn much about an informant's character structure and psychopathology if they treat his early memories not as historical truths (or half-truths) but as thematic representations or prototypical dilemmas, life strategies, and role paradigms around which he defines his relationship to himself and to his personal world.

REFERENCES

Ansbacher, H. L. Adler's place today in the psychology of memory. *Individual Psychology Bulletin*, 1947, *6*, 32–40.

Babcock, C. G. The manifest content of the dream. *Journal of the American Psychoanalytic Association*, 1966, *14*, 154–171.

Beck, A. T. & Ward, C. H. Dreams of depressed patients. *Archives of General Psychiatry*, 1961, *5*, 462–467.

Claparede, E. Recognition and me-ness. Chapter 3 in D. Rapaport, *Organization and Pathology of Thought*, New York: Columbia U. Press, 1951.

Eisenstein, V. W. & Ryerson, R. Psychodynamic significance of the first conscious memory. *Bulletin of the Menninger Clinic*, 1951, *15*, 213–220.

Erikson, E. H. The dream specimen of psychoanalysis. *Journal of the American Psychoanalytic Association*, 1954, *2*, 5–56.

Federn, P. *Ego Psychology and the Psychoses*. New York: Basic Books, 1952.

Freud, S. Screen memories (1899). Standard Edition *3*, 303–322. London: Hogarth Press.

Freud, S. Childhood memories and screen memories (1901). *Psychopathology of Everyday life*, Chapter 4. Standard Edition, *6*, 43–52. London: Hogarth Press.

Freud, S. Leonardo da Vinci and a memory of his childhood (1910). Standard Edition, *11*, 59–137. London: Hogarth Press, 1953.

Freud, S. Remembering, repeating and working through (1914). Standard Edition, 145–156. London: Hogarth Press.

Freud, S. Constructions in analysis. *International Journal of Psychoanalysis*, 1938, 377–387.

Greenson, R. On screen defenses, screen hunger and screen identity. *Journal of the American Psychoanalytic Association*, 1958, *6*, 242–262.

Kris, E. The recovery of childhood memories in psychoanalysis. *Psychoanalytic Study of the Child*, 1956a, *11*, 54–88.

Kris, E. The personal myth. *Journal of the American Psychoanalytic Association*, 1956b, *4*, 653–681.

Langs, R. Earliest memories and personality. *Archives of General Psychiatry*, 1965, *12*, 379.

Lewin, B. D. Sleep, the mouth, and the dream screen. *Psychoanalytic Quarterly*, 1946, *15*, 419–434.

Lewin, B. D. *The Psychoanalysis of Elation*, New York: W. W. Norton, 1950 (p. 72).

Martin, P. A. One type of earliest memory. *Psychoanalytic Quarterly*, 1959, *28*, 73–77.

Mayman, M. Early memories and abandoned ego states. Southwestern Psychology Association, April, 1959. *Proceedings of the Academic Assembly on Clinical Psychology*, Montreal, McGill U. Press, 1963, pp. 97–117.

Mayman, M. & Faris, M. Early memories as expressions of relationship paradigms. *American Journal of Orthopsychiatry*, 1960, 507–520.

Noble, D. A study of dreams in schizophrenia and allied states. *American Journal of Psychiatry*, 1951, *107*, 612–616.

Plank, E. Memories of early childhood in autobiography. *Psychoanalytic Study of the Child*, 1953, *8*, 381–393.

Richardson, G. A. & Moore, R. A. On the manifest dream in schizophrenia. *Journal of the American Psychoanalytic Association*, 1963, *11*, 281–302.

Roth, N. Manifest dream content and acting out. *Psychoanalytic Quarterly*, 1958, *27*, 547–554.

Saul, L. J. The utilization of early current dreams in formulating psychoanalytic cases. *Psychoanalytic Quarterly*, 1940, *9*, 453–469.

Saul, L. J., Snyder, T. R., & Sheppard, E. On earliest memories. *Psychoanalytic Quarterly*, 1956, *25*, 228–237.

Sheppard, E. Systematic dream studies: Clinical judgments and objective measurements of ego strength. *Comprehensive Psychiatry*, 1963, *4*, 263–270.

Presidential address, Society for Projective Techniques, September 4, 1967, Washington, D.C. One of a series of studies on the use of early memories in clinical assessment carried out under the auspices of the Psychotherapy Research Project of the Menninger Foundation, currently supported by the NIMH, Grant number MH 8308. The work of the project was previously supported by the Foundations' Fund for Research in Psychiatry and by the Ford Foundation.

Chapter 8

Psychoanalytic Study of the Self-Organization with Psychological Tests

MARTIN MAYMAN

Several levels of conceptualization in a theory may give that theory greater scope and power, but only if the various levels are not confused with each other and each remains clearly coordinate with the others and with the primary data to which they all refer. The current ascendancy of the most abstract level of conceptualization, psychoanalytic metapsychology, in psychoanalytic thought sometimes creates the impression that psychoanalytic theory is a rather monolithic structure. This is not the case; psychoanalysis is a complex, multi-leveled theory.

The conceptual language of psychoanalytic metapsychology is not the conceptual language of the patient's treatment hour. Psychoanalysis consists in fact of three coordinate and not always clearly distinguished sets of concepts. The language employed by the psychoanalyst in his exchanges with his patients is a language closer perhaps to poetry than to science. At this level of expression he tries to capture and make explicit those nuances of feeling which seek expression in the multifarious forms of thought and behavior which come under the scrutiny of the psychoanalytic eye. Later, outside the consultation room, the psychoanalyst may employ a "middle language" of essentially "empirical constructs" (Koch) which help him to formulate certain clinical generalizations about a patient. Psychoanalysis has developed a rich set of such middle language concepts, but these appear in clinical rather than theoretical papers, and perhaps for this reason do not command the same prestige among theorists as do the more "systematic or 'hypothetical' constructs" of psychoanalysis. These latter belong to the third and most abstract language of psychoanalytic metapsychology, a system of essentially impersonal constructs which examine the psychic organi-

Reprinted with permission from the *Proceedings of the Academic Assembly on Clinical Psychology.* Montreal: McGill University Press, 1963, pp. 97–117 © 1963 by McGill University.

Table I.   Coordinate Terms of the "Middle" and "Meta" Psychological Concepts of Psychoanalysis

METAPSYCHOLOGICAL TERMS which, as ordinarily employed, refer to ego structures viewed "from the outside," i.e., in essentially third-person terms.	MEDIATING (MIDDLE LANGUAGE) TERMS which designate ego structures in more subjective terms, i.e., more nearly in keeping with the subjective experiences of the patient himself.
Ego structure; ego-organization; ego apparatuses; ego-state (as defined by Gill and Brenman)	The self; the ego-identity; identity fragments; ego boundary; self-feeling; ego-syntonic; ego-alien; depersonalization; ego state (as defined by Federn)
Structural regression; ego disruption; ego disintegration; primary and secondary process thinking; ego weakness	Ego split; ego-id nucleus; partial identifications; identity confusions; conflicting identifications; identity diffusion.
The id; the instincts; affect-charge; cathexis; impulse-derivative	Repressed ego states; repressed affect-states; unconscious (split-off) infantile ego—object relationships; love; hate; "urge" or "drive"; the source, aim, object (and subject?) of an instinct
Superego	Hostile (and loving) introjects
Libido (oral; anal; phallic; and genital)	Sensuous or voluptuous sensori-affective feeling-state.
Object-cathexis	Parental "imagoes"; parental introjects; internalized others; transference paradigms.
The system "Ucs"; the system "Pcpt-Cs"; attention cathexis; hypercathexis; cognitive and perceptual structures	Latent content; unconscious phantasy; repressed thoughts and affects

zation of a patient in more objective, third-person terms, rather than in more intimate first-person or second-person terms employed at the more empirical or middle language levels of the theory (Table I).

The use of psychological tests to study behavioral and personality change would be much enhanced if psychoanalytic ego psychology were to systematize its middle language concepts of ego organization to parallel the systematization which has been taking place in its metapsychological theorizing. Psychoanalysis is well along in the development of a clinical, or middle language, ego theory (Jacobson, Erikson, Sutherland), but this development has not yet been extended systematically to psychological test data as was done by Rapaport for the structural theory of psychoanalysis. When this extension occurs, there will emerge a psychoanalytic psychology of the "self" rather than of the "ego." And unlike much self-concept research today, this psychoanalytic theory of the self would reach behind a person's avowed (conscious) self-image, to the *tacit* (preconscious and unconscious) self-conceptions expressed *implicitly* in his life style. More particularly, it would seek to understand the transference patterns which govern a person's evolving relationship with his therapist. The patient repeats—replays on the therapeutic stage, so to speak—deeply ingrained expectancies which shape each important new relationship he establishes. Psychoanalytic self-concept research would take care not to lose touch with this more deeply personal, less conscious dimension of self-experience. There is more to oneself than one can himself see. One *is* a particular self more fully than he *knows* that self, and he is *that* self to the exclusion of other possible selves he unconsciously fears or hopes to become. Conscious reflection about oneself can at best be only a limited source of knowledge about the self in all of its depth and complexity.

More revealing would be a study of the conscious purposes served by being the kind of person one has become.

Consider, for example, the case of a nurse who, throughout the early phase of her treatment, maintained a fixed role in relation to the therapist—that of "the nurse." She was prim, precise, controlled and deferential. Her symptoms and her feelings were reported by her with a detached objectivity as if she and the doctor together were studying a third person, the patient. She awaited the doctor's directions respectfully. It soon became apparent in her treatment that this fixed role she maintained would have to be undone before she could become involved in a more meaningful, more helpful therapeutic experience.

Subsequently, the deeper meaning of her "character-armor" became apparent. It represented, in part, the patient's attempt to rid herself of any resemblance to a mother from whom she recoiled with distaste. Her image of her mother was that of a volatile, emotional, crude woman of whims and passions. The theme of one of her TAT stories, told during her pre-treatment evaluation, presented in plastic representational form the conflicting choices with which she was faced.

There were two women in the picture. One, running along a beach, was seen by the patient as a spontaneous, openly expressive, but also sloppy and coarse woman; the other, watching with disapproval, but also a little wistfully, was seen as precise, calm, well-modulated, someone in whom any such affective outburst would be out of the question. The patient projected onto this picture the two representations between which she steered a life-course: the preferred self-image (or better, perhaps, the preferred "self-role"), and its converse, the hated model represented by the mother whom she feared, and at the same time unconsciously yearned to become.

For this patient a number of character traits (prim, precise, controlled, deferential), and a characteristic defensive style (detached, objective, monotonous and affectless in her self-descriptions and complaints) had congealed into a single meaningful behavior pattern centering around her internalized relationship with her mother introject. On the surface she was the nurse reporting to the doctor about this patient, herself, whom they were studying together. At a deeper level she was the rational, controlled, orderly and competent woman who was determined to prove herself in every way the direct opposite of her mother. At a still deeper level she felt herself closely identified with this mother. Her initial behavior toward the therapist—and her way of relating herself to other important figures in her life—showed the impasse created by her incompatible identity-models, and the emptiness of the solution she tried to impose.

Diagnostic assessment of character structure by means of psychological tests usually focuses upon a patient's preferred defense mechanisms, and the effectiveness of these and his adaptive structures in forestalling regressive ego changes. With tests we generally seek to establish a patient's vulnerability to disruptive attacks of anxiety (and its inverse, the capacity to tolerate and cope with such tension states); the deficiencies in ego strength such as are reflected in disturbance of the reality testing function; gross deficiencies in the modulation and affective channeling of feelings and impulses; and the ability to maintain reality-adapted thought organization against intrusions of primary process images, fantasies, and modes of thought.

But an equally tenable approach to diagnosis of character structure and psychopathology would be to organize the diagnosis around an analysis of the patient's identity-patterns, as for example in the case of the nurse. It is our assumption that diagnoses of this sort would require a careful content analysis of test productions: contents which carry in them traces of a person's object-representations, self-representations, significant introjects, and the relation of all to certain core neurotic conflicts. The cohesiveness and scope of a person's ego-synthesis will rest heavily upon the synthesis he can achieve of the various partial identities which crystallize out of the various object-relationships which in the course of his development have played a central organizing role in shaping the budding ego. It is through these identity patterns that a person channels his biological urges and infantile yearnings. And it is in terms of these patterns that he progressively defines his preferred relationship tendencies and limits the range of relationships he can enter into. It is these identity patterns which become ingrained and are then subsequently repressed which become the transference paradigms that the patient will later tend to recreate in his social intercourse.

The relevance of this kind of analysis to the study of psychotherapeutic change need not be belabored. Attempting such an analysis through the ''blind'' interpretation of psychological tests would, ideally, be based upon test data which sample the hierarchal layering of character structures. Such a test analysis would seek to inter-relate the patient's (a) manifest behavioral style and behavior predispositions; (b) the supporting attitudes, values and conscious images of self and others which help to sustain these major behavioral dispositions; (c) the specific impulses which the patient seems to be defending against by means of this character structure, inferred from impulse-derivatives which come to expression in his fantasies or fantasy fragments on projective tests; and finally, also by way of elicited fantasy fragments, (d) inferences about the core neurotic conflict as it has been carried along in fantasy representations of the major infantile neurotic dilemmas, involving significant introjects and the ego's relationships to these introjects.

THE RESEARCH INSTRUMENT: EARLY MEMORIES

One phase of the Menninger Foundation's Psychotherapy Research Project is the attempt to study such relationship- and transference-paradigms as they appear and are worked through in the course of treatment. We found it useful to include as one of the projective techniques employed for this purpose, a collection of the patient's earliest memories.

In the discussion which follows I shall try to show that the analysis of a patient's set of early memories can contribute valuable, and sometimes indispensable, data to the analysis of a person's identity-structure. In order to use early memories as projective test data, we were required to make these assumptions: That early memories are in fact projected (and more or less disguised) reconstructions of an earlier and still regnant intrapsychic reality; that such reconstructions are unconsciously selected so as to conform with, and confirm, deeply ingrained images of oneself and of his significant others, and therefore point to nuclear self—other relationship predispositions; and that the adult ego synthesis was subjected to the same organizing principles as intrude projectively into the structure and content of one's early memories. In short, we assume that a person's collection of early memories will reveal the imprint of core conflicts upon the forms and qualities of his self-experience, and that, as with Thematic Apperception Test stories, one may sift the productions for intrusive interpersonal themes which may define that person's enduring view of himself and his enduring expectations of others.

Table II lists some of the questions one can attempt to answer in his analysis of a set of early memories. The list is not meant to be exhaustive, but only to show the conceptual directions in which such data may lead us in any effort to understand patients through projective tests. The assurance that an early memories inventory can yield valid answers to such questions must await more research.

Table III lists the kinds of themes which commonly occur in early memories. We have found it an encouraging source of indirect validation of the test rationale that these themes distribute themselves along a continuum of prototypical object relationships much like that described by Erikson in his analysis of relationship modes which characterize the developmental stages in infancy and childhood. Moreover, these themes can be culled from a set of early memories with satisfactory inter-rater reliability.

Table II.   Clinically Meaningful Aspects of The Analysis of a Set of Early Recollections

Relationship Paradigms

1. To what extent does one represent himself as living in lonely isolation? In close interaction with others? How wide a range of relationships comes spontaneously to mind? To what extent do mother, father, other family members, and friends, "people" the patient's intrapsychic world?

2. What forms of relatedness seem most congenial, most ego-syntonic, easiest to maintain?

3. What is the quality and intensity of feeling implicit in these relationships? What is the "level" of relationship—impersonal? anaclitic? imitative? mutual?

4. Is there evidence of particular psychosexual paradigms serving as models for interpersonal relationships? Evidence of preferred psychosexual positions to escape from other more dangerous positions?

Coping Style

5. Does the patient represent himself as active or as passive in his relationships? If active, how? compliant? courageous? venturesome? defiant? autonomous? assertive? self-sufficient? If passive, what form of passivity? timid? self-abasing? compliant? limp? "feeling" and "watching," rather than "doing?"

Self-Structure

6. Where is a person's "self-feeling" most fully invested? In which modalities of experience? sensual? kinaesthetic? effective? introspective? extroceptive? What forms of activity does the person readily invest himself in, and in which can he not invest himself?

7. What kinds of life-experiences seem ego-syntonic and which, by exclusion, ego-alien? Which qualities of experience remain split off from the self? Which threaten to disorganize the sense of self (i.e., are not only estranged but bring on some depersonalization)?

Imagoes

8. What are the principal representations of mother, father, and self? What is the principal representation of the self in relation to others? In what roles are the significant-others cast?

9. Are there traces of multiple or conflicting representations of significant-others and of oneself?

10. Which self-representations seem to have been encouraged or fostered by the parents? Which seem to have been incorporated into the ego-ideal?

Defense Modes

11. To what extent do "primal" or archaic memories occur?

12. To what extent is there a masochistic fixation upon fears, disappointments, dangers, injuries, pain, or illness?

13. How much repression do we encounter? To what extent does the patient feel himself cut off from his infantile origins, i.e., early sources of pleasure and early objectives? How vague or nebulous are the memories? How selective is the memory process?

14. What defenses other than repression appear in the way in which the story is told? isolation? reaction-formation? projection? denial?

15. To what extent are memories phobic? depressive? self-punitive? counter-phobic? withdrawn? conflict-avoidant? shallow? self-preoccupied? warm and human?

However, the ultimate test of any such projective method is its usefulness in assessing individual psychopathology and character structure. In any such application of the method we should be especially attentive to ways in which the test serves to implement the "middle language" clinical theory of ego organization. I should like to illustrate how the analysis of early memories may serve both these purposes.

Table III. Prototypical Interpersonal Themes in Early Memories *

I. "Oral" Configurations—Anaclitic Relationship Paradigms

    1. Themes of basic mistrust:

        a. Danger of personal extinction by abandonment, starvation, suffocation, being swallowed; sense of engulfing evil and impending doom. (Reminiscent of M. Klein's "paranoid position.")

        b. Bleak, empty aloneness; anaclitic depression; themes of getting lost, being sent away from home more or less permanently, death of parents; themes of traumatic separation and of depression verging on despair. (Reminiscent of M. Klein's "depressive position.")

    2. Deprivation or insufficient supplies of attention, food or love: oral pessimism, dissatisfaction, bitter resentment, sense of unfulfillment (rather than of despair as in I.1.).

Oral
Pessimism

        a. Temporary separation from others: parents are off by themselves and not aware of the child; child is sent off to school or to other relatives; feeling left out of some adult activities; all of which give rise to a poignant sense of not belonging.

        b. Other themes of deprivation: insufficient supplies of comfort, reassurance, love, attention, care or food; dissatisfied with one's lot.

        c. Loss of some treasured object.

        d. Suffering an unpleasant or dangerous illness.

    3. Aggressive reactions to deprivation or frustration: demanding or grasping needed supplies rather than merely yearning for them as in I.2.

        a. Suffused with impotent rage.

        b. Greedy hunger for what one does not have: taking and holding onto, appropriating by snatching away, grasping, or biting.

        c. Resentment—and/or malicious treatment —of younger sibling.

        d. Meets with punishment, criticism or "accidental" injury as a direct consequence of oral-aggressive behavior.

    4. Gratification themes: sense of basic trust, expectation of fulfillment, oral optimism, sense of personal worth.

Oral
Optimism

        a. Snug pleasures of sleep, bed, breast, bath, food, or physical closeness.

        b. Comforting care during an illness.

* Early memories can be "scored" by using the notational schema employed in this table.

Table III. *(Continued)*

---

        c. Close comforting attentive presence of mother or mother surrogate. (Father may fill this role at times.)

        d. Receiving gifts as proof of love with ensuing sense of warmth, belonging, and fulfillment.

        e. Being helped by an adult to learn to look after oneself, e.g., being taught one's name and address, how to tie one's shoes.

    5. Gratification themes with a reversal of roles so that one becomes the giver rather than the recipient of nurturant care.

        a. Taking the nurturing parent role toward a younger sib, pet, friend or sick parent.

II. "Anal" Configurations: Self-Differentiating Relationship Paradigms

    1. Retentiveness: willful stubbornness, defiance, passive-aggressive noncompliance.

Passive
Aggressive

        a. Withholding from adults; sulking.

        b. Defiance by refusal to comply with adult's requests—including food fads, refusal to eat, refusal to go to bed.

        c. Passive aggressive "inability" to produce what is asked for or expected by adults.

    *add [p.] if: Meets with punishment, ridicule, or attack upon one's self-esteem by a superego-figure due to one's retentive behavior.

    2. Expulsiveness: hurting self or others by dirtying them or treating them like dirt.

Hurting
Self

        a. Insufficient sphincter control (usually with memory of shame, guilt or punishment); other forms of being dirtied or feeling oneself to be unclean.

        b. Being the object of vilification; being treated by other "like shit."

Hurting
Others

        c. Defiance by vilification, spitting, demeaning others, throwing things (especially rocks, dirt or mud); treating others "like dirt" or extruding others by pushing them away or keeping them at a distance.

    *add [p.] if: Meets with punishment, ridicule, or other injury to one's self-esteem due to one's extrusive-aggressive behavior.

    3. Sublimations or reaction formations:

        a. Doing what one is supposed to do, avoiding conflicts with coercive parents.

        b. Attention to cleanliness, cleaning up, being clean.

        c. Preoccupation with one's own or another's possessions, with emphasis on quantity, orderliness and ownership.

III. "Phallic-Intrusive" and "Phallic-Locomotor" Configurations: Pleasure in Mastery; Pleasure in Proofs of One's Prowess, Strength or Competence.

* A "p." (punishment) "score" is added to a previous score when an activity meets with some form of injury, narcissistic hurt, or punishment.

Table III. *(Continued)*

1. Active forms:

    a. Expressing initiative, independence or eager curiosity; going off on one's own, wandering away to explore one's surroundings.

    b. Boisterous play usually with peers; vigorous activity including physical attack; mischievously teasing play.

    c. Active use of "phallic-locomotor" conveyance, with emphasis on the vehicles which carry one to adventures and new places; riding a bicycle, riding a horse, going on a trip. (Being taken for a drive should be listed as III.2b.)

    d. Competitive games: enjoyment of competition, pleasure in conquest, insistence on asserting one's dominance over people or impersonal obstacles (to be distinguished from the "greedy hunger" of I.3b). Proving one is not inferior—being as good as someone else.

    e. Identification with father; admiring father and wanting to be like him, to use his tools like him, to fix things as he does.

    f. Setting fires and enjoying the ensuing excitement.

*add [p.] if: Any of these activities culminate in physical injury, narcissistic insult or physical punishment.

2. Passive forms:

    a. Passively watching large moving vehicles or other wondrous objects; watching fires (but not setting them); watching the feats of others.

    b. Being taken for a ride by an adult.

    c. Being teased, being tossed about playfully by an adult, or carried by father in horse-and-rider play.

    d. Admiration and envy of phallic objects of others (symbolic or real); disappointment and unfavorable comparison with one's own phallic object or prowess; yearning to do as well as one's ego-models.

*add [p.] if: Any of these activities culminate in injury, narcissistic insult, or punishment.

3. Being the object of a phallic-aggressive assault.

    a. Being knocked down and overpowered by brute strength; fantasy of being whipped or beaten.

    b. Fear of dangerous, brutish creatures (including ghosts and bogey-men).

    c. Being shy, timid, fearful of exercising initiative.

    d. Themes of physical injury: actual injury to the genitals, symbolic castration themes.

    e. Being hurt physically by a doctor; tonsil or other operation on body members.

IV. "Phallic-Sexual" Configurations: Activities which are Frankly Sexual or Veiled but Recognizably Sexual in Nature.

1. Intrusive forms: moving outward to make contact with a sexual object.

149

Table III. *(Continued)*

    a. Playful, sexually-tinged curiosity or exhibitionism; sex play or secretive, sexually-tinged play with peers; interested examination of the sex organs of others but only as a "passive bystander."

    b. Proud or excited self-display, usually sublimated in dancing, singing or performing in some other manner before an audience of potential admirers. The accent here is on *doing* something to win favor, not *standing* by, *waiting* or *expecting* to be admired as in IV.2b.

    c. Shame or embarrassment rather than pleasure following intrusive self-display.

*add [p.] if: Intrusive sexual activity leads to physical injury, narcissistic insult, or physical punishment.

2. Inceptive forms: trying to excite a sexually desired object to make a frank or veiled sexual approach.

    a. Being fetchingly coy, seductive; trying to make oneself attractive and endearing; teasing others in a sexually provocative manner.

    b. Pleasure in one's appearance; attention to pretty clothes, attractive grooming; pleasure in being looked at, noticed, admired or photographed.

    c. Shame or embarrassment rather than pleasure following inceptive self-display.

*add [p.] if: Inceptive sexual activity leads to physical injury, narcissistic insult, or physical punishment.

V. "Oedipal" Configurations:

1. Male relationship patterns:

Hostile
Competitive
    a. Jealousy or rivalry (with father or a sibling) for the affection of mother or a mother surrogate; interest in mother's doings with another male.

    b. Failure to win mother's love, often accompanied by self-blame for one's personal inadequacy.

    c. Resentment or fear of the father as an overt or tacit rival for mother's love.

    d. Conflict between parents in which the child sides with the mother and rejects the father; angry at father for hurting mother.

    e. Denial of Oedipal conflict by stress on the warm, harmonious relationships with both mother and father.

Postive
Harmonious
    f. Doing things with mother which are pleasureful and exciting, with the father tacitly excluded.

    g. Pleasure in bringing mother a phallic gift.

2. Female relationship patterns:

Hostile
Competitive
    a. Jealousy or rivalry with mother or a sibling for the affection of father or a father surrogate; interest in father's doings with another female.

* A "p." (punishment) "score" is added to a previous score when an activity meets with some form of injury, narcissistic hurt, or punishment.

Table III.   *(Continued)*

	b. Resentment or fear of mother as an avowed or tacit rival for father's love.
	c. Failure to win father's love, with accompanying sense of personal inadequacy.
	d. Conflict between parents in which the child sides with father and rejects the mother.
	e. Denial of Oedipal conflict by stressing the warm, harmonious, non-competitive aspects of one's relationship with mother in the family triangle.
Positive Harmonious	f. Doing exciting or pleasureful things with father, with mother tacitly excluded.
	g. Interest in having a baby as mother did; or receiving some symbolically equivalent phallic gift from father; interest in pregnancy and childbirth.
	h. Playing house, playing with dolls, dressing up in mother's clothes, or in some other way doing as mother does.

VI.   "Latency" Configurations: More Sublimated Peer-Group Activities.

    1.   Productivity and positive self-esteem.

        a.   Socialization with peers; group play with well-differentiated roles.

        b.   Industriousness, learning to do things, constructing and planning with others in a common endeavor.

        c.   Turning manipulative skills to creative accomplishment.

    2.   Inferiority:

        a.   Withdrawal from, isolation in, or rejection by one's peer group.

THE SYNTHESIS OF DISHARMONIOUS "EGO STATES": A CASE EXAMPLE *

Recently I happened upon these lines in a novel by Colette: "In each place where my desires have strayed, I leave thousands and thousands of shadows in my own shape, shed from me: One lies on the warm blue rocks of the ledges in my own country, another in the damp hollow of a sunless valley, and a third follows a bird, a sail, the wind and the wave." This figure of speech seemed a beautifully fitting metaphor for a person's early memories, which are indeed "shadows in one's own shape," shed once, but lingering on, ghosts of former selves which were once alive and real. Some shadows of an earlier self are cherished, and in moments of reflection, savored and embellished; others, darker

* Some of the biographical data have been altered so as to insure anonymity, but keep the essential features of the patient's life and character structure undistorted.

shadows, are turned away in shame or dread. One may be so busy being his current self or becoming his projected future self, as to be largely unconcerned with, or even oblivious to, such earlier selves, but they are never wholly superceded. These shadows of former selves, these residues of earlier and more impressionable stages in the formation of one's sense of self, mark the many choice points in one's growth, the evolving articulation of one's personal identity, and the many abandoned selves one might have become.

Consider, for example, the early memories of a forty-five-year-old, childless, married woman who decided to seek psychiatric help when spells of tiredness, lassitude and incipient depression grew increasingly incapacitating at home and at work. She had spent most of her life, and most of her energies, in a career as a rehabilitation worker in a hospital for crippled children. She had been a key figure in developing a professional organization of rehabilitation workers in her state, and was still one of its leading lights. At eighteen, she married a pleasant, passive, unambitious man who neither encouraged nor interfered with her professional activities. They remained childless and the patient worked throughout her marriage.

Two paragraphs from her psychological test report describe some of the patient's emotional state and character structure at the time she came for examination.

> Depression is as prominent in this patient's test performance as it is clinically, but even when the patient was at her worst, she did not seem to give in to her depressed feelings. Rather, she criticized herself for every failure, correcting her mistakes and insisting that she would have to do better. . . .

> Her compulsiveness was even more impressive when as testing went on the depression receded. The emphasis on making demands upon herself, the unwillingness to tolerate any weakness or failure in herself, and the inability to allow herself to express or even to experience angry feelings took clearer and clearer shape. Whatever happened she tried to smile or at least isolate off any resentful feelings she may have had. Severe reaction formations against her angry feelings were integrated into a self-image (and ego ideal) of a person whose life is spent in the service of others in an austere world of stern duties, values and standards. It seems clear that her ego has become thoroughly fused with a severe, uncompromising superego.

Her early memories, when analyzed into their component themes, sort themselves into three distinct thematic clusters. One cluster fits well the austere, highly principled and stoically long-suffering way of life which characterized this woman at the time she presented herself for treatment. Her very earliest memory tells of being unjustly coerced, threatened and then punished by father, who wanted her to confess to something she hadn't done; she stoically and with stubborn adherence to principle accepted all of the punishment rather than tamper with the truth. Another memory in this cluster describes her being forced to eat when she didn't want to. Still another told of her being disappointed one time at her father's failure to get for her one of the noisemakers that other children in the neighborhood had for Holloween: She added, "I was disappointed, but of course I couldn't show it."

A second cluster of memories shows us a girl rather different in quality from the woman we see today. Their emphasis was not on injustice or deprivation, but on doing things with (and for) mother and sister. Her sense of duty and obligation seem warmer and more giving, and were not yet tinged with sternness, bitterness or self-denial. They conveyed a more relaxed feeling of belonging and participation. This is how she remembers herself in her relationship with mother and sister following her father's death when she was five. She told several anecdotes from this phase of her life, all of them sufficiently detailed and sufficiently consistent with each other to justify the conclusion that this second self-representation, with its distinctive affect-state and ego-organization, might very well have served her once as the basis for a viable way of life. One incident, which according to the patient is the memory in which she felt herself to be "most fully herself," was a time when the sister went off to camp. The patient tells not of taking advantage of the sister's absence to enjoy mother's full attention—a response one would normally expect, but rather says this provided the opportunity to make three new dresses for her sister to surprise her with on her return. Another anecdote was of herself, mother and sister reading bedtime stories in the evening. These would be sad stories and her mother before she finished reading would break into tears and be unable to continue. The same happened when the sister tried to read, so finally the patient, who was the youngest of all, had to take over and finish the story for the three of them. It should be added that this cluster of memories was placed by her in the period between age five (when her father died) and eleven, in her representation of life as she believes she lived it.

The third cluster of anecdotes about herself is the most surprising of all. These self-representations came almost as an afterthought, and they were not really "memories" at all. They reveal a self she knows of only through others, one which now seems to her a totally alien, repressed ego-state. This cluster of stories consists of family anecdotes about her before the age of five, and portray a spontaneous, energetic, outgoing, vigorously alive little girl, who does with carefree self-confidence whatever she pleases. She tells, for example, about often running away from home, but running away in a very special sense; she was not running *from* anything, but *toward* new experiences. She once wandered into a store where she saw a women's hat lying on a counter. She picked it up, put it on her head and walked home dressed in style. Another time, instead of going to the movies as she was supposed to do she stayed out in the rain, took off all her clothes and was found dancing around in the nude. Still another time she was found sitting in the back row of a classroom, having decided to join the older children who were already going to school. These incidents were told by the patient with wry amusement but without any recollection of a time when she was such a vigorous, outgoing, zestful, hedonic and self-sufficient person. This third self is now so thoroughly repressed as to seem to her wholly ego-alien. It is part of herself with which she has lost all empathic touch.

This patient has unwittingly put before us three distinct self-representations, one very familiar and congenial to her, another somewhat less familiar, and a third which strikes her as totally strange. Each of these self-representations could provide the basis for a viable way of life, that is, each refers to a feasible ego structure. Each of the three self-representations embodies a particular ego-ideal image which once formed might have set the pattern for her subsequent ego-development. We can, for example, easily extrapolate a course of development patterned after the considerate, more maternal ego-ideal implicit in the second cluster of memories, and arrive at a different person from the one we see today. Had she continued to pattern new relationships so that they would be congruent with this particular self-image and this particular mother-daughter relationship, she would probably also have preserved intact those feelings, wishes, sublimations and ways of insuring a sense of self-worth, which are all implicit in that particular self-organization. This means, too, that she would have preserved the impulse-defense configuration upon which that particular self-image rested. We may borrow a term from Federn and refer to this entire structural-phenomenological complex as a particular "ego-state."

In this case, the compulsive, stubborn, long-suffering but stoic, ego-state was assumed to be the dominant one now only because the attitudes and values expressed on other tests indicate the pervasiveness of her compulsive-masochistic ego structure. It may be, of course, that the patient fluctuates in her adult life between two or more ego-states, or, more likely, that she achieves in some functions a partial synthesis of the affects, ego-ideals, and relationship paradigms belonging to two or more ego-states. In her work, for example, we may sometimes feel the complaisant satifactions of "Mama's good little helper" insinuating itself into the fiercer satisfactions of the more compulsive, more hard-driving adult.

But how well does the "good little helper" ego-state mesh with the temperament and the impulses which found expression in the uninhibited, action-oriented, mischievous, irrepressable ego-state of earliest childhood? To what extent was the later ego-state a natural outgrowth of the earlier one? Was it, rather, superimposed repressively upon the earlier one, to the detriment of the growing ego? In her case we may speculate that these two ego-states were, in fact, quite basically incompatible, and that one of them had to be displaced by the other if a relatively stable ego-structure was to be established.

Perhaps it was with the onset of adolescence that a resurgence of affects threatened to upset this more good-natured, more giving ego-state. Whatever the cause, more and more auxiliary defense mechanisms seem to have been called into play to help maintain equilibrium, and the intermediate ego-state gradually gave way to the one which characterized her adult life. As intrapsychic tension mounted, the patient seems to have adopted an increasingly compulsive way of life, and come to rely more and more heavily on reaction formations against the spontaneous impulsivity of childhood as well as against the anger she must have felt at its loss.

In this formulation, the transition from one to another ego-organization was traced in chronological terms, but this was done largely for schematic convenience. Actually, it would be more correct to speak only of different levels of ego-integration which coexist in any adult ego and are maintained in some hierarchical relationship to each other. Probably no ego-state is ever so effective that there remain no unassimilated ego-states in repression. In work with patients, it would be helpful to know which of a person's abandoned ego-states, though repressed, remain sufficiently compelling to exert a regressive pull on the character structure. It would be helpful, too, to know to what extent a person's adult character structure is impoverished by an overly restrictive, much too exclusive rejection of some earlier, more infantile ego-states.

Let me close with several brief postscipts.

Ego psychology has for many years focussed on ego structures and defense mechanisms which block or re-direct impulse discharge. The early memories data reported above direct attention not so much to defense mechanisms, nor even to a particular defense-style, but to an integrated life style in terms of which an individual may structure relationships, experience affects, and bring impulses to expression. It has become customary to think of intrapsychic conflict as essentially *inter*-systemic, that is, as conflict between ego and id or between ego and superego. In this paper I suggest that we may also conceive of *intra*-systemic conflict between overlapping and incompatible ego-states.

I am aware that I have only illustrated, not defined, "ego-state" in my presentation. I hope it has become apparent, nevertheless, that the term "ego-state" used as I have used it in this paper, is not a new concept at all to psychology nor to psychoanalysis. It has only fallen into disuse.

It is a concept closely related, in fact, to the meaning Freud gave to the term "ego" and "affect-state" in his earliest writings. Subsequently, he redefined ego in more meta-psychological terms, but without in any way denying the clinical usefulness of the earlier, more phenomenological concept. "Ego-state" has from the earliest years of psychoanalysis connoted a germinal psychoanalytic theory of the self, in contradistinction to the more structural theory of the ego which has been spelled out so carefully by Rapaport.

An analysis of ego-structure in terms of a more phenomenological concept like that of "ego-state" has a place in psychoanalytic theory, if only to provide a link between the more abstract language of theory and the more subjective language of the therapeutic hour. It may make more meaningful a view of therapy as the search for abandoned, repressed or superceded facets of the self which a patient may unconsciously seek to revive and reintegrate in the course of treatment. If successful, then the affect and libido buried with the repressed ego-states may once again be available for re-investment in more appropriate, more promising new relationships.

SUMMARY

There is great potential value for diagnostic testing in a set of concepts from psychoanalytic ego psychology which have thus far contributed little to the development of diagnostic test rationale: such concepts as ego nucleus (Glover), ego state (Federn), self-representation (Jacobson), and ego-identity (Erikson). The intent of this paper has been to show with one projective device that this deficiency can be corrected.

Chapter 9

Schizophrenic Thought Organization, Object Relations, and the Rorschach Test

GEORGE ATHEY, JR.

This paper addresses itself to the relationship between a patient's responses on the Rorschach test and his reactions to and behavior in treatment. More specifically, it will demonstrate how the schizophrenic patient's thoughts as organized on the Rorschach test parallel the way he experiences object relations in the transference during psychotherapy. This correspondence may be considered a special instance of the general metapsychological relationship between thought organization and object relations.

ASSUMPTIONS ABOUT SCHIZOPHRENIC THOUGHT ORGANIZATION

In trying to understand and explain schizophrenic thought organization many authors make various assumptions which, unfortunately, are not always explicit and may covertly affect conceptualizations of the schizophrenic process. For example, in the notion of "thought disorder," which has attained central diagnostic significance in assessing schizophrenic thinking, at least two such covert assumptions can be identified.

The Assumption of Deficit

The very term "thought disorder" connotes a deficit. Many authors view schizophrenia as involving a loss of some crucial function which results in or defines

Reprinted with permission from the *Bulletin of the Menninger Clinic*, 1974, Vol. 38, No. 5, pp. 406–429, © 1974 by The Menninger Foundation.

the psychosis. These authors describe the deficit in schizophrenic thinking variously: loosening of associations (Bleuler 1911); thematic interpenetration (Cameron & Magaret 1951); overinclusiveness resulting in loss of conceptual boundaries (Cameron 1939); loss of differentiation between an object, its representation, and associated verbal signifier (Werner & Kaplan 1963); concreteness (Benjamin 1944; Goldstein 1944); flouting of formal logic by transductive reasoning (Arieti 1948, 1959); assuming identity of predicate to indicate identity of subject (Von Domarus 1944); assuming that logical relationships are symmetrical at all times (Matte-Blanco 1959); loss of reality testing (Weiner 1966); loss of the capacity to direct attention (McGhie & Chapman 1961; Chapman & McGhie 1962) or hold a "mental set" (Shakow 1962); failure to screen relevant from irrelevant information (Lehmann 1966) or to assimilate discrete percepts (McReynolds 1960); incapacity to withstand or filter emotional stimulation (Venables 1964; Buss & Lang 1965). However, these authors do not describe the deficits in schizophrenic thinking in ways that could lead to further exploration of either the process by which these deficits occur or the organization of basic psychological functions which might contribute to their manifestation. As a result, these authors view schizophrenic thinking as a state of primary, static deficit in isolation from object relations and more general ego functioning.

The Assumption of Unidimensionality

Another problem with the term "thought disorder" is the implicit assumption that it is a unitary phenomenon. Differential diagnosis too often determines only the presence or absence of thought disorder. Even when the diagnostician describes the specific conditions under which he observes disordered thinking— for example, in heightened anxiety, diminished external structure, threat of loss of dependency relationships, etc.—the systematic delineation of different syndromes of disordered thinking remains unfathomed. By describing thought disorder in a global manner, diagnosticians continually stop short of differentiating distinctive patterns of organization which may exist in a patient's disordered thinking.

OBJECT RELATIONS AND SCHIZOPHRENIC THOUGHT ORGANIZATION

In explaining how thought organization bears on object relations and vice versa, many object relations theorists elaborate ideas similar to those of Federn. He hypothesized that psychotic regression involves a loss of ego boundary

(1952) and an associated loss or alteration of ego feeling and bodily awareness— all due to a basic inability to distinguish internal from external sources of sensation and perception. However, in their writing, object relations theorists emphasize understanding the meaning of the psychotic state through descriptions of *relationship paradigms*, such as: loss of interpersonal boundaries in the context of symbiotic relationships (Searles 1965; Mahler 1968); fusion of self- and object-representations (Jacobson 1954a, 1954b, 1964); and extreme splitting of the ego to perpetuate infantile, incorporative relationships (Fairbairn 1940).

The unresolved problem which this paper addresses is the nature of the relationship between these regressed ways of experiencing object relationships and the patient's thought organization. Ego psychologists assume that cognitive disruption may or may not cause disturbance in the experience of object relations. Federn (1952) in particular observed clinically that while perceptual distortions occur in acute phases of schizophrenia, object relations were maintained. On the other hand, some object relations theorists assume that cognitive disruption is secondary to the fragmentation of the sense of identity intrinsic to symbiotic or undifferentiated psychotic relationship paradigms (Rosenfield 1952; Bion 1957, 1958; Searles 1959, 1961). While some investigators (Freeman 1962; Freeman *et al.* 1965) observe that parallels exist between the deterioration of cognitive functions and object relationships in schizophrenics, the relationship between these two aspects of the patient's functioning remains to be explored systematically.

My own thinking follows that of Shevrin and Shectman (1973) in their definition of mental disorder: ". . . *the disturbance of certain psychological functions bearing on specific personal relationships*" (p. 474). In this definition, psychological functions—conceptualization, anticipation, judgment, attention, concentration, memory, affect, and motivation—constitute the formal features of mental life, while object relations constitute the significant content organized by these functions. Indeed, a representation is a thought or image—an idea formed on the basis of experience—which may exist at various levels of concreteness, depending on both the cognitive and emotional maturity of the individual. The clinical examples to be offered later demonstrate the utility of this assumption.

Shevrin and Shectman's approach differs from that of other authors (Blatt & Wild 1971; Blatt & Ritzler 1972) who, in order to bridge the gap between object relations and thought organization, postulate a superordinate concept of "boundary deficit." Accordingly, loss of the experiential "boundary" between self and other is like the loss of a conceptual boundary between one idea and another. However, while these authors point to parallels that may exist in the disorder of relationships and of thinking, they fail to describe the process by which the interpersonal and ideational "boundary" becomes "deficient."

SCHIZOPHRENIC THOUGHT ORGANIZATION AND THE RORSCHACH TEST

Rationale for Employing the Rorschach Test

The Rorschach test was selected for this study because it reveals various aspects of thought organization more sensitively than other psychological tests. Of course, diagnostic formulations concerning thought organization and other pertinent issues are usually made from a test battery; and using test results from the Rorschach alone, as in this study, limits the scope of psychodiagnostic information to some degree.

Rationale for Selecting Test Variables

This study focuses primarily on Rorschach variables concerned with the patient's thought organization. Excluded from consideration are form level and drive content classifications since these factors emphasize the outcome of a thought process (percept-stimulus fit or blatancy of aggressive and libidinal thought content, respectively). Each variable retained for consideration assesses thought process to a greater extent than do form level or instinctual drive content and has been termed a Thought Disorder Indicator (hereafter referred to as TDI).

Diagnostic Use of TDIs

The TDIs employed in this study are the standard set described by Rapaport *et al.* (1946, 1968) as well as some additional measures developed by Holt (1956, 1968; Holt & Havel 1960). Brief definitions of these are as follows: (1) *Fabulized combination* consists of attributing some relationship to well-perceived proximal areas of the blots when such a relationship is illogical. Thus, reality considerations are arbitrarily set aside, and the blot becomes organized on the basis of an ideational relationship which is of high valence to the patient but flouts reality. (2) *Confabulation* involves allowing a thought process to be guided exclusively by the patient's associations, disregarding the relationship of these associations to the reality of the blot stimulus. (3) *Contamination* occurs when there is a condensation among basic frames of reference which violates the boundaries of conceptual realms.

Rapaport *et al.* are of the opinion that these three major TDIs form a continuum of increasing pathognomic severity. However, their rationale for assuming this continuum is vague: Such responses are thought either to be caused by distortions of secondary process logic or to be a result of the ''loss'' or ''increase'' of ideational distance from the ink blot. In their analysis, the basic psychological processes operating in such responses remain incompletely examined, limiting the utility of TDIs as a source of inference about the patient's psychological functioning.

A number of studies employ TDIs either as a specific group of measures or in combination with other Rorschach indexes to differentiate clinical groups and thereby demonstrate their diagnostic validity. Both Watkins and Stauffacher (1952) and Powers and Hamlin (1955) derived a composite score based on all TDIs and were able to differentiate normal, neurotic, and psychotic groups. With increasing presence of TDIs, the severity of the diagnostic grouping increased. Focusing on contamination, Zucker (1958) and Jortner (1966) found greater incidence of this score in hospitalized schizophrenics than in other patients. In another investigation, Hertz and Paolino (1960) found that a composite score termed "organization level"—comprised of location, form level, and TDI variables—differentiated paranoid schizophrenic patients from neurotic patients.

Still other investigations have concentrated on the general quality of thought process implied by TDIs. Illogical thinking has been found to differentiate schizophrenic from nonschizophrenic psychotic patients (Dudek 1969). More refined measures of altered thought quality (quantified in two scales based on a combination of "conceptual loosening" and "arbitrary tightening" of the thought process) differentiated schizophrenic from nonschizophrenic patients (Bower et al. 1960). Further refinements of scaling were carried out in a recent study (Quinlan et al. 1972) in which thought quality (peculiar, bizarre, autistically reasoned responses), overspecificity (fabulation, autistic elaboration, intrusiveness, irrelevances, confabulation), and affective elaboration (attribution of affective qualities) were found to differentiate between schizophrenic and depressed patients and to correlate significantly with other Rorschach scores suggestive of thought disorder (i.e., fabulized combination, contamination, F − form level, and blatant instinctual drive content). Thought quality and overspecificity also correlated with ratings of bizarre behavior. Finally, one recent study (Blatt & Ritzler 1972) established that patient groups using only fabulized combinations, confabulations, or contaminations showed a linear increase in the likelihood of a diagnosis of psychosis over one of neurotic or character pathology.

These studies focus on differentiating by test scores those groups known to be grossly different in pathology. While supporting the validity of the thought disorder measures, they do not demonstrate their utility in understanding individual cases. Although correlations of group Rorschach pathology with group behavior ratings certainly point to the potential for such understanding, they do not show precisely how thought organization and object relations match in the individual case. By conceptualizing TDIs as more than simply a set of diagnostic signs, this study demonstrates their utility in assessing the emergence of qualitatively different levels of regressed psychological processes in the stream of thought and their operation in the patient's experiences with and representations of object relations with other persons during treatment.

Method of Approaching the Clinical Data

This study stays close to the level of observation in two independent sets of data: Rorschach test responses and treatment progress notes. In concrete fashion, the way the patient responds to a Rorschach card will be compared to the way he behaves in treatment. Couching the examination in terms of the basic psychological processes involved in both arenas of functioning, this study seeks qualitative distinctions in thought organization which can be useful in anticipating qualitatively different events in the treatment relationship.

The two patients whose Rorschach protocols and treatment records are to be presented belong to a larger group of twenty schizophrenic patients. These two patients were selected to illustrate specific notions derived from an examination of the larger group of patients. One patient manifests a thought organization dominated by contamination, the other patient confabulation. Examples of their responses on the Rorschach test illustrate how the patients' distinctive styles of primary process thinking emerged; and the incidents drawn from the treatment progress notes illustrate crucial interactions within their transference relations.

CASE A: A "CONTAMINATOR"

Rorschach Responses

The patient was 35 years of age when she was tested during the initial phase of her two-year hospitalization. On the Rorschach test her capacity to regulate her associations was erratic and capricious. As her associations became more fluid, she turned more and more to reversal and displacement in an attempt to undo peculiar thoughts. Her fluidity reached a peak in the following response:

Response (Card VII):   "An elephant again. [D₃] It's more like a devil than an elephant. The devil is made into a shape like cookies. It looks more like a bear than a devil and its beak. It could be an elephant or a devil. [Choice?] A devil. The eye of a devil. [Cookie?] It's sort of lumped like a cookie would be. The texture of a cookie."

Commentary: Fluidity was apparent in the way the response proceeded from one idea to the next with little transition, without sorting out the relationships among them. The patient manifested autistic logic when she offered a strange thought as a basis for justifying her response when in fact her fluidity was increasing (i.e., it looks more like a devil because a devil is made into a shape like cookies). Actually, this very sequence of "reasoning" introduced a verbal condensation: A cookie can be made into the shape of a devil, but not vice versa. This response was not only a reversal but also involved a violation of the conceptual boundary of each idea by the other, resulting in absurdity.

On inquiry, she used the texture of the card as the basis for the idea of a cookie, but did not correct the mixing of semantic frames of reference. Also notable was the oral content (cookies) which intruded upon phallic content (elephants with long trunks, and devils with tridents and long tails), reminiscent of a strong oral preoccupation implied in her earlier responses such as "cannibals" and "Siamese twins" (in utero). Even the devil was made phallic in an oral manner by being given a beak.

Condensation emerged more clearly in her subsequent responses. In the first response that follows, the patient was still fighting condensation, although less successfully; while in the second response, it was met with little resistance:

Response (Card VIII):   (Card inverted.) "This looks like some sort of ghost again [D$_2$]. Like two sheets being hung on a line [D$_1$]. Ghost. [Q] A great big sheet over the head and arms [D$_2$], big flaps of sheets here [D$_1$]. [Sheets?] One and another, flat and the way they went up."

Commentary: Although the association "ghost" was followed closely by "sheet," they were at first related to separate blot areas. Then these two areas were combined into one, and the ghost became a figure with a sheet over it. The sheets and the ghosts were the same. This confusion stemmed from her failure to recognize the difference between a ghost and someone who puts on a sheet to look like a ghost. It is important to note that "ghost-sheet" is not an unusual verbal association, and the patient appeared to be recovering in her shift from the idea of ghost to that of a person wearing a sheet. However, she had such difficulty maintaining the distinction between fantasy and reality that the verbal association compelled her to confuse the idea of a ghost with that of a person wearing a sheet and then to reveal this confusion by integrating two previously differentiated images into one perceptual area.

Again, the patient could not keep related ideas separate. Her capacity to observe her thoughts and sort them out failed in the face of regressive themes (e.g., ghosts, cookies). In the following response, the condensation occurred with much less resistance, emerging rapidly out of a brief, fluid association sequence.

Response (Card IX): "Two witches on each side [D$_2$], pointing their fangs [area where a finger or hand is usually seen in the act of pointing]. Here is the hood of the witch, and these would be the fangs. [Fangs?] More like a hand.''

Commentary: Again, the patient engaged in a syntactical verbal condensation. "Fangs" was used in place of "finger," mixing frames of reference. The crucial event was the violation of the realm of one idea (finger) by another (fang); fangs would be bared, not pointing. And again, there was a shift from a phallic action (pointing a finger) to an oral aggressive action (pointing/baring a fang). The idea of a witch pointing a finger gives rise to a notion of oral attack more appropriate to a wild animal which becomes condensed with and expressed through the original idea.

Summary of Thought Organization

While there is some affective elaboration and excessively specific ideational embellishment to some of her earlier responses, the most outstanding quality of her thinking is a contaminatory style which emerges blatantly from her associative fluidity despite her occasional efforts to rationalize and document the basis for her responses.

Reactions to and Behavior in Treatment

Observations

Two months after admission to the hospital the patient suddenly developed a psychotic transference to the hospital therapist, apparently reacting to a minor incident: An aide interrupted the patient's discussion with the hospital therapist five minutes early which caused the patient to complain that the aide was trying to take her "whole Ph.D." away from her (one of the patient's goals in treatment was to complete her Ph.D. in biology). On another occasion, when the hospital therapist saw the patient during her prescribed activities, she ran from the building feeling that the therapist was preventing her from getting her Ph.D.

After a month's remission from the symptoms that had brought her to the hospital, the patient began to threaten suicide and finally eloped from the hospital. After being returned to the hospital, she expressed the belief that the hospital therapist was not only trying to take her Ph.D. away but was also trying to poison her with medication. When the therapist ordered special nursing care for her, the patient responded by saying the therapist was "sending her away into the care of strangers."

Commentary

Certainly the patient was fantasizing about her Ph.D. However, there was no clear demarcation between fantasy and reality, the patient's condensation of events peremptorily bridging this gap: (1) Losing five minutes of her time with her hospital therapist meant losing her "whole Ph.D."; she equated a partial loss of her relationship with the doctor (M.D., the person) with the total loss of her Ph.D. (the degree). (2) She condensed the idea of being in treatment with the idea of receiving her Ph.D.; thus, losing treatment time meant losing her Ph.D. (3) Referring to her Ph.D. as if she had already obtained it indicated that she magically experienced the fact of simply being in treatment (i.e., being in conversation with her doctor) as the outcome of treatment accomplished (getting the Ph.D.). (4) By equating the aide with her doctor when he visited her at an activity, she saw the doctor as trying to take her Ph.D. away. (5) Following her elopement and suicide threat, she expressed the belief that the doctor was abandoning her and trying to poison her.

These events illustrate the way in which reality events and the patient's subjective state were equated in her mind. The patient condensed real events with the anticipations she had about the outcome of such events in fantasy. For instance, the patient condensed an actual change in her relationship with the therapist (e.g., his coming to activities) by expressing representations of changes she experienced in fantasy (taking the Ph.D. away or, more generally, losing treatment or the therapist). Different functions and levels of representation were superimposed. In fact, the shifting quality of her condensations paralleled the fluidity revealed in her Rorschach responses.

The patient's social history gives a clue to the source of the Ph.D. fantasy. At age eight, her mother pressured her to achieve in school at a time when the patient was anxious about leaving home; and the patient was unable to handle the double message of "achieve to get love but leave home to do it." This conflict emerged more clearly later in the transference as the central feature of the patient's infantile relationship to her mother. Thus, the idea of the hospital therapist sending her away to receive something she did not want or giving her something harmful to obtain her cooperation was a re-creation of her original double bind with her mother. Her experience of being given medication and receiving special attention was suffused so completely by her fantasy (i.e., being poisoned, being sent away to strangers) that the distinction between fantasy and reality was lost.

Summary of Remaining Treatment Developments

Initially, the patient's infantile conflict was condensed with and expressed directly through her reality relationships. The therapist could simultaneously represent himself, the patient's mother, and the intruder who took the mother away. As the patient began to sense reality support in her relationship with the therapist—support that continued despite her condensation of it with her fantasies of losing it—she was able to talk about her wishes and feelings. To the patient the therapist became a figure having an external reality beyond her fantasies. As this differentiation of the therapeutic relationship from her fantasy developed, she was able not only to look at the multiple levels of meaning many of her communications had condensed but also to link these different meanings with object relationships from various periods of her life, as well as her ongoing relationships with hospital staff. With these gains she was able to enter into a viable psychotherapeutic relationship in which her self-exploration continued. Her experience with the psychotherapist became even more focused on the "here and now," providing a reality stage on which her infantile conflicts could be dramatized, experienced, and examined with increasing contact with reality.

Near the end of psychotherapy she still revealed a potential for condensation when her transference feelings became intense. For example, she was planning an open house party to celebrate her move from the hospital to an apartment. When her psychotherapist asked her to reflect on the meaning of why she had invited him to the party, she became quite angry. She thought he was rejecting her and told him not to come; then suddenly she believed she had harmed him physically. Thus, she arbitrarily perceived the therapist's inquiry as a rejection and reacted with the anger that would have been appropriate if she had been rejected; then she experienced her *verbal* rejection of him as an act of *physical* attack. However, her gains in treatment by this time were such that these lapses were easily overcome.

CASE B: A "CONFABULATOR"

Rorschach Responses

The patient was 23 years old at the time psychological testing was administered as part of a diagnostic evaluation at the beginning of what turned out to be a four and a half year hospitalization. On one of the early Rorschach cards, she showed promise of keen self-observation as well as a capacity to relate her fantasies to culturally relevant modes (e.g., films or art). However, as pressure to express affect built up within her, the idiosyncratic nature of her thinking began to emerge in florid, drive-laden fantasies. At the same time, her self-observation became more reactive than anticipatory, helping her to rationalize but not to correct herself or to stave off the eruption of fantasy.

Response (Card III): "A torture chamber with a butterfly background. Two women are perhaps preparing something in a pot. The two red things hanging down [D₁] appear to be some sign of its being a torture. They seem to be swinging like they're about to knock their heads off into the pot. And the women have penises. They look like something in chains that are in flames. Something with weight that would hurt; the sides caused these two women to catch on fire. The butterfly [D₂] is a symbol of something and is a strange contrast to these torture things. The butterfly in the center is a paradox to these two red hanging things in relation to the women being held here for some reason. Maybe it's a sacrifice on their part. [Butterfly?] It seems to be right there, significantly involved, though not functionally. It's a symbol in the sense that it is red and in the same sense as these two knocker things—the delicate side of life in contrast to the hard, harder side."

Commentary: The patient appeared to luxuriate in her associations which were clearly confabulatory since they were guided almost totally by affect and fantasy. There was also a tendency toward the more usual type of confabulation: The patient linked the meaning of the center red detail to the upper red detail by sole virtue of a concrete similarity (color). Before this linkage occurred, the color was used symbolically (to indicate "torture"), but the symbolic aspects of the response remained interwoven with intense affect and overly specific fantasy. The autistic direction of her thought remained evident as she peremptorily reasoned that it *must* have been a symbol because it was red. In a similar manner she concluded it was a symbol because of the paradoxical contrast between the butterfly and the "knocker things." That the symbol became swamped by fantasy indicated that what appeared to be a creative ideational style was not sufficiently supplied with conceptual end points. Thus, at this point, the patient seemed to lack the capacity to use symbolism to regulate her regression and therefore maintain continuity of subjective meaning and communication.

Response (Card IX): "A woman [D_5 + Dr_2 + dS_2] going up to heaven. This is insane. And she is passing through a kind of gateway. Almost receded, not distant, standing, as if her will is someplace else; her will is not in her body. She is shooting out of this red stuff, as if propelled. The colors are very light, and all that makes me think it's very heavenlike. The discharge like when you shoot off a rocket."

Commentary: The patient's unrestrained elaboration, which itself took off like a rocket, was clearly confabulatory. The impressionistic style and the simile with which she terminated the response seemed to indicate some capacity for recovery; but they were also indications of her comfort with this sort of thinking. The confabulation began abruptly, overriding her evanescent observation "This is insane"; and the control features implicit in her later impressionism and simile seemed more reactive than anticipatory. The tenuousness of her ego boundaries yielded to depersonalization ("her will is someplace else . . . not in her body"). It is to the patient's credit that she could describe such an experience to the examiner during the response without experiencing it herself at the time. Therefore, even in the midst of disordered thinking, she demonstrated some capacity to maintain a task orientation.

On several occasions the patient approached contamination in her thought process. However, condensation did not occur. For example:

Response (Card VII): "Two little girls [total sides of the card] playing in the mud. They're connected. Three years old, facing each other; mud because their faces are blotched up and dark; connected at the bottom because of that real sharp connected thing. [Q] At the bottom it's a sharp line that connects them. [Q] Like a sexual connection, that sort of soft, rubbery line again. [Q] Like their vaginas were together. [Q] They didn't have any legs.''

Commentary: Elements of the two readily available responses were combined in this response—human figures (in the large details) and vaginas (in the small detail in the middle of the bottom of the card). By stipulating the figures had no legs she made it possible to see the line where their vaginas would join, although adding this proviso spoils the fit between the percept and the blot area. The response was a specific type of confabulation in which the introduction of the "sharp connected thing" resulted in an abrupt shift in the relationship between the figures—moreover, a shift that did not become visible in the patient's associations. This shift is distinct from a contamination for the shift was not in the identity of the percepts themselves but in the relationship between them.

That the initial sharpness of the connection became a "soft, rubbery line" indicated the tenuous differentiation of objects that she tried to reaffirm while still maintaining some sort of close, "attached" relationship. There was a sense of intense contact hunger that underlay her apparently genital strivings, as if she strove to kiss with her genitals. It is important to note that the merging of objects which the patient had only approached did not occupy a role in the formal aspects of her thinking (as it would in condensation).

Summary of Thought Organization

In the formal organization of her thinking, patient *B* exhibited a consistently confabulatory style to the almost complete exclusion of any other deviations. Thus, her case is illustrative of the second classification of schizophrenic thought organization with which this paper is concerned. In the context of her fantasies she often revealed the tenuousness of her sense of self; yet she never engaged in the sort of condensation characteristic of patient *A*. Rather, several of her responses seem to reflect a tenacious striving to maintain some sense of a relationship even when faced with the *potential* experience of fusion and condensation of thoughts. In addition, her content remained on a more phallic level, even when suffused by a quality of contact hunger. Overall, rather than manifesting condensation of her thoughts, this patient substituted intense affect discharge and fantasy elaboration for understandable communication of her thoughts.

Reactions to and Behavior in Treatment

Observations

In the initial phases of patient *B*'s relationship with her hospital doctor, she would burst into tears over intrusive thoughts and sudden experiences of intense feeling. The hospital structure was strictly maintained and expressive outlets diminished because of her perceived inability to "tolerate closeness." However, once she demonstrated a capacity to make use of clinical relationships despite continuing fantasies and intense feelings, she was referred for psychotherapy.

Her opening statement in pyschotherapy was, "I like you. The difficulties I wish to work on are my problems in relating to people with whom I get too involved; I can't put on the brakes with either males or females, and I lose my identity." She reported a dream of beginning a beautiful therapy relationship, but the dream then became frightening as it shifted to having therapy with herself in a mirror. According to her therapist, the patient exhibited "affective flooding, blocking of her thoughts, fragmentary thoughts, along with attempts to please the therapist with discussion of oedipal triangles, regression, penis envy, and seductive attempts to discuss the sexual fantasies she was having." The therapist also noted, "She described herself as being like the clay she used in ceramics—she was amorphous, shapeless, and like feces." On one occasion when the therapist wondered with the patient what significance an upcoming trip had for treatment, she talked about drawing a black curtain down on therapy, asserting that when she went on the trip it would destroy the therapist. As she became aware of her increasing disorganization, she began to relate it to various concurrent stress factors.

Commentary

The patient entered therapy with a markedly intense transference and a flood of affect and drive-laden thoughts. Behind her omnipotence and narcissism was a great deal of primitive fear about her identity. She spoke of her tenuous identity as a feeling of amorphousness, a quality which was evident in the object representations that occurred in her confabulations on the Rorschach. However, she was able to talk about such amorphousness without actually experiencing a loss of identity at the time, just as the intensity of her confabulations on the Rorschach did not entail condensations.

She feared that if her fantasies should get out of control she would regress further; and she anticipated in her dream the consequent loss of identity, specifically fusion with the therapist. She feared that if she let her feelings go in the initial "beautiful therapy relationship," the relationship would be replaced by a fusion experience: The therapist would be lost and, instead, there would be only a relationship between one part of herself and another—the therapist becoming only a reflection of herself. Thus, she feared the sort of condensation of fantasy and reality that patient A actually did experience; what might be a form of narcissistic splendor was also partially an experience of fusion.

In anticipating separation, she had thoughts that the therapist would magically be destroyed. However, these were thoughts that the therapist would be destroyed in the future, not a conviction that he was destroyed or hurt in the present because of her intent to go on the trip. Thus, she retained the differentiation between intention and actuality, present and future, anticipation of loss of the therapist and recognition of his actual presence. Her thoughts were only fantasies to her, and her ego weakness was conveyed by her temporary inability to gain distance from these fantasies except through a magically powerful symbolic metaphor ("black curtain").

Summary of Remaining Treatment Developments

As her psychotherapy progressed, patient B's transference became increasingly focused on separations and, to the exclusion of almost any other type of communication, consistently took the form of sustained, overwhelming affect states accompanied by withdrawal into sadistic fantasies. Essentially, her fantasies existed side by side with the actual relationship, resulting in distortions, and at worst took the place of communications about the actual relationship. However, her fantasies were always fantasies and were never condensed with her actual interchanges with the therapist. Despite her fantasies of rejection and death, the patient became able to sense the continuing presence of an accepting, living relationship. As she sensed that her fantasies did not destroy the relationship and that they could be verbalized without losing the therapist's protection, she spontaneously began to document parallels between her current experience and her past relationships, thereby gaining insight into her relationship with the therapist.

It is interesting to note changes in her use of the "black curtain" metaphor throughout treatment. Initially, "drawing a black curtain on therapy" meant "destroying the therapist." As her conflict over dependency and anticipated loss became more intense, she experienced a "black curtain dropping" between herself and the therapist—the metaphor becoming an expression of her fantasy in her immediate subjective experience, from which it was only tenuously differentiated at times. Then her experience became "as if a curtain drops," indicating greater distinction between the change in her subjective state and her experience of or anticipation of loss in the actual events of separation. Finally, she spoke of herself "letting the curtain drop," reflecting increasing awareness of how her withdrawal into sadistic fantasy and her insulation from people in general were responses that she actively made to actual or anticipated loss and that only served to intensify her distress at the time.

DISCUSSION

Thought Disorder as an Active Process

In the examination of these two cases, I have described two distinct levels of regression. However, each patient at times showed a potential for functioning at other levels. For example, patient A (the "contaminator") became capable of a more confabulatory mode of functioning once she began to separate the different levels of meaning which had been condensed in her relationship with the therapist. Indeed, by providing her with a consistent structure, her treatment team gave her an opportunity to experience a stable reality which attenuated her insistent sense of ultimate, pervasive object loss; and she was therefore able to increase her attempts to test the reality of her reactions. As her relationship with her therapist became more firmly represented in her mind, she became capable of tolerating sustained expressions of intense affect and urgent fantasy.

By contrast, patient B (the "confabulator") was already capable of experiencing a relationship apart from her fantasy life. However, her affect and fantasy could build to the point where they would replace reality. She feared that her intense affect and vivid fantasy would carry her beyond the bounds of her treatment relationship with the result that the relationship would no longer exist separately but would become fused with her subjective state. By experiencing a continuing relationship, despite the emergence of her intense fantasy, she eventually recognized this fear and became able to look at the relationship in a more conceptually (although arbitrarily) circumscribed manner. In a sense, by building a backlog of experience with a continuing relationship, which strengthened her autonomy, fears of fusion abated. She could then progress to a level of functioning where she experienced the therapeutic relationship (although in certain arbitrary ways) without gross distortion.

In light of this clinical material, thought disorder may be viewed as an active process of regressing to more urgent, peremptory manifestations of internally represented infantile conflicts. A speculative inference from this finding is that this regression may involve a full rekindling of a mode of organization of psychological processes appropriate to the age of the person when the infantile conflict was taking shape. More speculatively, it may be that it was on the basis of such an organization of representational functions that the conflictual relationship was originally internalized. The diagnostician of schizophrenic pathology must therefore assess the level of organization of basic psychological functions by which the transference relationship is likely to be experienced. His assessment will include a description of the various ways these functions contribute to the internal representation of relationships when the patient is under pressure from infantile conflicts. (Essentially, this same process is followed in the psychoanalytic/psychological diagnosis of neurotic and character pathology.) Thus, while the final path of regression in different forms of schizophrenic pathology may be the same (Bellak & Loeb 1969), it is important to attend to the different degrees of precipitousness with which this path is approached.

Distinction Between Content and Process

Diagnosis can be based on thought *content* or thought *process*. Content may be more or less primitive, but the degree of ego integration will be reflected by the process in which cognitive structures can be employed to modulate and express any content. Thus, a patient may say to a therapist, "I feel fused with you," indicating by way of content a concern about a primitive form of relationship. However, the formal quality of this communication contradicts its content: In the statement, the patient shows clear recognition of the difference between "I" and "you." To be concerned with fusion in a relationship may certainly indicate the presence of deeply regressive preoccupations; but it is not yet evidence for the experience of such regression in the relationship. For the clinician to assume that fusion has occurred would result in an underestimation of the patient's ego strength. Of course, why the patient should feel constrained to communicate such thoughts is another question requiring attention to the overall patterning of the relationship and the patient's motives with regard to it.

Evaluating content in light of process is at variance with approaches suggesting that ego integration may be read from content directly—for example, from the integrity with which the body image is represented in Rorschach responses (Fisher & Cleveland 1958). Patient B (the "confabulator") showed a great deal of "body boundary" tenuousness in her representation of figures but without contamination in her thought process. Patient A (the "contaminator") gave responses (not cited above) in which object representations were partially fused; however, she was able (at least during the initial emergence of her regressive preoccupations) to conceptualize such object representations within the mitigating context of fantasy figures, reflecting a noteworthy degree of ego strength in her ability to maintain the integrity of her thought process. Despite the later emergence of a contaminatory thought process, patient A's partial ability to contain conceptually such deeply regressive preoccupations was reflected in her treatment process: She was able to make effective use of a reality supportive relationship in order to differentiate the multiple levels of meaning in her experience of that relationship.

Certain contents may be sufficiently bizarre to be considered ideational representations of the distorted body experiences of schizophrenic patients (Federn 1948; Pious 1950; Erikson 1956; Winnicott 1958). However, the integrity of the relationship within which such contents are communicated (Schafer 1958, 1960, 1967) and the patient's capacity to draw upon an integrative thought process during incipient regression *toward* infantile ego states (Federn 1952) must be considered.

Levels of Organization of Regressive Experience

Earlier in the discussion schizophrenic pathology was considered part of an active process of regression through which primitive relationship paradigms from the patient's past life were activated. However, while schizophrenic functioning may be viewed as an alteration in the experience of relationships (as emphasized by Fromm-Reichmann [1959]), schizophrenic regression may also be viewed as qualitatively distinct configurations of regressed object relations. Yet, the problem with any such object relations model is that it may lead away from specifying the basic psychological processes which constitute the necessary (but not sufficient) psychological substrate for the emergence of these regressed object relation states. In what follows I shall attempt to make these specifications explicit:

The Confabulatory Mode — Unalloyed Affect-Laden Fantasy Relationships

While in a confabulatory Rorschach response the percepts are at first clear, the patient's associative process and implicated affects go well beyond the limits of the original response which becomes replaced by a fantasy imposed on the reality of the blot. Similarly, the patient who experiences this type of regression in the transference will encounter intense affect and fantasy, and reality will be replaced by fantasy.

By contrast, in a fabulized combination of the Rorschach, clear conceptual boundaries are apparent which limit the extent of distortion. In this case, the relationship between the accurately perceived objects is unrealistic and reflects a preoccupation with certain kinds of self-other relationships. For example, if on Card VIII a patient sees a weasel climbing on a butterfly, it suggests a tendency to peremptorily experience relationships in a sadomasochistic manner, although without gross distortions (if both percepts are well perceived).

Thus, the regressive shift from fabulized combinations to confabulations involves losing the reality basis for representing relationships and replacing reality with affect and fantasy. In this sense, the patient who initially has only an arbitrary preoccupation with the sadomasochistic implications of relationships becomes immersed in sadomasochistic fantasies that are no longer coordinated with what actually occurs in the relationship. Nonetheless, the concept of a self-other relationship is maintained.

On the other hand, progression to the confabulatory level from a contaminatory level of experience involves differentiating the internal self- and object-representations comprising the fantasy relationship.

The Contaminatory Mode — Condensation of Frames of Reference

The contaminatory mode of regressed experience may be seen as the loss of conceptual distinction among basic frames of reference (which in the extreme is manifested in full-blown condensations). The frames of reference are the conceptual dimensions by which reality experience is veridically represented internally and which exist as superordinate structures (Rapaport 1957)—processes normally with a lower rate of change than the flux of experience from which they have been derived and for which they provide a context. Such structures include conceptions of time as manifested functionally in memory (differentiation between past and present) and in anticipation (differentiation between present and future). They include conceptions of space (differentiation between here and there), of concrete sensory events and their symbolic representation (differentiation between action and thought, sensation and meaning, affect and idea), and of personal identity (self versus other). Condensation results in shifting frames of reference and leads in turn to the bizarre thought organization observed by ego psychologists and the bizarre self- and object-representations observed by object relations theorists. The basic psychological process of condensation leads the patient to experience a thought as an action, an anticipated event as an accomplished event, a memory as a current actuality, a sensation as a thought, a feeling as a concept, an object-relationship as an inner state. In his object relations, the patient condenses fantasy shifts with changes in the reality of the relationship. As a result, the awareness of the other person becomes more dim and eventually the patient condenses the changing events in the relationship *completely* with alterations in his subjective state, resulting finally in alterations of only the experience of himself.

Patients differ in the extent to which these two levels of regression coexist as well as in the pervasiveness with which such regressions are prone to occur. The quantitative relationship between the number of contaminations or confabulations on the Rorschach and the likelihood of such regression in clinical behavior has not been explored. However, the clinical likelihood of regression taking such forms will be affected by the nature of the treatment setting within which the patient's transference develops. In applying these concepts, it must not be forgotten that any patient's functioning can best be described by a probabilistic model—functioning at different levels under different conditions.

In light of these considerations, it might be of interest to examine again the response of patient A to her psychotherapist when asked to reflect on why she had invited him to her house party. Initially, she perceived his question as a rejection, viewing his request solely in the light of her own feeling, but clearly retaining a sense of herself and the therapist as different people in a given relationship. Her functioning was like a fabulized combination in which both percepts are well seen but the relationship between them is constructed arbitrarily. Then she became quite angry, reacting with an intense outpouring of affect that reflected the incipient elaboration of her interpretation of his action into an affect-laden fantasy about his unjustified rejection of her. Thus, she began to confabulate. Finally, she became afraid that she had physically harmed the therapist—a contaminatory experience in which a thought or feeling was confused with an action. This incident not only illustrates shifting across levels but also lends support to the notion postulated by Rapaport *et al.* (1946, 1968) that fabulized combination, confabulation, and contamination form a continuum of regressed modes of organization of experience.

Implications for Psychoanalytic Models of Psychotic Functioning

The findings presented in this paper are meant to illustrate the utility of assuming a correspondence between the basic psychological processes in object relations and thought organization of psychotic patients. But the ideas that have been presented also have implications for theory which should be clarified.

Object relations theorists have described the psychotic state as a fusion of self and other in regression to a symbiotic relationship such as between mother and child in early infancy. While this view is not questioned by these findings, it does appear that psychotic transference reactions can occur short of actual fusion, although with the potential threat of fusion clearly present (as with patient *B*). Object relations theorists apparently have not sufficiently considered the forms in which such regressed transference relationships emerge as modulated by ego functions.

Earlier psychoanalytic writers attempted to deal more directly with this facet of psychotic regression. The first step was considered variously as withdrawal of cathexis from external object ties (Abraham 1908), total loss of internal object ties (Freud 1911), complete loss of *part* of the person's internal object ties by detachment of cathexis while maintaining investment in some residual internal object relations (Freud 1914), and total loss of the *veridical* aspects of crucial internal object representations (Freud 1915).

By using the model of a continuum of thought organization from fabulized combination through confabulation to contamination, several results follow which aid in defining regression: (1) Arbitrary disregard of the fit with reality of one's interpretation of a relationship (fabulized combination) is a step prior to uniquely psychotic experience. (2) Psychotic experience begins when overwhelming affect states and intense fantasy result in a sustained loss of the reality basis for experiencing the relationship (confabulation), as suggested by Freud's (1915) emphasis on the crucial loss of veridical internal representations. However, the fantasies which replace reality are also a form of "restoration" of relationships (Freud 1914), expressing the infantile conflictual relationships in a peremptory manner. (3) Finally, the expression of the infantile relationship via condensation of fantasy with reality is a more extreme outcome of this same "restorative" process. The transference appears in its most intense form as an experience of fusion with the therapist in which the experience of a relationship with a separate figure is condensed with and then experienced completely as an alteration in an internal state. Reinvestment of cathexis in the ego (Freud 1911) and the establishment of relationships with oneself to substitute for relationships with objects from which one has become detached (Freud 1914) would appear to be narcissistic maneuvers intrinsic to the patient's turning to autistic (confabulatory or contaminatory) modes of expression of the earlier infantile relationship.

Future research should be directed at further exploration of (1) the nature of levels of organization of regressed experience, particularly in mixed and chronic cases, and (2) the crucial difference between the functioning of less severely regressed chronic patients and the more severe borderline patient and manic depressive patient, particularly in regard to the meaning of confabulation in their thought organization.

REFERENCES

Abraham, Karl (1908): The Psycho-Sexual Differences Between Hysteria and Dementia Praecox. In *Selected Papers of Karl Abraham, M.D.*, Ernest Jones, ed. London: Leonard & Virginia Woolf, 1927, pp. 64–79.

Arieti, Silvano: Special Logic of Schizophrenic and Other Types of Autistic Thought. *Psychiatry* 11:325–38, 1948.

———: Schizophrenia: The Manifest Symptomatology, the Psychodynamic and Formal Mechanisms. In *American Handbook of Psychiatry*, Vol. 1, Silvano Arieti, ed. New York: Basic Books, 1959, pp. 455–84.

Bellak, Leopold, & Loeb, Laurence, eds.: *The Schizophrenic Syndrome*. New York: Grune & Stratton, 1969.

Benjamin, J. D.: A Method for Distinguishing and Evaluating Formal Thinking Disorders in Schizophrenia. In *Language and Thought in Schizophrenia*, J. S. Kasanin, ed. Berkeley: University of California Press, 1944, pp. 65–90.

Bion, W. R.: Differentiation of the Psychotic from the Non-Psychotic Personalities. *Int. J. Psychoanal.* 38:266–75, 1957.

———: On Hallucination. *Int. J. Psychoanal.* 39:341–49, 1958.

Blatt, S., & Ritzler, D.: Some Order in Thought Disorder. Unpublished manuscript, Yale University, 1972.

Blatt, S., & Wild, C.: Schizophrenia as a Disturbance in the Capacity to Establish Boundaries. Unpublished manuscript, Yale University, 1971.

Bleuler, Eugen (1911): *Dementia Praecox or the Group of Schizophrenias*. New York: International Universities Press, 1950.

Bower, P. A. *et al.*: Rorschach Diagnosis by a Systematic Combining of Content, Thought Process, and Determinant Scales. *Genet. Psychol. Monogr.* 62:105–83, 1960.

Buss, A. H., & Lang, P. J.: Psychological Deficit in Schizophrenia: I. Affect, Reinforcement, and Concept Attainment. *J. Abnorm. Psychol.* 70:2–24, 1965.

Cameron, Norman: Schizophrenic Thinking in a Problem-Solving Situation. *J. Ment. Sci.* 85:1012–35, 1939.

Cameron, Norman, & Magaret, Ann: *Behavior Pathology*. Boston: Houghton Mifflin, 1951.

Chapman, James, & McGhie, Andrew: A Comparative Study of Disordered Attention in Schizophrenia. *J. Ment. Sci.* 108:487–500, 1962.

Dudek, S. Z.: Intelligence, Psychopathology, and Primary Thinking Disorder in Early Schizophrenia. *J. Nerv. Ment. Dis.* 148:515–27, 1969.

Erikson, E. H.: The Problem of Ego Identity. *J. Am. Psychoanal. Assoc.* 4:56–121, 1956.

Fairbairn, W. R. D. (1940): Schizoid Factors in the Personality. In *An Object-Relations Theory of the Personality*. New York: Basic Books, 1952, pp. 3–27.

Federn, Paul: *Ego Psychology and the Psychoses*, Edoardo Weiss, ed. New York: Basic Books, 1952.

Fisher, Seymour, & Cleveland, S. E.: *Body Image and Personality*. Princeton, N.J.: Van Nostrand, 1958.

Freeman, Thomas: The Psychoanalytic Observation of Chronic Schizophrenic Reactions. In *Aspects of Psychiatric Research*, Derek Richter *et al.*, eds. London: Oxford University Press, 1962, pp. 294–314.

Freeman, Thomas *et al.*: *Studies on Psychosis: Descriptive, Psycho-Analytic, and Psychological Aspects*. New York: Tavistock Publications, 1965.

Freud, Sigmund (1911): Psychoanalytic Notes on an Autobiographical Account of a Case of Paranoia. *Standard Edition* 12:3–82, 1958.

——— (1914): On Narcissism: An Introduction. *Standard Edition* 14:73–102, 1957.

——— (1915): The Unconscious. *Standard Edition* 14:161–215, 1957.

Fromm-Reichmann, Frieda: *Psychoanalysis and Psychotherapy: Selected Papers of Frieda Fromm-Reichmann*, D. M. Bullard, ed. Chicago: University of Chicago Press, 1959.

Goldstein, Kurt: Methodological Approach to the Study of Schizophrenic Thought Disorder. In *Language and Thought in Schizophrenia*, J. S. Kasanin, ed. Berkeley: University of California Press, 1944, pp. 17–40.

Hertz, M. R., & Paolino, A. F.: Rorschach Indices of Perceptual and Conceptual Disorganization. *J. Project. Techn.* 24:370–88, 1960.

Holt, R. R.: Gauging Primary and Secondary Processes in Rorschach Responses. *J. Project. Techn.* 20:14–25, 1956.

———: Manual for the Scoring of Primary Process Manifestions in Rorschach Responses. Unpublished manuscript, New York University Research Center for Mental Health, 1968.

Holt, R. R., & Havel, Joan: A Method for Assessing Primary and Secondary Processes in the Rorschach. In *Rorschach Psychology*, M. A. Rickers-Ovsiankina, ed. New York: Wiley, 1960, pp. 263–315.

Jacobson, Edith: Contribution to the Metapsychology of Psychotic Identifications. *J. Am. Psychoanal. Assoc.* 2:239–62, 1954a.

———: The Self and the Object World: Vicissitudes of Their Infantile Cathexes and Their Influence on Ideational and Affective Development. *Psychoanal. Study Child* 9:75–127, 1954b.

Jortner, Sidney: An Investigation of Certain Cognitive Aspects of Schizophrenia. *J. Project. Techn.* 30:559–68, 1966.

Lehmann, H. E.: Pharmacotherapy of Schizophrenia. In *Psychotherapy of Schizophrenia*, P. H. Hoch & Joseph Zubin, eds. New York: Grune & Stratton, 1966, pp. 388–411.

Mahler, M. S.: *On Human Symbiosis and the Vicissitudes of Individuation*. New York: International Universities Press, 1968.

Matte-Blanco, I.: A Study of Schizophrenic Thinking: Its Expression in Terms of Symbolic Logic and its Representation in Terms of Multi-dimensional Space. In *IInd International Congress for Psychiatry: Congress Report,* Vol. 1, W. A. Stoll, ed. Zurich: Swiss Organizing Committee, 1959, pp. 254–59.

McGhie, Andrew, & Chapman, James: Disorders of Attention and Perception in Early Schizophrenia. *Br. J. Med. Psychol.* 34:103–16, 1961.

McReynolds, Paul: Anxiety, Perception, and Schizophrenia. In *The Etiology of Schizophrenia,* D. D. Jackson, ed. New York: Basic Books, 1960, pp. 248–92.

Pious, W. L.: Obsessive-Compulsive Symptoms in an Incipient Schizophrenic. *Psychoanal. Q.* 19:327–51, 1950.

Powers, W. T., & Hamlin, R. M.: Relationship Between Diagnostic Category and Deviant Verbalizations on the Rorschach. *J. Consult. Psychol.* 19:120–24, 1955.

Quinlan, D. M. *et al.*: Varieties of "Disordered" Thinking on the Rorschach: Findings in Schizophrenic and Nonschizophrenic Patients. *J. Abnorm. Psychol.* 79:47–53, 1972.

Rapaport, David (1957): Cognitive Structures. In *The Collected Papers of David Rapaport,* M. M. Gill, ed. New York: Basic Books, 1967, pp. 631–64.

Rapaport, David *et al.*: *Diagnostic Psychological Testing,* Revised Edition, R. R. Holt, ed. New York: International Universities Press, 1968.

Rosenfeld, H.: Transference-Phenomena and Transference-Analysis in an Acute Catatonic Schizophrenic Patient. *Int. J. Psychoanal.* 33:457–64, 1952.

Schafer, Roy: Regression in the Service of the Ego: The Relevance of a Psychoanalytic Concept for Personality Assessement. In *Assessment of Human Motives,* Gardner Lindzey, ed. New York: Holt, Rinehart & Winston, 1958, pp. 119–48.

———: Bodies in Schizophrenic Rorschach Responses. *J. Project. Techn.* 24:267–81, 1960.

———: *Projective Testing and Psychoanalysis: Selected Papers.* New York: International Universities Press, 1967.

Searles, H. F.: Integration and Differentiation in Schizophrenia: An Over-All View. *Br. J. Med. Psychol.* 32:261–81, 1959.

———: The Evolution of the Mother Transference in Psychotherapy with the Schizophrenic Patient. In *Psychotherapy of the Psychoses,* Arthur Burton, ed. New York: Basic Books, 1961, pp. 256–84.

———: *Collected Papers on Schizophrenia and Related Subjects.* New York: International Universities Press, 1965.

Shakow, David: Segmental Set: A Theory of the Formal Psychological Deficit in Schizophrenia. *Arch. Gen. Psychiatry* 6:1–17, 1962.

Shevrin, Howard, & Shectman, Frederick: The Diagnostic Process in Psychiatric Evaluations. *Bull. Menninger Clin.* 37:451–94, 1973.

Venables, P. H.: Input Dysfunction in Schizophrenia. *In Progress in Experimental Personality Research,* Vol. 1, B. A. Maher, ed. New York: Academic Press, 1964, pp. 1–47.

Von Domarus, E.: The Specific Laws of Logic in Schizophrenia. In *Language and Thought in Schizophrenia,* J. S. Kasanin, ed. Berkeley: University of California Press, 1944, pp. 104–14.

Watkins, J. G., & Stauffacher, J. C.: An Index of Pathological Thinking in the Rorschach. *J. Project. Techn.* 16:276–86, 1952.

Weiner, I. B.: *Psychodiagnosis in Schizophrenia.* New York: Wiley, 1966.

Werner, Heinz, & Kaplan, Bernard: *Symbol Formation: An Organismic-Developmental Approach to Language and the Expression of Thought.* New York: Wiley, 1963.

Winnicott, D. W.: *Collected Papers: Through Pediatrics to Psycho-analysis.* New York: Basic Books, 1958.

Zucker, L. J.: *Ego Structure in Paranoid Schizophrenia: A New Method of Evaluating Projective Material.* Springfield, Ill.: Thomas, 1958.

This paper was supported in part by NIMH Training Grant No. MH5279-24 and was completed while Dr. Athey was a Postdoctoral Fellow in Clinical Psychology at the Menninger Foundation. The ideas in this paper grew out of the fellowship program's seminars on primary process and research and were refined through discussions with Dr. Howard Shevrin who directed these seminars.

PART THREE

Issues in the Communication of Diagnostic Understanding

Over the years there has been a shift in the nature of the diagnostic test report. Instead of findings akin to lab results, reports are now unique conceptual documents which may serve as blueprints for clinical action (Appelbaum, 1970). The accuracy of such diagnostic conclusions depends as much upon the abilities of the psychologist as on the validity of his testing instruments. In fact, one observer of the clinical scene asserts that, "Properly speaking, we do not validate tests, but rather the statements that are made with the aid of tests. Generally this means validating individual psychologists" (Tallent, 1976, p. ix). And part of such individual validation includes the diagnostician's capacity to communicate his findings in a credible way which invites receptiveness. Tallent (1976) notes that "The best psychological instruments in the hands of an otherwise knowledgeable psychologist are to little avail if that psychologist cannot generate with their use, and effectively present, statements that likely will be pertinent to his clients' needs . . . 'writing, communication itself, is also a psychological problem' " (p. ix; p. 106).

How such communication is a problem, and how that problem may be addressed, are issues examined in the first two chapters in this section. Sydney Smith and Fred Shectman each take seriously the idea that communicating diagnostic understanding is itself part of the clinical process. As such, they discuss how communications about diagnostic matters are subject to the same pitfalls as are other parts of the clinical interaction and hence are worthy of the same attention. Each of the two authors in his own way uses the psychological testing situation as a frame of reference to illustrate his thesis, but the applicability of the principles and issues discussed goes beyond testing per se.

Smith and Shectman thus present a way of thinking and model of working which exemplifies this special perspective on diagnosis. More properly, they mean the term ". . . diagnosing, to indicate its transitive, continuing nature, its look toward the future rather than toward something static or past" (Menninger, 1974–1975, p. 9). This view of diagnosing as fluid and unfolding fits with the viewpoint of Smith and Shectman which is forward looking by explicitly including the referring colleague and his further work with the patient in their conception of the diagnostic process. They stress the special importance for the diagnostician to 'include as part of his task an internal re-creation of both the patient's and the consumer-colleague's inner experience. Examples in their chapters illustrate how this internal attunement can facilitate better acceptance and implementation of the diagnostic information.

The chapters by Mary S. Cerney and Jon G. Allen reflect an application of the point of view inherent in the preceding two papers. Cerney takes as her starting point the psychological test report's usefulness in predicting psychotherapy outcome. In so doing she extends and amplifies the professional literature attesting to the crucial impact which test reports can have in shaping treatment. For example, Klopfer has boldly stated that "to deliberately blind himself and handicap himself as the psychotherapist by refusing to use the tools of assessment available to him, would seem a practice so questionable as to border on the unethical" (1964, p. 392). DeCourcy (1971) and Lambley (1974) provide case studies of the dangers of therapy without prior assessment.

Cerney also illustrates via case examples how the test report can serve as an auxiliary supervisor to help formulate overall strategy, guide interventions, and alert the therapist to countertransference pitfalls. Cerney thus extends the process approach inherent in other papers in this volume by demonstrating that diagnostic understanding need not be filed away once read in a report but can be used periodically to facilitate the developing treatment process.

Earlier we noted an evolution of the diagnostic test report from a listing of psychometric scores to a sophisticated conceptual document. This growth is paralleled by a change in the role of the psychologist from technician to consultant. Tallent (1976) distinguishes these two roles:

> The technician . . . does not interpret his findings, make a judgment as to which of his findings are relevant and which are not, or make recommendations. He is not sought out by the person who made the referral to discuss possible implications of his findings or the need for additional tests or subsequent retests . . . the consultant, by contrast, . . . must have a grasp of both broad and specific knowledge and the ability to reach decisions that may be of major importance . . . he must then decide on what kind(s) of data to seek, which of his findings have relevance, and how these can be most effectively presented. (pp. 13–14)

Indeed, today the psychologist is less a reporter of test scores and more a full-fledged consultant-colleague (Weiner, 1976). Allen specifically addresses the role of the psychologist as diagnostic consultant in his chapter. He notes that historically and traditionally such consultation has taken the form of psychological testing. He goes on to discuss how one can be a consultant without necessarily regarding oneself as a subordinate technician, even within the relatively circumscribed context of psychological testing. From that standpoint, diagnostic testing becomes a tool used by the psychologist to enhance a consultative role, rather than being a limited and limiting psychometric procedure. Allen uses clinical examples to illustrate how the psychologist as consultant can utilize the testing situation to both clarify diagnostic understanding and help formulate treatment considerations.

William H. Smith's chapter rounds out this group of papers by raising several currently topical issues relevant to "open records" and the sharing of diagnostic findings directly with patients. Fischer (1970), for example, endorses "coadvisement" based on discussion of the testing situation by patient and tester. Craddick (1972) advocates mutual interpretation with the client, as well as interpreting the test protocol to both the client and his therapist simultaneously. Mosak and Gushurst (1972) also write of the effectiveness of

> a "double interview" where the major therapist presents his findings to a second therapist who serves as a consultant. The cards are placed on the table: The therapist says what he thinks, and the patient is encouraged to respond with a similar openness. . . . (p. 541)

These authors believe such openness makes the diagnostic process more effective because it is more humanistic. In his chapter, Smith discusses the gains of such openness but also wisely raises cautionary concerns and even drawbacks, while in addition offering some specific suggestions. Smith also provides a way of thinking about issues implicated in the increasing practice of open records. This conceptualization very much grounds his views in the theoretical context of this volume and thereby increases the generality of his viewpoint.

Tallent's reminder of an aphorism by the writer Sydney Smith also reflects a common thread which weaves this section of papers together: "Everything which is written is meant either to please or to instruct. The second object is difficult to effect, without attending to the first" (1976, p. 51). In short, we need to be as rigorous in our attention to how and what we communicate in writing and to our colleagues, as we are in direct clinical contact with the patient. Indeed, the chapters in this section serve to breathe life into Santayana's belief that "The great difficulty in education is to get experience out of ideas."

REFERENCES

Appelbaum, S. Science and persuasion in the psychological test report. *Journal of Consulting and Clinical Psychology*, 1970, *35*, 349–355.

Craddick, R. Humanistic assessment: A reply to Brown. *Psychotherapy: Theory, Research and Practice*, 1972, *9*, 107–110.

DeCourcy, P. The hazard of short-term psychotherapy without assessment: A case history. *Journal of Personality Assessment*, 1971, *35*, 285–288.

Fischer, C. The testee as co-evaluator. *Journal of Counseling Psychology*, 1970, *17*, 70–76.

Klopfer, W. The blind leading the blind: Psychotherapy without assessment. *Journal of Projective Techniques and Personality Assessment*, 1964, *28*, 387–392.

Lambley, P. The dangers of therapy without assessment: A case study. *Journal of Personality Assessment*, 1974, *38*, 263–265.

Menninger, K. Hope. *Menninger Perspective*, 1974–1975, *5*, 4–11.

Mosak, H. and Gushurst, R. Some therapeutic uses of psychologic testing. *American Journal of Psychotherapy*, 1972, *26*, 539–546.

Tallent, N. *Psychological report writing*. Englewood Cliffs, New Jersey: Prentice-Hall, 1976.

Weiner, I. (Ed.) *Clinical methods in psychology*. New York: John Wiley and Sons, 1976.

Chapter 10

Psychological Testing and
the Mind of the Tester

SYDNEY SMITH

Psychiatry and clinical psychology share a unique affliction. They are the only branches of the human sciences where the value of diagnosis is a matter of dispute. A diagnostic statement in psychiatry is likely to be clouded by differences in theoretical persuasion, contradictions stemming from terminological fads, confusions over the usefulness of idiosyncratic diagnostic systems (like Kelly's personal construct theory or the language of Daseinanalysis), or disagreements about definitions of even the most basic terms. *Schizophrenia*, for example, or the term *borderline state* have almost as many definitions as there are writers about these conditions. Generally a medical diagnosis is more straightforward, more likely to be based on laboratory observations, and more likely to result in a specific treatment prescription whose course or outcome can be predicted with a fair degree of accuracy. In contrast, the psychiatrist is likely to use the same treatment on his patients regardless of the diagnosis. Whether the patient is suffering from depression or schizophrenia or a form of character disorder, he will most likely be treated with phenothiazines.

The fact that such difficulties exist in diagnosis has not characteristically served as a spur to resolving these conundrums, but have more often been seized upon as a rationale for the notion that diagnosis does not much matter. In many psychiatric settings, the practice of continuing to assign a diagnosis to a patient is done more out of habit or because of institutional requirements than out of any conviction of its usefulness. Of course, if the treater has only one therapeutic arrow in his quiver, then diagnosis loses its meaning, at least in the sense of differentiating one disorder from another in a way that allows a choice of appropriate treatment. If all one has to offer, for example, is a form of behavior modification or electric convulsive therapy, then diagnosis is mistakenly deni-

Reprinted with permission from the *Bulletin of the Menninger Clinic*, 1976, Vol. 40, No. 5, pp. 565–572, © 1976 by The Menninger Foundation.

grated as having no value, thus missing the importance of distinguishing this patient's complaints from every other patient's complaints. But if the treater is sensitive to the role of conflict, to the existing varieties of ego states, to the conditions of adaptive strength or weakness, to the range of human defenses and resistances and to their pathological implications, then the treater will appreciate the fact that all this information may point up the wisdom of choosing one treatment modality over another.

But this argument is a global one; indeed, these broader issues of deciding whether a patient would most benefit from supportive psychotherapy or psychoanalysis, from marital counseling or hospitalization, from individual or group treatment, can often be satisfactorily decided without the help of psychological tests. Or if the evaluator is interested only in describing the hysterical person or the obsessional character, then one is dealing with concepts so overdetermined as not to be useful in a specific clinical instance. But the psychological tester deals with real cases, with individual patients, not with the generalized person. Or at least the hope is that the final report on the test results will reveal the uniqueness of the particular patient, portraying those life paradigms that describe only that individual's psyche.

A case could be made for saying that bringing all the test references on a single patient together in all their uniqueness into a test report is a manifestation of poetic expressiveness. I am not speaking of rhapsodical writing. I am talking about lean, disciplined prose with a minimum of objectives and a commitment to brevity. The test report should have an evocative power because it is written for someone who will work therapeutically with the patient or someone who may have to make a subtle treatment disposition. The kind of empathic participation the examiner takes in the patient's test responses can stir the reader of the report to an understanding of the same nuances. A careful amassing of evidence from the tests or a sparingly picked sample response can convey with vivid poignancy the nature of the patient's inner world. This task is an essential part of the clinical situation, and we ought not to settle for a dry, mechanical analysis which might be diagnostically correct but does nothing to make the patient come to life. Here are two examples taken from two different test reports on two different patients but ostensibly describing the same diagnostic condition:

Example 1.   The patient could be described as an infantile personality, overlaid by narcissistic, masochistic, and hysterical features. Her infantile core is reflected by her pervasive immersion in affect-laden, wish-fulfilling fantasy, her predominant concern with receiving nurturant supplies in relationships with others, and her minimal tolerance for anxiety and depression. Her narcissistic features are manifested by arbitrariness, self-indulgent protection against harsh judgments, denial of inadequacy, subtle projection, and devaluation of others. Her external reality can become highly permeable and her thoughts drive-dominated. She defends against disorganization by undoing, rationalization, projection, repression, and detachment.

Example 2.   With deadening consistency, the tests roll up a mountain of evidence supporting a diagnosis of an infantile, narcissistic character structure. With her every utterance, one gets caught up in a tidal wave of egocentricity, tangential thinking, infantile demandingness, and a facetious flippancy that carries the examination procedure further and further away from its objective until it finally is cast on the barren rocks of her emptiness, her unreflectiveness, her remarkable incapacity to develop even rudimentary ties to other people. She has developed sufficient alertness and mimicry to pick up the standard clichés about "feelings" and "love" and "guilt." But invariably probing inquiry reveals only great hollows in her psychological development. With this patient, test inquiry is much like exploring an empty cave, where one becomes chilled from the absence of light and warmth, hearing only the echo of one's own probe tapping against the walls.

What one senses in these excerpts, brief as they are, is that the second writer, unlike the first one, was living out the responses of the patient in his own mind, had taken the patient for a brief moment as an object within himself so that the psychological knowledge the tester has of his patient becomes an inner experience. This conception means that the tester's understanding of the processes within the patient come about through a re-creation of those processes within himself.

Recently the historian Peter Loewenberg (1977) wrote a paper containing a remarkable paragraph describing the work of Wilhelm Dilthey, the German philosopher of history. Writing in the early part of this century, Dilthey articulated the task of the historian as: ". . . an inner reliving of the development of individuation. . . . [and] On the basis of this, [the] placing of oneself in the situation; [and in] this transposition, the highest form in which the totality of mental life can be effective in understanding, arises—imitation or identification." Loewenberg tells us that "Dilthey was the earliest conceptualizer of the use of sympathy and empathy as tools of cognition in historical research."

It seems to me Dilthey is saying something as a professional historian I am trying to convey as a professional psychologist: That a patient's feeling when it is lived empathically by the tester may be a pathway from the manifest to the latent content of the patient's response and thus also a way of reconstructing the past.

Freud wanted to show how the latent thought is derived from the manifest content. In a real sense the psychological tester has the same task in making inferences from his data. The way a person turns latent content into manifest thought speaks to the total structure of the personality. From the test responses it is often possible to reconstruct this process, a task probably more important than trying to trace the history of the latent thought. Actually it is the working through of the process of getting from the latent to the manifest content that leads to cure. That task is not the psychodiagnostician's, but it does lead to the realization that in one sense an analysis is nothing but a complete diagnosis. Reconstruction, then, is not merely a matter of reconstructing the past but of reconstructing the process that led to the present state in which the patient finds himself. Even the job of analysis is something more than digging up the past. Freud himself was more a process-thinker than an archeologist. It is also true that as one reconstructs the process, one also discovers the past. This function is not unique to psychology; every science has engaged in it. What is unique in psychodiagnostics, as in psychoanalysis, is the nature of the subject matter for such discovery.

We can approach this task in part through an analysis of the patient's verbalizations. I am referring to the patient's style of thought, outlook on life, his subjective experiences of thinking and feeling. These data always occupy an important place in understanding the patient. They represent formal aspects of the test even though we have no scores for them. They are not "test content" because such things as a patient's style of thought cut across all the tests and run through every patient's verbalizations. And the inferences one draws from these data can extend in all directions—dynamic, genetic, adaptive. There is no one facet of the personality to which analysis of verbalization is restricted. Again, this task represents a poetic aspect of test analysis, and it will probably always remain poetic.

There are three major obstacles to accomplishing the task we have set out for psychological testing—the patient, the tester, and the tests themselves. As psychologists we have to be concerned about the adequacy of our instruments: Are they going to tell us what we think they will and will they tell us reliably? But probably these questions represent the least of our troubles because almost any task can serve as the proving ground for the projective hypothesis. Dr. Herbert Schlesinger used to demonstrate to classes of wide-eyed neophyte clinicians how he could turn the chance contents of his pockets into a respectable sorting test. The tests we use with regularity, of course, do have certain advantages. For one thing they have been developed with an eye toward standardization which allows for the development of established norms. The patient's functioning can in this way be systematically observed; and the psychologist, on the basis of repeated experience with the same tests under the same testing conditions, develops his own internalized norms. The idea that this sensitive job can be relegated to a technician is based on the idea that the tests can yield nothing but a mechanical result. But the good psychotherapist who wants the help of test findings knows that it takes another highly skilled and experienced psychotherapist-tester to recognize what a treater needs to know about his patient.

The patient may also be an obstacle to the diagnostic task in testing, not because he may resist the process—his resistances in testing as in treatment are grist for the mill—but because his illness or his symptomatology may not be accessible for study. We are all aware of the fact that with some patients we can establish the presence of thought disorder within a short period of testing, whereas with other patients to arrive at the same finding may take considerably more time, and even then the result may remain a matter of dispute among experienced testers. This difficulty may be related to the nature of the pathology. As Kendell (1975) points out in his short monograph on diagnosis, there are consistent differences in the reliability with which a diagnosis may be secured. In general the psychoses can be established with greater reliability than the neuroses, the organic psychoses with greater reliability than the functional psychoses, and so on. When the illness possesses features specific to itself—as in anorexia nervosa—the diagnosis is easy, but if no such features characterize the illness, the job becomes more difficult.

Of course the psychological tester is not so much concerned with diagnostic issues as broad as those I have just described, but it is true that in multifaceted symptom pictures, the answers to diagnostic questions may be more ambiguous.

But the most serious obstacle to the task of diagnostic testing is the examiner himself. Schafer (1954) has explicated this point so well I do not need to dwell on it. The psychologist is his own primary instrument of research. He is not only the collector but the perceiver and interpreter of his data. In subtle ways, this process can go awry. For some psychologists, testing represents an assault on the patient. On some level of awareness, the psychologist may look upon test inquiry as a lethal weapon, not to be used in probing the patient because it may do great damage. (These same magical notions may exist in the psychiatrist, making him reluctant to refer patients for testing.) To what extent this attitude represents a reaction formation in the examiner, masking his wish to do the patient damage, or to what extent the examiner's reluctance to inquire into the patient's test responses is an effort to defend himself against an expected arousal of hostility or aggression in the patient would have to be determined in the individual case. Or there are those further instances in which the tester refuses to see pathology but attempts to explain away the patient's every quirk on cultural or sociological grounds. This approach is a way of neutralizing the test findings and always represents an abandonment of the intrapsychic.

There are also those puzzling instances when good diagnosticians who are also psychotherapists feel that in taking on a new therapy case the test results would contaminate their own thinking about the patient. To avoid any influence from the test data they would rather forego—at least for a time—any study of what the tests might contribute to an illumination of the patient's pathology. At this stage of the professional development of psychological tests this attitude is as outrageous as would be a modern traveler who in venturing forth on a long and complicated journey refused to look at a roadmap because it might influence his personal choice of direction.

What I have recounted in this brief communication about testing are some evidences of its value, the need for professionalism in its application, and some of the pitfalls in the way of its proper pursuit. Even when the psychodiagnostician may be committed to psychological testing and to the diagnostic process—even when he is convinced intellectually of its soundness and its vitality—we have to remember that, just as in the process of psychotherapy or psychoanalysis, psychological testing brings the examiner into close range with the patient's pathology. It is not surprising, then, that all the pitfalls to be found in transference and countertransference phenomena apply with equal force to the testing experience. We are not dealing merely with a psychometric process carried out by a technician on a neutral object of observation, as suggested in the early literature on testing, but a relationship between the tester and his patient which in its very complexity encompasses all that we know about the nature of the human condition.

REFERENCES

Kendell, R. E.: *The Role of Diagnosis in Psychiatry*. Oxford, England: Aberdeen University Press, 1975.

Loewenberg, Peter: Why Psychoanalysis Needs the Social Scientist and the Historian. *International Review of Psychoanalysis*, 1977, *4*, 305–315.

Schafer, Roy: *Psychoanalytic Interpretation in Rorschach Testing, Theory and Application*. New York: Grune & Stratton, 1954.

Chapter 11

Problems in Communicating Psychological Understanding

Why Won't They Listen to Me?!

FRED SHECTMAN

Difficulties (if not outright antagonisms) exist between providers and consumers of psychological understanding, that is, between diagnostic testers and their referral colleagues (Appelbaum, 1977), between managerial consultants and their organizations (Leavitt & Pondy, 1973), and among social science investigators, granting agencies, and the public (Shaffer, 1977).

The controversy over the role, utility, and future of personality assessment is a case in point. Many investigators toll the death knell for the professional role of conventional diagnostic testing. Critics drawing on survey data (Shemberg & Keeley, 1970; Thelen & Ewing, 1970; Thelen, Varble, & Johnson, 1968) have implied that clinical and training programs are deemphasizing the role of traditional assessment and that such a function is playing an increasingly less meaningful role in the professional lives of clinical psychologists.*

In view of such dire predictions, it is interesting to note that "the same surveys that identify a continuing place for psychodiagnosis in the graduate clinical curriculum are frequently cited as evidence for its educational demise" (Weiner, 1972, p. 543). As Weiner pointed out, often only certain data are selected to support one conclusion, and diametrically opposed data are overlooked. Indeed, during the past few years a steady flow of other survey findings has demonstrated that competence in personality assessment is required of most clinical psychologists who serve the public (Brown & McGuire, 1976; Levy &

Reprinted from the *American Psychologist*, 1979, Vol. 34, No. 9, pp. 781–790. *Copyright © 1979 by the American Psychological Association. Reprinted by permission.*

* See Weiner (1972) and Wade and Baker (1977) for well-balanced overviews of such allegations.

Fox, 1975; Lubin, Wallis, & Paine, 1971; Ritzler & Del Gaudio, 1976) and is recommended by practitioners as an essential skill that newcomers to the field should be able to offer (Garfield & Kurtz, 1973; cf. Smyth & Reznikoff, 1971). For instance, the American Psychological Association's newly proposed accreditation criteria include specific attention to broad training in assessment ("Proposed Accreditation Criteria," 1978).

THE PREMATURE DEATH KNELL: IMPLICATIONS OF A LARGER ISSUE?

If indeed diagnostic assessment is not about to lie down and be buried, why is it that so many seek to bring that about through selective data presentation? The answer is, of course, multifaceted, and many aspects of it have been discussed over the years (Holt, 1967; Wade & Baker, 1977).

In this article, I deal with one often overlooked factor that causes dissatisfaction and can lead to the incorrect conclusion that the fault lies in our instruments rather than in ourselves. I am referring to the multiple problems that interfere with our effectively conveying our knowledge and better informing our constituencies. I refer to *constituencies* because I believe that the issues and principles I discuss below cut across narrowly defined task boundaries and professional roles and have wider applicability. Thus, much of what follows refers specifically to problems that interfere with diagnostic assessment results being usefully conveyed and received by consumers. Though I hope to offer ideas about how to improve this important interaction in applied psychology, my broader aim is to spell out principles that can be generalized to interchanges between psychologists and nonclinicians as well, including members of the nonpsychological public.

Below, I use examples from my own work involving the assessment situation and process to show (a) the narrow goal of going beyond findings based on this or that battery of tests and illustrating a viewpoint that can apply as readily to objective and paper-and-pencil tests as to projective tests, and (b) the wider purpose of extending this way of thinking and feeling to the work of nonclinicians, like industrial–organizational psychologists and even research psychologists who have the difficult task of communicating with the nonscientific public, including grant-giving agencies. Thus, my use of the term *patient* in this article refers to the object of our efforts, whether it be an individual, an industrial group, or a public agency. In brief, as psychologists we need to employ what we understand about people in order to improve our own ability to communicate to others what we have to offer.

ILLUSTRATING THE PROBLEM, OR WHAT'S WRONG WITH THEM?!

Most dynamically oriented clinicians hearken to Freud. I am no exception, but I want to use something from his writings to depict a way of thinking rather than the content of a theory per se. When Freud first began his clinical work, he regarded the patient's uncooperativeness as a nuisance to be circumvented. In describing his treatment of Elizabeth von R., for example, he wrote:

> It often happened that it was not until I had pressed her head three times that she produced a piece of information; but she herself would remark afterward: "I could have said it to you the first time."—"And why didn't you?"—"I thought it wasn't what was wanted" or "I thought I could avoid it, but it came back each time." In the course of this difficult work, I began to attach a deeper significance to the resistance offered by the patient in the reproduction of her memories. (Freud & Breuer, 1895/1966, pp. 194–195)

Only later did Freud become aware that this seeming impediment was an integral part of the psychological process and not something to be simply detoured by applying a technique. These resistances taught Freud the significance of the nature of the interpersonal relationship—of responding not to the problem that resides in the person but to the person who has a problem.

As psychologists in general and as psychodiagnosticians in particular, we too frequently react as Freud first did and experience the referring source's unreceptiveness to our communications as an irritant or disappointment—something to be grudgingly tolerated or verbosely overridden by the sheer weight of results that support our viewpoint, as if quantity alone would silence and convince the colleague. When we behave in this all too human way, we lose the opportunity to take Freud's next step, to turn our diagnostic light on difficulties arising between the provider and the consumer. When we regard such problems themselves as diagnostic issues to be understood and grappled with, however, we are able to think about them in a more systematic way, analogous to how one might think about a patient's psychological functioning, or a problem in group dynamics within an organization, or a difficulty in communicating technical findings to a nonprofessional audience. In this article I offer a point of view, a way of thinking about such difficulties.

INTRACLIENT SOURCES OF DIFFICULTY AND SOME GUIDELINES

The first line of defense against a breakdown in a consultative relationship is to recognize the developing disagreement and the temptation to become pejorative about the consumer–colleague. If one relinquishes that pleasure and takes the budding friction seriously enough to try to understand it, that psychological act will itself become a powerful safeguard against playing out the discord. As a consequence, several options become available. One can review the assessment protocols with an eye toward detecting themes, paradigms, or at least clues that help place such interactions in the psychological framework of the patient and make them more comprehensible, just as one can seek to relate the disagreement to particulars in the context of what one is communicating, whether it is clinical understanding or not.

Possible breakdowns in a working relationship between clinical professionals may be due to the patient's playing out divisive conflicts in his or her own personality by having the provider and consumer battle via ostensibly professional disagreements; that is, the patient expresses and perhaps lives out intrapsychic conflicts via interpersonal interactions. Such patients certainly include the kind described by Main (1957) in his classic paper, summarized by Burnham (1966) as follows:

> In a study of twelve special-problem patients, all women, Main beautifully described their special appeal, which evokes in the staff member a great desire to help, equally great distress and guilt at failing to help, feelings of massive responsibility for the patient's welfare, and omnipotent urges to rescue her from mishandling by others. He pointed out the patient's unremitting demand for a primitive but impossible form of love, a demand that arouses latent staff rivalries. He added that at least in the later stages of her hospital career the patient may actively split the staff in an effort to relieve her ambivalence and to control the imperfections of the world by dividing it into good and bad portions. (p. 106)

Burnham went on to delineate some of the psychological functions and purposes involved in the behavior such patients elicit, for example, the patient's experience and self-presentation as reflected in internal splits played out externally. We can be alert to these issues in our assessment protocols, and in noting the complementary divided responses by professionals to the patient (or to research results or grant proposals), we can learn more about our own needs and better use that understanding to help our clients, be they patients or not.

Similar to Main's special-problem patients, other patients can unwittingly recreate a family constellation or organizational structure by casting the professionals in certain parental or administrative roles, thereby generating a process parallel to that of the family or work situation. Disagreements in the diagnostic team, for instance, may reflect projected patient and family conflicts which are also expressed via team countertransference reactions (Staff of the Menninger Foundation Children's Division, 1969). A sign of this situation is when one feels absolutely convinced that one really knows best and can best provide for the patient, that is, regarding the other person's complementary competitiveness as his or her blindness. Under such conditions it may help to think about collegial disharmony not so much as divisiveness but as the patient's unconscious attempts to communicate something in the only way available, because the patient cannot yet express such inner struggles in words (Shectman, 1979).

In short, I am proposing that a thorough diagnostic understanding of such patients needs to include what roles the patients may play in creating difficulties in having their assessment findings (and their implications) properly received.

SOURCES OF INTERPROFESSIONAL DIFFICULTY AND SOME SOLUTIONS

Many problems in communication are not necessarily due to the dynamics of the patient or the organization per se but are linked instead to certain impediments between professionals.

More Is Not Better

One such interference is *information overload*. Diagnosticians typically know more about the patients than they should include in their communications to the referring colleagues. In fact, part of the task of all psychologists is to choose just what needs to be communicated out of the wealth of material at their disposal. A crucial question diagnosticians should ask of themselves is, What do consumers really need to know to help them make the decisions they will be faced with? In the clinical area, for instance, the findings should be geared to treatment issues. Otherwise, if one subjects the colleague to excessive (if not overwhelming) understanding, the essential findings will be diluted or obscured.*

We're All Human, But We're Not All Alike

There is another interfering issue that is also related more to professionals than to patients or other targets of our efforts. Today, poor communication between colleagues could easily arise out of the current interdisciplinary friction between the two professional societies (APAs) and how that reverberates and filters down to possible problems between individuals. Psychologists and psychiatrists are thus especially vulnerable to playing out strife via only too human battles over who is most competent or best able to care for the patient.

---

* Siebolt Frieswyk reminded me of these ideas, which Herbert Schlesinger and Howard Shevrin have raised in their meetings with Psychology Fellows in the Menninger Foundation's Post-Doctoral Training Program.

Nevertheless, there is more to professional differences than just the contemporary rivalry, and a sense of those differences may help to understand better why diagnostic findings are not as well received as one would like. Research has related differences in viewpoint among disciplines to differences in training inherent in discipline affiliation (Colson & Coyne, 1978):

> Our data suggest that differences in point of view and in basic premises about clinical concepts are more the rule than the exception. . . . For example, when making judgments about severity of disturbance, nurses focus on disruptive and explosive behavior, social workers on social skills and social attractiveness, and treating psychiatrists on peculiarity and alienation. . . . Thus, what may at first be seen as differences in opinion should in fact be appreciated as differences in conceptualization and point of view. This research may help us recognize that differences in points of view are a natural and inherent part of . . . [our] work and should not necessarily be viewed as disputes or personality clashes. Rather, at its best, the emergence of such differences should be seen as an indication of effective team communication and of a team atmosphere which facilitates diagnostic work. The research supports the conjecture . . . that division and disruption in . . . [collaboration] will most likely occur when differences in perspective are ignored or suppressed. (pp. 420–421; see also Chance, 1963)

Thus, the provider who responds to the referral issues alone and not to the person making the referral repeats Freud's mistake and that of diagnosticians who respond to referral questions as if they existed in a vacuum. In short, such providers forget that they, too, are in an interpersonal relationship, just as they were with the patient during the assessment process, and just as referring colleagues were and will be before and after that process. Such forgetting makes the psychologist more vulnerable to missing the unspoken needs of the referring colleague and having the assessment findings go unheeded—hence the need to appreciate the different viewpoint the colleague may be bringing to bear. Taking that into account but not slavishly submitting to it, perhaps we can better recognize what the treater needs to know about the patient that we can provide. *All too often, I fear, we write for our supervisors or each other under the guise of writing for a colleague.*

CONSUMER'S EXPERIENCE AND THE GOLDEN FLEECE EPISODE: A CASE IN POINT

The importance of taking the consumer's experience and cognitive set into account is dramatically illustrated by the controversy surrounding Senator Proxmire's "Golden Fleece Award." In this very Journal, Shaffer (1977) used this controversy as a case study in public misunderstanding of the nature of knowledge. . . .

If students, or Congressmen, do not understand the epistemological assumptions of social science, they will use "common sense" as a basis of evaluation. Against such a background, basic research in social science will not be appreciated. (pp. 814; 819)

Shaffer rightly challenged us to take into account such differences between ourselves and our constituencies, noting for instance that "clearly, technical language obscures the nature of the study and its value to the nonprofessional" (p. 822).

Bevan (1976) also issued a call for psychologists to take seriously the need to help the nonprofessional public better understand their hard-won knowledge:

I begin with the premise that the public's confidence in science and technology as significant instruments of social purpose will depend ultimately on an understanding of the character of these fields as social institutions and the activities associated with them as the reflection of a particular way of looking at the world. (p. 481)

MISTAKEN ASSUMPTIONS ABOUT OUR ROLE

Mutual dissatisfaction and disappointment also occur when the consumer expects more than the contracted-for service can deliver. When this happens, consultation with a colleague is more useful than are assessment results. For instance, what Schafer (1954) called the "oracular aspect" of the clinical tester's role can lead the consumer to expect *the* answer. And who is immune to succumbing to the temptation of omniscience? That longing can readily be stimulated by the current professional rivalry and the all too human wish to demonstrate one's unassailable expertise by dispensing pronouncements wrapped in the cloak of scientific objectivity. But we pay a price for such a stand. The higher our pedestal, the farther we eventually have to fall—and regrettably, our patients with us.

For instance, the referring clinician may ask if a patient is suicidal or in need of hospitalization. Is it really within our ability to answer such questions in the form in which they are asked, that is, in an absolute and static way as if the answer could be *yes* or *no*? Do the evaluation data contain all the information necessary to answer such a question? Hardly, because a prediction is being requested, and "measures of personality processes alone cannot and should not be expected to predict behavior, unless the key situational influences happen to be closely tied to personality variables that are validly assessed by the diagnostic measures being used" (Weiner, 1972, p. 535). Thus, unless one has knowledge of the environment in which the patient will be functioning, such questions cannot be answered. What the diagnostician can do, however, is help to specify

(a) the patient's vulnerabilities to resort to certain actions (e.g., impulse control problems, intolerance of sadness, etc.), (b) the conditions that could trigger a suicide attempt, and (c) the conditions under which the patient is less likely to act in a self-destructive fashion.

Should the patient be hospitalized? Test-based statements can be used to answer under what conditions and in what treatment environment the patient has a reasonable chance to be helped. But if one says more on the basis of the assessment data alone, one risks "cantilevering himself beyond his assessment data" * and will eventually compromise one's credibility. "Modesty and stipulated degrees of confidence reassure the . . . [consumer] that the psychologist knows the limitations of his tests, of himself, and of the prediction of human behavior" (Appelbaum, 1970, p. 353).

What this implies is a hard-earned sense of professional humility and restraint. The importance of these attitudes is demonstrated by Gibb's (1961/1973) pertinent research on "defensive communication":

> In the writer's experiment, listeners often perceived manifest expressions of certainty as connoting inward feelings of inferiority. They saw the dogmatic individual as needing to be right, as wanting to win an argument rather than solve a problem, and as seeing his ideas as truths to be defended. This kind of behavior often was associated with acts which others regarded as attempts to exercise control. . . .
>
> One reduces the defensiveness of the listener when he communicates that he is willing to experiment with his own behavior, attitudes and ideas. The person who appears to be taking provisional attitudes, to be investigating issues rather than taking sides on them, to be problem-solving rather than debating, and to be willing to experiment and explore tends to communicate that the listener may have some control over the shared quest or the investigation of the ideas. If a person is genuinely searching for information and data, he does not resent help or company along the way.
>
> The implications of the above material for the parent, the teacher, the manager, the administrator, or the therapist are fairly obvious. Arousing defensiveness interferes with communication and thus makes it difficult—and sometimes impossible—for anyone to convey ideas clearly and to move effectively toward the solution of therapeutic, educational, or managerial problems. (pp. 248–249)

Thus, awareness of one's limitations and role also helps guard against being idealized as an oracle. Clinicians know all too well that the other side of such idealization is envy—an experience that can lead consumers to seek out psychologists eagerly, only not to hear their findings. The consumer may lose the

---

* Herbert Schlesinger has used this graphic expression in his cautionary remarks to Psychology Fellows in the Menninger Foundation's Post-Doctoral Training Program.

security of having a consultant with *the* answer, but he or she can gain in having a consultant who can help him or her deal with the anxiety raised by such questions—a coprofessional who can help the referring colleague better reason about treatment or other alternatives. Moreover, the diagnostician may also be helpful in alerting the colleague to what the patient is evoking in him or her— perhaps crucial experiential diagnostic information which may have direct treatment implications and on which the assessment data may shed light.

TOO GOOD FOR OUR OWN GOOD?
A KNOTTY PARADOX

One reason assessment procedures are so powerful is that they are able to clarify the principles by which the patient implicitly develops his or her world. They illuminate not only the patient's dynamics but the structural organization of that personality as well, that is, not only the content of the container but the way in which the container itself is constructed. David Rapaport (1950/1967), the father of many current assessment approaches, made the following assumption on which diagnostic testing is based:

> Every behavior segment bears the imprint of the organization of the behaving personality, and permits—if felicitously chosen—of reconstruction of the specific organizing principles of that personality. . . . It is assumed that these behavior segments bear the imprint of the organization of the subject's personality, and therefore it is expected that the test performance will be revealing of that personality. (pp. 339–340)

The very power of diagnostic testing to illuminate what is not so easily accessible clinically is, of course, just why colleagues seek out psychologists. Nonetheless, the ability of diagnosticians to discuss what is not so evident may also paradoxically work against their ideas being accepted. Specifically, what these clinicians infer may not conform enough with the clinical picture to be accepted by consumer–colleagues. According to the results of the Menninger Foundation's Psychotherapy Research Project (Appelbaum, 1976):

> A study was made of the relative effectiveness of psychological testing compared to all other sources of psychiatric information with regard to global diagnostic understanding, treatment recommendations, and treatment predictions. Both the testing done for research purposes and the ordinary clinical test reports were better predictors for all three questions than was the psychiatric material. (pp. 562–563)

Although the test report alone was a more accurate predictor, it was apparently ignored, for when disagreement occurred between test and nontest (clinical) data, the psychiatrists incorrectly believed the nontest information (Appelbaum, 1977). This finding is all the more striking because "the clinical test report demonstrates its superiority over the psychiatrist, despite the psychiatrist having the clinical test report's information at his disposal" (Appelbaum, 1977, p. 260). In other words, the test information was diluted when it was combined with other (nontest) information, despite the oft heard banality that the more information available about the patient, the greater the understanding! In fact, Appelbaum boldly asserted that "the unvarnished fact of the matter is that major questions about these patients would have been better answered if the examinations had consisted solely of testing" (p. 260).

Such an assertion could unfortunately further stimulate the oracular wishes previously noted and cause psychodiagnosticians to make pronouncements far beyond their limitations. In fact, one likely reason for the demonstrated accuracy of the test findings in the Menninger Foundation's Psychotherapy Research Project is that the psychologists were predicting to a situation they knew well, namely, treatment; they were able to assess many of the crucial variables which make for success or failure in that special environment.

But what can account for the finding that psychiatrists did not use the test information they had? Appelbaum (1977) proposed that "in the minds of the psychiatrists, nontest data were more compelling and convincing" (p. 261). One reason for this may well be that the gap between the clinical findings and the test implications was too great for the psychiatrists to overcome, since one's own ideas about a patient are usually far more persuasive than another person's. And this may be especially so when one believes the patient to be healthier than the testing suggests, a rather frequent occurrence. An explanation for why the test information was downplayed comes from the finding that "the largest single source of error was in the psychiatrist's ignoring the clinical test report findings of the severity of the patient's difficulties" (Appelbaum, 1977, p. 262).

THE CRUCIAL IMPORTANCE OF OUR IMPACT ON THE CONSUMER'S EXPERIENCE

Consumers are apt to experience too much gloom and perhaps feelings of nihilism when a patient's (or organization's) difficulties are so amply portrayed by assessment reports or when research results are so unexpected and disconcerting in their implications.* They may then protect themselves against this sense of hopelessness by ignoring the test report, especially if in their work with the

---

* Part of the ongoing heated controversy over alleged racial differences in intelligence may well be due to such a factor.

patient they see little of the severity of illness. Unfortunately, psychologists are more adept at describing psychopathology than health. This is not surprising, since they earn their bread and butter primarily by elaborating the less evident bases for the patients' distress, which brings them to seek help in the first place. I am not implying that diagnosticians should water down the severity of what they discover; minimizing disturbances would certainly be no service to the patient! Instead, psychologists should improve their ability to articulate what is right with the patient as well as what is wrong.

I do believe, however, that findings would be received better by the consumer if psychologists would consider the consumer's psychological state. The now classic Hawthorne experiments (Roethlisberger & Dixon, 1940) illustrate just this point: With the introduction of each new incentive, worker productivity grew. And these increases were sustained and even rose after the workers' return to the original working conditions. It appears that the workers were motivated not as much by external incentives as by the increased internal good feeling based on their experience of being cared for as individuals rather than as mere cogs in an industrial machine.

Similarly, we need to take the consumer's experience into account by presenting our findings in a way that evokes an empathic participatory involvement. As Gibb (1973) submitted, "One way to understand communication is to view it as a people process rather than as a language process. If one is to make fundamental improvement in communication, he must make changes in interpersonal relationships" (p. 242).

The Need for Internal Re-Creation

One way to facilitate just such changes is to communicate our findings in a way that goes beyond test data or research results. We need to bring to life the person who generated the data, or spell out the research implications meaningful to the consumer. Just as Freud needed to temper his emphasis on technique by taking the patient and the relationship into account, so we need to be more patient and consumer centered and less oriented to data or results per se. Specifically, the more clearly the patient or situation is discussed and understood from the inside, rather than described from the outside, the more likely it is that the consumer will experience what we communicate and perhaps be more receptive to the findings. In the clinical domain, the way these understandings are conveyed

> should have an evocative power because . . . [they are intended] for someone who will work therapeutically with the patient or someone who may have to make a subtle treatment disposition. The kind of empathic participation the examiner takes in the patient's test reponses can steer the reader of the report to an understanding of the same nuances. A careful amassing of evidence from the tests or a sparingly

picked sample response can convey with vivid poignancy the nature of the patient's inner world. This task is an essential part of the clinical situation, and we ought not to settle for a dry, mechanical analysis which might be diagnostically correct but does nothing to make the patient come to life. (Smith, 1976, pp. 566–567)

Of a psychologist who does make the patient come alive in his report, however, one might say that he

was living out the responses of the patient in his own mind, had taken the patient for a brief moment as an object within himself so that the psychological knowledge the tester has of his patient becomes an inner experience. This conception means that the tester's understanding of the processes within the patient come about through a re-creation of those processes within himself. (Smith, 1976, p. 568)

Just as the psychologist needs to re-create internally the processes within the patient that give rise to the understanding of the patient, so the psychologist maximizes the chance of his or her findings being well received if he or she creates a parallel process with regard to the referring colleague. To put oneself truly in the role of the other is, of course, no small feat. For one to achieve this internally re-created state, one must be able to empty oneself temporarily of one's self; in other words, to sense from the inside what life is like for the other person, whether client or colleague; to look at things from a mutually shared "inside" while simultaneously keeping a sense of separateness and one's own frame of reference against which the other person's viewpoint and experience are contrasted.* Erikson (1958) called this "disciplined subjectivity."

Perhaps only via an internal re-creation of the referrer's role can one sense an important but unasked question or issue—maybe because it is covert and only at best partially conscious for the referring colleague. Moreover, when one is in this internally re-created state, one is better able to distinguish a request for assessment per se from the referrer's dimly perceived need for consultation with a colleague, which may unwittingly take the form of an assessment request as a ticket of admission or way of asking for help. If this is undetected, the assessment findings may be unreceived because they are not basically what was wanted. The same point applies to pseudoquestions asked of an organizational consultant and to special projects assigned to a researcher.

Static Versus Process Orientation: The Impact of Language on Experience

Related to the importance of an internal re-creation is the impact of the language used to convey our findings. Language carries with it a conceptual viewpoint

---

* I am indebted to Cesar Garza for helping me make this point explicit.

that makes for differentially elicited experiences in the consumer. Thus, I think we tend too much to present our findings (e.g., patient disturbance) in static statements—as if that is just the way it is. As consumers ourselves, we know how it feels to have such disheartening information dumped on us (with all the meanings of *dumped on*).

But note the potential for a different experience if the same findings are presented less from a descriptive (external) point of view and more from an experiential (internal) point of view, as mentioned above (cf. Shectman, 1979). For instance, it is one thing to describe with deadening impact the severity of the patient's thought difficulties and how perplexed and even autistic he can become. It is quite another thing to add that the patient uses his disorganized and unstable thought organization to thwart and befuddle others, thereby disparaging them and consequently hiding, protecting, and amusing himself in the process. Similarly, one can stop at spelling out the multiple indices of a patient's disturbance that lead one to think of a chronic condition. Or one can go on to state that the patient has not succumbed to this state but is vulnerable to it as a way of inviting others and the patient herself to regard her state as a hopeless one—thus avoiding what she would otherwise need to face if she took the risk of having hope. Such ways of understanding and communicating invite the consumer's empathy for the patient, based on an appreciation of the patient's need to be a certain way in order to manage certain psychological issues. In this instance, the patient is appearing hopeless to protect herself against getting her hopes up and then being vulnerable to disappointment. The implication here is that the patient is in an ongoing process with aims and purposes, rather than statically fixed and frozen. This implication carries far more hope that things might be altered if certain maladaptive problem-solving efforts were worked on, thereby lessening the potential of the consumer to feel as defeated and helpless as the patient.

THE NEED TO CHALLENGE ONESELF

This way of thinking about their clinical contribution challenges psychologists to view patients (and people in general) as ever engaged in activity; that is, however inexplicable it may seem, people do things for reasons and create their own experiences, situations, and activities. This model of the person is reminiscent of Frank's (1948) view of "the personality as a dynamic process, the continued activity of the individual who is engaged in creating, maintaining, and defending that 'private world' wherein he lives" (p. 8). As Harty (Note 1) asserted:

> The test report that follows [such] principles . . . is more likely to be read, understood, and used by persons engaged in the therapeutic work with the patients. This

is because [these principles] . . . force the test report writer to address the questions of greatest relevance to the therapist in his work. Simply put, these questions are: What is the person doing? What do his actions mean to him? What are their purposes? What else might he be doing if he were not doing this? It is at this level, and in this language, that therapists talk to their patients. . . . [From this viewpoint, then] the essential task of the treater becomes not to discover the patient's secrets, but to describe his secret-keeping; not to expose his weaknesses, but to clarify how he weakens himself; in short, not to diagnose what the patient is, has, or contains, but rather to understand and convey as fully as possible what the patient is doing. (pp. 8–9)

And what the patient is doing will be done to and in a relationship with the diagnostician and the treater. Thus, the more such action can be made explicit by the diagnostician, the more direct relevance his or her assessment results will have, and the more likely it is that they will be received by the colleague. Instead of just another chronic patient, the aforementioned patient may, for example, be experienced and presented as someone in an ongoing acute state who has an investment in being chronic and who is therefore actively doing something to others to elicit just that reaction.

It is traditional to regard a psychiatric condition as chronic if it has existed for a long time, as if it were a temporal matter alone. What is missed in that viewpoint, however, is that a patient may have been struggling for a long time against succumbing to her disturbance. Thus, some of her psychological functions may be intact and others may not. But either way, the assessment of psychological functions (and their degree of impairment) would be the key because such an assessment is linked to current functioning, not to a temporal dimension. Thus, the struggle itself may be chronic but the resolution may not. From this standpoint, a patient who has successfully been warding off the inroads of her disturbance for a long time would appear to be in an acute state, which is a way of thinking about her that is more in tune with her frame of mind than one that would regard her condition as chronic because she has been troubled for many years. The more the psychologist can help the colleague be in tune with the patient's frame of mind, the better the chance for meaningful treatment to occur.

One key to being in tune is an understanding of the patient's psychological functions, their impairments, and the patient's attitude toward his or her impairments, that is, the stance of the ego—and that is well within the psychologist's domain. In fact, understanding and experiencing the patient in the way I propose facilitates one's being in tune with the referring treater, for it is the patient's functioning with which he or she will be confronted. And instead of just presenting what one will have to contend with, such findings will be much more palatable if one can specify the conditions under which shifts occur, and perhaps how the diagnostician used himself or herself to facilitate the shifts, that is, firmness at one point, accepting encouragement at another point in the assessment process, and maybe an interpretation of how the patient is dealing with certain issues in response to the evaluation (e.g., giving up easily on some items in order to protect his or her self-esteem). The impact of such an interpretation on subsequent test performance would be important diagnostic information. The consumer is then in a position to draw his or her own conclusions regarding the treatment implications of such information. The consumer will be more receptive to the findings because he or she can then feel that something can be done with them, rather than feeling discouraged or ignoring the findings.

THE NEED TO RISK ONESELF

This way of assessing the patient implies an active interaction that includes but goes beyond being the passive observer and recorder of test responses. Even more, it requires an entering into the patient's inner object world via an internal re-creation of it. This disciplined permeability or interpenetration of the patient's and diagnostician's inner worlds requires a delicate internal balance and is quite psychologically demanding. It is probably because this is so effortful a state to develop and sustain that many examiners tend to focus on test scores and dry, mechanistic inferences instead of the processes that give rise to such responses. If one uses one's self in this different way, one is vulnerable to risking one's own sanity every time one truly meets with ("takes in") a patient (Searles, 1959).

A major reward of working this way, however, is that one is able to provide one's colleague with an understanding of the patient that makes the patient feel deeply understood. Consequently, the patient may experience the special togetherness felt when one is truly understood. It is not the cognitive understanding alone that is so satisfying. It is the simultaneous experience that the helper is experientially attuned to the patient and hence psychologically together with him or her. *When one feels thus understood, one does not feel alone.* And a colleague may experience some of that as well. The colleague is less professionally alone when the psychologist at least partially re-creates the colleague's inner world and provides understanding that enables him or her to do the job better—be that treating patients, helping an organization with a problem, or better communicating with a nonscientific segment of the public, like many grant-giving agencies.

BRIDGING THE GAP BETWEEN PROVIDER AND CONSUMER

But what if the psychologist does not take his or her colleague into account? And what if the assessment results lead the examiner to disagree with the clinical picture of the patient and the issues raised? Does not the psychologist unwittingly invite the referrer to discount the findings if he or she just flat out presents an unexpectedly different picture? Even if the referring colleague accepts the assessment findings, they may be so different from what he or she has experienced first-hand with the patient that it may be hard to assimilate them experientially—unless the colleague has an internal anchoring base that can be used to bridge the gap between the clinical and the assessment findings. One way to bridge the gap is for the psychologist to "express his own surprise at various test findings, thus leading the reader along empathically as well as intellectually toward the shared discovery of the hitherto overlooked aspects of the patient. By the end of the report the reader has made his own discovery, so that it is now easier for him to manage whatever difficulties he may have in revising his opinions" (Appelbaum, 1970, p. 351).

Another way of bridging the gap is by using a discontinuity in the clinical picture as a pivotal issue around which to organize one's findings (Shevrin & Shectman, 1973). By focusing on a crucial incongruity the colleague will have to face, the psychologist can use a mutually shared beginnning point. As a result, the colleague will be more involved in seeing the various issues that unfold from the shared clinical starting point. For instance, if an obviously intelligent college student complains of inability to concentrate and study, why begin the report with a statement about his IQ? Will the reader not be more engaged if one immediately addresses how not concentrating is a compromise expression of rebelliousness by a frightened patient? One might elaborate how the patient fears that his fragile sense of self will be further undermined if he does not protect himself by covertly balking at oppressively felt demands to conform.

CONCLUSION

It is just this simultaneous sensitivity to both the patient's struggles and the referring colleague's need to be able to understand and help do something about those struggles that is the challenge. In short, just as one assesses and facilitates a diagnostic and therapeutic alliance with a patient, so one needs to do that with a referring colleague—helping to develop a kind of consultative alliance in which the kinds of interprofessional and other difficulties I have discussed are themselves the objects of mutual scrutiny, open discussion, and collaborative endeavor. This is as essential for nonclinicians and their crucible of involvement as for diagnosticians and their patients.

REFERENCE NOTE

1. Harty, M. *Action language in the psychological test report*. Paper presented at the meeting of the Society for Personality Assessment, Tampa, April 1978.

REFERENCES

Appelbaum, S. A. Science and persuasion in the psychological test report. *Journal of Consulting and Clinical Psychology*, 1970, *35*, 349–355.

Appelbaum, S. A. Objections to diagnosis and diagnostic psychological testing diagnosed. *Bulletin of the Menninger Clinic*, 1976, *40*, 559–564.

Appelbaum, S. A. *The anatomy of change*. New York: Plenum Press, 1977.

Bevan, W. The sound of the wind that's blowing. *American Psychologist*, 1976, *31*, 481–491.

Brown, W. R., & McGuire, J. M. Current psychological assessment practices. *Professional Psychology*, 1976, *4*, 475–484.

Burnham, D. The special-problem patient: Victim or agent of splitting? *Psychiatry*, 1966, *29*, 105–122.

Chance, E. Implications of interdisciplinary differences in case description. *American Journal of Orthopsychiatry*, 1963, *33*, 672–677.

Colson, D., & Coyne, L. Variation in staff thinking on a psychiatric unit. *Bulletin of the Menninger Clinic*, 1978, *42*, 414–422.

Erikson, E. H. The nature of clinical evidence. *Daedalus*, 1958, *87*, 65–87.

Frank, L. K. *Projective methods*. Springfield, Ill.: Charles C Thomas, 1948.

Freud, S., & Breuer, J. *Studies on hysteria*. New York: Avon Books, 1966. (Originally published, 1895.)

Garfield, S. L., & Kurtz, R. M. Attitudes toward training in diagnostic testing: A survey of directors of internship training. *Journal of Consulting and Clinical Psychology*, 1973, *40*, 350–355.

Gibb, J. Defensive communication. In H. Leavitt & L. Pondy (Eds.), *Readings in managerial psychology* (2nd ed.). Chicago: University of Chicago Press, 1973. (Originally published, 1961.)

Holt, R. Diagnostic testing: Present status and future prospects. *Journal of Nervous and Mental Disease*, 1967, *144*, 444–465.

Leavitt, H., & Pondy, L. (Eds.). *Readings in managerial psychology* (2nd ed.). Chicago: University of Chicago Press, 1973.

Levy, M. R., & Fox, H. M. Psychological testing is alive and well. *Professional Psychology*, 1975, *6*, 420–424.

Lubin, B., Wallis, R. R., & Paine, C. Patterns of psychological testing usage in the United States: 1955–1969. *Professional Psychology*, 1971, *2*, 70–74.

Main, T. F. The ailment. *British Journal of Medical Psychology*, 1957, *30*, 129–145.

Proposed accreditation criteria. *APA Monitor*, July 1978, pp. 14–16.

Rapaport, D. The theoretical implications of diagnostic testing procedures. In M. M. Gill (Ed.), *The collected papers of David Rapaport*. New York: Basic Books, 1967. (Originally published, 1950.)

Ritzler, B. A., & Del Gaudio, A. C. A survey of Rorschach teaching in APA-approved clinical graduate programs. *Journal of Personality Assessment,* 1976, *40,* 451–453.

Roethlisberger, F. J., & Dixon, W. J. *Management and the worker.* Cambridge, Mass.: Harvard University Press, 1940.

Schafer, R. *Psychoanalytic interpretation in Rorschach testing: Theory and application.* New York: Grune & Stratton, 1954.

Searles, H. The effort to drive the other person crazy—An element in the aetiology and psychotherapy of schizophrenia. *British Journal of Medical Psychology,* 1959, *32,* 1–18.

Shaffer, L. S. The golden fleece: Anti-intellectualism and social science. *American Psychologist,* 1977, *32,* 814–823.

Shectman, F. Psychological testing and inpatient treatment: Dual anachronisms or clinical necessities? *Journal of the National Association of Private Psychiatric Hospitals,* 1979, *10,* 28–33.

Shemberg, K., & Keeley, S. Psychodiagnostic training in the academic setting: Past and present. *Journal of Consulting and Clinical Psychology,* 1970, *34,* 205–211.

Shevrin, H., & Shectman, F. The diagnostic process in psychiatric evaluations. *Bulletin of the Menninger Clinic,* 1973, *37,* 451–494.

Smith, S. Psychological testing and the mind of the tester. *Bulletin of the Menninger Clinic,* 1976, *40,* 565–572.

Smyth, R., & Reznikoff, M. Attitudes of psychiatrists toward the usefulness of psycho-diagnostic reports. *Professional Psychology,* 1971, *2,* 283–288.

Staff of the Menninger Foundation Children's Division. *Disturbed children.* San Francisco: Jossey-Bass, 1969.

Thelen, M. H., & Ewing, D. R. Roles, functions, and training in clinical psychology: A survey of academic clinicians. *American Psychologist,* 1970, *25,* 550–554.

Thelen, M. H., Varble, D. L., & Johnson, J. Attitudes of academic clinical psychologists toward projective techniques. *American Psychologist,* 1968, *23,* 517–521.

Wade, T. C., & Baker, T. B. Opinions and use of psychological tests: A survey of clinical psychologists. *American Psychologist,* 1977, *32,* 874–882.

Weiner, I. D. Does psychodiagnosis have a future? *Journal of Personality Assessment,* 1972, *36,* 534–546.

I am grateful to Virginia Eicholtz for her creative editorial contribution in the preparation of this manuscript.

Chapter 12

Use of the Psychological Test Report in the Course of Psychotherapy

MARY S. CERNEY

The problem which faces every psychotherapist is how therapeutically to maximize the time spent with the patient and how to avoid being trapped in the transference paradigms with which the patient struggles. A good supervisor can help both situations but it is possible to use something additional to enable one to regain the perspective necessary to assess accurately what is occurring within the therapy situation.

Individual tests have been found to be very predictive of therapeutic outcome (Aronow & Reznikoff, 1971; Frank, 1967; Shostrom, 1974; Vandenbos & Karon, 1971; Walker, 1974). Few psychologists, however, use just one or two tests in the inference process prior to writing the psychological test report. Perhaps what inhibits the study of predictions and inferences made from psychological test reports is that so much depends not only upon the capability of the psychologist to make inferences but also upon his or her ability to communicate findings.

That tests can be useful for predictive and descriptive purposes provided they are well written (Appelbaum, 1970, 1972) is generally accepted, but their usefulness need not stop there. For example, a study by Peterson compared the assessments made by both the testers and the therapists of selected patients. He found that as the treatment progressed, the assessments made by the patients' therapists, began at each succeeding measuring point to more closely parallel the assessments originally made by the testers until at the end they had reached the highest possible correlation (Peterson, 1969). His conclusion was that the assessments made by the testers could indeed be helpful to the therapist.

Reprinted with permission from the *Journal of Personality Assessment*, Vol. 42, No. 5, pp. 457–463, © 1978 by the Society for Personality Assessment, Inc.

It is possible to use a test report as an "alter ego," much like an auxiliary supervisor to warn of countertransference pitfalls, to guide interventions, and to develop overall strategy (Appelbaum, 1977). To illustrate the use of the psychological test report in this capacity, three psychotherapy case studies are reported in which the psychological test report, though initially read, was at first neglected as an ongoing help but then utilized more consistently for the remainder of the treatment. I had tested two of the individuals (Cases 1 and 2) as part of regular outpatient evaluations and had written the reports. At the time there was no indication I would be treating these patients later. Because I had done the testing, I felt I was well acquainted with the material and would remember it sufficiently to guide my work. From discussion with colleagues, something quite similar appears to be the general pattern. Case material, if read at all, is read prior to beginning treatment, and seldom if ever referred to again. The rationale frequently given is that it will be remembered. Others feel having the material beforehand might contaminate the treatment.

CASE 1

Sister A., a member of a religious community, was referred for an evaluation because of increasing difficulties in her living situation. She had been accused, according to reports she gave the interviewing psychiatrist, of being the cause of much internal discord within the community.

After an outpatient evaluation including psychological testing, the patient was referred for psychotherapy.

The test report contained the following caution:

> Because the patient appears so well-composed and apparently agreeable it may be easy to miss how frightened she is, and how very anxious and uncomfortable she is behind her apparent serene composure. She does show some potential to think psychologically though she is too troubled and wary of the as yet unintegrated, hitherto warded off side of herself. It will be important for her therapist to proceed sensitively and slowly in helping her to explore her highly charged areas of conflict, for it would be fairly easy to frighten her out of therapy or at least unnecessarily to increase her defensiveness.

There was also considerable material from the testing and from her history indicating the potential of this patient to get herself into the "victim" position. This was the area that caused the most difficulty in the course of therapy. This patient had a way of arousing considerable negative countertransference feelings. She would tantalize with comments such as "there's really something I would like to talk about but just can't," but would resist all efforts to explore the issue in question. Similar comments would be repeated throughout the hour punctuated with long periods of silence. This would go on for numerous sessions. Attempts to understand this maneuver or facilitate her talking were experienced as attacks and criticism; silence was seen as "not caring."

The patient had other ways of being provocative. She would begin crying just at the end of the hour and be in no state or condition to leave, necessitating a lengthening of the hour. Often she would report that she had told so and so what I had said on a particular topic and state the other person's hostile retort. These were generally misquotes and/or exaggerations of my comments or the other person's response. She had difficulty becoming aware of her own hostility in these references. She could be infuriating in her always obliging, subservient manner. She was so skilled in her maneuvers that it was frequently very difficult to detect what exactly made one feel so irritated. Furthermore, she seemed so well-organized that it appeared, contrary to what the tests had indicated, that she could handle a direct exploration of her behavior. But this only frightened her. She felt attacked and became more resistant, as the test report said she would. The part of the test report that spoke to the need to proceed sensitively and slowly—for it would be fairly easy to frighten her out of therapy or at least unnecessarily to increase her defensiveness—was easily forgotten under the impact of the feelings she aroused.

I began to feel so blocked and at such an impasse that I considered referring her to another therapist. It was easy to understand why she had been asked to leave a number of her community mission homes and was on the verge of being asked to leave her present home.

Rereading that psychological test report helped me to regain my objectivity. It alerted me that such a maneuver on my part would be a repetition of her past, and it helped me understand and resolve my negative countertransference. It reminded me that underneath the provocative behavior was not so much a stubborn, unwilling patient, but a very anxious, frightened woman struggling to control the disquieting thoughts and fantasies that invaded her consciousness.

Because she always appeared so much in control, it *was* easy to forget the frightened, anxious side of her so well masked by perfect composure. It was also easy to slip into the role of the all-bad authority figure for one could easily feel righteous indignation with her provocativeness and could empathize with her religious superiors who did not know what to do with her.

Utilizing the psychological test material, not only in the early stages of treatment but well into the treatment process, enabled me not only to regain objectivity but also to alter the course of psychotherapy so that she was able to avoid becoming again a victim of rejection. She gained considerable insight into her manner of provoking others to reject her and she was able to complete a two and one-half year treatment successfully.

Post treatment follow-up at three years indicated that the changes effected in the course of treatment were well-integrated. Her verbal intelligence which tested originally in the Bright Normal range showed a gain of almost 20 points, placing her well within the Very Superior range and indicating the lifting of many of the repressive barriers blocking her true potential. Her self-report, which is corroborated by those who know her, supports her improved functioning. Whereas formerly community groups did not want her to be part of their membership, she is now most welcome. She has become an outstanding teacher, well-liked by parents and students alike for her ability not only to teach but also to understand her students. She is better able to express anger appropriately and is not afraid to speak her mind. She knows how to set limits and no longer feels taken advantage of. Although she reports she still has ups and downs, she is better able to understand their cause and to deal with them.

The greatest change occurred in her interpersonal relationships. She is much freer, more spontaneous, and brings issues out into the open for discussion. She also has been most helpful in enabling others to seek psychiatric help. Now, almost five years out of treatment, she is becoming a recognized leader in her religious community.

Although this is a report of a successful treatment outcome, treatment itself may have been facilitated and both the patient and I might have been spared much pain and frustration if I had kept the test information more consistently in mind.

CASE 2

Without the psychological test report, Case 2 might never have begun. This patient, a 20-year-old girl, refused to come to my office for therapy and insisted I go to the hospital section to see her where she was a patient.

The test report stated that during the testing,

> The patient seemed to want and demand structure, yet fought against it consistently. But in spite of her threats and complaints, when she was not argued with but presented with a task with the implicit assumption that she would comply, she did.

I therefore consulted with her hospital therapist who approved of my plan to see her in my office. Three calls between the nursing staff and me were involved before she was brought to my office in a wheel chair. The wheel chair was not because she refused to come, even though she had initially insisted to the nursing staff that she was not coming. She was suffering from some possible but un-diagnosed neurological difficulty which made it difficult for her to walk. This, however, disappeared at least partially after three weeks of treatment.

The first session dealt extensively with her fear of therapy after having "out-witted and controlled so many therapists for so many years." She frequently, in the course of therapy, referred to the first session and the meaning of security that it had for her. She was frightened by her ability to terrify and intimidate others and yet she knew no other way to get what she felt she needed.

If it had not been for the test report, it might have been easy to miss her core difficulty. The test report stated that

egocentric, the patient needs to be the center of interest and attraction which has a helpless, mainly orally-determined, inappropriately demanding nature. She is given to the use of histrionics, repression, and symptom formation characteristic of the hysterical personality.

And in another part of the test report

egocentric and somewhat narcissistic, she would like to see herself as not needing others. But on a deeper level, she hates the artificiality she feels to be herself. She feels evil and capable of destruction, a part of her which she would like to have taken out of her.

Keeping these issues in mind, it was possible to deal with her resistances to explore these very important points. It was also possible to understand her behavior in a different light from what she tended to present. One of the most important of these issues was her struggle with symptom formation. Having a possibility of real neurological difficulty, this issue would have been easy to bypass.

The psychological test report was also most helpful in enabling me to understand how she related to others and to convey this information to the nursing staff. At times they saw her as an impossible patient whom we could not treat. They in turn were seen as all bad while I was seen as more helpful. She saw them very much as she saw her mother and only by helping them understand this were we able to work cooperatively in her treatment.

They did not give up on her and we were able to work together cooperatively so that she, too, had a successful treatment. During her After-Care treatment, she completed Montessori Training and within one year of termination of psychotherapy had established her own Montessori Training School and had already been chosen a "Montessori Teacher of the Year." She is now over five years out of treatment and continues to do well. She recently married a young man who has just completed his doctoral work in psychology. They plan to blend his behavioral orientation with her Montessori techniques in working with the mentally retarded. It is interesting to note that prior to establishing her own Montessori School, she was selected out of over two hundred applicants to teach behavioral psychology and Montessori techniques to the staff at a local neurological facility as part of a federally funded program.

CASE 3

Mrs. K. was an attractive 30-year-old Home Economics Teacher. She had been in therapy for about a year with a psychiatric resident who would soon be graduating. He, therefore, referred her for a diagnostic consultation about the possibility of her continuing in analysis. Psychological testing revealed a much more tenuous hold on reality with strong paranoid trends than was readily apparent. Analysis was not indicated. She, however, had formed a strong attachment to the female consultant and was deeply hurt by not being able to continue in therapy with her. This only came out, however, much later in the treatment with me. Because I was going on vacation, I did not consider it wise to begin therapy and then immediately interrupt it, so I met with the patient briefly to let her know that I would be her therapist when I returned from vacation.

Therapy began after my vacation. It was difficult to work with this patient because my remarks, be they clarifications, interpretations, or whatever, were experienced as narcissistic insults to her intelligence. The test report shed light on the underlying dynamics and allowed for a redirecting of the psychotherapeutic intervention.

The report stated:

Several problems make it hard for this woman to accept being helped and to learn from another person. One of her TAT stories deals with an evil man who attacks a good one out of envy. Contemptuous of women, she so envies "men" (someone with something good to offer) that she needs to destroy the good that could be taken in and used. She will likely vacillate between being envious and attacking the therapist, and projecting her 'badness' onto the therapist and feeling attacked because she has the goodness inside her.

She frequently referred to, but would not elaborate on the humiliation she had experienced in having a man for her therapist in her previous therapy.

The patient felt very embarrassed at letting her feelings show and saw therapy as a humiliating experience.

This patient was constantly looking for the all-good mother who died when the patient was but ten years old, but became terrified when she began to experience me in this role. Separations were particularly difficult, but she denied their importance. Her typical response was, "That's all right. What do you mean that I might have some feelings that you are going away? I'm a mature person and I can understand why you are leaving." This reaction made the issue difficult to explore directly.

The test report read that

> she is quite vulnerable to experiences of longing and yearning for a reunion with "missing" others. But the sadness is colored by much anger and resentment, which could make for spiteful-vengeful behavior—especially if she experiences the "lost" person as rejecting her in favor of another.

In spite of these technical difficulties, the patient made significant changes during the course of therapy. Her relationship with her husband improved markedly; she began to be able to set limits; she became more independent and felt less victimized. We were in the last stages of treatment and had been working on her fear of closeness and her fear of abandonment when I was gone twice within the space of two months. She cried for the first time over any of my absences, and expressed some feelings of regret. This, however, was followed by a depreciation of me as a person and as a therapist for "therapists are not real people, they are only objects," followed by an insistence that she terminate treatment. This termination was averted by working with her around the issue of how she reacts to separations and her fears that she will be left alone and abandoned just when she begins to trust another. But after I was gone a few days about a month later, she could not be diverted from her insistence on termination. Although I did not agree with her reasons for terminating treatment, I supported her right to do so. Her eyes filled with tears as she said good-bye, what she valued most was that I had always treated her with the utmost respect. I stated that if in the future, she ever felt the need to return, I wanted her to know the door was open. The patient pointed out that she had made considerable change in the course of treatment, which was true, and what remained she needed to work out directly with her husband. She thanked me for all I had done to help her and left.

The patient, however, did manage to remain in treatment with me for a period slightly over two years. Although I did not feel she was able to complete treatment, I did feel that the test report was invaluable in guiding a very difficult course of therapy. Whether my absence was the critical issue affecting termination is difficult to assess although I feel it was a deciding factor which would fit with the test material and also her history. She was at a critical point in her treatment where she could no longer blame others for her situation and where she was on the brink of assuming greater responsibility for her life. In order to make the transition, she needed the support of others in whom she could trust. My leaving was to her an indication that I could not be relied upon when she really needed me.

The treatment itself was clearly encapsulated in one of her TAT stories in which she told of an older woman becoming angry at a younger one who is ruining her life but won't listen to the wisdom of the older woman. The older woman does not want to hurt the other one but uses her anger to get the younger woman to listen to her. She tries to help the younger woman . . . without ridicule or domination but could not.

Follow-up after one year indicated that this woman was coping rather well, but was not so happy as she would like to be.

DISCUSSION

Freud's reporting of the case of Dora records the problems one encounters in the course of therapeutic work. Not recognizing or dealing with such transferential feelings frequently leads, as in that analysis, to the premature termination of treatment.

Although Freud is said to have discovered transference with the analysis of Dora (Freud, 1905/1955), it would be more accurate to say he rediscovered it. We know that as early as the "Studies in Hysteria," Freud not only knew of transference, but in the fourth chapter of this work, devoted to the psychotherapy of hysteria, showed a very clear understanding of the transferential phenomenon and of its repetitive nature (Freud, 1893–1895/1955). Freud's notion of the "repetition compulsion" arose when he observed, in children's play and in traumatic neuroses and dreams, a puzzling tendency to repeat over and over some painful situation (Freud, 1920/1955). The compulsion to repeat a painful situation was seen in the life of the Sister in Case 1 who had already managed to get herself rejected by numerous others and almost succeeded in getting me to continue the pattern.

In essence, Freud defined transference as the process whereby individuals react to one another on the basis of previous experience, anticipations, expectations, and stereotypes. Historically, the confusions and distortions in the patient's imagery were of prime importance to the therapist in the therapeutic process. In recent years, there has been a renewed interest in the effect of the therapist's counterdistortions on the therapeutic process (Salzman, 1962).

With so many years of practice and of "success," patients are very skillful in creating the very problematic situations that lead to their requesting psychotherapy (see Case 1). Yet they remain unaware of their role in the process. It is the work of the therapist to interrupt the sequence of events that lead to their achieving what they most fear: rejection.

In the course of therapy, however, even highly skilled therapists can slip unawares into the transferential paradigms and act like others in the patient's environment instead of maintaining distance and enabling the patient to observe his own behavior. The latter stance is greatly facilitated if one is forewarned of possible transferential paradigms. A supervisor can help one to recognize the signs and to avoid slipping into such a role. Where a supervisor may be unavailable, another possible way to gain distance is by re-reading the test report where predictions are made of what might occur and why. This point is not new but one which needs to be repeatedly reemphasized for it is so easy to be caught in the web of our own omnipotence and the unconscious resistance of the patient to change. For example, in Case 1, the provocative behavior that led to the patient being transferred from two other mission houses where she had been assigned was being re-enacted in the therapy. My efforts to enable her to understand "why" she behaved in such a way were stymied. I felt helpless with everything I tried ending in failure. I was frustrated. The patient was successfully projecting onto me her own feelings of helplessness.

My earlier understanding of the dynamics inherent in this transferential situation were forgotten. A re-reading of the test report at this time may have helped me to maintain my perspective rather than to be drawn into reacting to her behavior. Instead of attempting to enable her to understand her behavior, it would have been more helpful initially to empathize with her fear, a fear which had many levels and which prevented her from accepting my interpretations. At one level, she was becoming more terrified of the implications of our relationship. Would I reject her as the others? She was fearful that if she allowed herself to be vulnerable, I would overpower her and that she would lose all control and suffer annihilation. Furthermore, her alienating behavior was a way of protecting me from her own devouring destructive feelings toward me. I needed to know, understand, and be aware of these various levels of inference, but more important at this point in her treatment, I needed to be accepting and to allow the patient to grow in trust, strengthening her ego capacities to deal constructively with her behavior. She did not need my interpretation at this point, but she did need my acceptance and understanding.

In Case 2, the test report information, perhaps due to more experience on my part, was more consistently used preventing the repetition of this patient's early childhood experiences. The more important contribution of the test report in this case was its utilization outside of the psychotherapy proper in enabling me to work with her treatment team to prevent a split occurring between them and me. Thus she was not able to recreate two warring factions as she had between her mother and father.

Countertransference feelings were strong in Case 3, but here with a greater utilization of the test report, I was able not only to be more aware of these feelings, but also to utilize them more productively. Understanding her pathology enabled me to handle her hostile attacks more effectively without acting on feelings of wishing to retaliate. These feelings were instead an indicator of how persecuted and attacked the patient felt by whatever I said. It afforded the opportunity instead to examine why she needed to feel this way and to explore the underlying feelings against which her attack and retaliation responses were a defense. However, in this case, that was not enough. When the patient was at a point where she could no longer maintain her defensive stance, where she was uncomfortable with the way she was but fearful of becoming someone different, she had to flee. Understanding her pathology and the struggles in which she was engaged also lessened the narcissistic blow of losing a patient before "in my estimation" treatment was completed. My being gone twice in the space of two months gave her the excuse she needed.

In summary, the understanding which is contained in a well-written test report can be a valuable resource in the treatment of patients. Test reports, however, should not be read and neatly filed away, but used in a somewhat "supervisor" or "alter-ego" role through the entire course of treatment. Although this article deals principally with the usefulness of the test report in this regard, there also can be no adequate substitute for competent supervision and one's own personal analysis. Perhaps the test report becomes an even more valuable tool once one has experienced the other two.

REFERENCES

Appelbaum, S. Science and persuasion in the psychological test report, *Journal of Consulting and Clinical Psychology,* 1970, *35,* 349–355.

Appelbaum, S. A method of reporting psychological test findings. *Bulletin of the Menninger Clinic,* 1972, *35,* 535–545.

Appelbaum, S. *The anatomy of change.* New York: Plenum, 1977.

Aronow, E., & Reznikoff, M. Application of projective tests to psychotherapy: A case study. *Journal of Personality Assessment,* 1971, *35,* 379–393.

Frank, G. A review of research with measures of ego strength derived from the MMPI and the Rorschach. *Journal of General Psychology,* 1967, *77,* 183–206.

Freud, S. Beyond the pleasure principle. In *The complete psychological works of Sigmund Freud* (Vol. 18). London: Hogarth, 1955. (Originally published 1920).

Freud, S. Fragment of an analysis of a case of hysteria. In *The complete psychological works of Sigmund Freud* (Vol. 7). London: Hogarth, 1955. (Originally published 1905).

Freud, S. The psychotherapy of hysteria. In *The complete psychological works of Sigmund Freud* (Vol. 2). London: Hogarth, 1955. (Originally published 1893–1895).

Peterson, P. The clinical utility of projective techniques. *Dissertation Abstracts,* 1969, *30,* 2913–14b.

Salzman, L. Countertransference: A therapeutic tool. In J. H. Wasserman (Ed.), *Current psychiatric therapies.* New York: Grune & Stratton, 1962.

Shostrom, E. The measurement of growth in psychotherapy. *Journal of Personality Assessment,* 1974, *38,* 144–148.

Vandenbos, G., & Karon, B. Pathogenesis: A new therapist personality dimension related to therapeutic effectiveness. *Journal of Personality Assessment,* 1971, *35,* 252–260.

Walker, J. The Word Association Sentence Method as a predictor of psychotherapeutic outcome. *British Journal of Social and Clinical Psychology,* 1974, *77,* 13, 219–221.

Chapter   13

The Clinical Psychologist
as a Diagnostic Consultant

JON G. ALLEN

While the role of the clinical psychologist has greatly expanded since the inception of the profession, a central function continues to be conducting psychological testing and providing diagnostic consultations. Given the attack on the validity of psychological testing from within psychology, in conjunction with the interprofessional rivalry between psychologists and psychiatrists, the psychologist who acts as a psychodiagnostician often finds himself in an embattled position (Shectman 1979). In this paper I shall specifically focus on the psychologist's role as consultant to all the mental health disciplines (e.g., psychiatrists, social workers, other psychologists), which is by no means limited to testing.

Even in the relatively circumscribed context of psychological testing are various tasks that are related to the psychologist's level of skill and experience. At one level is the psychometrician whose work is limited to administering and scoring a variety of psychological tests. With considerable training, this individual could administer such complex instruments as the Wechsler Adult Intelligence Scale or the Rorschach test. At the next level is the psychologist who not only administers and scores various measures but also interprets the results and writes reports summarizing the test findings. In practice, this psychologist often bases his written reports on tests administered by a psychometrician. At the highest level is the individual I call the consulting psychologist. This psychologist has the broadest professional skills and engages not only in psychodiagnostic testing but also in diagnosis, treatment, and consultation.

In some respects, psychodiagnostic consultation is similar to the consultations utilized in general medical practice. To assist in the process of formulating a psychiatric diagnosis, the psychiatrist orders psychological testing just as the

Reprinted with permission from the *Bulletin of the Menninger Clinic*, 1981, Vol. 45, No. 3, pp. 247–258, © 1981 by The Menninger Foundation.

general practitioner orders appropriate tests (e.g., blood chemistry profiles, electroencephalograms, skull films) to help determine the medical diagnosis. Within the medical domain exists a range of skill comparable to that among psychologists. That is, the psychometrician's counterpart is the medical technician, and the consulting psychologist's counterpart is the hematologist, the neurologist, or the radiologist. These psychological and medical specialists are consulted because they are skilled not only in providing diagnostic information but also in suggesting possible treatment interventions.

That a psychological consultation is analogous to a consultation in one of the various medical specialties is an important point because the consulting psychologist must conduct himself as the psychiatrist's colleague and not as a subordinate. For the consulting psychologist to feel subordinate to the psychiatrist who requests the consultation blurs the distinction between the roles of consultant and technician. Indeed, the consulting psychologist who unwittingly views himself as a technician severely limits the contribution he can make to the diagnostic process. Although delegating psychological test administration to a psychometrician is a common practice in some settings, the yield of the data-gathering process would be much enhanced by the consulting psychologist's skills. For example, skillfull interventions in response to a patient's resistances (e.g., constriction, suspiciousness, passivity) not only contribute to an understanding of the patient's functioning but also enhance the validity of the evaluation by enabling the patient to provide a more complete test record. This enhancement of the testing procedure constitutes a difference in degree, if not in kind, between the psychological consultation and many medical consultations. In the latter domain, a well-trained technician is often able to collect data for the consulting physician that serve the diagnostic purpose as well as those data the physician could gather by administering the techniques himself.

PSYCHOLOGICAL TESTING AND CLINICAL DIAGNOSIS

It should be axiomatic that one cannot treat without diagnosing, at least in the broad sense of systematically formulating the problem for which treatment is sought. Although the use of formal psychiatric diagnostic labels has been widely debated (Shevrin & Shectman 1973), most psychologists, particularly those in institutional settings, are requested to utilize the psychiatric nosological system when they act as diagnostic consultants. Ideally, the assignment of diagnostic labels constitutes a step in the diagnostic process rather than a conclusion; the label is, in effect, a "psychological ball park" within which more refined inquiry takes place (Holt 1968).

However, when psychiatrists ask psychologists to act as consultants in arriving at clinical diagnoses, there is potential for competitiveness and territorial battles.

At worst, the psychologist and psychiatrist disagree about the diagnostic label and engage in open combat about who is "right." Shectman (1979) points out that such disagreements may, upon reflection, yield additional information about the multiple facets of the patient's functioning. To avoid battling for the dubious distinction of assigning the correct label, the psychologist and psychiatrist should agree in advance what the psychologist is expected to contribute regarding the clinical diagnosis. Notably, the psychologist whose role is confined to psychological testing may not be in the best position to specify the diagnosis; testing provides a cross-sectional view of the patient, whereas the diagnosis often depends on a longitudinal view such as would be elicited in the clinical history (e.g., in the diagnosis of bipolar disorder). On the other hand, the psychologist, because of the refinement of his methods, may often be in an optimal position for making a central contribution to the diagnosis (e.g., using the patient's responses to the Rorschach test for assessing subtleties of thought organization). To make such a contribution, however, the psychologist ideally should be capable of making a diagnosis, that is, capable of obtaining a clinical history and of integrating it with a cross-sectional assessment from the tests.

An appropriate response for the psychologist who is requested to provide diagnostic consultation is to summarize the features of the cross-sectional data that bear upon the diagnosis and to integrate the cross-sectional findings with the pertinent historical data. Such considerations can be summarized in the psychological test report under a heading such as "diagnostic understanding" (Appelbaum 1972). For example,

> Mr. Smith has been given the tentative diagnosis of schizophrenia, paranoid type; this patient's history of severe depression also raised the possibility of a major affective disorder or schizo-affective schizophrenia. There was no reported history of mania. At the time of initial testing, Mr. Smith was severely depressed and disorganized. After receiving antipsychotic medication, the patient improved clinically; further testing (repeat Rorschach) was done to clarify the nature of the improvement. The considerations pertinent to diagnosis were spelled out in the psychologist's test report:
>
> > Mr. Smith's current functioning is most consistent with the diagnosis of a major affective disorder inasmuch as his affective symptoms are considerably more prominent than his thought disturbance. Specifically, his thinking is most disturbed in the context of depression. Although there is no history of mania, the findings are suggestive of a bipolar or cyclothymic syndrome. Mr. Smith was observed to shift over the course of testing from a state of severe depression to some consolidation of hypomanic defenses. In addition to the disorganization, Mr. Smith shows impaired interpersonal adjustment and, when depressed, he is prone to retreat into a state of alienation. These latter features of his functioning, while consistent with schizophrenia, could also be attributable to severe character disturbances, namely, a mixture of schizoid features and narcissistic defenses

at a borderline level of personality organization. Thus, the current clinical picture suggests an affective disorder superimposed on significant character problems. Whatever diagnostic label is assigned, the psychological evaluation underscores the predominance of the affective disturbance in Mr. Smith's current functioning.

Sometimes a patient is referred for psychological testing after a definitive psychiatric diagnosis has already been made. In such a case, the psychological evaluation may focus on treatment considerations. Even when given a definitive diagnosis in advance, however, the psychologist can still make a contribution to diagnostic understanding. When there are multiple diagnoses for a patient, for example, the psychologist may be in a position to assist in the formulation of an integrated understanding of the patient. For example,

> Mr. Green was referred for psychological testing with several well-established diagnoses: bipolar disorder; substance use disorder; mild organic brain syndrome, probably secondary to substance abuse; and dependent personality disorder. The consulting psychologist integrated these various facets of the patient's difficulties in his report:

>> Mr. Green is desperately trying to stave off depression associated with the sense of deteriorating to a state of barrenness and even death. He wards off depression by manic defenses manifested in a flood of ideation along with a range of turbulent affective states. His capacity to control and integrate this psychological turmoil is severely impaired, not only because of the disorganization inherent in the manic state, but also because organic impairment has eroded his cognitive functioning and capacity for self-regulation. His self-esteem is severely threatened by a developmental crisis in relation to aging that is exacerbated by the deterioration partly associated with organicity. Mr. Green's characterological dependency is a mixed blessing: on the one hand, he can take sustenance from a benign relationship which enables him to function successfully and somewhat independently; on the other hand, his dependency has roots in primitive wishes to fuse with another and leaves him vulnerable to depression associated with a sense of abandonment and concomitant feelings of helplessness.

PSYCHOLOGICAL TESTING AND TREATMENT

Just as it should be axiomatic that one cannot treat without diagnosing, it is also true that one cannot diagnose without treating. In the realm of the psychologist's work this statement has two meanings. First, the diagnostic process is hampered if the psychologist is not also a capable therapist. Indeed, the psychologist who has experience in treating a range of patients with a variety of modalities will be most skilled in his diagnostic work with patients and will be most knowledgeable in formulating treatment recommendations. Second, patients tend to experience the process of testing as part of their treatment programs.

Psychological Testing as Treatment in Microcosm

Psychological testing, like diagnostic interviewing more generally, might be viewed as the treatment process in microcosm, for it is a systematic investigation of the nature and meaning of the patient's psychological problems. This description is also applicable to the process of psychotherapy and, to some extent, to hospital treatment. In addition, the patient-examiner relationship provides the central context within which the test findings take on meaning. Thus, all of the concepts that are employed to understand the therapeutic relationship (e.g., alliance, transference, countertransference) are central to the testing process. Moreover, psychologists who are experienced therapists are in the best position to make diagnostic use of these phenomena in the testing situation.

Psychological evaluations require a particularly active involvement on the patient's part. In psychotherapy this involvement is called the therapeutic alliance or working alliance (Greenson 1968), which can be briefly described as the realistic, positive, collaborative relationship between the patient and therapist, predicated on the patient's experiencing the therapist as a trustworthy helper. This dimension of the relationship applies equally to the diagnostic situation, where the psychologist and the patient should be engaged in a collaborative effort to understand the latter's problems. Pruyser (1979a) described this relationship as a "diagnostic *partnership*" (p. 251) wherein the patient becomes "fully engaged in self-diagnosis with the help of a particular expert" (pp. 255–56).

In stark contrast to this positive view of the patient enthusiastically collaborating in the process of self-diagnosis is the negative experience of having virtually to drag a hospitalized patient out of bed so he can "take the tests." Another negative extreme is represented by the patient who has the delusional conviction that the examiner is reading the patient's mind and is using the information to plot the patient's demise. Short of these extremes are the many patients who feel that the tests will only expose their inadequacies and weaknesses or who feel that they will fail in some sense or other. While the examiner might experience these reactions to testing as frustrating his aim of achieving an alliance with the patient, these ostensible impediments, in fact, constitute the very essence of the diagnostic material, the realm of transference and countertransference. Like any clinical encounter, the patient-examiner interaction is enlivened by the feelings, fantasies, and distortions of both the patient and the examiner. These phenomena need to be understood not only because they embody the patient's core conflicts and struggles, but because they also foreshadow major treatment dilemmas. An examiner who is aware of his countertransference is able, for example, to alert those who will treat the patient to the dangers and pitfalls that are likely to emerge in the subsequent treatment process. Thus, the examiner who allows himself to enter into a significant relationship with the patient will be able to provide the richest information (Shectman 1979; Smith 1976).

The effort to build a diagnostic alliance has a significant effect on the whole conduct of testing. Throughout the testing process, the patient is repeatedly invited to be a collaborator in the investigation, for the diagnostic work entails a discovery of the conditions under which the patient is able to do so and of the interventions that promise to be most helpful. There are many concrete methods of inviting the patient's participation. For example, the psychologist may begin the process by asking the patient how he thinks the testing might be helpful and what questions he has about himself that might be explored. Not every patient will readily provide such clues, but when he does, an avenue for an alliance is opened. Another means of encouraging the patient's participation throughout the testing process is to engage the patient in exploring the meaning of his responses. For example, when the patient runs into difficulty, his understanding of and feelings about this difficulty can be explored then and there. This kind of exploration can also be built directly into the tests. For example, on the Thematic Apperception Test, the patient is asked to make up stories about a series of pictures; after having completed this task, he can be asked to go back through his stories and provide his own explanation or interpretation of their meaning. This process of engaging the patient in working out the meaning of his test responses and productions is directly analogous to the process of psychotherapy. So conducted, the testing situation becomes a microcosm of the treatment situation, providing the best basis for translating the test findings into the treatment plan.

At this point, some questions might be raised. Why bother with testing? If one wants to generalize from an analogue to the treatment situation, why not simply conduct a clinical interview? Indeed, all that I have said about testing as treatment in microcosm applies equally to diagnostic interviews; not only do they have intrinsic therapeutic value for many patients but they also mirror the treatment process directly. I answer these questions by suggesting that psychological testing be viewed as a special type of stuctured interview, the test materials providing a rich context for clinical interviewing. The standardization of the procedures and materials allows the psychologist to build up experience with responses to various items and to develop a keen sensitivity to individual nuances and idiosyncrasies.

Even more than standardization, the comprehensiveness of the test battery provides diagnostic power. First, unlike a clinical interview, which follows selected paths of inquiry in response to the patient's presented complaints, a battery of tests covers a full spectrum of psychological *content* (e.g., eliciting themes of sexuality, aggression, dependency, achievement). Second, a test battery enables the psychologist to assess the full spectrum of psychological *func-*

tions (e.g., perceiving, remembering, reasoning, judging, fantasizing, feeling, reality testing), in effect, sampling various facets of the patient's activity *in vivo* (Pruyser 1979b). Third, a test battery provides a wide range of *structure*. The highly structured tests provide clear guidelines for the patient's response (e.g., many intelligence test items have only one correct response). The loosely structured tasks, such as on the Rorschach test, not only present ambiguous stimuli but also allow a vast range of possible responses; moreover, most patients have little idea what dimensions of their responses are of significance to the examiner. It is a common finding that the more disorganized the patient, the more structure he needs to function effectively (e.g., perceive accurately, think logically). Thus, the amount of structure a patient needs to succeed in the testing situation can be used to gauge the amount of structure required in the treatment program. For example, a patient who becomes disorganized while working on the ambiguous and fantasy-eliciting Rorschach test is not a suitable candidate at that time for an expressive, exploratory treatment like classical psychoanalysis. Thus, by virtue of having worked with the patient in contexts varying in structure, the psychologist can provide predictions about the patient's functioning in various facets of treatment (e.g., hospital milieu, psychotherapy).

Clinical Examples

The following clinical example illustrates how a consulting psychologist used his relationship with the patient and the patient's responses to his interventions to formulate a treatment strategy. When the patient was referred for testing, there was no question about the diagnosis—schizophrenia, paranoid type. Therefore, the consulting psychologist addressed himself to the central issue in the referral, which he summarized as follows: "There are concerns about the chronicity of the patient's difficulties with serious doubts concerning her ability to rebound from her present decompensated state or to establish trustful relationships with treatment staff members in the face of her intense persecutory concerns." After describing the patient's central conflicts, self-concept, and views of others, the consulting psychologist addressed treatment issues directly:

> Not only did Miss Thompson welcome the structure of the tests which enabled her to perform at more adequate levels, but also she was able during the course of the testing to develop a somewhat trusting relationship with this examiner. At one point during her telling of the Thematic Apperception Test stories, she requested that I assist her to follow the story format by asking her specific questions. An important treatment paradigm appears to be implicit in this exchange. She may fear closeness, intrusion, and control, and may seek to rebel and isolate herself. Nonetheless, she appears also to wish for support and structure which assist her to function more adequately. Thus, the treatment process will

be demanding from the staff members' standpoint. It will require awareness of Miss Thompson's fear of intrusion, domination, and control, but responsiveness to her wish for helpful intervention.

The next clinical example reflects an even closer link between the testing and the actual treatment process. In this case, the consulting psychologist, working in collaboration with the treatment team, incorporated treatment interventions in the course of the testing and thereby directly influenced the patient's attitude toward treatment.

> Just prior to the first testing appointment, Mr. Jones formally declared his intention to leave the hospital, thus planning to quit the treatment before the testing would be completed. He explained that he felt drained and did not feel he had what it takes to embark upon treatment. On the Rorschach test administered on the second day of testing, he provided material that poignantly portrayed his internal struggles and turmoil. He gave a number of responses in rapid succession which reflected shifts among feelings of anxiety, depression, hypomania, rage, and fear; he then ended by saying, 'It evokes sadness, which scares me; on the other hand, it could be a rainbow!' Thus, he concluded with manic denial. After the Rorschach was completed, the examiner read back this series of responses to Mr. Jones, pointing out to him the tumultuous inner experience that they implied. The examiner also observed more generally that, in the context of such turmoil, Mr. Jones's thinking became quite unrealistic and illogical. The examiner empathized with Mr. Jones's feeling of being depleted in the face of this turmoil; nevertheless, the examiner confronted Mr. Jones with the fact that his inner turbulence was not consistent with his plan to leave the hospital and explicitly advised him to remain in treatment. Mr. Jones experienced the observations as empathic interventions and subsequently decided to remain in the hospital, encouraged that his dilemma could be deeply understood.

Boundary Issues

The clinical psychologist's consulting role can be clarified by analogy to the medical model of diagnostic consultation. Yet, psychological testing differs from medical consultations inasmuch as the examination procedure is so much like the treatment process itself. That is, the techniques and process of the examination overlap considerably with those of treatment; thus, one of the major distinctions between diagnosis and treatment is the time-limited perspective of the former. Nevertheless, because of the overlap in procedures, the boundaries between the diagnostic consultation and the treatment can be blurred.

The usual expectation of a diagnostic consultation is that the consultant will not engage in a treatment process unless specifically requested to do so. However, the view of psychological testing I have outlined suggests that therapeutic interventions are likely to be part of the diagnostic process. As Pruyser (1979a) contends, "the diagnosis does not stand alone, but is caught up in curative efforts, in which indeed the whole diagnostic process may be embedded from the start" (p. 249). Psychological testing includes, at the very least, considerable psychological exploration. It is also likely to include, broadly speaking, some interpretive work; that is, in response to the patient's productions, the examiner formulates meanings that go beyond the patient's current awareness. In addition, as in the case of Mr. Jones, confrontation and even direct guidance may be part of the psychological testing process. In that instance, the consulting psychologist was working closely with the treatment team and consciously reinforcing what he knew to be the team's position. Nevertheless, this style of testing raises a general question: where does one draw the line between doing the work necessary to provide the diagnostic consultation and providing treatment for the patient?

CONCLUSION

The interprofessional boundaries in the areas of psychological diagnosis and treatment cannot be conclusively established by fiat. They must be negotiated in the individual relationships among professionals. Like their clinical counterparts, these consultative relationships are open to considerable conflict and distortion (Schafer 1954; Shectman 1979). In this presentation, rather than attempting to propose solutions, I have raised the issues that warrant resolution in these relationships.

The success of the consultative relationship is determined not only by the manner in which the consulting psychologist is viewed by the referring psychiatrist but also by the way in which the psychologist views himself. Psychologists have created considerable difficulty for themselves by attacking the validity of their tools. The validity of the tests needs to be researched, but the debate is often polemical, perhaps fueled by psychologists' conflicts about their role as consultants. Indeed, if psychologists experience themselves as technicians in the consultative role or believe that they are so viewed by referring physicians, they are likely to rebel; attacking the tests, however, is a displacement!

I believe that the central issue is not the validity of the tests but rather the skill of the psychologists using the tests. The extent to which a particular psychologist can provide valid and useful diagnostic information is determined both by the validity of the tests and by the psychologist's ability to interpret and apply test findings. This ability is a direct derivative of his general professional experience; that is, in addition to knowledge of the tests, the psychodiagnostician must also have a thorough understanding of psychological development, personality theory, and psychopathology; moreover, he must be competent in the treatment processes about which he is making forecasts. Only then can he provide useful consultation to those who want to know the best ways to treat the patient.

REFERENCES

Appelbaum, S. A.: A Method of Reporting Psychological Test Findings. *Bull. Menninger Clin.* 36(5):535–45, 1972.

Holt, R. R.: Editor's Foreword. In *Diagnostic Psychological Testing,* Rev. Ed., David Rapaport *et al.* (R. R. Holt, ed.), pp. 1–44. New York: International Universities Press, 1968.

Pruyser, P. W.: The Diagnostic Process: Touchstone of Medicine's Values. In *Nourishing the Humanistic in Medicine: Interactions with the Social Sciences,* W. R. Rogers & David Barnard, eds., pp. 245–67. Pittsburgh: University of Pittsburgh Press, 1979a.

———: *The Psychological Examination: A Guide for Clinicians.* New York: International Universities Press. 1979b.

Schafer, Roy: *Psychoanalytic Interpretation in Rorschach Testing: Theory and Application.* New York: Grune & Stratton, 1954.

Shectman, Fred: Problems in Communicating Psychological Understanding: Why Won't They Listen to Me?! *Am. Psychol.* 34(9):781–90, 1979.

Shevrin, Howard & Shectman, Fred: The Diagnostic Process in Psychiatric Evaluations. *Bull. Menninger Clin.* 37(5):451–94, 1973.

Smith, Sydney: Psychological Testing and the Mind of the Tester. *Bull. Menninger Clin.* 40(5):565–72, 1976.

Chapter 14

Ethical, Social, and Professional Issues in Patients' Access to Psychological Test Reports

WILLIAM H. SMITH

Psychologists in training have always been admonished about carefully protecting written clinical documents to keep them from falling into the wrong hands, including those of the patient. Teachers of clinical psychology feel comfortable in explaining to the novice that one professional writes a test report for another professional in a specialized language which not only can be different from the usual mental health jargon but which also can often be specific to the tests themselves, thus making the report misleading and incomprehensible to the patient about whom it is written. To see in black and white his exact I.Q. scores or to read diagnostic labels such as "schizophrenia" or "inadequate personality" could certainly be of no constructive use to the patient, and to read descriptions of latent or tenuously defended against characteristics and tendencies could be nothing but upsetting. For a patient to look at his test report would be, at best, uninformative or misleading and, at worst, damaging.

In a parallel vein, a patient is routinely informed that his file belongs to the professional, not to the patient, and that nothing but harm could come from a patient reading his own file. For a patient to express the wish to see his records implies a lack of trust in the professional, a trust the clinician finds to be indispensable in a successful treatment relationship. Therefore, the message is that a patient had better cooperate with these values if help is to be forthcoming.

These three concepts—(1) that confidentiality restrictions include the patient as well as others, (2) that records belong to the professional rather than to the

Reprinted with permission from the *Bulletin of the Menninger Clinic*, 1978, Vol. 42, No. 2, pp.150–155, © 1978 by The Menninger Foundation.

patient, and (3) that in order to be helped the patient must place a high degree of trust in his treater—are currently being subjected to serious review, if not open attack. While the public is interested in maintaining privacy and confidentiality, it is increasingly intolerant of all kinds of professionals keeping secrets *from them*. Indeed, recent legislation heavily endorses a patient's right to question and to have explained the nature of, the reason for, and the common side effects of all medications and treatments prescribed. In these laws, the word *treatment* clearly implies psychological as well as chemical-somatic approaches.

Under most legal circumstances, psychological test reports are included in what are referred to as "medical records," * and courts seem increasingly inclined to grant patients access to their medical records during or after treatment. Despite the erosion of privileged communication in many states, most state laws still do not require professionals to give reports to patients except in specified instances. The federal Buckley-Pell amendment, for example, which allows students over eighteen years of age and parents of minor children access to any records maintained by an educational institution, clearly distinguishes clinical records from educational ones by stating that "educational records" do not include records "created or maintained by a physician, psychiatrist, or psychologist."

Although a patient can obtain a copy of his clinical records through such legal means as court order or subpoena, current laws only recognize the patient's legitimate claim to the "content" of these records. While these laws require professionals to communicate such content clearly to the patient, they do not require that the patient be given a copy or an actual reading of the document. Neither is a psychologist required on ethical grounds to provide a written report to the patient. A proposed revision of principle 8 in *Ethical Standards of Psychologists* provides that the client has the right to have and the psychologist has the responsibility to provide explanations of the nature and the purposes of the test and the test results in language that the client can understand unless, as in some employment or school settings, there is an explicit exception to this right agreed to in advance. Besides the focus on explanation rather than open access to documents, the phrase "in language that the client can understand" is significant since few test reports are written in such language. Psychologists are well acquainted with the problems of communicating test findings to those outside the discipline. Social workers, physicians, teachers, nurses, and paraprofessionals all have different educational backgrounds, different languages, different conceptual approaches to understanding patients, and different expectations of a test report. Indeed, the necessity and techniques of tailoring a report for a particular consumer is a fundamental skill in report writing. Adding the patient

---

* This situation may be a price psychologists pay for the profession's alliance with medicine for such benefits as insurance reimbursement.

to the list of a report's intended or potential readers compounds the communication problem considerably.

Can a test report be written specifically for a patient to read? Certainly. Would it be the same report written for a psychiatrist or another psychologist? No more than a report written for an internist would be the same as one for a psychoanalyst. Can test reports be written that not only are suitable for patient reading but that do not compromise their information value to other professionals? I seriously doubt it. Some clinicians abuse the presumed privacy of their communications by using excessive jargon, by making inferences that far exceed the data, or by engaging in extravagant speculations; but these evils should be corrected for other reasons. A clinician who writes a report without reasonable certainty that it will be read only by the intended professional loses a considerable degree of freedom in frankness as well as language and style.

How can we understand the changes in society that challenge practices such as privileged communication and confidentiality which have seemed to serve the professional community well in providing optimal service to clients? One response is to question whether the professional community has indeed been successful in its mission. Is it not now reaping a bitter harvest for insensitively treating patients, for insisting on needless degrees of secrecy, and for unnecessarily patronizing patients? What is generally called the "consumer movement" coupled with the public's increasing reluctance to endow professionals automatically with trust and to behave toward them with passive compliance are significant elements in the patients' rights movement and the resulting legal trends. Until recently, the legal system protected professionals very well, perhaps better than it protected the citizens, and this balance or imbalance is now changing. However, in stripping away professional prerogatives, society may gain in some respects while losing in others. Deprived of the ability to function as they best see fit, professionals may not be able to deliver optimal service—a high price for the privileges gained by the consumer-patient.

With the trend toward patients increasingly gaining access to their records, professionals are confronted with the problem of how to resist or how best to comply. In some individual cases, judges accept the professional's opinion that material in the record is potentially injurious to the patient, and access is denied. In many court hearings, however, the judge is not convinced. In point of fact, no persuasive evidence that patients have been harmed by reading their own medical records can be marshaled, which paralyzes those who plead to the contrary. To resist the increasing encroachment upon privilege and privacy in treatment relationships, professionals must document their convictions with case reports. Until such evidence can be gathered, professionals must learn how to operate within the constraints of openness; however, their goal must continue to be optimal service to patients.

In considering the presumed sources of harm to the patient who reads his own psychological test report, the question arises of whether psychological test reports are more or less potentially harmful than other "medical records," such as psychiatric examinations or social work evaluations. I suppose this matter is debatable, but it does appear that patients are even less aware of what they are revealing about themselves in response to projective test materials than they are in their disclosures to other clinicians.

I believe there are two general sources of potential harm to the patient who reads his own psychological test report: (1) misuse of the knowledge the patient gains, and (2) impairment of the patient's trust in the clinician.

1. *Misuse of knowledge:* If the aim of the various modes of psychological treatment is increased self-knowledge, what harm can there be to a person who learns about himself by reading what another has learned about him? Diagnosis and treatment are two sides of the same coin; and as the clinician refines his diagnosis, he should be sharing it with the patient, if by *diagnosis* the clinician means an understanding of the patient and not merely a label. Self-understanding, however, does not typically arrive all of a sudden; rather, it proceeds gradually as readiness develops in concert with the willingness and capacity to understand and to change. Knowledge gained prematurely may easily become empty intellectualization which is useless and may even serve a significant resistive function.

2. *Impairment of the patient's trust in the clinician:* It is difficult, if not impossible, to write a psychological test report that is complimentary to a patient. Even the gentlest interpretations offered before a good working relationship is established can have a stinging, assaultive effect upon the receiver. Simply seeing the words and phrases describing such attributes as a patient's "narcissism," his "impulsiveness," his "limited capacities to cope under stress," his "tenuous hold on reality," his "meager capacity for empathy" will almost certainly make that person feel belittled, criticized, humiliated, and resentful toward his "accusor." As an adolescent female patient who literally stole her test report from the hospital nursing station said, "How could that nice old man say such nasty things about me?" A good working relationship is ultimately the vehicle through which information becomes experientially real and useful in a process of self-discovery and change.

Harrower (1960) and Aronow and Reznikoff (1971) offer examples of how the content of psychological test reports can be effectively used in the treatment process; and Shervin and Shectman (1973) show how this information can be used in the diagnostic process preparatory to treatment. To illustrate this latter possibility, I quote from a memo that a psychologist received from a psychiatrist:

> I thought you might like to know that Mr. X asked me to go over your test report with him in detail so that he could learn as much as possible from it. I did this

last Saturday, taking the report in hand and going over it almost line by line, usually 'translating' your statements into the everyday language used in psychotherapy. The patient got a great deal out of this session, by his own account and by my observation as well. His use of sarcasm as a defense, his tendency to put himself down in order to beat a potential critic to the punch, his efforts to cover up his sad feelings, the way anxiety interferes with his intellectual functioning, and the sharp dichotomy he attempts to maintain between 'male' and 'female' attributes were, among other things, helpful topics for discussion. At several points during the interview he said, 'I will have to think more about that,' or 'This is something I would like to work on.' I have never discussed test reports with patients with the report in my hand in this way, always giving the patient feedback from the test report in a general way, and focusing on the issues that seemed to me most relevant to the immediate psychotherapeutic task or to the wrapping up of a formal diagnostic study. When we had finished going over your report, the patient asked to see it, and I told him that he was certainly welcome to read it but that he should be warned that the technical language of such reports sometimes hurt people's feelings, and that if he noticed such a reaction while reading the report he should tell me so and we could discuss it fully. As a matter of fact, he simply wiped his eyes over the test report very quickly and did not even finish reading it. It seemed that it was more a test to see whether I would allow him to read it than a genuine wish to peruse the report.*

Other examples can be found, of course, of colleagues quoting test findings in much less constructive ways, such as to overcome resistances or persuade the patient of something, like the undeniability of the diagnosis, the need for hospitalization, or the seriousness of a thought disorder. Such uses are either thinly disguised attacks on the patient or the desperate efforts of an inept clinician to gain some leverage with a patient whose resistances are greater than the helper's skill.

Although psychological test reports can be written specifically for patients, the problem with such reports is that they may of necessity be somewhat superficial and may even have the quality of a horoscope. Such a report may communicate characteristics in a somewhat static way, conveying to a patient that he has now gotten the "final word," that there is little left to be understood about him, that he possesses no possibilities for change, and that he consists of no more than appears on the printed page. If such a report runs seriously counter to a patient's self-experience, it may evoke dire pessimism about the capacity of professionals to understand him and weaken not only trust but motivation.

In the face of these difficulties, I offer a few concrete recommendations:

_____

* The author is indebted to Drs. Ann Appelbaum and Richard Maxfield for this clinical example.

1.   The psychologist should suit the test report to the clinical purpose at hand—a task that involves answering specific referral questions with specific answers and leaving answers to unasked questions dormant in the raw test data. This approach reduces the number of areas of psychological functioning that may become points of difficulty should the patient read the document.

2.   While many other reasons exist for doing so, jargon and highly technical language should be avoided because of the potential communication gaps with the patient-reader.

3.   Focusing on the patient's self-experience rather than on description in purely structural or abstact terms may allow the patient to feel that an effort is being made to understand him rather than feeling he is being "talked about." *

4.   A patient's wish to see his test report almost always seems to be the product of either an unsuccessful treatment relationship or a feeling of antagonism toward the clinician involved. Discussion with the patient in advance of the testing about how the information will be used and discussion of the results following the testing will probably keep such requests to a minimum. Reviewing findings can also help the patient understand the report should he happen to read it later. As in the example, having a patient read the test report in the company of a professional who can answer questions, translate, and work with the feelings involved is a far better arrangement than having the patient read it alone.

As indicated in the example, a patient's request or demand to read the test report should not be taken at face value; rather, it should be taken as communicating some specific or general apprehension the patient has about himself or about the clinician. "I want to know my diagnosis" may be a way of asking "Am I hopeless?" "Will you show me your report?" may be a question about the clinician's intention to dominate, to criticize secretly, or to deceive. Clinical sensitivity and skill in responding to the "questions behind the question" may go a long way toward rendering confrontations over access to records unnecessary.

REFERENCES

Aronow, Edward & Reznikoff, Marvin: Application of Projective Tests to Psychotherapy: A Case Study. *J. Pers. Assess.* 35(4):379–93, 1971.
Harrower, M. R.: Projective Counseling—A Psychotherapeutic Technique. In *Creative*

* Sargent (1951) nicely illustrates these two styles of approach.

Variations in the Projective Techniques, M. R. Harrower, ed., pp. 3–39. Springfield, IL: Thomas, 1960.

Sargent, H. D.: Psychological Test Reporting: An Experiment in Communication. *Bull. Menninger Clin.* 15(5):175–86, 1951.

Shevrin, Howard & Shectman, Frederick: The Diagnostic Process in Psychiatric Evaluations. *Bull. Menninger Clin.* 37(5):451–94, 1973.

PART FOUR

Diagnostic Understanding and Treatment Implications: Forging the Connecting Links

Explicitly devoted to treatment planning, this last series of papers focuses on the rationales and actual techniques of intervention. The first three papers deal with hospital treatment issues. Psychiatric hospitals have been targets for social and scientific criticisms for decades, but they remain an essential component of our country's health care system (Brill, 1981). While pharmacological developments, increased outpatient treatment resources, and a decline in involuntary commitment have reduced the total hospital census, recent estimates still put psychiatric beds at over 300,000. Whether long-term or brief, the need for hospital treatment that is both humane and effective is undeniable.

In contrast to a view of hospitalization as a necessary evil or a "last ditch" alternative, sophisticated inpatient care can be seen as facilitating change and growth in positive, constructive ways. Many patients lack the control over thoughts, feelings, or impulses that would make outpatient treatment possible. Their lack of self-awareness, inability to know or communicate conflicts, and need for externally imposed limits or structuring calls for a sensitive milieu that detects the various needs and provides the required supports, outlets, or containment. Hospital treatment need not be strictly behaviorally or educationally focused, and certainly can be more than confinement while type and dosages of medication are determined. William C. Menninger's 1950 *Guide to the Order Sheet*, recently republished in the *Bulletin of the Menninger Clinic* (1982), was the first effort to spell out how the various components of a treatment milieu, including staff behavior, could be prescribed following an assessment of the patient's treatment needs. The chapters in this section broaden Doctor Will's ideas, and provide treatment formulations from a more modern theoretical perspective.

In the first chapter, Philip S. Holzman and Herbert J. Schlesinger address the importance of admission procedures in setting the stage for treatment and actually serving as the beginning of it. An examination follows of the patient's complex motives for admission, the psychology and diagnostic significance of this particular way of beginning to the various parties, and the ways institutional forces may be antithetical to treatment.

In the following chapter, the same two distinguished authors describe the general and specific factors in the hospital milieu that promote a patient's recovery and growth. While the general factors include health-promoting characteristics presumed good for all patients, the specific ones may be selected and prescribed, not for diagnostic "conditions," but in accordance with the patient's particular needs, abilities, and limitations. William H. Smith's paper on the analysis of activities uses the game of chess to illustrate how components of a therapeutic milieu can facilitate specific treatment aims.

Just as there is no question of *whether* hospital treatment will be done, only *how*, recent research on psychotherapy increasingly justifies its conduct and calls for continued efforts at refinement (Smith and Glass, 1977; Landman and Dawes, 1982). Having thus proceeded beyond the "pseudo" question of whether psychotherapy is effective, we must consider the more meaningful ones of what sort of intervention is helpful to what sort of person having what sort of difficulty? The second set of chapters in this section addresses such issues.

One pivotal consideration is that of theory; what guides the therapist's thinking? Fred Shectman addresses some basic conceptual problems posed by various theoretical viewpoints. He contrasts a psychoanalytic approach with behavior modification, encounter groups, and primal therapy. In an interesting and novel "dialogue" format, he teases out fundamental differences in the ways these orientations view the nature of adjustment problems and the pathways to change.

Building on the theme of how change actually comes about, Stephen A. Appelbaum's chapter calls into question the often-assumed inherent value of insight in the process of therapeutic change. He cautions the reader against idealizing insight, reminding us that it is a means to an end rather than an end in itself. How insight can facilitate—or hamper—change is a question too little asked by therapists, but one which treatment planning should unfailingly include.

Shifting from the internal ingredients of psychotherapy to its boundaries or "frame," in the next chapter Appelbaum examines the role of time and its experience by patient and therapist alike in influencing the nature and pace of the therapeutic work. Parkinson's Law may well apply to psychotherapy, and giving it less, rather than more, time to fill may hasten or facilitate treatment, at least for some patients. Economic, as well as humanitarian, values dictate that every effort be made to explore whatever factors may affect the duration of treatment.

Economic issues are sometimes at play when group treatment is considered, but more should and can go into such a decision than the typically lower fee. In his chapter devoted to borderline and narcissistic patients, Leonard Horwitz describes the typical intrapsychic and interpersonal characteristics of these often difficult to help patients and explains how specific factors in group therapy can be expected to influence them. His careful linking of treatment factors with specific patient characteristics to be influenced makes informed prescription possible. Such linking also allows a therapist to monitor whether the treatment is in fact having the desired impact. While some borderline patients should not be treated in groups, Horwitz concludes that some of these patients can benefit considerably, especially if a supportive individual relationship is provided concomitantly.

Matching the treatment interventions specifically with the patient's difficulties is also the theme of Herbert J. Schlesinger's "diagnosis and prescription" chapter. Formerly the chief clinical psychologist at the Menninger Foundation, as Horwitz is now, Schlesinger argues that using terms like "supportive" and "expressive" to describe therapeutic modalities seriously underestimates the specificity we can actually employ when recommending or planning a treatment. Using a case example, he shows how diagnostic information helps us decide *what* to support, *when*, and *how*; also, *what* should be expressed, the timing of its expression (*when*), and *how* such expression might be facilitated.

The last chapter in this section is in some ways the most specific of all, as it directly links diagnostic understanding to actual treatment interventions. Using psychological test findings, Rowe L. Mortimer and William H. Smith illustrate how the focus of psychotherapy can be planned and carried out in accordance with the specific patterns of assets and liabilities of the patient. Defining in advance what is to be addressed and what ignored, where the time and energy will be spent, can be as crucial in long-term therapy as it is in brief, and it can make a marked difference in treatment effectiveness.

The term "cost effectiveness" is more managerial-sounding than it is clinical, but who would argue that a person's treatment should take no longer or cost no more than absolutely necessary? Though originally written with "effectiveness" as the only aim, these papers are entirely consistent with the "cost" consciousness of our country's current economic ills.

REFERENCES

Brill, H. The present and future of the psychiatric hospital. In S. Arieti & H. K. H. Brodie (Eds.), *American handbook of psychiatry*, Vol. VII. New York: Basic Books, 1981, pp. 734–749.

Landman, J. T. and Dawes, R. M. Psychotherapy outcome. *American Psychologist*, 1982, *37*, 504–516.

Menninger, W. C. Guide to the order sheet. *Bulletin of the Menninger Clinic*, 1982, *46*, 3–112.

Smith, M. and Glass, G. Meta-analysis of psychotherapy outcome studies. *American Psychologist*, 1977, *32*, 752–760.

Issues in Hospital Treatment

Chapter   15

On Becoming a Hospitalized
Psychiatric Patient

PHILIP S. HOLZMAN AND HERBERT J. SCHLESINGER

The importance of the beginning phase of hospitalization for the patient's successful treatment is hard to overemphasize. If "well-begun is half-done" in any endeavor, it is certainly so for the hospital treatment of psychiatric patients. Yet many of the details of the admissions procedure, the processes through which a person becomes officially a patient, seem to be designed for administrative convenience rather than to facilitate the patient's beginning treatment. Unless they take particular care, institutions of all kinds, hospitals included, tend to become "closed systems" responsive principally to their own internal pressures and relatively insensitive to the needs of the clients they serve. Even procedures originally designed for effective treatment practice can lose touch with their original purpose and become institution-serving (or even nonfunctional) and self-perpetuating. They may even call for additional practices that are designed to maintain them, and that further remove them from responsive participation in the mission of the institution.

But we are not preparing the reader for yet another indictment of the psychiatric hospital as one of those institutions which, although designed to serve humanity, instead degrades the human condition. Another such one-sided discussion of the relations between man and his institutions could easily be written, and would be true insofar as the facts related are considered only in the light of the position taken. But we would have to regard that polemic as only partly true in that it considers only the hospital as the active partner. Yet even in the best-run hospitals, forces within the patient conspire against him and ally themselves with the obstacles offered by the hospital.

To a greater or lesser degree, a patient offered the opportunity to change may seem intent on repeating the maladaptive behavior patterns that cause him so much distress. He may even involve the hospital in his illness, breaking the rules

Reprinted with permission from the *Bulletin of the Menninger Clinic*, 1972, Vol. 36, No. 4, pp. 383–406, © 1972 by The Menninger Foundation.

designed to protect him and to further his treatment, and thus provoke unhelpful responses from the staff. He seems driven to make them and the hospital join the parade of disappointing and punitive figures who have marched through his life. He seems to have an uncanny knowledge of the weak points of the hospital structure, and he exploits them to embarrass the institution rather than use what is good in the institution to help himself. He sometimes seems totally ungrateful for the help offered him but instead attacks the hospital for "making him sicker."

A considerable body of theory has evolved to explain the paradoxical behaviors of patients. Such concepts as transference, defense, resistance, ambivalence, the tendency to repetition and the tendency to convert passive experiences into active ones help us to understand and intervene helpfully in these behaviors. But no such parallel body of psychological theory exists for the treating agents except for the concepts involved in countertransference. There is a body of sociological and social psychological theory that attempts to explain the behavior of organizations and their interactions with individuals, but this body of knowledge is not easily placed in the service of rational therapeutics. It is not usually available to the staffs of our hospitals.

To make maximal therapeutic use of hospitalization in the treatment of psychiatric patients, the treating personnel would need to be as familiar with the forces that guide and misguide their own efforts as with those complementary forces that guide and misguide their patients.

From the point of view of the hospital, as for any treating agency, a suffering person is not a patient until he has been admitted. It is essential that formal acknowledgment be made that (some) responsibility for the patient has been taken by the hospital before any diagnostic or treatment procedures can begin. But the necessity that may be felt by the hospital staff to do something to, for, or with the patient newly in their hands may obscure an important fact—that for the patient, perhaps as well as for the hospital, the treatment process has begun long before this formal ceremony of admission. The patient has already begun his relationship with the hospital in fantasy from the time hospitalization has been discussed with him and surely before he has finally accepted the idea. For the admitting staff, the relationship with a new patient also may have begun earlier than his actual arrival if any communications about the patient preceded his admission. From these communications the staff, too, begins to form impressions about the sort of person and problem they are about to deal with.

THE MECHANICS OF ADMISSIONS

The procedures by which a person officially becomes a patient should, of course, be an integral part of the beginning of his treatment. The initiation of treatment requires that certain information be exchanged between hospital staff and patient;

exchanges that have to do with getting to know each other. There are also forms to be signed, valuables to be checked, financial responsibility to be ascertained, and many other details. In busy facilities some of these procedures tend to be delegated to people other than those who will be directly involved in the patient's treatment. In such instances, these essentially supportive and "record-keeping" arrangements may unwittingly become the focus of the admissions procedure rather than its adjunct. One reason for this emphasis is that the procedures are tangible and they are necessary; regulations require that they be done. It is far easier to deal with concrete procedures and paper forms than to deal with the patient in a more open-ended way. Indeed, some patients, themselves, find it less burdensome to be "processed" than simply to be met.

Thus, from the point of view of those responsible for these functions, the admission of a new patient may be regarded not as the beginning of a treatment process but as a mechanical matter, a kind of processing in which the setting up of a clinical chart, a financial record, and other administrative details are the chief concerns, and the patient is merely the vehicle. In this routinization, what is likely to be overlooked is that the admission procedure is the first occasion not only for the patient to be assessed, but also for the patient to examine the hospital and its staff and to begin to feel what it is like to become a patient in this psychiatric hospital. It is an important anchoring point for the patient's expectations about treatment.

During the admission procedure itself, both patient and institution begin to experience the discrepancies between what the hospital holds as its purpose and what it actually conveys to the patient by its action toward, with, and about him, and between what the patient proclaims is his problem and the nature of the help he wants, fears, and despises.

The contrast between the needs of the patient and the apparent indifference of the institution is epitomized by the waiting room of a typical public hospital. There will be a number of patients sitting in a large inhospitable room that may be crowded, but the patients are each alone, usually silent, staring at the floor or looking at a magazine. There may be unwanted piped-in music or an unwatched television set. Off in a corner there may be a little enclosure from which patients are barred and in which sit one or more clerks who are to function as receptionists but who seem preoccupied with matters other than patients. From time to time a clerk will approach a patient with a form in hand and ask the patient to answer some personal questions and then withdraw again to his own affairs. The effect is to define the patients as "non-persons," as those who have lost their individuality and are there waiting for something to happen to them, to be picked up, perhaps soon, perhaps not, and taken into the depths of the hospital.

It is easy to wax indignant about this literally inhumane kind of treatment. But it may be more useful at this point to wonder why hospitals inflict it and why patients put up with it.

The Complicity of Hospitals

The ease with which some hospitals lose the view of the forest of their treatment goal for the trees of administrative treatment procedures suggests a similarity to an overloaded system, one that has too many inputs to process effectively and adapts by shutting itself off from certain inputs. Milgram[2] has used this system analogy to describe the adaptation people make to each other in crowded cities. Urban living, he noted, involves a persistent overload which distorts patterns of living. One adaptation is that relationships with people become superficial and transitory. Another way of reducing input is to set up barriers to new inputs threatening to enter the system. Milgram mentions such devices as using unlisted telephone numbers to discourage telephone calls, or assuming unfriendly facial expressions to deter personal contact.

For hospital staff to intrude helpfully into the troubled lives of patients, as for a patient to "intrude" into a busy hospital, may produce a strain comparable to that of the city dweller's experience of overload. The raw impact of an encounter between a patient and his would-be healers can be mitigated for both by setting up barriers to the encounter or by deflecting attention to the mechanical aspects of the admissions procedures. And all too often the delegation of admissions functions to nonclinical personnel tends to keep the patient at a distance or even turn him away. This tendency is exaggerated in busy hospitals whose overworked staff must continuously try to reduce the personal demands made upon them. Thus, procedures originally designed to expedite treatment may become obstacles even to beginning it.

In considering the factors that permit a hospital to treat its patients in a way that puts them down and irritates them, it may be helpful to look at the particular nature of the hospital as a service organization. A comparison of the usual city hospital or psychiatric hospital with commercial service organizations may be instructive. They, too, have the problem of dealing with large masses of customers. But inasmuch as they exist in a competitive situation, they realize the importance of appealing to the individual consumer to make his contact or transaction with the organization gratifying if possible, not only through the adequate delivery of an appropriate service, but through the very atmosphere in which that service is delivered.

Compare, for instance, the practices of the various airlines that compete over a given route. Even though the actual service offered the public by each airline is substantially identical, each will try to provide it in the context of amenities which seem to offer the potential passenger more. The approach will be made to seem individualized, the passenger will be made to feel important, to feel that his personal needs are being served and that he is wanted and valued. In most instances these offerings amount to little more than advertising gimmicks—a stereotyped "thank you for calling our airline." Sometimes these amenities seem grotesque when the service itself is deficient, e.g., when flights are oversold or schedules are not maintained—but there is no intrinsic need for these conflicts to take place.

Competing service organizations realize very well that their existence depends upon pleasing their customers, not just serving them adequately. In this respect the usual hospital almost completely lacks the kinds of commercial, competitive and personal pressures that serve to keep the commercial organization on its toes. The usual hospital does not serve people electively. Its customers are patients who come because they have to, and usually they come to the only place they can. While the hospital can be compared in this way to the public utility that advertises, "We may be the only phone company in town, but we try not to act like it," the usual hospital *is* the only place in town and makes no effort not to act like it.*

For these reasons, if the psychiatric hospital in pursuit of its therapeutic goals wants to pay attention to these aspects of the personal relationship to its patients, it must generate internally those forces which competition furnishes automatically to the airlines, the hotel, the department store and other service organizations.

The reason for "pleasing the customer" is not the same for the hospital as for the commercial establishment. After all, the hospital would be more than delighted if its "satisfied customers" would never return. It is rather that the service the (psychiatric) hospital offers has more to do with "treating the whole person." Its program tries to communicate better ways to live than the patient has found hitherto, to let him discover that it is safe to let others know him, to learn that the respect of others does not require the expensive defenses and dissimulations he has felt forced to use. In short, the effective communication of these messages that are essential to any psychotherapeutically-based psychiatric treatment requires the hospital not merely to say the messages but also to act them toward the patient. Respect for the patient as a person even when he himself may be so disturbed or regressed as to have little respect for himself, even when he may invite mistreatment or retaliation, is essential to the hospital's treatment program.

The Complicity of Patients in Their Own Mistreatment

To some extent the antitherapeutic atmosphere of the waiting room persists because patients do not complain about it, at least not until they are out of the

* To digress in this comparison—the patient who "shops around" among doctors is usually despised by all doctors. It is true that such a shopper may be shopping for the wrong reasons—he may be looking for a treatment that pleases rather than the treatment that cures, and thus he does "waste the doctor's valuable time." But those who know the present state of health care delivery would have to concede that for a patient to have a shopping attitude may be for him the wisest course in all situations that do not require emergency treatment.

hospital. There are several reasons for this. We must remind ourselves that there are forces in the patient that make him an unwitting accomplice against himself. Before the patient comes to the hospital, he has already been processed many times in his life—through schools, the military, job-seeking—and he knows what is expected of him when he comes as a supplicant to an institution. Thus, he will be resigned to wait, to obey, to repeat the same demographic information over and over again to individuals who have no particular interest in hearing it. In short, he will become less like himself and more like the idealized, generalized patient that the institution seems to have been designed for. This tendency is present in all of us but it becomes exaggerated when we are feeling needful.

The patient may literally be intimidated by the fact that he is ill and helpless and in need of what the hospital has to offer. He feels in no position to challenge anything about the hospital, not even the rudeness of the least of its functionaries. The patient may wisely choose to ignore these slights, preoccupied as he is with more important concerns. But the very fact of being ill, the more so being psychiatrically ill, is accompanied by a state of aloneness, an aspect of the kind of alienation that fosters a split in the patient's view of himself. The impersonality and indifference of the waiting-room staff fits with and aggravates the rejection of the "sick part" by the patient himself. Further, to be ill unconsciously connotes immorality for many of us. It implies that one has been bad, and is being justly punished. Acquiescence to the maltreatment of the waiting room can be assimilated to the self-punishing tendency that already exists within the patient. Thus, the spectacle of the quiet, isolated, infinitely passive patient enduring the waiting room is the product of a history of socialization, of institutionalized indifference, of the self-preoccupation of underpaid nonprofessional and ill-trained staff, and also of dynamic reinforcements within the patient's personality.

But not all patients are long-suffering in this way. An occasional patient will show minimal tolerance even for the unavoidable delays or lapses in attention that occur in generally considerate settings. The patient who blusters angrily or storms off complaining about mistreatment may be demonstrating less his independence of spirit than his anxiety about seeking help while excusing his flight by the poor reception.

Hazards of Mechanization

Generally speaking, the message a cold or mechanical reception conveys to the patient is that he can expect impersonal care, and little understanding or direction in his treatment. The absence of "someone in charge" to whom the patient is important compounds the anxiety about having to come to a psychiatric facility for help. In contrast, the therapeutic effects of having someone at the "front door" who can guide the patient in this initial period are inestimable. Later experiences with his psychiatrist may do much to inspire confidence in the treatment program, but first the patient will have to overcome the distancing effects of the routine administrative admissions procedures.

There is an additional hazard for the subsequent treatment program in such a chilling reception. The very contrast between a cool reception and the later more personal care of the psychiatrist serves to separate the opening encounter with the hospital from the beginning treatment process with the psychiatrist. It also reinforces a tendency, which is natural enough in human life but which is exacerbated during times of regression (especially that attending illness), to deal with one's mixed feelings by dividing the world into "good or bad" portions. Rather than seeing all humans and all institutions as complex, having both good and bad aspects, the patient in regression, to a much greater extent than the rest of us, tends to idealize some persons (and institutions) and to despise others. It is a frequent enough occurrence in psychotherapy for therapists to be idealized at one time and rejected at another and therapists learn to understand these shifts in terms of changes in the patient's internal motivations. To work effectively with the patient in such terms, however, requires that reality provide little support for either idealization or its opposite. When, as in such instances as the thought-less admission "routine," the treatment has gotten off to a bad start, the patient's tendency to idealize the doctor and denigrate the hospital may be so strongly reinforced by these reality events that an important aspect of the patient's treatment, the understanding of both the patient's beginning fantasies, wishes, and fears, and his ways of dealing with ambivalence, may be severly impaired.

In some hospitals, there is a further short-circuiting of the beginning treatment process. Information will have been taken from the patient by unidentified people; sometimes even a fee will have been collected; yet no contract for treatment has been made and no service as yet rendered. In some instances, no one in the receiving area is quite sure why the patient is even there. This impersonal structuring would seem to work at cross purposes to any conception of adequate treatment, particularly for those patients who come to a hospital to solve a psychiatric problem.

Here are some retrospective comments (written at the request of one of the authors) by patients at a large state hospital about the way in which they were admitted to the hospital:

> At the time of my admission I was quite confused as to where I was going, what my status was, etc. As a matter of fact, I recall that I was under the impression that I was entering a ward devoted entirely to the administering of psychiatric tests in a medical hospital. When I finally was informed that this was a mental institution, I was rather startled and immediately recalled a chapter from Ray Bradbury's *Martian Chronical* correlative to mental hospitals on Mars and a great variety of weird and exotic images ensued. Mr. A's search of all my personal possessions reminded me of a militaristic deprivation of civil rights. Shortly afterwards came the simple thought that I had been and still was bad. Then came the shock of

entering the ward which wasn't too bad after all, and then came what I call Dr. B's inquisitive intelligence probe for the benefit of the enemies' G-2 section. The last of these horrors was the shower which I thought of as being the decontamination period prior to entry to a Jewish health camp sponsored by the Third Reich.

Another patient wrote:

The procedure for my admission to this hospital was like this. I filled out the admission papers at the outpatient clinic. I was told to walk up to the hospital building and give my name. I told them that I had a suitcase at a hotel uptown and could I get it first. They said I should go right up to the hospital now. The aide wrote some things on a form and asked me questions. I don't remember what they were. He tried to make me feel at ease, that this was a real nice place. I thought, yes, but it's a mental hospital. Dr. J. then came in and interviewed me. He made me feel very nervous, uncomfortable when he asked me about my sexual problems. I was then given a physical, not as thorough as some I have taken. Also I was asked a question that seemed to be designed to show how clearly I was thinking. Then I was taken into the shower room and there was instructed to take off all my clothes. Rather like coming into a prison, I thought. It reminded me of missions I've been through. Rather as if I were unclean. And I forgot about my suitcase. When Dr. J. interviewed me I told him about my suitcase being at the hotel room. He said it would be taken care of. A week later I found it had not been taken care of. I felt I had been lied to.

A third patient wrote:

Immediately upon entering I was slightly accosted [sic] at the urgency that dis-possessed me of the few articles with which I arrived. No sooner had I arrived than I found myself giving an inventory of these articles. Somehow the hospital had been given the idea that I was a combative patient. This of course explained the welcoming committee. After a short interview with my admitting physician I entered the ward without partical [sic] information of what I might expect to find there. I feel that I could have been made to feel a little easier if I had been given more information on some of the hospital procedures surrounding admission and early treatment.

A fourth example:

A man telephoned a psychiatrist at an outpatient clinic in a large general hospital. The man had been having marital troubles and was not certain whether he should consult a lawyer, minister, psychiatrist or marriage counselor. The psychiatrist invited him to come to the clinic to discuss the problem and to see if he could help him decide on the appropriate person to consult. When the man arrived at the clinic, he was told by the clerk to fill out some forms that requested demographic information, including marital status, amount of income and business address. The man became indignant because he did not yet consider himself a patient, and he refused to complete the forms. The psychiatrist, however, had no inkling that this contretemps had preceded his contact with the patient. During the course of the interview, nothing was said about the man's encounter with the admitting clerk. The outcome of that interview was that no treatment contract was made but, if the man felt the need to consult the psychiatrist again, he could do so. The psychiatrist accompanied the patient to the door and on the way back the clerk stopped him and said, "Boy, that is the worst patient I ever came across." The psychiatrist asked him why and the clerk replied that the man had refused to sign the papers and to give him the information required for the clerk to have a complete record. The psychiatrist then told the clerk he could supply the needed information because indeed he had obtained much of it during the course of the interview.

Ideally the completion of medical record forms, fee setting, and other administrative procedures should be part of the treatment process rather than separated from it. The actual treating personnel should be the ones to collect needed information in the course of beginning the treatment with the patient. This information, and especially the *way* in which the patient gives it, are important data for the diagnostic assessment. Such an integration also helps the patient to see that there are real administrative aspects to the treatment process as well as intrapsychic aspects. Further, by dealing with the administrative aspects of the hospitalization in the same context as the intrapsychic ones, the hospital conveys that it considers the patient to be a whole person rather than a collection of administrative portions, medical portions, psychiatric portions, etc. He is not encouraged to form a concept of the hospital in which the doctor is on "his side" in opposition to "the administration," which views the patient only as a source of income and a potential deadbeat rather than as a person needing help.

THE PSYCHOLOGY OF BEGINNINGS

Turning now from examining the impact of the initial encounter on the patient and on his treatment, we can list the factors that contribute significantly to the complexity of the beginning interaction between the new patient and the hospital staff. These include: (a) the motives that led the patient to seek hospitalization; (b) the general dynamics of the "beginning process," whether of hospitalization or any other human interaction; (c) the "philosophies" of treatment or the "ideologies" held by the hospital and the patient about mental illness and its treatment, and the degree to which the hospital's practices in regard to patients are congruent with its official stance.

Motivation for Entering the Hospital

Patients come to psychiatric hospitals by different routes. Some few seek hospitalization themselves, others are referred by their outpatient therapists. Some are brought by their families or under order by a court. These various routes of access imply different views of the patient and his illness held by both the patient and society, views that will influence the meanings hospitalization will have for the patient and for his family.

For the patient, entering the hospital may mean—in part—an escape from a situation of imminent failure at work, or a crisis at home, or even an avoidance of prosecution. It may stand for a retreat from a slowly worsening situation that exceeds the patient's endurance. Entering the hospital may also express defiance or reproach or revenge upon another family member, as "look what you've driven me to"—so "I'll bleed you dry." It may also express a wish to turn the clock back and, by making a gesture of serious intent to change, to attempt to regain a spouse who is about to leave, or as a way of showing one's family how weak and helpless and needful one really is. Entering the hospital may also represent a wish finally to do something about the bad state of one's life, perhaps even as a last resort before giving up entirely. Several motives usually converge in the decision to seek hospitalization and it is an important part of the process of beginning treatment to help the patient and his family to understand the mixture of motives that brought about this step.

In discussing motives as an essential aspect of the beginning process, we do not imply that the concept of motivation is important only at the time of admission. But at the beginning one can usually see clearly many of those motives of which the patient is conscious and those which, although not acknowledged by the patient, are visible to the trained observer. The deeper layerings of the patient's motives will often not become apparent until after careful examination and often not until the patient has been in treatment for some time.

The layerings of motives that precede a patient's entrance into the hospital can be illustrated by the following case example:

A young mother was beset by the multiple responsibilities of having to care for a new baby and having to accept her husband's frequent absences on business trips. She was living in a community far from her parents' home and her unacknowledged sense of dependence was exacerbated to the point that she herself felt a desperate need for the care that her own baby was receiving. The decompensation of her previously fragile, hysterical adjustment made the home situation increasingly difficult for all. The patient finally brought herself to tell her husband she needed to be in a mental hospital because of fears she might harm the baby.

Although such a set of antecedent motives may appear to be relatively uncomplicated, the account does not mention the patient's conflicting feelings about "being a mental case" and needing to be hospitalized. Once the patient was safely in the hospital, these feelings came to the surface and the inner and outer reality situations that led to her hospitalization were explored. Exploration of those feelings continued after she was discharged from the hospital into outpatient treatment.

In the foregoing example, hospitalization resulted from the patient's own open, though conflicted, choice. But the role of the patient's choosing should not be overlooked in those instances when the patient seems to enter the hospital against his better judgment or even against his will, or in those instances when the patient finds it difficult to accept his own need for hospitalization.

A youth was brought to the hospital by his parents who were concerned about his failure in school and his use of illegal drugs. The boy maintained it was his parents' and society's problem, not his. But the patient was the one who brought his difficulties to his parents' attention and, though he protested about coming, he complied with the admissions procedures and did not make use of his keen wits to escape from the situation as he well might have if that were his primary goal. Clearly the boy had a sense of his own difficulties and was aware of his need for help but could not ask for it directly. Recognizing the boy's need to be admitted, but only under duress, the staff could allow him to enter the hospital in a way that did not immediately challenge his denials.

For some patients to ask openly for help involves a shattering admission of failure. They may find it easier and less humiliating to seek help by having what appears to be a major "nervous breakdown" that provides an acceptable reason for someone else to seek hospital care for them.

A newly promoted business executive, pressed with uncertainties, fearful of competition, and increasingly anxious, found it easier, rather than diagnosing himself as weak, neurotic, or maybe "crazy," to develop alarming somatic symptoms and a generalized state of "nervous exhaustion." These symptoms provided the impetus for his superior to recommend hospitalization after a searching medical work-up found no organic basis for the patient's complaints. It became the psychiatrist's task to help the patient see what put him on the course that led him to be hospitalized, why this particular method of communicating distress was chosen, and why it seemed to be an "honorable" solution to his dependency problem.

Another patient, unhappy about her chaotic work adjustment, could not bring herself to ask for psychiatric help. Such a request would have conflicted with her lifelong stance as an independent person who supported her entire family. She let her anxieties mount until they compounded her intolerable life situation; retreating into psychosis which required hospitalization was her only refuge. Following the remission of the psychotic episode, the doctor had the task of helping the patient stay in treatment until her life problems could be worked through.

Akin to the patient who avoids the implication of yielding to passive needs by developing a major breakdown is the patient who when given the recommendation that he should be hospitalized indicates he is willing to comply but only over his better judgment. He yields, though unconvinced, to "superior force." He makes clear that the dire consequences that are sure to follow will be on the heads of those who urge this course on him. The principal therapeutic focus at the beginning of hospitalization may need to be on helping the patient accept some of the responsibility for his coming into the hospital. So it was with one patient who blamed her therapist for her own return to the hospital. When she could see she herself had precipitated this return and that the therapist had simply responded to the cues the patient provided him, she was well on her way to being able to leave the hospital and again take on the responsibility for steering her own life.

An indirect return to the hospital can be illustrated by the following case example:

> A patient was discharged from psychotherapy and did well for many years. When new crises entered his life, he resumed using narcotics. Instead of returning to the hospital, he chose instead to go to other doctors. Finally he did go to his former therapist who was practicing in another city. Only by accumulating several recommendations to place himself in a hospital could he do what he knew he should have done in the first place. The point of his complicated approach was to demonstrate that he was sent by others, that he did not come of his own will and did not even think it was a good idea. In working with such a patient, it is often necessary neither to accept his story at face value, nor to discount it completely, but rather to work with his feelings about himself in order to understand the necessity for the circuitous return to the hospital.

It should be clear from these illustrations that the task of the doctor is to recognize not only the manifest motives that bring the patient to admission, but also those more covert, latent patterns of motives that influence the context of the admission and therefore set the direction for the rest of the hospital course.

This view implies that whatever the ostensible circumstances and whatever the degree of external compulsion seemingly involved, in *every* instance the patient has had some essential part in bringing about his admission to the hospital. If he has not literally decided to come into the hospital at a particular time, it can probably be demonstrated he has been aware of having acted in such a way as to encourage or require others to assume responsibility for him.

The hospital is willing, as a temporary expedient, to assume some responsibility and authority over the patient's life, but only as much as is needed and for as short a period as possible in order to accomplish the purpose of hospitalization. That purpose is (generally) to strengthen the executive functions of the patient sufficiently so that he is again able to exercise them effectively without the help of the hospital. Put in these terms, the hospitalization of a patient would seem to be a fairly straightforward transaction. But the rationality of a two-party encounter is most obvious when the status of each party is equal and when the transaction between them is relatively unambiguous. The situation alters radically when one person approaches the other feeling needful or with a sense of help-lessness, not really knowing what he wants from the other who is an "expert."

Thus, the hierarchy of motives that leads the patient to the hospital does not alone shape his initial experience in the hospital. The reasons for coming may even be overshadowed for a time by the problems about entering a new set of relationships with unknown persons in a strange milieu and by the interplay between his fantasies, expectations and experiences in the new situation in which he finds himself.

The Dialectics of the Beginning Process

Entering the hospital has much in common with other beginning processes such as entering a new school, taking a new job, going on a blind date, or starting outpatient psychotherapy. The beginning phases of each of these human en-counters are similar. In each instance, at least one of the parties will wonder: Will they understand me? Do I dare let them know me? Will they reject me if I do? Is this person competent to do what I need to have done? And, conversely, am I worth his bothering with me? Can I meet and afford his requirements?

Thus, whatever the patient brings in the way of his first communications—verbal and nonverbal—can be understood in part as reflecting the way in which he, in common with all people, begins a relationship with others who may become important to him as authorities, as potential helpers, as sources of gratification or punishment. He begins a testing process in which he must deal with his mixed fears and hopes. His defensiveness will likely show as he tries to conceal, conventionalize, and otherwise tone down, distort, or control the impact upon him of this important event.

In most transactions between parties who are ostensibly equal in their potential to fulfill each others' needs, each is likely to perceive an imbalance of power, frequently in favor of the other. But there are times when the relationship is in actuality unbalanced by one person's greater need for the skills, services and protection of the other. At such times, the tacit acceptance by each of the implicit power imbalance is embodied in the complementary roles (e.g., doctor and patient) each assumes. Thus, the imbalance may obscure the real business each has to accomplish with the other, and reflect more the unrealistic interactions between the experienced power-need discrepancy and the role-stereotypes. Put in another way, the usually unverbalized conditions and purposes in an encounter provide fertile soil for the flowering of transferences. The more vague, unspec-ified or ambiguous the primary purposes and conditions are for the encounter, the more the role of fringe intentions or expectations with their capacity for mobilizing transference becomes prominent. The beginning of a psychotherapy relationship illustrates this point nicely.[1] The party who feels helpless or driven by pain feels he has little choice or freedom of action and is at a psychological disadvantage. He is likely to attribute to the other omniscience and even more control over his future than he actually has and to minimize his own power and opportunities for alternative courses of action.

When the transaction is not only between two individuals, as for example, doctor and patient, but also between an individual and an institution, such as a hospital, then the patient's sense of powerlessness will be determined not only by his fantasies regarding the doctor and the hospital but also by his actual experiences with the hospital's procedures, routines, schedules, and even architecture. It may be difficult for the doctor or nurse who feels himself identified with the hospital, or who regards himself as only a powerless worker in it (e.g., ". . . I only work here") to disentangle what is real and what is fantasy in the patient's reports of his relations with the hospital. To the extent that the hospital's procedures are impersonal and institutional, they will be felt by both parties as externally imposed on their relationship and controlling it. The hospital may become for both doctor and patient a convenient scapegoat to blame for their difficulties in getting together. And each may regard it as unchangeable, as a part of nature rather than as a contrivance of man.

The patient admitted to a psychiatric hospital may show a greater tendency to obscure, deny or to remain unaware of the reasons for his admission than the patient, for instance, who is admitted to surgery. For unlike many physical illnesses, which allow the patient to feel there is something wrong with only a part of him, a psychiatric disorder severe enough to require hospitalization is more likely to be experienced by the patient as totally involving and to imply a negative evaluation—that he is weak, inadequate, and even bad. Such a view of oneself fosters regression, the adopting of more infantile modes of relating oneself to others, and hence augments the transference loading of the initial encounter with the hospital and its staff. These infantile, regressive forces are, however, opposed by the forward thrust provided by the patient's desire for relief from his suffering, his need for self-respect, and his wishes to attain competence and independence.

Whatever meaning the patient's symptoms had before hospitalization, they acquire additional meanings when he enters the hospital. The symptoms become a language through which the patient communicates with his doctor. They also are his "ticket of admission" to the hospital, i.e., the justification for his claim for attention. For many patients, symptoms are the only way they have found to communicate their distress. Words fail them and they are forced to reenact their conflicts in some totally or partially disguised way. Especially when the patient's symptoms have been exacerbated by recent stresses, entering the relative peace and quiet of the hospital is often sufficient to bring about considerable relief from these symptoms. Some patients who formerly could not sleep without drugs are able to get a good night's rest without them. Similarly, some patients' anxiety and tension states may lose their edge and even psychotic symptoms may remit within a few days of admission without specific treatment. The hospital staff must be alert to such changes in the patient's symptoms and the conditions under which they came about. Such changes inform about the dynamic significance of the symptoms and help to predict the patient's response to hospital treatment.

The doctor also realizes that should symptoms continue or even become worse, the patient may be communicating a fear of relinquishing them. Such fears have many dynamic meanings among which may be the following: For some patients, to face the doctor without symptoms might mean they are not entitled to be patients and will be forced to leave the hospital; for some, being hospitalized implies a yielding to passive wishes that can only be excused or tolerated by being "sick." For other patients, symptoms may have acquired secondary adaptive meanings and thus, paradoxically, are valued by the patient even though he suffers from them.

Discussing the patient's symptoms in this way might leave the impression that we are concerned only with their secondary functions. Our emphasis, however, is meant to convey that at times of special stress during hospitalization, such as entry into the hospital and separations of various degrees leading ultimately to discharge from the hospital, it is important for the doctor to recognize not only the primary gain of symptoms, but their communicative value as well. At such times, the secondary, later-acquired significance of a symptom can be of critical importance. In accordance with the principle of multiple function,[3] the predominance of one function of a symptom over another shifts depending on the dynamics of the current situation.

We do not advocate that the patient be eased into the hospital noiselessly and painlessly in order to make a "good" (i.e., compliant) patient out of a troubled person. Well-intended, manipulative attempts to reassure patients by being excessively agreeable and "giving" (whether of attention or psychoactive drugs) are all too commonly misunderstood to be synonymous with "good treatment." Instead, such attempts may be antitherapeutic to the extent that their effect is to hide from the patient and the staff the fact that the patient's anxiety and fearfulness are important and partly realistic aspects of his experience of entering a new and problematic situation. It should not be the purpose of the admission procedure to dispel all of the patient's anxieties and fears as a first order of business, but rather to begin a treatment process which aims at more than the alleviation of immediate distress. For, by words and example, the doctor and staff communicate what treatment is like from the very beginning. It is not meant to mollify, to soothe or to provide all manner of need-satisfying experiences. Nor is it meant deliberately or unthinkingly to frustrate and cause pain. The goal of the psycho-analytically-oriented psychiatric hospital is the *ultimate** alleviation of unnecessary suffering through understanding, leading to alteration of behavior.

As noted before, often the mere removal of the patient from his home environment to the hospital with its more "hygienic" regimen may alter the patient's symptom picture markedly. Thus, if the doctor does not understand that the patient's symptoms serve several functions, he may yield to one of two temptations: to speed the patient's symptomatic recovery and aim for a rapid discharge, or to discount the symptomatic improvement entirely and insist on treating the "deeper illness" he is sure is lurking there. Both ought to be avoided as *a priori* positions. A more appropriate position is to attempt to understand the patient's need to communicate with the hospital staff through his symptoms or other complaints and to make an explicit effort to help him find a more direct way of communicating about the problems that resulted in his hospitalization. Assuming that the patient is disturbed enough to warrant extensive treatment, the problem is to help the patient convert the presenting complaint into motivation to change those conditions in his life that led him to experience pain in the first place.

We are not advocating a puritanical or stoical ethic that holds pain to be good for one and, therefore, that nothing should be done to make the patient more comfortable. Our position rather is that mercy should be tempered with wisdom, and that direct efforts to relieve pain should find their proper place in the overall diagnostic and treatment goals for the patient. One implication of this point of view is that while ataractic drugs are a merciful and important adjunct in treatment (particularly the phenothiazines for the treatment of schizophrenia and lithium for manic psychoses), the doctor should regard drug therapy as part of the entire treatment program and not the program itself. Thus, the immediate prescription of psychotropic drugs may not always be the most helpful first step in a treatment program. Indeed, frequently these drugs may interfere with a proper diagnostic assessment.

The newly hospitalized patient faces a dilemma. He wants help to straighten out his troubled life and resume control of himself as rapidly as possible and hence would like to give up as little autonomy as he must in order to get the help he needs. But he is also burdened by a more or less conscious expectation that he should assume the traditional "good patient" role. "Good patients" in

---

* "Ultimate" in this context should be understood merely as implying "not as the first order of business." Proper, rational treatment is based on diagnostic understanding. The "first order of business" for the hospital, therefore, is to establish those conditions that facilitate understanding the patient's condition, including at least distinguishing among the underlying problems, the "crisis" that precipitated admission and the feelings and motives that belong to the admission itself.

a general hospital are expected to follow their doctor's advice unquestioningly; they agree that the doctor's time is valuable and theirs is not; they take the bitter medicine that is prescribed for them uncomplainingly; they submit to the painful diagnostic and treatment procedures; they suffer graciously the indignities and deprivations that treatment of one's ailing flesh frequently entails. But if this concept of the patient's role in treatment were to be carried over erroneously to the psychiatric hospital and followed to its ultimate implications, it would put the patient on a path opposed to what we think would be the most direct course toward renewed health and autonomy.

The enlightened doctor, too, has his dilemma. He, too, subscribes in principle to the idea that the patient should surrender only as much autonomy as he must. He would like to help the patient cooperate in his own treatment in a far different sense than mere unthinking submission to medical authority. But he, too, is burdened by the complementary traditions and attitudes of the "good patient—good doctor" role. Furthermore, the hospital in which he works, as we discussed earlier, has institutionalized these attitudes in a hierarchical organization. The many procedures, routines, rules and customs promulgated and rationalized as necessary to provide good treatment for all patients tend often to infantilize individual patients, discourage their initiative, and in other ways undermine the very therapeutic ideology the doctor explicitly subscribes to. And all too often patients acquiesce in this role assignment, partly out of passive resignation and partly to avoid the painful awareness of their own role in bringing about the crisis that led to hospitalization.*

The Philosophy of Treatment Held by the Hospital and by the Patient

We have observed that the patient's verbal and nonverbal behavior at admission communicates his expectations of the coming treatment process. These expectations can also be framed as articles of belief, as "ideologies." We have phrased them in more or less opposed pairs to indicate they are most usually seen in conflict. Needless to say, the listing is not exhaustive and the pairings not exclusive. Further, in succinct phrasing, they may seem like caricatures.

I need help but I don't really know what's wrong. I'd like to believe that it's physical and that a pill or treatment of some kind you can give me will make it all go away.

Or, perhaps it is somebody else's fault, and you can help me find him and blame him so I don't have this nagging feeling of having failed.

* A fuller statement of this point would demonstrate that the crisis leading to hospitalization was in itself a solution to other personal dilemmas.

I'm afraid to enter the hospital because I don't want to give up control of myself.

But I know to be a good patient I have to follow your orders and I am therefore prepared to swallow whatever medicine you tell me to take because I want to get well as quickly as possible. I will give you no trouble.

I'm so afraid of myself and of what I have been thinking that if you knew what was going on in my mind you'd never let me out of here. So I am afraid of you; I can't let you know what I am thinking.

But, if I could only tell you, or better if you could only read my mind so I wouldn't have to tell you and then, if you would let me know that everything is really all right, maybe I could trust you and get better.

I'm afraid I'm different from everybody else. No one ever had feelings or thoughts like mine. I must be dirty or immoral or weak or sinful and I don't deserve to be treated well or sympathetically. How can I when I failed at those things we all agree are the standards by which people should be judged? I don't respect myself and I don't expect you to respect me either.

But really I am not different from a lot of people—everyone has his weak spots and his weak moments. Why have you locked me up in here? I have committed no crime. If you don't let me out, I'm afraid I'll go crazy.

I have such great demands and so many needs that no one could possibly meet them. Maybe if I make myself into a small child, you'll treat me like a loving parent or a punitive one.

But I'm scared to be so small. I'd better grow up fast and not need anybody or anything. Just let me out of here and I'll behave myself.

In the same way, the doctor's and the hospital's verbal and nonverbal behavior toward the patient conveys the hospital's ideologies—the usually unstated and often conflictual sets of beliefs, attitudes and practices that govern the hospital's actions toward the patient. These also can be stated as pairs of more or less opposed attitudes but are neither exhaustive nor exclusive.

We want to help you to communicate what is wrong, to help you understand the sources of your pain rather than to try to relieve your pain first of all.

But you're causing us a great deal of trouble by coming to the hospital. In view of that, have some consideration for us; let us get our job done for you as efficiently as possible. We'll have you processed in no time if you'll only cooperate.

Only people can help people and we rely mostly on people and relationships among them, rather than on gadgets or drugs, though they are available if needed.

But you are "different"—unclean—we'll have to bathe you before we allow you into our sterile hospital. You are untrustworthy; we'll search your baggage to make sure you're not sneaking anything in that you shouldn't have. You're weak or degenerate, we have rules to guide you so you're not likely to get into trouble and bother us or the other patients.

You are a person as well as a patient and we respect you as well as your pain and illness.

But we know you are a demanding type; you're used to getting your own way and look where it got you. Here you'll find it different.

We expect you to respect us and the other patients here as people. We also expect you to respect our efforts to help you as rapidly as you can come to understand them.

But this is a hospital, not a hotel. The doctor's time is important and you have nothing better to do than to wait for him. Please remember we have many other patients to deal with other than yourself. Wait your turn. You're not all that important; we'll get around to you as soon as we can. In general, this hospital is much too good for you. Don't expect any rewards from us for failing outside. You probably should be punished rather than coddled.

We want to take only as much responsibility for your life as is necessary to help you regain full control over yourself. Thus, you're invited and even expected to participate in your treatment program and to understand what is being done in your behalf.

But, do as you're told; the doctor knows best. These are the orders he left for you; it's too late to disturb him now; stop being troublesome. How do you expect to get better if you're always fighting us who are here to help you. We have a lot of important things to take care of in regard to your admission.

One must keep in mind that a person entering the hospital experiences pressures to regress stemming both from his illness and from the significance of becoming a patient in a hospital. He is invited by old connotations of the word "patient" to surrender autonomy and responsibility. The doctor, for his part, has to avoid adding to the pressure to regress from these two sources while maintaining a diagnostic watchfulness as he carefully notes the lines of regression open to the patient and the extent of regression he undergoes. If the doctor himself, out of a wish for an untroublesome or a docile "patient," unwittingly reinforces the pressures to regress, he will complicate the diagnostic problem. He will find it difficult to know how much of the manifest regression is attributable to the situation, to the illness, or to his own unwitting interference.

We do not imply by this statement that the doctor should display intolerance for illness and for regression, but rather that he should not unthinkingly undermine the patient's ability to take responsibility for himself. It is difficult to avoid clichés and banalities in describing the general principles that ought to govern a patient's admission procedures. They tend to sound dismayingly like psychiatric versions of the golden rule. Yet, it is essential, since first impressions are lasting, that we start getting our therapeutic messages across to the patient at the very beginning and with minimal self-contradiction, for this is the time when the patient is most sharply attuned to our intentions toward him. Thus, the nature and success of admissions procedures must be judged in terms of what it is in general the hospital wants to say to its patients. And each act and encounter with the patient in the beginning must be judged in terms of its contribution to or detraction from that general goal.

We are overlooking other factors affecting hospital ideology, for example, the "official missions" and particular social functions assigned to the hospital. Whether it is a receiving and disposition center, or whether it carries nontreatment functions such as supporting the teaching of one or more mental health professions, or has certain research missions, will influence the way it fulfills its therapeutic responsibilities. These several functions will conflict with each other in complex ways, at least at certain times, as when residents or other students change services or when data must be collected. These interrelationships are important and deserve separate consideration.

In an effort to ease the admission process, many hospitals have prepared handbooks for prospective patients to familiarize them with some aspects of the hospital before they come. Although such handbooks can be useful, it would be folly to assume that a handbook can provide more than a general orientation to the institution, some intellectual understanding of what the patient may expect and something of the hospital's official attitude toward the patient. Perhaps its most important function is that by its very existence, rather than by anything it says, it conveys to the patient that he has a right—even an obligation—to know about the hospital, that he can ask questions and that he is expected to understand and participate in his treatment program in an active way and not merely as a passive recipient of the treatment. It also serves to remind the staff of these ideas and thus may help to reduce the amount of conflict between explicit and covert attitudes.

Our position is that there is no single best way to conduct the admission of a new patient. Any set of procedures must derive from the treatment goals and philosophy of the hospital as well as its customs, facilities, and the local conditions of practice. We wish to emphasize that the admissions procedures, like other aspects of psychiatric inpatient treatment, require constant attention on the part of those responsible for them lest the forces we have described push the procedures insidiously into serving ends other than the treatment of the patient.

REFERENCES

1. Ekstein, Rudolf: Structural Aspects of Psychotherapy. *Psychoanal. Rev.* 39:222–29, 1952.
2. Milgram, Stanley: The Experience of Living in Cities. *Science* 167:1461–68, March 13, 1970.
3. Wälder, Robert: The Principle of Multiple Function. *Psychoanal. Quart.* 5:45–62, 1936.

Chapter 16

The Therapeutic Aspects
of the Hospital Milieu

Prescribing an Activities Program

HERBERT J. SCHLESINGER AND PHILIP S. HOLZMAN

Since its beginning the Menninger Clinic has pioneered in the innovative use of the hospital milieu as a therapeutic agent. Dr. William C. Menninger in 1943[1] devised a guide for prescribing hospital activities and attitudes based on psychoanalytic drive theory. More recently Dr. Karl Menninger has written about the prescribing of hospital activities as part of the larger framework of the psychiatric case study,[2] an approach to milieu treatment cast in an educational framework.

Our present effort takes its inspiration from both of these sources. We shall discuss the broadly therapeutic influences of the hospital milieu on all patients as well as the prescription of activities programs for individual patients based on an understanding both of the patient and the activity from the points of view of psychoanalytic ego psychology and of drive theory.

Because the psychiatric hospital permits a degree of manipulation of the environment, it offers the patient an opportunity for new and significant life experiences that may be more therapeutically effective at some stages of his treatment than reliance on "talk" alone. The hospital milieu may also be seen as supplementing the hospital-doctor and patient relationship or psychotherapist and patient relationship in that it may provide opportunities for the patient to work out in a real context what has been talked about in psychotherapy and to practice trying to change or to regard himself differently. The milieu may also generate problems for psychotherapy, in that the patient lives in a known environment that imposes graded and realistic demands upon him, and his failures

Reprinted with permission from the *Bulletin of the Menninger Clinic*, 1970, Vol. 34, No. 1, pp. 1–11, © 1970 by The Menninger Foundation.

and successes in adapting to or mastering these provide current material for his psychotherapeutic interviews.

We can divide into two groups, general and specific, the factors in the hospital milieu that promote a patient's recovery. The *general* factors take their rationale from the assumption that many patients need psychiatric hospitalization because they have experienced excessive stress in their daily lives, whether in the area of work, marriage, family, or their relations with themselves. The experienced discrepancy between environmental demands and their own inner demands may force a regression to an earlier level of functioning, to an impairment of some aspects of ego structure.

The *general* therapeutic factors of the hospital milieu include first of all removing the person from the noxious environment, from the overwhelming tasks of daily life and from the people with whom he had been interacting. Thus, in the hospital there may be less of a sense of pressure than he has experienced before. The hospital offers him sympathetic attention, an atmosphere in which he and others around him are respected, and a regular mode of life which assures the patient an adequate diet, rest and exercise. The patient may not starve himself or overeat, may not go without exercise or wear himself out with too much activity. Thus, hospitalization interrupts the disturbed pattern of his life, and substitutes a hygienic moratorium. These factors reflect a general understanding of human development and human needs, the self-perpetuating nature of some mental illness, and the self-healing nature of others. They involve no necessarily specific understanding of any particular patient's personality or illness.

The general therapeutic factors of the hospital milieu imply a system of values, some of which are held also in a large segment of our culture and all of which are implicit in modern psychiatric treatment. A partial list of those values that are of particular relevance for an activities program are: (a) It is good for people to live up to the best that is in them; human potentiality should be exercised, not allowed to stagnate. (b) One should appraise oneself realistically, and expect neither too much nor too little of oneself. (c) While developing one's own sense of values one should be open to new experiences and remain in communication with the world. (d) While trying to do one's best, one should be reconciled to the likelihood that one will occasionally fail. Temporary impasses and regressions may occur but they need not lead to continued incapacity; it is important to keep alive the hope for better things. (e) One should feel a sense of obligation to one's fellow men, to want to give as well as to receive. (f) "Togetherness" up to a point is good; the capacity to be alone is also important. (g) Conflict is part of life, and one should be able to tolerate awareness of and some expression of one's infantile needs without shame or guilt. (h) One should be moral, not moralistic. (i) A balance of work and play is important for healthy living. (j) There is pleasure to be gotten not only from the satisfying of one's needs and desires, but from loving and aggressing in sublimated or attenuated forms, and, not least, from doing well what one is capable of doing.

The *specific therapeutic factors* of the hospital milieu include the intentional and selective use of the hospital's facilities and its staff based on an understanding of an individual patient's personality, the form of his illness, the pattern of his breakdown, and his expected course of recovery. From the point of view of the milieu an individualized program of treatment can be devised by selecting and prescribing activities from among the many that the hospital affords, by selecting particular staff to work with the patient and even by prescribing the modes of interpersonal interaction and "attitudes" that would be desirable for staff to cultivate. It is important to remember that the *general* values we have described above are (or should already be) built into the hospital setting and into its activities and programs and that it is not necessary to reiterate these for each patient but rather to specify what is different or unique about him and therefore what *specific* attributes of the milieu need to be called upon.

In order to prescribe milieu treatment one can look at each life setting or activity in the hospital from three points of view:

1. As a setting in which the patient may pursue educational aims, learn more about the world, about art, music, literature, and develop skills that could make him more useful to others and to himself.

2. As a set of opportunities to exercise and strengthen particular ego capacities such as attention, concentration, memory, delay of impulses, motor coordination; to facilitate making decisions or following instructions, to plan a task and to finish it; to minimize a sense of awkwardness and futility; to increase tolerance for frustration, as well as tolerance for boredom and routine; to be less meticulous and rigid, or to be neat and more regular.

3. As offering many possibilities for therapeutic interaction with staff and other patients; to work with people cooperatively or against people competitively but within rules to permit constructive or relatively harmless expression of aggressive drives.

By listing such specific purposes we may seem to imply that we mean to categorize activities *a priori* in terms of the therapeutic values they contain and the pathological conditions for which they would be suitable. Indeed, such efforts at categorization have been made (for instance, the *Guide to the Order Sheet*[1]). We want to emphasize, however, that any such categorization constructed on the basis of the activity names without reference to the specific facilities, social context, ecology, personality and level of skills of the activities therapist, etc., would be futile. Elsewhere we will try to analyze several activity therapy settings in terms of these values to demonstrate this point more clearly.

The prescribing of any activity depends not merely on the diagnostic understanding of the patient concerned, but also on the predilections and skills of the person who makes the choice and those of the persons who actually will work with the patient. For instance, knowing only that a patient is upset, it is possible to consider helping him by offering him a relaxing atmosphere—either a warm tub or a sedative or a back rub and some gentle mothering to promote an acceptable degree of regression. Another staff member might more appropriately treat such a patient by involving him in some energetic activity, by turning his attention outward, perhaps by taking a brisk walk, or by a game of paddle tennis. A third person might choose to sit and talk with the patient. We offer these alternatives to suggest that the choice of any one of them should depend on knowing why the particular patient is upset and on an understanding of the properties of the activity in mind and the attributes of the person who is to engage in it with the patient. Thus any categorization of activities should be thought of as simply a guide intended to emphasize particular qualities of these activities and not as a way of drawing boundary lines between kinds of treatments.

In milieu treatment as in any other form of psychological treatment we do not treat diagnostic category names. There is no single treatment for "depression," but there can be many appropriate treatments for people who are depressed depending upon what they are depressed about, what their ego capacities are, what their life situation permits in the way of change, and other variables, all of which should be clarified in the diagnostic process. Just as there are no treatments for diagnostic names, neither are there any milieu therapy activities which can be thought of as specific for any one condition.

The choice of a specific activity for a given patient thus is made with several considerations in mind: What do we want the patient to accomplish? What capacities are to be exercised? What harmful tendencies should we avoid stimulating? All things being equal it is preferable that the activity be con genial to the patient. The activity is more likely to be therapeutic if the patient can carry on the activity for inner reasons, although in the beginning external pressure may be necessary to get him started. Even if the patient does not actually like what he is doing, he should be able to develop the feeling, "I'm doing it because it's good for me," or "It's good in the eyes of someone else whom I value."

Any activity has rules of its own and ends of its own. One should not expect a patient to enter an activity if his needs or capacities are too widely at variance with what the task stands for. Any great discrepancy between the task requirements or social expectancy and the patient's needs or capacities could negate treatment efforts. For instance, to ask a patient to take a job in a store only for the "experience of meeting people" is likely to be as unrewarding for the patient as for the store management, unless the patient is able to adopt the values and attitudes appropriate to working in a store. For most activities (perhaps other than those that involve only, for instance, a disturbed patient in an individually supervised activity) the patient has to fit the activity as much as the activity fits him, and the prescription of an activity must thus take into account the patient's readiness to adapt to the task or social requirements.

To sum up, in prescribing an activity program one should keep in mind three points of view:

1.   From a broadly educational point of view, the activity should fill a gap in the patient's experience, or help him to improve skills that have remained dormant, or continue his development in an area in which he has had some previous experience.

2.   The activity should be chosen for the cognitive, affective and motor functions it requires of patients. The diagnostic examination of the patient will assess the intactness of his psychic functioning and show the presence of psychological deficits and areas of strength and will lead to the selection of certain activities that require broad or narrow attention, much or little social interaction, large or fine motor movements, creative abilities or rote functioning, or more or less in the way of social controls over impulsive or idiosyncratic behavior.

3.   The activity should be viewed as an occasion for a desired interaction either with other patients or with members of the staff or as an opportunity to generate experiences to be discussed with the patient's doctor.

The following case examples illustrate each of these aspects of the specific factors in the milieu treatment of hospitalized patients.

1.   *The milieu as an educational experience*:

CASE A

For thirty years a 55-year-old, successful, "self-made" businessman had "put all his eggs in one basket," his business. But as he grew older he became increasingly aware that his own powers were diminishing. His son's refusal to enter his company left him with the feeling that he had no clear purpose in going on in life. While he was discussing the dynamics of his depression with his doctor and coming to see why his potential for becoming depressed was mobilized by this precipitating event, he was also engaged in an activities program designed to provide him with a variety of interpersonal experiences different from those he had in his single-minded attention to business. Activities were chosen that provided other ways of renewing his self-esteem and these also offered new ways (to him) for acquiring "things of value" to replace his children and his job in his life. His program was a way of "reintroducing him to the world" as well as offering him a moratorium from the situation in which he had become depressed.

CASE B

An acutely disturbed woman with auditory hallucinations had previously been financially successful at her work, but her reputation had been built largely on factors other than her own talent. She never believed that she, herself, was honestly contributing to her fame. The activities recommended at first for this woman were principally those that would occupy her attention and promised a gratifying outcome but which did not require more concentration than she could muster in her disorganized state. Later, activities were chosen that would allow her to produce something that required more creativity, something that she, herself, could respect. The compliments that she received from these products she could properly regard as earned. One of her first projects of this kind was to make a mosaic table. She had to cut thousands of little pieces of mosaic tile, cement them in place, mix the grout and apply it, a task that took a considerable amount of time, yet kept her limited capacity for attention focused on the task. After the patient had considerably recovered from the psychosis, she was able to entertain the idea of selling the table and there were many interested buyers.

CASE C

A woman hospitalized for alcoholism had led a life that looked superficially comfortable, but had so shielded her from educational or vocational challenges that she had never had a chance to find out what she could do. It became an important part of the milieu treatment to provide her with a series of tasks that were graded in difficulty to allow her to find out what her capacities and interests were. Through experiences of success she came to believe that her efforts could achieve a result that she could respect. The development of skills together with the understanding of herself she gained in psychotherapy facilitated the late blossoming of a personality that no longer needed to rely upon intoxication to overcome boredom and to make life bearable.

2. *The milieu as ego strengthening*:

CASE A

An adolescent patient who had a history of many asocial and aggressive acts had great difficulty in making friends and keeping those he had. His egocentricity and low frustration tolerance made any kind of social accommodation difficult for him. His doctor soon learned that the patient could play the trumpet, and assigned him to play in the band as a part of his activities program. Here he had to learn to get along with the others in the band, to coordinate his playing with the others, to control himself in the service of ensemble playing. It was possible for him to modify his customary impulsive behavior because of the pleasure he obtained in playing music with his peers, because of the respect he soon developed for the music therapist who was an accomplished musician and teacher, and because of the gratification he obtained from playing at concerts attended by the rest of the patient group. A slow generalization of social skills began with his first successes in his "combo" and band relationships.

One can also devise an activities program to help the patient alter certain psychological defensive structures to facilitate working on the patient's problems in psychotherapy.

CASE B

A patient was hospitalized because of disturbed behavior resulting from fear of her homosexual impulses. She felt everyone around her was trying to seduce her into perverse practices and she had been making threatening gestures to her neighbors and showed other paranoid symptoms. The major burden of the treatment program was borne by her relationship with her doctor. But the milieu program was needed to assist in the process. Her defense of externalizing her conflicts inevitably involved her in conflicts with other patients and with staff members, and these relationships within the hospital were explored with her by the doctor, turning them into corrective experiences for her. As she found that staff members, particularly, neither were seductive nor would involve her in relationships beyond the intensity that she could tolerate safely, nor would reject her for her thoughts about them, she discovered repeatedly that her experiences contradicted her expectations. The carefully regulated hospital program made it possible to prescribe the kinds and intensities of relationships she would encounter. She was neither allowed to isolate herself to avoid seduction, nor to choose as close acquaintances those persons who actually did have these tendencies, to which she was acutely sensitive. Depending on the stage of her treatment, her doctor prescribed activities in which she had to come in closer contact with others, or activities that permitted greater interpersonal distance. He later found it useful to allow her to undertake some "masculine" activities, which had long appealed to her but which she had to deny herself, and, at another time, to undertake activities which had a particularly feminine cast in order to heighten her sense of herself and her conflict about her sexual identity, and thus to provide additional material for psychotherapy.

3.   *The milieu as the setting for therapeutic interactions*:

CASE A

A schizophrenic woman was slowly recovering from a seriously disorganized state. With some superficial indications of gratitude she brought to her doctor a ceramic ashtray she had made. The ashtray was of extremely poor quality, something that might have been expected from a kindergarten child, and it was clear to the doctor as well as to the adjunctive therapists that the patient was capable of much better work. The doctor then had the dual problem of dealing with the patient's ambivalent feelings toward him—the wish to show her gratitude and her resentment as well, and to test him—could he accept her in spite of her illness? Did he think that she was capable of nothing better than what she had produced? Would she be distinguished from her products? For our present purpose we merely want to point to the complexity of the interaction and the many layers of meaning contained in the apparently simple act of bringing this gift. The doctor and the patient spent many useful hours disentangling these several messages and the patient was helped to express her feelings toward the doctor and toward herself verbally, rather than in such highly condensed acting-out.

There are times when the potentially therapeutic aspects of interaction in the hospital may be lost sight of if the patient develops sexually- or aggressively-colored transference feelings to other patients and staff.

CASE B

After a year in the hospital, a young female patient, who was on a program encouraging her to earn love and self-esteem and to tolerate closer interpersonal contacts, had begun to respond. The staff, however, did not recognize the degree to which they had been successful with her because one of the expressions of the patient's response was a display of erotic feelings both toward other patients and toward one of the staff members to whom she had become close. Her warm feelings together with sexual stirrings led to some mild attacks of anxiety in the presence of a particular male staff member. She had also been seen holding hands with another schizophrenic patient and this behavior was looked upon with considerable misgivings by the hospital staff who, in an effort to curb the patient's "acting-out" attempted to break up the relationship.

The staff member toward whom the patient was attracted became uncomfortable since he did not understand her feelings or what he might have done to encourage them. He therefore attempted to withdraw and "cool off" the relationship. Thus, through the inappropriate expression of her growing involvement in her treatment program and with her doctor, the patient was in danger of breaking up the very relationships her treatment program was designed to encourage. As if to demonstrate that she knew her feelings and behavior were inappropriate, she begged her doctor not to take her out of this activity which had come to mean so much to her.

One could readily see how her self-esteem would have been hurt had she been rejected for experiencing the closeness that she was encouraged to feel. But one can also see that she had managed to bring about what we can presume to be a replica of some of the original traumata that led to her illness, that is, a kind of seduction resulting in rejection and a consequent loss of structure within her own personality.

In order to continue her treatment successfully from this point, the staff had to recognize that if they encouraged her to form closer relationships, she would react in ways that would express both her wishes to be more intimate and her anxieties about this wish. They would have to expect that she would try to test the limits of the staff's tolerance and hence their "sincerity." They also had to understand the metaphoric meaning of her "sexual feelings." In a person of such fluid psychic structure one feeling may easily be replaced by another, and "sexual feelings" may be the final common path to express many kinds of affect experiences. The staff had to be able to separate out from the sexual metaphor her increasing willingness to let someone else into her life and her fears about closeness. They had to help her to approach them safely, not by taking the sexual feelings at face value but by understanding their multiple meanings, which included, "To see if you really mean it, I'm going to show you my worst side." Or, alternatively, "I'm going to do with you the same way I did with Daddy, and I'll bet you'll reject me also."

Erotic feelings are of course not the only way a patient's growing involvement can be expressed. The wish to be close may arouse such a sense of shame or guilt that withdrawal or hostile activity may be the only obvious sign. The staff has to be prepared to understand a patient's responses to the treatment program in the "language," whether behavioral or verbal, that he is able to use.

The three points of view around which we have built our presentation are not the only ways in which one can approach the prescribing of milieu therapy. One advantage of this schema is its simplicity and the fact that while it is congenial with psychoanalytic drive and ego theory, the schema itself is not committed to that theory. If one were to study more systematically the prescribing of milieu therapy and its effects upon the hospitalized patients, one would want to consider the multiple reverberations of a patient's interaction with the milieu for his total personality. For this purpose one would need a more refined schema. A schema that reflects more sensitively the multiple functions of any patient's involvement in the hospital milieu can be derived from the five points of view of psychoanalytic metapsychology:

1. Structural: (a) to correct ego attitudes; (b) to exercise and strengthen ego functions; (c) to make superego demands more realistic and sanctions more appropriate; (d) to allow appropriate id expression.
2. Economic: (a) to provide opportunities for drive discharge in aim-inhibited or sublimated forms or to channel off or redirect surplus energies; (b) to intensify interests as expressions of higher order motives.
3. Dynamic: (a) to offer "corrective emotional experiences," permitting a person to alter unconscious images of significant figures; (b) to allow time-limited regressive experiences, permitting regression in the service of growth to occur and allowing greater exercise and freedom for preconscious ego functioning.
4. Adaptive: (a) to enhance reality attunement through stressing the real aspects of life in the hospital, encouraging patients to do productive work and to begin activities and modes of relating themselves to others that can be continued after they leave the hospital.
5. Genetic: (a) for those patients who have suffered developmental arrest, to provide an opportunity to resume growth in cognitive, affective and motor areas; (b) to provide activities that are planned to be congruent with the patient's own pattern of psychosexual and psychosocial development and take into account his particular areas of success and failure in early development.

Each of the examples that we have provided could be used to demonstrate the applicability of this metapsychological schema, but it is *not* our purpose in this paper to provide an extended metapsychological analysis of the patient in the milieu.

SUMMARY

This paper examined the general and specific therapeutic factors in the psychiatric hospital milieu. The former includes those factors which are available for all patients: removal of the patient from a noxious environment and the providing of a more hygienic one with a tolerant and humanistic value system. The specific factors include those which are manipulable so as to bear effectively upon requirements of particular patients. Three points of view should be considered in prescribing an activity: 1. its intrinsic values as a human activity; 2. the specific functions—cognitive, motor and affective—which it calls upon; and 3. the opportunities it provides for therapeutic interaction with other patients, with the staff, or with the patient's doctor. Striking a balance among these three points of view provides one of the major challenges in applying milieu therapy.

REFERENCES

1. Menninger, William C.: *Guide to the Order Sheet*. Topeka, Kansas, the Menninger Clinic, 1943.
2. Menninger, Karl et al.: The Prescription of Treatment. *Bull. Menninger Clin*. 24:217–49, 1960. Also in *A Manual for Psychiatric Case Study*. New York, Grune & Stratton, 1962.

Chapter 17

An Approach to the
Analysis of Activities

The Game of Chess

WILLIAM H. SMITH

It is common practice in psychiatric hospitals to employ activities such as sports, games, and creative arts in treatment programs. How the therapeutic role of such activities is regarded, however, hinges on how the treatment process in general is conceptualized (Key *et al.* 1958). One widespread, highly influential view (Menninger 1948) emphasizes the role of activities in the expression and/or rechanneling of drive energies. In this view, the potential benefits that warrant the inclusion of these activities in a treatment program are that competition is an "outlet" for the "instinctive aggressive drive" and the act of creating serves the "erotic, constructive, or creative drive." Another point of view (Llorens & Johnson 1966), one less anchored in the early, drive-oriented psychoanalytic theory, regards activities as enhancing adaptive functioning through the practice and mastery of ego skills: "These include physical and motor performance skills as well as skill in psychological, social and interpersonal interaction" (p. 179). Still another point of view (Barnard 1954) places most weight on *inter*personal rather than *intra*personal considerations: "Even more important than the specific activity is the emotional atmosphere in which the activity is carried on, and the relationships created between the patient and the therapist who guides the activity" (p. 22).

The thesis I shall advance here is that in evaluating activities for use in treatment, each activity should be regarded as a complex, multifaceted event— no dimension should either be ignored or attended to exclusively. The selection of activities that will further (or at least be compatible with) treatment aims can best proceed from a broad, thorough analysis of their characteristic elements. A framework or matrix within which such an appraisal of activities could be made

Reprinted with permission from the *Bulletin of the Menninger Clinic*, 1975, Vol. 39, No. 1, pp. 93–100, © 1975 by The Menninger Foundation.

would facilitate clinical decisions regarding the potential benefits or disadvantages of a given activity for a particular patient. I propose the following framework for such analysis. Descriptions should be made of: (1) the formal aspects, such as materials and space required; (2) the physical and intellectual prerequisites for participants; (3) the interpersonal aspects; (4) the opportunity afforded for gratification of needs and discharge of drive energies; and (5) the task demand from a cognitive, affective, and motoric-muscular standpoint.* As a demonstration of this framework, I present an analysis of the game of chess.

FORMAL ASPECTS

Chess is a table or board game. Two players sit opposite one another across a game board upon which are thirty-two chess pieces, sixteen for each player. Each piece has a value commensurate with its freedom of movement and its consequent power to "capture" the opponent's pieces—except the king whose movements are limited but whose importance is paramount. The rules of the game are easily obtainable and need not be presented here. Suffice it to say that the object of the game is to direct the pieces according to their prescribed moves in a fashion designed to capture and remove the opponent's pieces until an opportunity is created to put the opponent's king in a position of capture—the checkmate.

All that is necessary beyond the pieces, the board, and the two players are two chairs, a table, and a lighted room sufficiently quiet to allow the players to concentrate.

PHYSICAL AND INTELLECTUAL PREREQUISITES

No physical activity is required except that necessary to move pieces around the board without upsetting the others. Seeing the board and the pieces is, of course, necessary unless the set has been especially adapted for the blind. Exceptional intelligence is not required to play the game; however, a high level of intelligence (at least of a certain sort) is necessary for one to become an expert player. Most people can learn the basic elements of the game within a few hours instruction. There is evidence that once acquired, the ability to play chess is not lost in psychosis (Fine 1956) and that patients described as schizophrenic can be taught to play (Pakenham-Walsh 1949).

---

* I do not intend to suggest that these considerations are independent of one another, only that for purposes of analysis they may profitably be separated.

INTERPERSONAL ASPECTS

The interpersonal aspects of the game can occur on two levels—the cooperation and competition between the opponents, and the symbolic representation of human events through the characters and actions of the pieces. Beginning with the two players' agreement to begin the game, the entire activity is one of interdependency. Each player must await the move of the other before his own move, and each move must be calculated with regard to the opponent's preceding move. There must exist, then, an interpenetration of minds, with each player continually wondering what the opponent is thinking.

It is often said that there is no element of chance in chess. While this remark may seem an overstatement when applied to the play of novices, there is, even then, no doubt about where responsibility for the move lies. With no plausible latitude for rationalization or excuse, a loss is undeniably a loss, and a victory a victory; the responsibility for the outcome rests squarely on the players. In some activities, such as bowling, a player's performance can be assessed in absolute terms, i.e., his score is not contingent on his opponent's performance. In chess, however, a move is "good" only in terms of the threat it poses to the opponent, and a move is "poor" only in terms of the opportunities it presents to the opponent. The competitive aspect of the game is clear; the point is to defeat the opponent. Chess is exclusively an intellectual contest and, as such, is particularly provocative for those whose intellectual performance is a source of self-esteem. Only improved performance in a rematch can attenuate the sting of defeat; and in each game the players face anew the prospect of losing, winning, or tying, for the game is not over until one of these outcomes is clear.

Since the interaction between players may be almost exclusively nonverbal, those who have difficulty talking to others may keep verbal interaction to a minimum while actually interacting quite closely, in the sense described above. When the two players are a therapist and his patient, as Fleming and Strong (1943) demonstrated, chess can be a valuable avenue of communication and even a primary therapeutic medium. Depending upon the skill and training of the therapist, the game can become an opportunity for interpretation of some of the patient's conflict areas, those manifested in his style of play and in the ways he experiences playing, winning, and losing.

A great deal has been written about the symbolic aspects of the game.* For example, Coriat (1941) said that: "The unconscious symbolic significance of the chess pieces and their manipulation in the game are essentially a reanimation of the player's family conflict resulting from the Oedipus complex. The protection of the Queen from loss is for the purpose of retaining her as long as possible to

* See Fine (1956) for a good summary of these ideas.

attack the King. Whatever the character traits of the player or his rationalized conscious attitude during the game, the unconscious primary purpose is the same, a reenactment of the fundamental Oedipus conflict'' (p. 35). The basis for the assumption about the symbolic oedipal nature of the game lies in the fact that the destruction of the king is the aim of the game. The prohibitions against this ''father murder'' are nicely observed in the fact that the king is never actually captured and removed from the board. While this interpretation of the nature of the game has been ''confirmed'' by clinical observations of chess players, it seems possible that the symbolic significance of the activity may vary from player to player, though perhaps with this as the richest possibility. Indeed, Menninger *et al.* (1963) wrote, ''In every chess game there are trillions of possible moves and there are almost as many combinations of symbolic gratifications for the players'' (p. 143).

GRATIFICATION OF NEEDS AND DISCHARGE OF DRIVE ENERGIES

Many writers (Coriat 1941; Jones 1951; Fine 1956) have emphasized the rich oedipal symbolism of the game as the major source of gratification, seeing it as touching upon conflicts around aggression, narcissism, homosexuality, and masturbation.* Narcissistic gratification may be derived through demonstration of intellectual prowess and through identification with the king. The mastery of a complex skill (or at least the improvement of one's ability to perform a difficult intellectual task) may also be a source of gratification. Since the game is generally considered a pastime of the intellectually gifted, some measure of social regard may be reaped, even though quite spuriously, from association with the game.

The discharge of energies in the game occurs in highly sublimated form, i.e., far removed from direct drive expression. Fine (1956) states, ''in the chess player . . . the ego is strong: it is capable of tolerating a great deal of libidinal stimulation, it can renounce primitive gratification with original objects and it can neutralize the drive energies to a high degree'' (p. 28). To the extent that the game is a symbolic reenactment of an internal struggle, some gratification may be afforded by the projection of this painful struggle onto substitute inanimate objects, through partial drive expression via symbolic enactment and some degree of mastery over the conflict. The principal avenues of gratification in

---

* This view of the game may partly account for the fact that it tends to be more attractive to men than to women.

chess, therefore, are intellectual-narcissistic and highly sublimated aggressive ones.

TASK DEMAND FROM A COGNITIVE, AFFECTIVE, AND MOTORIC-MUSCULAR STANDPOINT

Since chess requires a minimum of physical involvement, strength, dexterity, coordination, and the like are of little relevance in this activity. The most salient aspect of chess is its emphasis upon intellectual processes. The rules of the game are strict, and the nature of play complex. Therefore, a standard of reality via rules is set forth against which numerous task demands emerge.

Although unflagging vigilance need not be rigidly maintained, concentration must be sufficient to allow the player not only to take careful note of the opponent's moves and strategy but also to pursue a series of mental trial actions—"if-then" propositions that will guide his decisions (e.g., if I move my pawn here, he will move his bishop there; if I then move my knight here, he will have to defend his queen with either his bishop or his knight, etc.). Each action must be preceded by thought and the consequences of each move carefully weighed. The player must be alert to what the opponent hopes to achieve by each of his moves and must plan each of his own moves accordingly; no information may be disregarded. A number of separate elements (e.g., values and positions of various pieces) must be appraised and coordinated in a systematic, organized way. Flexibility, i.e., continual reevaluation of the situation, is also critical, for a plan will need to be modified or abandoned according to those changes introduced by the opponent's responses.

While the emphasis is upon logical and systematic thought, the thought must eventuate in action; but no action should be made impulsively or carelessly. No move should be made without benefit of prior thought. A player must maintain control over any affective stirring that might prove disruptive to judgment or attention.

Chess is an anxiety provoking game. To quote Karl Menninger (1942): "Whatever else it is, chess is not a relaxing game. Playing chess is a very intense and exciting experience which only one who has gotten well into it can fully appreciate" (p. 81). Anxiety may be mobilized around winning or losing or symbolic aspects of the game. A constant threat may be posed by the fear that what is symbolic may become real, depending on the intactness of the players' ego defenses; but some reassurance is no doubt gained by the fact that it is, after all, only a game. The necessity for constant thought also helps bind anxiety. In summary, the exercise of intellectual processes not only in executing the play of the game itself but also in controlling the affective potentialities attendant to the game's real and symbolic aspects can be said to be the principal adaptive challenge posed by chess.

DISCUSSION

Finding that chess serves certain intrapsychic and interpersonal purposes for some persons does not, of course, mean it will do so for everyone. For that matter, the issue of whether adaptive capacities can be strengthened through exercise or practice is by no means an established fact (Reider 1967). While it is inviting and even somewhat compelling to assume that such capacities as persistence in the face of frustration or careful, meticulous planning and execution of a project would generalize to areas of life other than those in which they are practiced, this is an empirical issue which is far from conclusively established.

However, case history reports (Fleming & Strong 1943; Slap 1957) have indicated that for *some* patients chess may be a powerful treatment tool. Fine (1956) suggested that for one expert player chess actually warded off a psychosis for a time. He also quoted a prison psychologist as saying that prisoners who learned chess during their incarceration were less likely to be recidivists, since the appeared to have learned better ways of handling their aggression.

While my purpose in analyzing the game of chess was not to promote the use of chess in treatment, some comments about its application might illustrate the potential use of such an analysis. As part of a program of reinstating orderly, logical, goal-directed thinking, playing chess might be encouraged for those suffering a breakdown of ideational defenses. To foster the interposition of thought between impulse and action, the careful weighing of consequences before acting, it might be encouraged for people whose difficulties include impulsivity. Someone for whom verbal communication is too anxiety provoking could use chess as a vehicle for establishing an interacting relationship. Encouraging the expression of aggression in controlled, socially appropriate ways, that is, to offer chess as an avenue of sublimation, might also prove helpful for those whose aggressive impulses are not well controlled. The game might be discouraged for those whose narcissistic valuation of themselves and/or their intellect is a problem. Also to be discouraged from playing might be those who tend to have difficulty relating to others in other than intellectually pretentious or competitive ways. These few examples show how once the various elements of an activity are spelled out, it can be recommended or discouraged for use in a treatment situation, depending on the treatment goals for the given patient.*

---

* In offering this framework for analysis of the intrinsic qualities of activities, I have not touched upon the personal characteristics of the treatment personnel or the relationship established between staff personnel and patient. This omission is by no means a tacit implication that such relationships are not important; it is only that such considerations are not the focus of this paper.

A treatment team, having analyses comparable to the one presented here for all the activities at its disposal, could prescribe a combination of activities coordinated to serve complex treatment aims. For example, one activity might be included in a patient's schedule principally because it allowed him to experience self-esteem building gratification in completing projects that eventuate in a product (such as ceramics, woodworking, etc.), another because it promoted careful thought and control over impulsivity (such as chess, radio repair, etc.), and another because it involved cooperation with a number of peers (such as a drama group, patient newspaper, etc.). Prevailing treatment philosophies and theoretical persuasions ultimately guide the use of any activity: the characteristics of the patient that are deemed important to modify, the point at which an activity is introduced into a treatment process and for what specific purpose, etc. By the same token, activities comprise only a portion of a therapeutic milieu and may play a much larger role in the treatment process for some patients than for others. However, for whatever uses activities are put in a treatment program and with whatever treatment philosophy prevails, the outline offered here for analyzing the elements of the activities employed may prove helpful, since it offers a comprehensive view of any activity.

REFERENCES

Barnard, Ruth: Milieu Therapy. *Menninger Q*. 8(2):20–24, 1954.

Coriat, I. H.: The Unconscious Motives of Interest in Chess. *Psychoanal. Rev*. 28:30–36, 1941.

Fine, Reuben: Psychoanalytic Observations on Chess and Chess Masters. *Psychoanalysis*, Vol. 4, #3, Monogr. 1, 1956.

Fleming, Joan & Strong, S. M.: Observations on the Use of Chess in the Therapy of an Adolescent Boy. *Psychoanal. Rev*. 30:399–416, 1943.

Jones, Ernest: The Problem of Paul Morphy: A Contribution to the Psychology of Chess. In *Essays in Applied Psychoanalysis*. Vol. 1: *Miscellaneous Essays*. London: Hogarth Press, 1951, pp. 165–96.

Key, W. H. *et al.: Project 52: A Study in Adjunctive Therapies Coordination*. Topeka: Washburn University, 1958.

Llorens, L. A. & Johnson, P. A.: Occupational Therapy in an Ego-Oriented Milieu. *Am. J. Occup. Ther*. 20:178–81, 1966.

Menninger, Karl: Chess. *Bull. Menninger Clin*. 6:80–83, 1942.

Menninger, Karl *et al.: The Vital Balance: The Life Process in Mental Health and Illness*. New York: Viking Press, 1963.

Menninger, W. C.: Recreation and Mental Health. *Recreation* 42:340–46, 1948.

Pakenham-Walsh, R.: Chess as a Form of Recreational Therapy. *J. Ment. Sci.* 95:203–04, 1949.

Reider, Norman: Preanalytic and Psychoanalytic Theories of Play and Games. In *Motivations in Play, Games and Sports*, Ralph Slovenko & J. A. Knight, eds. Springfield, Ill.: Thomas, 1967, pp. 13–38.

Slap, J. W.: Some Clinical and Theoretical Remarks on Chess. *J. Hillside Hosp.* 6:150–55, 1957.

Issues in Psychotherapy

Chapter 18

Conventional and Contemporary Approaches to Psychotherapy

Freud Meets Skinner, Janov, and Others

FRED SHECTMAN

As you know, I am interested in the potential of three relatively new treatment orientations: encounter groups (Back, 1972), behavior modification (Agras, 1972), and primal (scream) therapy (Janov, 1970).

And, as you know, my commitment is primarily to a more traditional psycho-analytic approach that has stood the test of time.

If we look at some divergences between what is contemporary and what is more conventional, perhaps both orientations can profit and even be advanced by the cross-fertilization that may ensue. New and old may emerge even more worthwhile than before, just as a gene pool can create a more vigorous and richer strain when infused by "new blood." A step in that direction has been an attempt to note contrasts and similarities between a psychoanalytic approach and a be-havioristic one and to provide some ideas about integrating the two (Shectman, 1975).

Fair enough. And may I propose that your viewpoint be titled "Everything You Always Wanted to Know About the Behavior Modification of Primal Screams Shrieked in a Nude Group Encounter Gestalt Marathon But Were Too Afraid to Be Conscious Of—Let Alone Ask!"

Very funny—and very revealing as well. For such a snide remark perhaps reflects a tendency to be prejudiced, if not outright antagonistic to new treatment ideas and methods. To the extent that such biases operate to foreclose on our really investigating such approaches, then we have not only lost the opportunity to broaden our own horizons but have failed as scientists to fairly evaluate new efforts designed to help people change.

Reprinted from the *American Psychologist*, 1977, Vol. 32, No. 3, pp. 197–204. *Copyright 1977 by the American Psychological Association. Reprinted by Permission.*

You are correct in chiding me. Perhaps we could better guard against prejudices by being aware of some sources.

Well, one origin of prejudice is that a treatment method can easily be judged on the basis of how it fits with conventional approaches—so that to be different is reason enough to be suspect. From this viewpoint, however, you would do well to remember that a conventional treatment approach like psychoanalysis was attacked for just that reason when it was the newer and more controversial treatment method. And I think you were implicitly resorting to such a bias just a moment ago when you referred to a psychoanalytic approach as having stood the test of time—as if its having been around a long time were, in itself, a basis for believing that it is superior. But charlatans have also been around a long time and claimed much success, yet we would hardly accept their longevity as proof of the efficacy of their approach.

Linking my remarks to an analogy about quacks! Whose prejudice is showing now!!

All right, all right.

Anyway, I do agree with your point. But just as longevity does not necessarily make a treatment modality worthwhile, so being new does not in and of itself necessarily make a treatment approach better than its predecessors—despite the fact that new treatments often generate initial enthusiasm and appeal just because of their newness.

OK. And neither should a treatment method be evaluated by the impression made by the practitioners of that method. The actions of a controversial person or a charlatan may well color the way we regard such a person's approach—however separate the treater and the method might be. But an indictment of the way an individual uses (or abuses) a method is not an indictment of the method itself.

Fair enough—I know how I react when someone evaluates a psychoanalytic approach on the basis of those who practice "wild analysis."

And may I add that another source of bias is that, like it or not, your conventional approach is in competition with newer ones. And you know that it is not unusual to hear dynamically oriented therapists complain about the periodic decline in requests for their treatment, due to some siphoning off by contemporary forms of treatment advertised as quicker, less expensive, and less psychologically effortful and painful. And it must come as no surprise to you that competition can breed anger (if not envy) and that one way of handling such feelings is by deprecating the source of them, that is, the competitors.

But as therapists, we compete not only for patients and for financial well-being. We also compete in the marketplace of ideas—competing for the hearts and minds of students and for the belief by educated people in our preferred way of thinking about psychological distress and, ultimately, in our particular view of the nature of human beings. A psychoanalytic approach can be char-

acterized in many ways. One of these is to view it as a long-standing love affair with reason. As in a serious love affair, psychoanalysis' commitment to its lover (understanding) is both deep and intense. As such, it does not take kindly to newer approaches that relegate the role of understanding to a lower priority— if not discount it altogether. Indeed, one reviewer of the encounter movement has written:

> *Much of the activity . . . within sensitivity training . . . is a concerted effort to turn away from the emphasis on the intellect . . . on mediation of any experience through reflection, and to push the participants toward a direct experience that is not thought about and is not analyzed. (Back, 1972, pp. 207–208)*

Along this line, a colleague* has told me of a university professor who not long ago wrote on his blackboard the credo ''What feels right is right.'' As my co-worker pointed out, this dictum calls to mind the parallel Victorian standard: ''What feels right is wrong.'' Both are on the same level of unreflective judgment. Exhibition has simply been substituted for prohibition, but in neither case is there room for considering what makes the feeling right or wrong or how we have arrived at these quite general judgments in the first place. As such, these modern calls to action easily clash with psychoanalysis' cherished belief in the value of thought preceding and guiding action, not being subordinated to it. It would thus be only human for psychoanalytic therapists to want to retaliate by belittling such approaches.

Human yes, but not necessarily wise. Surely you must be questioning in your attitude, and I am *not* suggesting an uncritical acceptance of any and all new approaches out of a misguided benevolence. But you also must not confuse being critical, in the sense of being discerning, with criticizing, in the sense of denouncing that which is different.

Fair enough, but now let's get down to specifics. One selling point of the newer approaches, and certainly one of their promised advantages, is the elegant straightforwardness of their techniques. Each of the approaches of which you are in favor emphasizes—in its own way—the role of technique and minimizes the role of the relationship between the treater and the client. For example, as touched on earlier, experience itself is extolled as inherently worthwhile by encounter group advocates, whereas adding understanding to that experience is seen as being likely to spoil it. One way of looking at the encounter group, then, is to see it as relying on techniques for generating intense, rapid, and unthought-about experience and feeling. But you know more about all this than I do! Perhaps you should elaborate on the techniques employed.

---

* I am grateful to Howard Shevrin for this example and for his discussion of its implications with me.

Thanks for letting me get back into the discussion. But I'm not so sure I agree with you about "techniques" being used. Participants are just encouraged to reveal themselves more than they have done and to utilize the experience of the moment as it unfolds in the group.

You imply that because "only" self-disclosure is stressed, no techniques are used—because self-disclosure is presumed to be on a par with just being "natural"—as if exposing oneself in a group were not a technique in itself, with its own set of assumptions and implications, for example, that such self-disclosure fosters "genuineness"; that such "openness" is good for one's psychological well-being; and that these psychological states promote intense emotions that are inherently beneficial.

But you leave out that people are also encouraged to "own" their feelings and not just to pour them out!

Even so, aren't certain techniques used to foster just that? For example,

The authority of the therapist-expert is discarded; . . . the pursuit of long-range personal goals is replaced by the immediacy of experience in the here-and-now; . . . the role of reason in understanding one's interpersonal operations is disparaged; the experiencing of strong affect is seen as a value in its own right; the long-term aspects of interpersonal relations are temporarily suspended in favor of affection, gentleness, and "understanding" from strangers; and openness, spontaneity, self-expression and the experiencing of affects are viewed as [desirable]. (Strupp, 1973, p. 122)

I would put it somewhat differently. Group members are encouraged to take responsibility for their actions and their feelings as representing choices.

But there is still an implication that complete openness should be regarded as tantamount to what is good in providing psychological growth and well-being. Surely you don't believe that disclosure is inherently valuable, independent of the particular context or relationship in which it occurs? *

Tut, Tut. Don't let your bias enter in now.

All right, but the role of the relationship between encounter members, and especially between the members and the group leader, is minimized if not explicitly thrown out in favor of mutual directness, spontaneity, and revealing what has been private.

No, the relationship of the moment is being emphasized and thereby freed of past encumbrances.

Not at all! The way the person experiences that current relationship is bound to be colored by past ones. And you need not take my word about that. Simply

---

* For an incisive critique of the encounter group movement and its image of humans, see Koch (1973) and Marin (1975).

observe the diverse reactions of people in almost any group who are exposed to the same occurrence. While the relationship of the moment may be felt, its particular significance for individual group members may be diluted simply because its various individual meanings are not thought about and put into the context and perspective of each person's life as it was before the group experience. Thus, by not linking it to the past, the present is not enriched.

Behavior therapy and primal therapy in principle also do not attend to the relationship between patient and therapist. By not regarding the nature and role of that relationship as an element in treatment, they, too, are able to avoid the messy, complicated, and often quite troublesome vicissitudes of what goes on between the two parties. Instead, they emphasize a method—be it the formulation of contingencies to positively reinforce certain behaviors and not others, the systematic desensitization of certain anxiety-producing stimuli, or efforts designed to release pent-up painful feelings and their associated memories. These treatments, then, are impersonal in quality. In terms of the explicit rationale given for these forms of treatment, they could be applied by machines and do not depend on a personal relationship between the patient and the therapist for their effectiveness.*

But ignoring such a personal relationship does not mean that it does not exist. In fact, there is research to suggest that in one study,

> the prevalence of behavior modification techniques in the therapy was not significantly related to outcome, whereas a variety of the patients' personal feelings about their therapists were. . . . The important elements of these therapies were interpersonal ones, much as has been demonstrated in psychodynamic psychotherapy. (Ryan & Gizynski, 1971, p. 1)

Are you implying that behavior modification, encounter groups, or primal therapy are ineffective in themselves and really due only to the influence of what goes on between the treater and the patient(s)?

No, clearly there is evidence to suggest that these approaches can bring about change in their own right. I do think, however, that therapists of these newer approaches limit their effectiveness and narrow the theoretical scope of their treatment method by excluding attention to the role of the personal relationship.

But there is little personal relationship unless the therapist actively enters into one with the patient, and these treaters tend not to do that.

But that is not so, for the research I just cited demonstrates that a great deal is going on in the thoughts and feelings of the patient about the therapist, however much it may be unattended to. From this viewpoint it is impossible for a relationship not to exist. The only choice is whether to recognize it and take it into

---

* I am indebted to Howard Shevrin for drawing my attention to this point.

account, because one cannot choose to have a relationship be absent since the patient will clearly form one anyway (cf. Shevrin & Shectman, 1973, p. 468). Winnicott's (1965) belief that there really is no such thing as an infant—that is, no isolated infant apart from a relationship with a mothering figure—applies here. To paraphrase Winnicott, I don't believe it is possible for there to be a patient without a relationship to a treater.

What if a teaching machine were used, so that the human treater would not have direct contact with the patient?

Even under those conditions, the influence of a personal relationship would still need to be taken into account. This is so because the patient's performance would be a function of how he perceived the therapeutic context; that is, his psychological functioning is influenced by qualities of the perceived relationship, for example, its "impersonality," "scientific purity," etc.* Clinical psychologists, especially Schafer (1954), have drawn attention to the importance of the influence of the patient-tester relationship as an important context in which test responses are obtained. And there is research evidence here, too, which demonstrates that the client-examiner relationship influences the patient's responses, and that the latter are not just lying dormant in the patient, waiting to be elicited independent of the relationship in which they emerge (Masling, 1966).

I can see that you are quite intent on this issue. What makes it so important to you?

I am making such a point of this because it is tempting to focus on techniques that can be applied and to forget that their application occurs in an interpersonal context. If this is indeed forgotten, then, as Santayana has said and our patients have taught us, "Those who forget the past are doomed to repeat it."

Freud began by focusing on technique and was forced to go beyond that and to take note of the role of the relationship between him and his patient. In describing his treatment of Elizabeth von R., he writes:

> It often happened that it was not until I had pressed her head three times that she produced a piece of information; but she herself would remark afterward: "I could have said it to you the first time."—"And why didn't you?"—"I thought it wasn't what was wanted" or "I thought I could avoid it, but it came back each time." In the course of this difficult work I began to attach a deeper significance to the resistance offered by the patient in the reproduction of her memories. (Freud & Breuer, 1966, pp. 194–195)

---

* I wish to thank Howard Shevrin for making me aware of this idea. This point is equally applicable to the biofeedback situation, in which it may superficially appear that there is only a person and a machine—which the person himself regulates. But recent literature reflects a growing appreciation of the role and influence of the interpersonal context within which biofeedback training occurs (Brown, 1974; cf. Balint, 1955; Certcov & Calvo, 1973).

By invoking the explanation that her thought was not what was wanted, the patient clearly was responding to the therapist and her imagined idea of what he wanted—just as she was reacting in part to him by wanting to avoid saying something unpleasant and painful. These resistances taught Freud the significance of the nature of the interpersonal relationship and opened the way to the importance of being aware of transference—of responding not to the problem that resides in the person, but rather to the person who has a problem.

I am frankly skeptical of your harkening back to Freud, unless you can buttress his ideas with some current research findings.

All right, from the Menninger Foundation's landmark Psychotherapy Research Project, which spans 20 years, come other findings that underscore the central role of the therapeutic relationship. Some patients who acquired very little insight during the course of their psychotherapy nevertheless made durable personality change. Something other than understanding alone must account for these changes. What is proposed is that these patients represent:

> *New instances of therapeutic change based in large part upon the curative factors inherent in the therapeutic relationship per se . . . a major contribution of this study is the indication that the therapeutic alliance is not only a prerequisite for therapeutic work, but often may be the main vehicle of change. We are proposing to account for the numerous observations of stable change associated with the development of a favorable therapeutic relationship as due to the internalization of the therapeutic alliance. (Horwitz; 1974, pp. 254–255)*

By utilizing the concept of "internalization," Horwitz makes explicit that certain features of the interpersonal relationship are essential ingredients in bringing about the stable change.

Are you saying that this point about the relationship is particularly germane to behavior therapy?

No, primal therapy also stresses a technique and minimizes the particular relationship between the patient and the treater. In this sense, then, what has been said about behavior therapy applies as well to primal therapy and to some encounter group therapists who underemphasize interpersonal relationships in favor of feelings that are to be expressed within the group.

Moreover, it is clear that the recovery, experience, and release of submerged affects is regarded as a central therapeutic agent in primal and emotive-encounter treatments.

So?

But the role of affect has from the beginning played a crucial role in psychoanalytic thinking about human functioning. Freud's (1896/1962) first model of psychological disturbance (the actual neuroses) conceptualized the etiology as the "damming up" of libido—a blockage to be dealt with by discharge through affective catharsis. In ignoring what analysts have learned since, the newer modalities are in danger of repeating psychoanalysis' own past, when short-term relief was thought to imply lasting change. But early psychoanalytic experience with so-called "abreactive cures" demonstrated that such cures were temporary, that the relief experienced because of the discharge of pent-up emotions was short-lived. The patient resisted facing and assimilating what had emerged under catharsis and so had to repeatedly recall and work through such experiences before enduring change occurred (Freud, 1914/1958).

While we are on this topic, I also have a real question as to whether these groups relying upon catharsis are treating those patients who might be helped by their technique, for example, emotionally inhibited and overintellectualizing patients. As Pruyser (1973) has submitted,

> There is good reason to think that the prevailing psychopathology of our time and our culture is no longer typified by restriction and hyper-repression, but rather by weakness of impulse control, narcissistic self-indulgence, loose thought organization, and externalization of conflicts. . . . Here, then, is a jarring note: many of the newer . . . therapies address themselves in theory and presuppositions to more or less Victorian psychopathologies, while many of the clients they attract, by a kind of drift in the absence of diagnostic screening, may possess the opposite kind of pathology requiring remedies toward containment and restructuring rather than fitful abreactions. (pp. 435–436)

My point here is that if different kinds of therapy attract different clienteles because of self-selection, without proper diagnosis the way is open for a mismatch between the patient and that type of treatment best suited to his need. Also, the way is closed for any systematic comparisons of the effects of different therapies.

I will grant that the ethos of the Human Potential Movement and the ways in which it offers experience to people do not lend themselves to systematic study of results. People are welcomed uncritically into encounter or Gestalt groups, for example. They have the experience and go on their way. Those who can benefit from it do so; those who are shaken by it are often skillfully helped to reintegrate themselves on the spot; those untouched by it are not heard from again. But please face the fact that very little systematic research has come out of psychoanalysis either. The work of the Psychotherapy Research Project is an exception—perhaps the only study of its kind done in nearly a century! Furthermore, to my knowledge, no one has yet proved that self-selection of treatment modality produces worse or better results than the matching you propose. And lacking such proof, are you not unfairly manipulating people when you pretend to know that a certain kind of treatment is better for them than the one they choose for themselves.*

---

* I gratefully acknowledge that Ann Appelbaum suggested and provided the inclusion of this paragraph.

You have made many good points, and I agree with much of what you say—but not all of it.

Somehow I anticipated that!

Well, with your emphasis on proof, you remind me of Nietzsche's comment that "That which needs to be proved cannot be worth much."

And Mark Twain wrote that "Faith is believing what you know ain't so."

All right, there are some data available about the deleterious effects of mismatching. Again, from the Psychotherapy Research Project comes the conclusion that

> the Psychotherapy Research Project had an influence on the practice of psychotherapy and psychoanalysis at The Menninger Foundation both in large and small ways. One definite finding which I believe infiltrated into our thinking and practice was the importance of a careful diagnostic study before embarking upon treatment, particularly psychoanalysis. Despite the current popularity of the new briefer therapies, there is still considerable conviction at our institution, reinforced by the present study, that analysis is an unrivaled method for the alteration of deep-seated character problems. But the research impressed upon us the great care that must be taken in the selection of cases for such treatment lest we spend much effort, time, and money to no avail. (Horwitz, 1974, p. xxi)

And, though not research, some analysts (e.g., Ticho, 1972) have published reports that are well grounded in hard-won clinical experience. These deal with the importance of the analyst's personality on the treatment process, and they highlight the importance of another kind of matching, that between treater and patient.

But such matching requires much thought and understanding before any particular patient can embark on any specific form of treatment; and in doing so much thinking and reflecting, one runs the risk of doing precisely what the newer forms of therapy seek to avoid—that is, overemphasis on what is intellectual at the cost of bypassing what is at the core of the patient's experience and feeling.

While it would indeed be unfortunate for reason to stifle feeling, wouldn't you agree that it would be equally undesirable to abandon reason in favor of feeling? Neither extreme is an integral part of diagnosis but is rather an abuse of true diagnosis, which would seek the optimal balance between thought and feeling for each patient. Furthermore, without a way of taking individual differences into account and tailoring treatments accordingly, you are vulnerable to violating those very humanistic interests in people as separate selves, which you, as an encounter-emotive enthusiast, so value (cf. Shectman, 1976).

But don't you think that all people need pretty much the same kind of treatment to get better anyway? For me, devising separate treatment plans for different patients smacks of unjust manipulation.*

---

* For an elaboration of these ideas, see Shevrin and Shectman (1973, especially pp. 454–458).

Manipulation may indeed be involved, but this is not necessarily unjust at all—just the opposite! For although "manipulation" has come to take on a pejorative connotation, one meaning of the term is "skillful management" (Shevrin & Shectman, 1973, pp. 459–460; Strupp, 1970). And that, in effect, is why the patient comes for help to an expert in the first place, isn't it?

Well, one thing I think we can agree on is the great temptation of polarization and argument! Not only have we shown that in our talk here, but one need only peruse the professional literature to recognize how clinicians have divided into antagonistic camps—except for some noteworthy exceptions.

Well put, and I think you will agree, however great the temptation for divisiveness is, that the need for integration of what is offered by each of the approaches we have considered is even greater. While the behavior and primal therapies emphasize technique to the exclusion of personal relationship, encounter and sensitivity groups tend to emphasize expression of feelings while not examining carefully enough the implications of their oft-used technique, abreaction. I think that perhaps only a psychoanalytically inclined mode of therapy has so far sought to conceptualize and integrate all these ingredients, for example, the significance of the personal relationship and the varied techniques that can range from interpretation to suggestion. The effects of these techniques have been shown to be closely tied to the nature of the personal relationship between the two parties (Klein, Dittmann, Parloff, & Gill, 1969), thus illustrating that both the relationship and the technique influence each other and need to be mutually attended to.

I think you are proselytizing here. And you too quickly gloss over the role of feelings. I think that is one area in which the primal and encounter group approaches have something to teach us, or at the very least, to remind us of. It seems to me that by self-selection, traditional therapy modes have attracted those who value the use of the intellect because of their belief in the importance of understanding and of proceeding according to that understanding. But it is so easy to confuse the therapist's need to understand intellectually in order to be able to help with what is helpful to the patient, who does not need to understand to the same extent as the therapist—or at least not at the same level. I think such confusion can lead to emphasizing the role of intellectual insight over that of emotional experience and understanding and to overlooking the importance of feelings as an integral part of change. And no less a person than Jerome Frank (1963) concluded in his review of various forms of influencing people by stating, "a further implication of this survey for psychotherapy is that the emotional components of the process deserve more attention" (p. 233). And I hardly need remind you that long ago, Alexander and French (1946) stressed that "the patient, in order to be helped, must undergo a corrective emotional experience suitable to repair the traumatic influence of previous experiences" (p. 66). Further, to pick up on something you mentioned, I think this underemphasis on the role of feelings has also come about in part because of Freud's experience that the effects of abreaction tended not to be permanent. This has led to some turning away from the role of emotions in making for change. Thus, it is as if these newer modalities wish to teach us that one can so stress "reason" that "feeling" is stifled and the essence of a person's experience is missed.

Good points. But to compensate for this onesidedness by swinging to the other pole and underemphasizing (if not altogether excluding) understanding is to miss the point by going too far in the other direction. That is, I think that you are confusing using one's intellect with intellectualization. It is one thing to use one's intellect to understand and quite another to use it to prevent oneself from having feelings. But to discard both uses in hopes of getting rid of the latter one is hardly warranted.

Fair enough. But if advocates of newer therapies tend to emphasize feelings over thinking, psychoanalytic therapists are inclined to stress the value of thought over action. Because they so value understanding, they too easily equate action with "acting out" and regard it in a pejorative fashion. As you said in the beginning of our talk, psychoanalysis cherishes thought over action. And so, psychoanalytic therapists may forget that thought can serve to prevent action, as in the case of obsessional patients, and that thinking can block constructive action such as necessary risk taking in new relationships and undertakings. Thus, too often, analytic therapists tend to regard action as inherently detrimental— seeing it one-sidedly as a substitute for what should be thought about. Rangell (1968) has observed:

> I have seen a wrongly moralistic, anti-action attitude which creeps into some analyses fortify the patient's own phobic avoidance of action and lead in some cases to almost a paralysis of the latter and a taboo against even the necessary actions of life. Such analyses may hit a snag somewhere after mid-point where a marked indecisiveness eventuates at the necessity to convert long-standing insights into effective action. (p.200)

In fact, though, I am heartened by the burgeoning number of conventional therapists who are recognizing this and are underscoring the importance of certain forms of action. Principal among them is Allen Wheelis (1969), who submits that

> We are what we do . . . and may do what we choose. Insight is not enough. Effort and will are crucial. The most common illusion of patients and, strangely, even of experienced therapists, is that insight produces change; and the most common disappointment of therapy is that it does not. Insight is instrumental to change, often an essential component of the process, but does not directly achieve it . . . personality change follows change in behavior . . . the sequence is suffering, insight, will, action, change. (pp. 57–59; 63)

Wheelis's emphasis on the importance of the patient's really wanting to put forth the effort to change harkens back to Kaiser's (1955) ideas about the personal responsibility of the patient in continuing on as before or in changing him- or herself. It also fits with more recent contributions by Shapiro (1970) and Schafer (1976). Shapiro (1970, p. 341) takes issue with "the marionette conception of unconsciously driven action" and accentuates the necessary role of intention and volition in personality change. And Schafer has begun to evolve an "alternative language" for psychoanalysis—one in which the patients are the actors, rather than beings passively acted on by unknown forces, and thereby accountable for actively behaving so as to perpetuate their misery or for altering themselves accordingly.

Our talk has certainly been heartfelt, and thought-provoking as well; so at least in our own discussion we have exemplified some of the very ingredients for change that we have been discussing. Now we must seek to translate these into action and to change.

On that we certainly agree. We do need to work toward an assimilation that integrates old and new, relationship and technique, understanding and feeling, and thought and action—in order that we can better treat our patients as the individual human beings they are.

REFERENCES

Agras, W. (Ed.). *Behavior modification: Principles and clinical applications.* New York: Little, Brown, 1972.

Alexander, F., & French, T. *Psychoanalytic therapy.* New York: Ronald Press, 1946.

Back, K. W. *Beyond words: The story of sensitivity training and the encounter movement.* New York: Russell Sage, 1972.

Balint, M. The doctor, his patient, and the illness. *Lancet,* 1955, *1,* 683–688.

Brown, B. B. *New mind, new body; Bio-feedback: New directions for the mind.* New York: Harper & Row, 1974.

Certcov, D., & Calvo, J. The problem of psychotherapy in psychosomatic medicine. *Psychosomatics,* 1973, *14,* 142–146.

Frank, J. *Persuasion and healing; A comparative study of psychotherapy.* New York: Schocken Books, 1963.

Freud, S. Further remarks on the neuro-psychoses of defence. In J. Strachey (Ed. and trans.), *Standard edition of the complete psychological works of Sigmund Freud* (Vol. 3). London: Hogarth, 1962. (Originally published, 1896.)

Freud, S. Remembering, repeating and working-through. In J. Strachey (Ed. and trans.), *Standard edition of the complete psychological works of Sigmund Freud* (Vol. 12). London: Hogarth, 1958. (Originally published, 1914.)

Freud, S., & Breuer, J. *Studies on hysteria*. New York: Avon Books, 1966. (Originally published, 1895.)

Horwitz, L. *Clinical prediction in psychotherapy*. New York: Jason Aronson, 1974.

Janov, A. *The primal scream; Primal therapy: Cure for neuroses*. New York: Putnam, 1970.

Kaiser, H. The problem of responsibility in psychotherapy. *Psychiatry*, 1955, *18*, 205–211.

Klein, H., Dittmann, A. T., Parloff, M. D., & Gill, M. M. Behavior therapy: Observations and reflections. *Journal of Consulting and Clinical Psychology*, 1969, *33*, 259–266.

Koch, S. The image of man in encounter groups. *The American Scholar*, 1973, *42*, 636–652.

Marin, P. The new narcissism. *Harper's*, October 1975, pp. 45–56.

Masling, J. Role-related behavior of the subject and psychologist and its effects on psychological data. In D. Levine (Ed.), *Nebraska Symposium on Motivation* (Vol. 14). Lincoln: University of Nebraska Press, 1966.

Pruyser, P. The beleaguered individual: Images of man in clinical practice. *Bulletin of the Menninger Clinic*, 1973, *37*, 433–450.

Rangell, L. A point of view on acting out. *International Journal of Psychoanalysis*, 1968, *49*, 195–201.

Ryan, V. L., & Gizynski, M. M. Behavior therapy in restrospect: Patients' feelings about their behavior therapies. *Journal of Consulting and Clinical Psychology*, 1971, *37*, 1–9.

Schafer, R. *Psychoanalytic interpretation in Rorschach testing: Theory and application*. New York: Grune & Stratton, 1954.

Schafer, R. *A new language for psychoanalysis*. New York: Yale University Press, 1976.

Shapiro, D. Motivation and action in psychoanalytic psychiatry. *Psychiatry*, 1970, *33*, 329–342.

Shectman, F. Operant conditioning and psychoanalysis: Contrasts, similarities and some thoughts about integration. *American Journal of Psychotherapy*, 1975, *29*, 72–78.

Shectman, F. Provocative issues in psychiatric diagnosis: A dialogue. *Bulletin of the Menninger Clinic*, 1976, *40*, 435–458.

Shevrin H., & Shectman, F. The diagnostic process in psychiatric evaluations. *Bulletin of the Menninger Clinic*, 1973, *37*, 451–494.

Strupp, H. Specific versus non-specific factors in psychotherapy and the problem of control. *Archives of General Psychiatry*, 1970, *23*, 393–401.

Strupp, H. The experiential group and the psychotherapeutic enterprise. *International Journal of Group Psychotherapy*, 1973, *23*, 115–124.

Ticho, E. The effects of the analyst's personality on psychoanalytic treatment. *Psychoanalytic Forum*, 1972, *4*, 137–151.

Wheelis, A. How people change. *Commentary,* May 1969, pp. 56–59; 63–66.

Winnicott, D. W. *The maturational processes and the facilitating environment.* New York: International Universities Press, 1965.

I wish to thank Ann Appelbaum and Michael Harty for their helpful comments and criticism in the preparation of this paper.

Chapter 19

The Idealization of Insight

STEPHEN A. APPELBAUM

CONTEXT AND ROLES OF INSIGHT

Freud's hard-won battle to show that a systematic understanding of oneself can lead to beneficial change is under renewed attack. Many of the new schools of psychotherapy and new ways of viewing man psychologically are organized around the following ideas: (1) psychoanalysts adhere to a rigid, monolithic technique with all patients; (2) the psychoanalyst does nothing except declaim interpretations (usually about the past); (3) insight is far less useful than psychoanalysis has claimed in bringing about change, if not harmful and inimical to change. Many of the critics who say these things are not trained in psychoanalysis; in order to justify their a priori beliefs they argue against bits and pieces of the various psychoanalytic theories developed over three-quarters of a century, and they ignore the historical and intellectual context in which the ideas they criticize are embedded. Deprived of the opportunity to learn and practice psychoanalysis by the restrictions placed upon membership in psychoanalytic institutes, some of these critics may have needed to establish a professional identity not only apart from but in opposition to psychoanalysis. Let us, however, move past an ad hominem dismissal of such criticisms and see whether, for the wrong reasons or not, there may be something right in the raising of these issues, something from which psychoanalysis can benefit.

In answer to the charge that psychoanalysis is a finished and rigid system, one can argue that in one sense psychoanalysis does not require external pressures as exerted by these new schools to examine and reexamine its beliefs and techniques. Psychoanalytic theory and technique are recognized in the literature as unfinished and as the object of continued questioning. Note the tentativeness, sense of ambiguity, and relativism in such remarks as those of Fenichel (1941) who says that different opinions exist about the technique of psychoanalysis as

Reprinted with permission from the *International Journal of Psychoanalytic Psychotherapy*, 1975, Vol. 4, pp. 272–302.

"a consequence of the fact that the personalities of various analysts express themselves differently in practice . . . also because there are often uncertainties as to the governing principles which should be common to all analysts." Greenson (1967) cites as evidence for his similar opinion Glover's questionnaire on common practices, and the panel on "Variations in Classical Psycho-Analytic Technique" held at the 20th Congress of the International Psycho-Analytic Association in 1957. Nonetheless, powerful cultural influences have made psychoanalysts sometimes act and sound (and consequently to some extent think and believe) as though they were practicing a finished, prescriptive treatment. If one holds himself out as a physician or therapist in Western society, he is expected to make reasonably accurate diagnoses leading to reasonably accurate treatment prescriptions and to the delivery of treatments which conform to the nature of the illness. To the extent that such a cultural expectation finds its way into an internal expectation, it is understandable that there should be a trend toward an acceptance of "psychoanalytic technique," as is, despite one's intellectual awareness to the contrary. This is perhaps one reason that technique has lagged behind theory. "It is amazing how small a proportion of [psychoanalytic literature] is devoted to psychoanalytic technique and how much less to the theory of technique . . . the scarcity of papers on technique remains astonishing" (Fenichel, 1941).

One might also consider in this connection that psychoanalysis, especially in its early years, was a research instrument, a means of observation, at least as much as it was a therapy. This was Freud's (1926) position, and one reason why he was hesitant to let psychoanalysis become a medical specialty: "I . . . want to be reassured that the therapy will not destroy the science." So the skepticism which is inherent in the scientific attitude runs in uneasy tandem with the practitioner's need for professional certainty.

As to the cartoon view of the analyst who says or does nothing but interpret, much in psychoanalysis can be construed to support this caricature. This state of affairs has led Karl Menninger (1958) to dislike the word "interpretation" itself because it connotes wizardry, linguistics, detection, and oracular utterances. The psychoanalytic process has been described metaphorically as a surgical procedure, with interpretation as the scalpel; as a piece of work, with interpretation as the main tool; and as a war, with interpretation as the chief weapon. Indeed, in reference to the basic model of psychoanalytic technique, Eissler (1953) says, "The tool with which the analyst can accomplish this task is interpretation. . . . The problem here is only when and what to interpret; for in the ideal case, the analyst's activity is limited to interpretation; no other tool becomes necessary." Roy Schafer (1973) writes:

> According to the [psychoanalytic model], the psychoanalyst limits himself to making interpretations; otherwise, he remains as nondirective as possible. He neither

instructs nor speaks personally. He believes that his speaking personally or emotionally will contaminate the analysis of the transference and that his instructing his patient will intensify the patient's resistance by encouraging the patient to intellectualize.

Merton Gill (1954) writes, "Psychoanalysis is that technique which, employed by neutral analysts, results in the development of a regressive transference neurosis and the ultimate resolution of this neurosis by techniques of interpretation alone." Greenson (1967) writes, "Interpretation is still the decisive and ultimate instrument of the psychoanalyst."

Now, to a discussion of the role of insight. The basic model is, indeed, a thing of beauty: supported by structural arrangements and the behavior of the analyst, the patient is invited to say whatever comes to mind, and quickly sees that he prevents himself from following that rule in ways which are characteristic of him. By way of associations to his present life outside the analytic hour, to his past life, and to his relationship with the analyst, the patient is enabled to see not only how he behaves but why he behaves as he does. Equipped with such insight the patient no longer needs to behave (or have symptoms) contrary to his best interests. The analyst's major activity is limited to helping the patient develop such insights through interpretation. This vision of psychoanalytic technique is, as Ramzy (1961) suggests, entitled to borrow Bertrand Russell's description of mathematics—"a beauty cold and austere like that of sculpture, without appeal to any part of our weaker nature, without the gorgeous trappings of painting or music, yet sublimely pure and capable of a stern perfection such as only the greatest art can show." With some patients the achievements which occur during and after such a procedure are remarkable, and what actually takes place does at least approach the ideal of the basic model.

Yet the facts of clinical life often fail to allow such a rarefied view, pristine practice, and gratifying result. Almost as soon as Freud laid down the basic model, which was derived from and designed for the treatment of hysteria, he was forced to introduce deviations from it. "Our technique grew up in the treatment of hysteria *and is still directed principally to the cause of that affection* [italics mine] [but a] . . . different kind of activity is necessitated by the gradually growing appreciation that the various forms of disease treated by us cannot all be dealt with by the same technique" (Freud, 1919). Departures from the basic model were labeled "parameters" and discussed systematically by Eissler (1953). He notes that such modifications in the basic model are necessitated by various symptoms as these reflect differing diagnostic categories and ego structures. A long series of papers repeats the same theme: while retaining basic psychoanalytic concepts and understanding we need to adopt interventions to fit the varying needs of different people, and some of these interventions may be vastly different from the insight-interpretation matrix of the basic method. This "widening scope"

(A. Freud, 1954) of patients which psychoanalysts try to benefit is said to have come about because the nature of people has changed since the turn of the century, because patients nowadays come from wider socioeconomic populations, because diagnostic acumen has improved so that we now see the needs of the patient in a more differentiated, sophisticated way than before, and because of the development of ego psychology and its influence on technique. All of these stimulate us to design the treatment to fit the patient rather than selecting only those patients who fit the basic method of treatment. Stone (1961) says, "[The basic model] is . . . more austere in the teachings and writings of good psychoanalysts than it is in their practice." Why psychoanalysts should teach and write about psychoanalysis in ways different from their practice of it is curious, a matter to which we shall return.

Despite this catholicity of outlook, there remains in psychoanalysis an idealization of interpretation and insight, as these are held to be used in the starkness of the basic model. Schafer (1974) calls attention to a slavish following of the basic model, an "honoring [of] the artificial and inappropriate psychoanalytic model" which results, among other things, in lack of attention to other means of working with patients. Ekstein (1959) notes the temptation of some analysts to place a value on the final form of interpretation, its translating function, as an intervention "on its highest level." He notes that psychoanalysis as a translating technique hearkens back to Freud's hypnosis-influenced belief that the curative task of the analyst was simply to recover the repressed traumatic memory. According to Ekstein, this has been a "continuing misconception" among some analysts. In "The Curse of Insight," a memorandum of many of the problems connected with insight, Brian Bird (1957) notes that even after emphasis upon the topographical model diminished, with lessened focus upon symbols and unconscious material, an emotional premium continued to be placed on the analyst's capacity for insight, as if this were the real and ultimate measure of analytic ability. Silverberg (1955) notes, "We have proceeded on the assumption that insight is a good thing for a person to have; the word insight as currently used among psychiatrists and psychoanalysts has 'good' connotations." A familiar task of those who teach neophyte analysts and beginning psychotherapists is to help them overcome the rigid, simplistic application of the basic model, so imbued have students become with the emphasis and value accorded interpretation and insight. All clinicians have heard patients described as being "good" patients because of their ability to develop insight and to respond in a preferred way to interpretations. The implication often seems to be that those patients who cannot use the basic model to develop insight and respond favorably to interpretations are inferior in general, not just in this ability.

It is curious that on the one hand analysts have long recognized the need to depart from the basic model, yet they act in what might be described as a phobic manner about departures from it, about parameters. The literature and clinical discussions are replete with anxious, if not acrimonious, reactions to "deviations" (itself a word with tendentious connotations). These deviations are often advanced as bold, if not new, though they may be available in the literature and discussed whenever analysts informally share ideas with colleagues. Note, for example, the formal introduction of the idea of the "real relationship" (Greenson and Wexler, 1969) some seventy years after the development of the basic model, even though Freud had offered the idea in his early papers on technique as well as his last one, in 1937. Consider the discussion which most analysts have had at one time or another about that group of optimal behaviors perhaps epitomized by such questions as when, how, and if to offer Kleenex to patients, to extend condolences, to allow the patient or oneself to smoke, to see a patient four instead of five hours a week. These issues can, of course, be laden with meaning and transference consequences. I call attention only to the ambience of psychoanalysis, which seems to me to be one of fearfulness (and sometimes counterboldness) in doing or saying anything which may deviate from the purity of the basic model. Even such obvious interventions as the asking of questions (Eissler, 1953) or the variety of ways one might talk to patients (Schafer, 1974) have been underemphasized in the literature on technique, and tend to be introduced defensively.

A subtle example of the suggested value judgment of the basic model may be seen in Eissler's (1953) choice of "parameter" as the term for a deviation from it. "Parameter," as a departure from an agreed-upon classical procedure or situation, is most directly and unambiguously used when it takes place less often than does the basic procedure. In psychoanalysis, however, parameters are departures from a clinical situation which nowadays is found hardly at all, and in fact is specified by Eissler himself more as an utopian ideal than as an actuality. The nomothetic facts of clinical life would be better conformed to if the basic model were the parameter instead of the other way around.

"Parameter" is an unfortunate choice of words in another way. The schism which it creates, between the basic model and parameters, casts the problem in adversary and polarized terms, which can give the impression that any departure, innovation, or even reexamination of psychoanalytic technique is outside "real" psychoanalysis. It fails to leave room for attitudes, technical devices, and emphases which lie well within the boundaries of the conservative application of psychoanalysis. Some of these are already practiced by some, probably many, analysts, and some could be experimented with and possibly adopted by others. As Ramzy (1961) has pointed out, "within the range of a purely interpretive approach there is enough leeway to conduct an analysis without sacrificing the basic tenets of the method." Freud (1914) went even further. For him psychoanalysis was defined merely by undoing resistances and interpreting transference.

If it is true that the basic model, featuring interpretation as the sole intervention and insight as the sole means of change, is idealized, then what may be the consequences? What effects does such a value judgment have upon the theories of psychoanalysis, the way psychoanalysis is practiced, and the political and social roles which it seeks to play, is forced to play, or is alleged to play?

I shall discuss some of these effects, and the dangers they pose to the extent that the interpretation-insight basic model is, in any particular situation and by any particular analyst, overemphasized. It is only then that the idealization of insight may restrict the range of observation, inhibit the ingenuity of practitioners to select other interventions, and stifle examination of the means by which insight, in and of itself, can be maximized.

SOME CONSEQUENCES OF THE IDEALIZATION OF INSIGHT

Discussed below are some of those aspects of technique and theory which lend themselves to being underemphasized as insight is overemphasized.

Cognition vs. Affect

From outside its borders psychoanalysis is being subjected to strident attack for being too intellectual, for explaining to the detriment of experiencing. From within its borders this is an old story. Reich (1949) argued for a consistent intellectual guidance in technique, while Reik (1933) was afraid that this would lead to intellectualizing and would diminish intuition, empathy, and experience. Fenichel (1941) wrote, "There are doubtless some analysts who would like to substitute knowledge for experiences and who therefore do not dissolve repressions but rather play thinking games with their patients." Fenichel made clear the dialectical excesses of the struggle between cognition and feeling:

> In the early days of psychoanalysis . . . the greater danger was the Scylla of too much talking or intellectualization. . . . Ferenczi's and Rank's book represented a reaction against this situation. They emphasized again and again that analysis is not an intellectual but an affective process . . . the authors certainly went too far to the other extreme. In their emphasis on experiencing they became admirers of abreaction, of acting out, and thus working through was the loser . . . in the history of psychoanalysis Scylla periods and Charybdis periods alternated and . . . it must have been very difficult to pass evenly between the opposite dangers.

The problem was set for psychoanalysis in its very beginning. Breuer and Freud (1895) first seemed to believe that once the stifled affect was released through catharsis the symptoms would disappear. But the release was in words, and the words soon led to an understanding of conflict and the unconscious. The goal then was to make the unconscious conscious, to understand verbally why the situation had led to strangulated affect. "By providing an opportunity for the penned-up affect to discharge itself in words the therapy deprives of its effective power the idea which was not originally abreacted" (Freud, 1895). "Abreaction, originally considered a curative agent, thus came to be employed as a technical tool in the process of acquiring 'insight' through interpretation with all its implications and consequences" (Bibring, 1954).

Elaboration of the discovery of unconscious meaning has proliferated through the decades, while a psychology of affect has lagged behind. One may speculate that the intellectual challenge and excitement of discovery which led to this emphasis was abetted by the self-selection of the verbal people who earned advanced academic degrees and entered the practice of analysis. A problem in the training of psychoanalysts has been to promote the recognition that verbal, intellectual understanding alone is insufficient to bring about change—that insight must be experienced emotionally. The difficulty of putting this formula into practice effectively was highlighted as psychoanalysis was increasingly applied to patients with pregenital difficulties, borderline personality organization, psychoses, and impulse disorders. It was further highlighted as analysts pushed for earlier and earlier material in order to gain understanding of early object relations. Difficulties whose geneses were primarily in the preverbal years, and presumably intimately tied with primitive ways of thinking suffused with affects, were difficult to recapture in the developmentally later language of the secondary process, though unintegrated storms of affect might be easily available. It remains for each practitioner to struggle with what is meant, for any patient at any moment, by the rule of thumb that insight should be accompanied by affect. Each analyst has had to decide for himself almost from moment to moment during a therapeutic process when to stop finding ways of helping the patient express affect in favor of encouraging insight, and vice versa.

The relative narrowness of the range of affect with which analysts usually work has recently been dramatized by the primal scream therapy of Janov (1970) which shares important similarities with Freud's early abreaction model of psychoanalytic practice. Janov says that under conditions of stimulus deprivation over extended time periods, shielded by soundproofed offices and especially as the result of a relentless pursuit of affect by the therapist, patients are capable of remarkably intense discharges of feeling. Coincident with these is the recovery of memories of intrauterine existence and the trauma of birth. Among the claimed results of this process are increases in size of feet, hands, and breasts. If only a fraction of such claims prove to be valid, the question is posed: would psychoanalysis benefit from a return to and an exploitation of abreaction, whose usefulness has been lost sight of in part because of the pursuit of insight? At a minimum we may discover that well within the range of even conventional technique we could work toward infusing the analytic process with increased affect, which, consonant with present theory, should better promote change.

(We should not overlook the fact that abreaction can also serve as a resistance, and that feelings can be produced spuriously for this purpose.) Although applicable, in principle, to all analyses, working with affect is especially necessary for those patients whose difficulties are decisively related to preverbal experiences (Blanck and Blanck, 1974).

The following case provides an example of technical error encouraged by idealization of insight. A long-time alcoholic and drug addict was in supportive-expressive psychotherapy begun when she was in a hospital. As she moved from the hospital, was able to attend school successfully, and give up drinking and drugs, the therapy shifted more toward the expressive end of the continuum. She showed encouraging growth of adeptness in thinking psychologically, and was being considered as a possible case for psychoanalysis. Hers were hard-won insights; she was neither an intellectual nor an intellectualizer. Out of enthusiasm for these changes and interest in the patient's increasing ideational productions, both the therapist (a psychoanalytic candidate) and his supervisor (a training analyst) somehow overlooked or minimized the fact that the patient was not keeping up her payments. She finally volunteered that she had reverted to drugs and alcohol, using money which otherwise would have paid her therapy bills. The patient's understanding and ideational productions were undeniable. But they were not accompanied by affective meaning appropriate to the primitive levels of the patient's ego organization, and therefore were unable to sustain her through the anxiety inherent in the new challenges she was taking on. They were, however, sufficiently impressive to bemuse clinicians into overlooking what they are ordinarily alert to.

The Existential Danger of Insight

What might be called the existential danger of insight is illustrated in Eugene O'Neill's play, *The Iceman Cometh* (see also Appelbaum, 1976). A group of derelicts, each with his own comforting illusion, is visited by Hickey, a traveling salesman, who joins them from time to time on monumental benders. This time, however, Hickey insists that they give up their pipe dreams and face the stark reality of their failings. One by one, under his verbal lash, they make abortive attempts to behave differently, fail in the midst of intense anxiety, and return to their peaceful down-and-out adjustment. In his pursuit of insight as if it were a universal good, Hickey was unable to realize that self-knowledge has to be matched with the ability to solve the problems which, once avoided, are now starkly seen. Freud (1917) wryly noted that melancholics are capable of piercing self-recriminatory insights without deriving benefit from them. Camus espoused the idea that when one asks the basic questions about existence one opens himself to a recognition of absurdity from which suicide is easily derivable. Clinicians are aware of the dangers of psychosis and suicide should patients be exposed to more insight than they can absorb without undue regression, or than their environments can accommodate without untoward reaction. Careful diagnostic work, especially the assessment of basic ego functions, is used in order to identify those patients who cannot absorb unlimited insight safely. For such patients Knight (1953a, 1953b) recommends ego-supportive interventions as alternatives to insight. Guntrip (1968), in an object relations context, discussed the dangerous limbo in which one has to exist between insight and the establishment of a new equilibrium:

> . . . the classical psychoanalytic technique is indispensable [to the solution of conflict. But] the result may well be . . . that the patient . . . is rather deprived of a main defence against the ultimate problem, the profound sense of inner emptiness . . . if he loses his internal bad objects while not yet feeling sure enough that his therapist will adequately replace them, he will feel that he is falling between two stools, or as one patient vividly expressed it, "plunging into a mental abyss of black emptiness."

A new view of oneself raises new questions as it answers old ones. The truth sets many people free, but not everyone. We may ask ourselves to what extent any excess zeal for insight results in taking more from the patient than it replaces, whether we act upon an implicit belief that if some insight is curative, more insight is more curative regardless of the patient's capacity to tolerate and integrate it. As with Hickey's clumsy intervention, does the attraction of truth overcome considerations of technique and considerations of existence?

Research data are available to support the idea that for some patients with some therapists the development of insight is no guarantee of maintained gains. In the Psychotherapy Research Project of the Menninger Foundation patients were examined before treatment, at termination, and at a follow-up point two years after termination. On the basis of psychological test examinations of twenty-eight patients at termination and follow-up, seven who had done better at termination had become worse two years later. Three of the seven had achieved the highest amount of insight on a four-point scale, and one had achieved the next highest amount (Appelbaum, 1977).

Meaning of Interpretation to the Patient

Silverberg (1955) writes that the good reputation of insight follows the recognition, "that insight has a liberating effect, like education: 'and ye shall know the truth, and the truth shall make you free.' " Yet Silverberg's patient, whose intransigence had encouraged these remarks, did not change his behavior. Although Glover (1955) pointed out the usefulness for some purposes of inexact interpretations, the implication in Silverberg's paper is that the insight repeatedly offered to the patient was an exact one. In the course of pursuing correct insight it may be that some analysts overlook two other requirements for insight to be effective. One has to do with the way the insight is offered. Just as a good script can be ruined by poor acting, setting, or lighting, so can the hoped-for effect of a correct interpretation be minimized by poor timing, clumsy choice of words, wooden or objectionable voice quality, or other contributions to inexpressiveness. Therapists vary in the degree to which they are evocative, and one would presume that, all other things being equal, the relative effectiveness of insights offered by them would vary commensurately (Appelbaum, 1963). Another variable which might go uncontrolled in the process of the development of insight is the unconscious meaning to the patient of being the recipient of the interpretive offering, quite apart from the specific meaning, correctness, or manner of delivery of the insights themselves. The offering of an interpretation is the major piece of action interrupting the relatively inactive mode of the analyst in the basic model. It is often what patients are implicitly waiting for. Occurring in the context of the heightened emotions of the transference neurosis, the getting of interpretations may be heavily invested with unconscious meanings which are often central to the patient's personality. Ekstein (1956) describes the developmentally earlier meanings which are stimulated by developmentally later symbolic language. Silverberg (1955) reports that until he recognized the meaning to the patient of being offered insight, he was surprised and frustrated that he could not interrupt with insight the patient's acting out. The insight only became effective when the analyst realized, and interpreted to the patient, that the patient was experiencing the giving of the insight as a disciplinary measure, which implied to the patient that the analyst was omnipotently able to assert his authority over him. Greenson (1967) also notes that interpretations of the patient's anger toward the analyst, especially in the first phases of analysis, often result in the patient's feeling that he is being criticized. He offered a case example of a patient who had projected his impulses to be a humiliator onto the analyst, and felt humiliated by the analyst's making of interpretations. Bird (1957) notes that a too avid pursuit of insight creates an unfair competition with the patient, and does not permit the patient to discover anything for himself. While these difficulties may in fact stem from the analyst's offering too much insight too quickly, they can also be a transference impression of the patient's. Bird also suggests that some patients may take interpretations as if they were nourishment from mother, and thus the interpretive work rewards dependency rather than being a stimulus toward growth. It seems plausible to assume that every patient at one time or another experiences the giving of insight in ways consistent with his relationship dispositions and psychosexual modes. While one patient may experience interpretations as nurture, another may experience them as poison. Others may accept them as gifts, as something to be negativistically refused, as entries in a contest, or as rapes.

One patient who characteristically crossed her legs while on the couch resisted the development of the therapeutic alliance and, especially, resisted thinking psychologically with the analyst. She had fantasied that her sister, born when the patient was three years old, was the child of her father and herself. This child was born damaged and died shortly after birth, a fact which apparently contributed to the patient's fear of the consequences of sexuality. In the course of the analysis it seemed clear that she had sexualized the process of thinking psychologically with the analyst, equating any insights that they created together as giving birth to an idea-child. Insights offered to her unilaterally were experienced as rapes, against which her legs were locked. The very correctness of the insights tended to arouse increased anxiety and consequent defensiveness in her. (For further elaboration of this case in the context of a delineation of psychological-mindedness see Appelbaum, 1973.)

Insight and the Curative Effects of the Interpersonal Relationships

A major finding of the Psychotherapy Research Project of the Menninger Foundation was that those patients who had developed insight in the context of psychological-mindedness and had achieved some conflict resolution did best of all the patients. Yet, at the same time, a number of patients made substantial gains even in the absence of insight, psychological-mindedness, and conflict resolution (Appelbaum, 1977). The latter finding was a surprise to most members of the Project, some of whom had formally advanced the idea through detailed predictions that the development of insight was a requisite for substantial, especially structural change (Horwitz and Appelbaum, 1966). Yet there is much in psychoanalytic theory, writing, and practice that would lead one to anticipate such a finding rather than to be surprised by it. Once again we might do well to consider the extent to which an overvaluation of insight, along with psychological-mindedness and conflict resolution, leads some of us to believe that substantial change can come about only in these ways.

By contrast, members of the British object relations school are explicit about believing change comes about in ways other than insight. Guntrip (1968) writes:

the analytical technique itself is more an instrument of research and of temporary relief than of radical therapy. The analyst's interpretations will be given to the patient as suggestions for him to respond to, not as dogmatic or authoritative pronouncements for him to accept blindly. . . . It is only the kind of self-knowledge that is arrived at as living insight, which is felt, experienced, in the medium of a good personal relationship, that has therapeutic value.

Contrast this with Freud's (1937) comment in one of his last papers, "*The therapeutic effect* depends on making conscious what is repressed. . . . We prepare the way for this making conscious by interpretations and constructions" (italics mine). Winnicott (1965) speaks of analysts who

> deal with more primitive mental mechanisms; by interpreting part-object relations, projections and introjections, hypochondriacal and paranoid anxieties, attacks on linkages, thinking disturbances, etc., etc. They extend the field of operation and the range of the cases they can tackle. This is research analysis, and the danger is only that *the patient's needs in terms of infantile dependence may be lost in the course of the analyst's performance.*

The curative functional task to be performed by the real relationship is to provide a second chance for the patient to grow. "Object-relations theory calls for the analyst to be a good-object in reality, in himself, just as the mother has to be a good-object in reality to the baby. . . . He must, in his own reality as a person, bring something *new* that the patient has not experienced before" (Guntrip, 1968). Freud (1937), Greenson and Wexler (1969), and Gitelson (1952) remark on the real, nontransference relationship but stop short of maintaining that relationship in and of itself has a curative function; and Edward Glover (1955) states, "It is obvious that many people cure themselves through their unconscious human contacts."

In American psychoanalysis a tradition of benefit through the interpersonal relationship has been asserted by, among others, Harry Stack Sullivan, Frieda Fromm-Reichmann, and Otto Will. A retrospective attempt from the Psychotherapy Research Project of the Menninger Foundation to explain how patients improved in the absence of insight was offered by Horwitz (1974); he cited ways patients may have used the interpersonal relationship to bring about their gains.

Psychoanalysts seem even to have minimized, for technique purposes, their own theory of normal child development, which posits change as occurring without insight, at least insight of the kind encouraged in psychoanalytic treatment. (Ernst Kris [1956], who posed the question whether insight had to be verbal at all, is an exception.) In such normal development crucial internalized self- and object-representations become imprinted into the personality. In interaction with such objects, the ego develops its functions, grows, differentiates, consolidates as part of a process of continued living with "adequate mothering" in an "average expectable environment." In pathology this growth sequence has been interrupted. Many patients suffer more from developmental arrest than from regression (H. J. Schlesinger, pers. comm.). Insight may be sufficient to overcome symptoms by supplying links between experience, by overcoming repression; but an interpersonal growth experience may be required to continue the arrested childhood one (Winnicott, 1965). (How to continue a growth process through adulthood is an existential question, which is at least implicit in many psychoanalyses.)

Reporting on the consensus of a group of analysts with respect to the treatment of schizophrenia, Philip Holzman (1974) remarks that psychoanalysis has developed as an interpretive discipline rather than an observational science, and one with limited sources of information and adaptations of technique. In commenting on this report Donald Burnham writes that the interpersonal relationship is the major and essential part of the treatment, deserving to be understood as such rather than "being referred to with scorn or shame as a deviation or as a 'parameter.' "

A seventeen-year-old boy had been a drug user and dropout from all other aspects of life since the age of ten. Despite the considerable disturbance implied by this and other aspects of his history, as revealed in the initial clinical examination and psychological testing, he was taken into analysis largely because of what seemed a latent capacity to think imaginatively and psychologically. Through the first year of treatment it was difficult for him to make constructive use of this capacity because, among other things, of his pervasive distrust that anyone could have his best interests at heart. For example, he would act in unpleasant ways toward his girlfriend so that when she rejected him as he fantasied she would it would be because of clear actions on his part and under his control rather than because he was an essentially unlovable person. While in some respects he made reasonable gains in analysis, he began to miss appointments, to provoke the people with whom he lived into wanting to be rid of him and the school staff in refusing to graduate him. He seemed to take attempts at understanding as just further evidence that he was to be dealt with at an emotional distance, deprived of what he needed, and forced to conform to what someone else wanted. The dramatic turning point occurred as an almost immediate result of the analyst's finding, in part through dealing with his countertransference, ways to make experientially and dramatically clear that he wanted the patient to come to the hours, and that the patient's presence as a person was something to be valued quite apart from any meanings which might be attached to his thoughts or feelings. The patient again began to attend the hours, he worked out a better relation with his girlfriend and the people with whom he lived, and graduated from school. (Without much additional work, interpretive or otherwise, he successfully went on to college, got his first job, and in many ways treated himself better, all understandable as stemming from first interpersonal, then intrapersonal, acceptance.)

Factors Common to All Psychotherapy

Some ameliorative forces apart from insight which occur by design or inadvertently in most therapies have been cited by major psychoanalytic writers. For example, Fenichel (1954) remarks that "relative allowance for rest and for small regressions and compensatory wish-fulfillments . . . have a recuperative effect," "verbalization of unclear worries alone brings relief," "the very fact that a doctor spends time, interests, and sympathy on a patient's worries [may be] a very substantial relief for lonely people [as may] information about emotional and especially sexual matters." Glover (1955) states, "The psychoanalyst has never questioned the symptomatic alleviation that can be produced by suggestive methods," either by way of transference cure or as the result of quasi or inexact interpretations. Ella Freeman Sharpe (1959) suggests the therapeutic usefulness simply of allowing the patient to talk with her. Writing about her first patient, a psychotic, she said, "I was too conscious of my ignorance and too frightened to do much interpretation. I listened for over 12 months for an hour a day to her. . . . By this very freedom to elaborate fantasy life, the patient got more grip on reality. *The foundation of technique lies there* [italics mine]."

Ekstein (1959) writes that, "The word 'correct' stands in our literature at times for 'true,' at other times for 'effective,' and often for both." He also wrote (1950), "The primary intent of an analytic interpretation is not to explain, but to cure." It may be that what is curative is the process of gaining the insight, regardless, at least to an extent, of the content and veracity of the insight. This would be a common factor in all of those therapies which proceed according to similar processes, a factor which is independent of much theory as well as of correctness (Marmor, 1964).

Outside of psychoanalysis, in a trend adumbrated by Rosenzweig (1936), systematic attention is being paid to the possibly curative effects of factors inherent in all therapeutic interactions. These factors may function apart from the awareness and technical range of the therapist (Strupp, 1973). All therapies may be helped along simply because the therapist behaves as if he believes change for the better is possible, that one need not be terrified of something unknowable, that there may be causes for behavior which are less awful than those the patient has assumed, that someone else cares enough to try to understand him. The nonoccurrence of dreaded events could extinguish fears (in learning theory terms) which may contribute to the beneficial effects of a corrective emotional experience. The latter may come about inadvertently, rather than through designed activity on the part of the analyst as suggested by Alexander and French (1946). The placebo effect (Shapiro, 1971) is one of the nonspecific factors held by Strupp to be "established facts" in psychotherapy. According to Frank (1971) common (nonspecific) factors in psychotherapy include (1) an intense, emotionally charged, confiding relationship with a helping person; (2)

a rationale or myth which offers an explanation of the patient's distress and leads to confidence in the therapist; (3) provision of new information about the patient's problems and ways of dealing with them; (4) the personal qualities of the therapist, which arouse hope and the expectation of help; (5) provision of success experiences which increase self-esteem and a sense of mastery and encouragement of emotional arousal.

In all interventions which have change, or therapy, as an avowed goal, there is a self-selection of people who combine readiness and need. One can notice this attitude at various junctures in life—times of tragedy, major decisions; it can be brought on by works of art, drugs, or other means of altering the boundaries of consciousness. At such times we may benefit even from a friend's casual remark. When one identifies himself as a patient, ready to make the investments which treatment requires, such openness is maximized.

Another common element is that upon becoming a patient one's attention is directed inward, a first step toward psychological-mindedness. There is a "give" in the many ways we use in order to minimize anxiety by looking elsewhere for explanations or through diverting attention. As a result the self becomes an external percept. This occurs, for example, when people hear the sound of their voice on a tape recorder. They are startled and shocked, attempt to disown it, notice that they may sound effeminate, raspy, and older. Yet they listen to their voices all day long without such reactions. As part of themselves, their voices are buffered by defenses. When their voices come upon them from the outside, without prior defensive processing, people become aware of themselves in new ways. Treatment situations similarly focus on the self as a percept, and attempt to keep it free of the distortions introduced by defense activities.

No one suggests that such common factors are solely responsible for beneficial change nor that insight or other means of change are therefore irrelevant. Rather, common factors should be assessed for their relative contributions to change. Such a point of view fits with the psychoanalytic belief in overdetermination and in the complementary series.

Insight and Action

An important polarity in human life, and therefore in psychology, is that of thought and action. Some systematic examples are Jung's (1923) distinction between introversion and extroversion and Hermann Rorschach's (1951) "experience balance," i.e., Rorschach test signs of the capacity for ideation as against a proclivity toward action. "The thinker" and "the doer" are figures in art and in everyday observation. Activity and passivity roughly correspond to this dimension (if one does not look too closely—there is much "passivity" in "activity," and much "activity" in "passivity" as systematically described by Schafer [1968]). With due regard to the grossness of the term "passivity" the basic model of psychoanalysis can be described as passive. In the limiting case, the analyst's one activity is interpretation; the rest of the time he silently listens to and accepts the patient's productions. The patient, too, is encouraged to be passive in many respects, such as in his recumbent position. The basic rule suggests that thoughts passively come to mind rather than being actively prepared or selected, and that insight, as a creative product, can come about through the passivity implicit in preconscious problem-solving. Menninger and Holzman (1973) dramatically present the heuristic model of an analyst whose unremitting passivity in the form of silence induces the patient to regress in analytically helpful ways. As analysts well know, passivity is not without seductiveness to all human beings, perhaps especially if leavened by the opportunity for authoritativeness and controlling pronouncements. While this is a caricature of the basic model, it is not entirely irrelevant to the facts of the situation.

Freud altered his model in the direction of taking direct action which was nonanalytic in the interpretive sense, sometimes to further the analytic process, and sometimes in departure from it. With the Wolf-Man he made an attempt to deal with resistance and further the process by telling him that they had only a year more to work and would end at that time regardless of the circumstances. He also promised the Wolf-Man that the treatment would benefit him, a maneuver maximizing suggestion rather than furthering the analytic process. He demanded that phobic patients face their phobias, and he called attention to those patients who make it necessary that one "combine analytic with educative influence," and "take up the position of teacher and mentor." "I think activity of such a kind on the part of the analyzing physician is unobjectionable and entirely justified" (1919). In *Studies in Hysteria* he has Fraülein Rosalie H. carry on a dialogue with a person important to her as if that person were present, much as would be done by a gestalt therapist nowadays (1919). He was willing to "psychoanalyze" a child through correspondence with Little Hans' father, and he endorsed Aichhorn's maverick ingenuity (1945). End-setting has since fallen into disrepute, although Freud (1937) is at the least neutral in his retrospective evaluation. His warnings about the timing of such end-setting seem to have been taken as proscriptions.

A prominent objection to such activities is that they will deleteriously influence the transference. Leo Stone (1954) addresses himself to this difficulty:

> I am inclined to agree with Eissler that the giving of a cigarette to certain patients, in a certain context, might create serious difficulty. In general, if this occurs as an *exception* to a general climate of deprivation, I would believe it more likely to cause trouble than, let us say, an appropriate expression of sympathy in a tragic personal bereavement—or even, circumspect, competent, direct advice in a real emergency which requires it.

By extrapolation, then, Stone is pointing out that the effect of an intervention has to be judged with respect to the baseline, or background, against which it occurs. The more passive, silent, "classical" the baseline is, the more harm might be expected from any deviation from it. By the same token, if various active interventions compose the baseline, then any particular active strategy may be expected to have less transference consequences. One may argue that such a baseline interferes with full utilization of the transference to begin with since it makes transference reactions more difficult to distinguish from appropriate responses to the analyst's behavior. That is a legitimate, empirical question.

I am not suggesting that all or any of the actions mentioned here are necessarily useful, and I am aware that such actions can be resorted to out of unrecognized countertransferences and frustrations borne of incompetence. I am suggesting that reasonable diagnostic and therapeutic thinking and research about such options may be hampered by emotional fealty to a passive mode of attempting to produce insight, along with the belief that only insight produces "real," enduring change.

To what extent does the analyst's shrinking from action influence the patient to do likewise? Rangell (1968) writes:

> I have seen a wrongly moralistic, anti-action attitude which creeps into some analyses fortify the patient's own phobic avoidance of action and lead in some cases to almost a paralysis of the latter and a taboo against even the necessary actions of life. Such analyses may hit a snag somewhere after mid-point where a marked indecisiveness eventuates at the necessity to convert long-standing insights into effective action.

A common transference resistance is for the patient to try to please the analyst with insights, and thus among other things prolong the dependent gratifications of an interminable analysis. A possibly not uncommon countertransference reaction to this is to be seduced into remaining the central figure for the patient, basking in one's capacity to encourage the development of insight, yet all within the analysis and unreflected in commensurate behavioral changes outside the hours. Bird (1957) writes, "Truly good insight implies using judiciously whatever is discovered and correlating its use effectively with the patient's life, present and future, as well as past. Insight lacking practical applications . . . is not good insight at all."

A similar, if not more pessimistic, assessment of psychoanalytic practice seems to have encouraged Allen Wheelis' (1950) observation that insight often does not result in changed behavior. He notes that change must come about through different means and quantities of energy discharge, and that discharges through insight are miniscule compared to discharge through changed life behaviors. He implies that the analyst may need to find ways to bring such changes in behaviors about. Without denigrating the usefulness of the basic interpretive-insight model, Wheelis calls attention to its capacity for inhibiting analytic thought about how to bring about change:

> the haze of familiar concepts—transference, derivatives, resistance, working through, and the like . . . they are the useful tools of his understanding. Yet they have the disadvantages intrinsic to all concepts: to some extent they blind him. . . . Precisely because they enable him to view certain familiar areas more closely, he becomes loath to use his unaided eyesight to look elsewhere. . . . [The] counterpart to the principle that the patient must experience and work out his problems in the transference is less well-known, though equally necessary. This principle is simply that he must also experience and work out these problems in real life.

In this article Wheelis stops short of encouraging behavioral change in the treatment session itself. His discussion has been concerned, he says, with "the theory of personality change, not with the technique of therapy," and he worries that the analyst's taking action in the form of encouraging or discouraging the patient's behavior would jeopardize what the analyst traditionally provides. Wheelis' remarks (1973) more than two decades later make it difficult to believe that at least in subtle ways technique would not be changed by his reformulation of the role of insight. After giving a case example of a symptom neurosis, for which insight would be necessary and sufficient, he says:

> Most psychiatrists know such cases only from reading examples like this one. Though other patients may have circumscribed symptoms, most of them suffer from problems of being, for which insight is not enough . . . the most common illusion of patients and, strangely, even of experienced therapists, is that insight produces change; and the most common disappointment of therapy is that it does not. Insight is instrumental to change, often an essential component of the process, but does not directly cause it.

Instead of the sequence "insight equals or produces change," Wheelis suggests, "The sequence is suffering, insight, will, action, change." In Wheelis' view, the patient must decide, equipped with insight, that he will take the action to produce change and that he must continue to take it, for "personality change follows change in behavior."

Insight into neurotic conflict results in actions which renegotiate old inefficient contracts and promises (Schlesinger, 1969). Schafer (1973) takes a similar position with respect to the actions which the patient takes, even in such "passive" modes as producing free associations and attending to the basic rule. The implication of these positions, as delineated by Schafer, is to question those aspects of psychoanalytic theory which cast the person as object rather than subject—

acted upon rather than acting. Such thoughts illuminate both the human and the psychoanalytic condition. They suggest that psychoanalytic patients, cultural institutions influenced by psychoanalysis, and psychoanalytic theory itself are the poorer through absorption with insight which is offered and accepted independent of action. According to Hartmann (1964) psychoanalysis has an inadequate theory of action. An adequate theory of action would lead to specification, weighting, and understanding of the technical ,consequences and opportunities of the roles in action of consciousness, cognitive style, perception, capacities for delay and for the making of decisions, responsibility, and the subjective experiences coordinate with all of these (D. Shapiro, 1970).

Insight as a Defense Against Change

Almost any behavior can be impressed into the service of defense and can function as an inhibition to change. Conformance to the basic rule and the production of insight, however, present special difficulties in that they are what we ask of the patient, and in the right circumstances are indeed necessary. Abraham (1919) noted this difficulty in his paper, "A Particular Form of Neurotic Resistance Against the Psycho-analytic Method," in which he described obsessional, narcissistic patients who produce "psychoanalytic" material in the service of defiance, self-protection, competitiveness, gratification, and envy, rather than change. Fenichel (1954) noted that, "The patient uses a new insight, acquired by successful interpretation, for resistance purposes—that is, for a reinforcement of other repressions." That is, the patient uses insight as a defense against other insight, as do patients with partial or inexact self-knowledge (Glover, 1955). Bird (1957) comments that "Insight becomes an end in itself, to the detriment of the changed behavior." What analyst has not faced situations in which patients use their insights as a means of deadening their feelings, or who attempt with explanations to divert the analyst's attention from thoughts or behaviors which are not so emotionally isolated? Freud's rule of abstinence warns us against insights being used in the analysis for gratifications which slow and diminish the process. This may come about through warding off further investigation, by lowering the motive power of anxiety, or through providing instinctual gratification, as for example in orally mouthing good things, anal gifts offered in pride, or competitive games as to who can come up with the best insights.

A young married mother came for analysis because of her overweight and for a variety of other dissatisfactions. According to the psychological test study made before beginning treatment, she already had copious intellectual insight. The tester cautioned that at times the analyst might assume that the patient was understanding things on the basis of her apparent insight, but that this understanding would not be the same one held by the analyst. The tester predicted that she might achieve many further insights, but it would be difficult for her to change on the basis of these. She would be less likely to be able to gain insight into oral disappointments and masochistic gratifications than into oedipal, heterosexual, and phallic conflicts. On the basis of the test study repeated at the termination of treatment she was assessed as having improved in a number of ways, although she seemed to be caught in an excessive struggle against unpleasant affects; and in the context of increased awareness of her fantasies and daydreams her ideational activity had become more ruminative. As predicted, she had been unable to achieve the depth of insight one might hope for in analysis, particularly into pregenital issues. On the basis of a third examination, two years after treatment, she was shown to be struggling even more with a decompensation of character and consequent troubled feelings, which had now resulted in a further surfacing of pregenital, especially homosexual, issues despite there being no "noteworthy lack of insight." One conclusion drawn from another and independent examination of the analyst's participation in the treatment was that he had taken her insights to mean that the analysis was progressing satisfactorily and, for this and possibly other countertransference reasons, had not sufficiently sought to encourage insight into the more primitive aspects of her personality.

EPISTEMOLOGY, AD HOMINEM, AND OPPORTUNITIES

The traditional pattern of most sciences is systematically to relate new discoveries and reformulations to what has gone before. Consequently, it is possible to trace the history of ideas and discoveries, and especially to know what is old and what is new, what has been kept, superseded, or discarded. This pattern in psychoanalysis tends to be adhered to more in form than in substance. Much in psychoanalytic literature, and at its academic meetings, is reacted to as if it were old hat even though for many analysts it may feel fresh if not novel. Much is taken as new when in fact it is readily available in the literature. What is known, believed, and especially what is emphasized in psychoanalytic theory and practice varies from one psychoanalyst to another, from one time to another, from one society to another, from one area of a country to another, and from one country to another. (One can conceive of this situation in general systems terms, with one idea or emphasis being forced to play one or another role by the overall system—the id role, the superego role, the orthodox role, the maverick role, the physical science role, the humanist role, etc.) There are many plausible reasons for this state of affairs. In the long shadow of history the first seventy-five years of analysis may turn out to be only a shakedown phase, early convulsions from the shock of Freud's momentous discoveries. Not many fledgling systems of thought have had their early practitioners suddenly and forcibly separated and spread around the world to be influenced by diverse cultures, as were the Central

Europeans in the 1930s. Freud (1937) was alert to such varying cultural influences, as when he suggested that the movement toward brief psychotherapy stemmed from the rapid pace of American life. Not only did this separation (the traumatic nature of which may in and of itself have exerted an influence) subject psychoanalytic explorers to diverse cultures, but at the same time it made communication and homogeneous development more difficult. The diversity of goals in psychoanalysis, as formulated by Freud from the beginning, is also an important plausible factor. He offered at one and the same time an instrument for research toward developing a scientific theory, and a method of treatment which was as much art as skill and as much education as medicine. He pursued these diverse lines of inquiry, attempting to use the language, concepts, and ways of thinking of the physical sciences in which he was trained. Just as easily he used the metaphors of art, a Socratic teaching style, and permitted himself the sweeping speculations of an armchair philosopher, all the while drawing upon and applying his thoughts to anthropology, history, politics, religion, and academic psychology. In the course of this monumental catholicity, he operated at different levels of abstraction, which gave rise to different classes of words referring to the same empirical observations. He was enormously productive and he continually changed his views. Each generation of psychoanalysts, and to some extent therefore their students, learned different versions or different emphases. Finally, because of the nature of psychoanalysis it is extremely difficult to subject it to clear, coherent, agreed-upon rules of research which in other sciences could serve as a referee or court of last resort. Instead, differences in psychoanalysis are often discussed at the level of debate, with data being collected by individual practitioners and subject to their idiosyncratic observations, selection, classification, inference-making, generalizing, and communicating. In view of all of this, the fact that psychoanalysis has achieved what it has in therapy, theory development, and influence on the world's thought is a testimonial to its sheer power. But with such an epistemological background, certainty and complacency are inappropriate.

According to Eissler (1969), the many differences observable among psychoanalysts the world over do not make for much difference. In his view, in the midst of apparent differences, a congealed orthodoxy has arisen to the point that there is even lacking within psychoanalysis the paradoxes with which to generate continued thought. Perhaps the following paradoxes would fail to meet Eissler's criteria, but they seem to me to deserve a good deal of attention: the psychoanalyst pays fealty to a model of work established for a kind of patient hardly ever seen, is encouraged to believe that insight is the single means of definitive change while simultaneously being encouraged to believe in other possibilities, believes in the consequences of affectively charged events in the preverbal years but is restricted to recovering these solely through verbal means, knows that explanations and formulations tend to remove a person from emotional experience yet tries to achieve both, notices that some people change their behavior apparently as the result of insight while others collect insight and remain otherwise unchanged.

This situation of ambiguity and fragmentation can be understood dynamically as well as historically. One would have to assume that all people, not just nonanalysts, smart and chafe against the narcissistic blow inflicted by Freud's assertion of unconscious forces determining behavior (knowledge of which is gained as insight). The continuing hostility of the nonanalytic world has made it possible for some psychoanalysts to deal with their own ambivalences alloplastically. In the face of a world constantly trying to deny the full import of Freud's discoveries, proponents of such discoveries may just as constantly feel the need to defend them, and to do so with less than dispassionate reflection. Such an impulse-defense configuration could be seen most clearly in the early years of analysis, where acrimony and open debate were the order of the day. More recently, with Freud's insights nominally at least absorbed by the culture, the struggle assumes quieter forms. For example, a "yes, of course," attitude can lead to insidious intellectualization, a surface acceptance minimizing the gravity of Freud's discoveries for each individual's life. The need for the ceaseless struggle against (broadly speaking) repression, which Freud warned against in his recommendation for periodic reanalysis, can be seen, symptomatically, in defenses and defensiveness. Unsure, still, some psychoanalysts are chronically anxious about any behaviors which might resemble nonanalytic or antianalytic interventions.

A more specific speculative hypothesis stems from Guntrip's (1968) opinion that " 'Analyzing' is a male function, an intellectual activity of interpretation." The "making" of an interpretation may be experienced as a phallic activity, as is implied in the words *in*sight and *in*terpretation, those *tools* of the metaphorical *surgical* and *military* trades of psychoanalysis. The historic hostility of organized medicine toward women is well known, as is the alleged overtechnologizing of obstetrics, the cross-cultural demeaning of menstruation and pregnancy, and the substantive position that "the repudiation of femininity can be nothing else than a biological fact" (Freud, 1914). The basic insight-producing model is a form of technology, and techology is supposed, stereotypically, to be the province of men. Medicine has traditionally used technologies to buttress its professional claims against nonprofessional purportations of healing. We see around us now the flowering of various nonpsychoanalytic means of change in a nontechnological, often nonprofessional, culture no longer dominated by males, a culture whose emphasis is on cure and help rather than science and knowledge (Appelbaum, 1979). Perhaps not by coincidence these cultural developments have occurred at the same time as has the assertion of the rights of women.

Many of the techniques and beliefs of these schools of change have been available within psychoanalysis from the beginning: abreaction; the real relationship; the emphasis on feeling, suggestion, manipulation; the importance of the body as a means of influencing neurosis, as a carrier of memories, and as a source of information (Sharpe, 1959), and meditative states of consciousness such as "free-floating association" (Freud, 1912). Yet these have been inadequately exploited, in print at least, and command less public psychoanalytic respect than does the production of insight. We may justifiably consider the extent to which adherence to the basic insight-producing model alone is emotionally determined by the wish to protect, exercise, dignify, and assert a phallic expression of masculinity, with the antagonism toward other means of change serving as a defense against, in effect, castration anxiety.

However, the psychoanalytic technology is not a pure exercise in phallic masculinity; it is more in the nature of a compromise. Before the analyst makes his interpretations, he indulges in a great deal of passivity—listening, allowing, receiving, relying upon "the female function of intuitive knowing" (Guntrip, 1963), and fulfilling of the function of mother (Winnicott, 1965). It probably includes also the anal derivatives of overwhelming words while inhibiting feeling and action. The nature of many compromise formations is to develop energetic defenses, such as unquestioning loyalty, isolation and dissociation, and zealotry.

One response to the question of "deviations," or nonstandard interventions, is a refusal to consider them seriously. This complacency may be expressed in open hostility or shallow, patronizing indulgence. But those who take this position are acting basically as if they fully believe that the results they achieve with their present technique are the best possible, for the most patients, at the least expense of time and money. To me this is a breathtakingly bold position. A more realistic assessment would be that results range from remarkably good to disappointing. An informed, objective assessment would also recognize that outside psychoanalysis techniques of impressive, if perhaps temporary, power are repeatedly being demonstrated with a wide variety of patients. It is indeed complacent for one to assume, without further investigation or trial, that such techniques have nothing to offer psychoanalysis.

Another reaction to the question of "deviations" is to say that analysts behave differently in their offices from the way they do in their writings or at meetings, that they frequently experiment or use nonstandard interventions without teaching or writing about them. Much of this paper has to do with just that paradox, which for the good of patients and the development of science is indefensible. When practitioners do things in such a bootleg manner, they cannot be expected to do them as well as they might with a clear conscience, aided by the corrections and improvements which usually come from public discussion. Further, if what they do is in fact helpful, then their secrecy deprives others of their experience.

Another reaction would be to accept uncritically and use any intervention which holds a priori promise, or yields intrapsychic or behavioral "movement" in practice. It is common knowledge that new techniques, even new drugs, are more effective when first tried than they are later. A restless search for improvement can degenerate into mere faddism. This is yet another version of complacency—that what one does is right, without its being subjected to disciplined questioning and experimentation. Intrapsychic and behavioral "movement" is not the same as achieving the goals of the enterprise, neither in psychoanalysis nor any other therapeutic approach. One can become bemused by an outpouring of affect, a declamation of a new view of self, or changed behavior based solely on an emotional glow or unrecognized suggestion. Fascination is no substitute for science.

A functional reaction to the ideas suggested here would be to consider the options, and select one or all for experimentation in thought and action.

1. One can give up or minimize the quest for insight (a) within psychological treatment by encouraging suggestion, transference cures, educational, inspirational, and cathartic methods; or, (b) outside of psychological treatment, as in meditation, yoga, or structural integration (rolfing). While not psychoanalysis, or sometimes not even psychotherapy, such measures may still be useful for narrowly defined cure, and ought, therefore, to be in the awareness, if not armamentarium, of anyone who sees patients for whom cure of symptoms, alone, rather than self-understanding or thoroughgoing personality change is the practical and appropriate goal.

2. One can in principle pursue insight and add to the process of developing insight other techniques, for example, allowing or encouraging patients to have sex therapy along with their attempt to achieve insight into their sexual difficulties, or allowing or encouraging them to subject themselves to the affective highs and insight-producing results of human-potential techniques. While these activities might be pressed into the service of resistance and influence the transference deleteriously, this is by no means a foregone conclusion, and even if it does occur, may, through analysis of resistance, abet self-knowledge and change.

3. The most promising option stemming from widening the scope of inquiry into how people change beneficially is to try to increase the usefulness of psychoanalysis in general, and insight in particular. I think one would have everything to gain and, if it is done with analytic care, nothing to lose, if technical decisions could be made with a view toward such issues as have been raised in this paper—e.g., finding ways to infuse the process with more affect, moving relatively from the "why" question to the "how" question, from idea to experience; attending assiduously to the meaning to the patient of the process of developing insight; being attuned to the influence of factors common to all treatment relationships; monitoring and exploiting the effects of the interpersonal relationship independent of self-knowledge; following up the stage of learning about oneself with the stages of asserting will and accepting responsibility for

oneself; and taking action in order to live out desired changes in behavior. In planning treatment strategies, in making tactical decisions, and in gently guiding awareness, the analyst might persistently ask himself: What are the relative contributions to this overall process and at this moment of the variety of plausible means of change? Paradoxically, less idealization of insight may well result in greater useful insight.

Could such shifts of emphasis still be called psychoanalysis? To the extent that they are only shifts in emphasis, it seems hardly possible to withdraw the name psychoanalysis from them. In the view of Leo Stone (1954), for example, even more extreme changes in the conditions in the therapeutic process can be encompassed within psychoanalysis:

> How far can the classical analytic method be modified, and still be regarded as psychoanalysis, "modified," if you wish, rather than another form of interpretive psychotherapy? I believe that any number and degree of parameters can be introduced where they are genuinely necessary to meet special conditions, so long as they are all directed to bringing about the ultimate purposes and processes of the analytic end requirements . . . to the maximum extent which the patient's personality permits.

After agreeing with Freud's criteria for psychoanalysis, undoing resistances and interpretation of transference Fenichel (1945) writes, "That procedure is the best which provides the best conditions for the analytic method."

Stone's remarks carry with them the implicit call for diagnosis of each patient at a particular moment in time, under particular conditions, and with respect to particular goals. This, indeed, is the sine qua non of any experimentation, indeed of any technical intervention. If there is any inviolable rule in psychoanalytic technique, it is that the psychoanalyst should be diagnostically aware of the shifting weights in the totality of influence upon him and the patient, and make his intervention on the basis of this awareness.

Finally, Ekstein (1956) offers some historical perspective on such rethinking and experimentation as has been suggested here:

> the master-apprentice method as well as the initial hostility against psychoanalysis have led to the formation of schools as well as to a vast number of special research interests which were frequently experienced by contemporaries as deviations and only later on were integrated into the total body of psychoanalytic theory and practice. The recent rapprochement between the "schools" of Melanie Klein and Anna Freud is a good case in point for the synthesizing efforts so necessary in all of psychological sciences.

It is ironical that psychoanalysis, of all systems of thought, should have to struggle to extricate itself from the effects of emotional and historical forces. It is fitting, however, that psychoanalysis, of all systems of thought, should as the result of such liberation exploit the possibility of increasing the effectiveness of insight, of providing helpful alternatives to the starkness of its use in the basic model, and of more accurately assessing the capacity of patients to take advantage of and benefit from informed interventions.

REFERENCES

Abraham, K. (1919), A particular form of neurotic resistance against psychoanalytic method. *Selected Papers on Psychoanalysis*. New York: Basic Books, Inc., 1954.

Aichhorn, A. (1945), *Wayward Youth*. New York: Viking Press.

Alexander, F., and French, T. (1946), *Psychoanalytic Theory: Principles and Application*. New York: Ronald Press.

Appelbaum, S. (1963), Speaking with the second voice. *Journal of the American Psychoanalytic Association*, 14:462–477.

——— (1973), Psychological-mindedness: Word, concept, and essence. *International Journal of Psycho-Analysis*, 54:35–46.

——— (1976), The dangerous edge of insight. *Psychotherapy: Theory, Research and Practice*, *13*; 202–206.

——— (1977), *The Anatomy of Change*. New York: Plenum.

——— (1979), *Out in Inner Space, A Psychoanalyst Explores the New Therapies*. New York: Anchor Press/Doubleday.

Bibring, E. (1954), Psychoanalysis and the dynamic psychotherapies. *Journal of the American Psychoanalytic Association*, 2:745–770.

Bird, B. (1957), The curse of insight. *Bulletin of the Philadelphia Association for Psychoanalysis*, 7:101–104.

Blanck, G. and Blanck, R. (1974), *Ego Psychology: Theory and Practice*. New York and London: Columbia University Press.

Eissler, K. (1953), Ego structure and analytic technique. *Journal of the American Psychoanalytic Association*, 104–143.

——— (1969), Irreverent remarks about the present and the future of psychoanalysis. *International Journal of Psycho-Analysis,* 50:461–471.

Ekstein, R. (1950), The Tower of Babel in psychology and psychiatry. *American Imago*, 7:76–141.

——— (1956), Psychoanalytic technique. In *Progress in Clinical Psychology*, ed. by Daniel Brower and Lawrence E. Abt. New York: Grune & Stratton, Inc.

——— (1959), Thoughts concerning the nature of the interpretive process. In *Readings in Psychoanalytic Psychology*, ed. Morton Levitt. New York: Appleton-Century-Crofts. Pp. 221–247.

Fenichel, O. (1941), *Problems of Psychoanalytic Technique*. New York: The Psychoanalytic Quarterly, Inc.

——— (1945), *The Psychoanalytic Theory of Neurosis.* New York: W. W. Norton and Company.

——— (1954), *Collected Papers of Otto Fenichel.* Second Series, "Brief Psychotherapy." New York: W. W. Norton and Co. Pp. 243–259.

Frank, J. (1971), Therapeutic factors in psychotherapy. *American Journal of Psychotherapy,* 25:350–361.

Freud, A. (1954), The widening scope of indications for psychoanalysis. *Journal of the American Psychiatric Association,* 2:607–620.

Freud, S. (1895), Studies on hysteria. *Standard Ed.,* 2:1–319. London: Hogarth Press, 1955.

——— (1909), Analysis of a phobia in a five-year-old boy. *Standard Ed.,* 10:3–149. London: Hogarth Press, 1955.

——— (1912), Recommendations for physicians on the psychoanalytic method. *Standard Ed.,* 12:109–120. London: Hogarth Press, 1958.

——— (1914), On the history of the psychoanalytic movement. *Standard Ed.,* 14:3–66. London: Hogarth Press, 1957.

——— (1917[1915]), Mourning and melancholia. *Standard Ed.,* 14:239–260. London: Hogarth Press, 1957.

——— (1918), From the history of the infantile neurosis. *Standard Ed.,* 17:3–123. London: Hogarth Press. 1955.

——— (1919), Lines of advance in psychoanalytic therapy. *Standard Ed.,* 17:157–168. London: Hogarth Press, 1955.

——— (1926), The question of lay analysis. *Standard Ed.,* 20:179–258. London: Hogarth Press, 1959.

——— (1937), Analysis terminable and interminable. *Standard Ed.,* 23:211–253. London: Hogarth Press, 1964.

Gill, M. (1954), Psychoanalysis and exploratory psychotherapy. *Journal of the American Psychoanalytic Association,* 2:771–797.

Gittelson, M. (1952), The emotional position of the analyst in the psychoanalytical situation. *International Journal of Psycho-Analysis,* 33:1–10.

Glover, E. (1955), *The Technique of Psychoanalysis.* New York: International Universities Press.

Greenson, R. (1967), *The Technique and Practice of Psychoanalysis.* New York: International Universities Press.

——— and Wexler, M. (1969), The non-transference relationship in the psychoanalytic situation. *International Journal of Psycho-Analysis,* 50:27–39.

Guntrip, H. (1968), *Schizoid Phenomena, Object-Relations and the Self.* New York: International Universities Press. Pp. 331–364.

Hartmann, H. (1964), On rational and irrational action. In *Essays on Ego Psychology.* New York: International Universities Press.

Holzman, P. (1974), The influence of theoretical models on the treatment of schizophrenia, reported by John L. Gunderson. *Journal of the American Psychoanalytic Association,* 22:182–199.

Horwitz, L. and Appelbaum, A. (1966), A hierarchical ordering of assumptions about psychotherapy. *Psychotherapy,* 3:7–80.

Horwitz, L. (1974), *Clinical Predictions in Psychotherapy.* New York: Jason Aronson, Inc.

Janov, A. (1970), *The Primal Scream.* New York: Dell Publishing Co.

Jung, C. (1923), *Psychological Types or the Psychology of Individuation.* New York: Harcourt, Brace. P. 401.

Knight, R. (1953a), Evaluation of psychotherapeutic techniques. In *Psychoanalytic Psychology and Psychiatry.* New York: International Universities Press.

———— (1953b), Borderline states. In *Ibid.*

Kris, E. (1956), On some vicissitudes of insight in psychoanalysis. *International Journal of Psycho-Analysis,* 37:445–455.

Levitt, M., ed. (1959), *Readings in Psychoanalytic Psychology.* New York: Appleton-Century-Crofts.

Marmor, J. (1964), Psychoanalytic therapy and theories of learning. In *Science and Psychoanalysis,* ed. J. Masserman, 7:265–279. New York: Grune & Stratton, Inc.

Menninger, K. and Holzman, P. (1973), *Theory of Psychoanalytic Technique.* 2nd ed. New York: Basic Books, Inc.

Ramzy, I. (1961), The range of spirit of psycho-analytic technique. *International Journal of Psycho-Analysis,* 42:497–505.

Rangell, L. (1968), A point of view on acting out. *International Journal of Psycho-Analysis,* 49:195–201.

Reich, W. (1949), *Character-Analysis.* 3rd ed. New York: Orgone Institute Press.

Reik, T. (1933), New ways in psychoanalytic technique. *International Journal of Psycho-Analysis,* 14:321–334.

Rorschach, H. (1951), *Psychodiagnostics.* New York: Grune & Stratton, Inc.

Rosenzweig, S. (1936), Some implicit common factors in diverse methods of psychotherapy. *American Journal of Orthopsychiatry,* 6:412–420.

Schafer, R. (1968), On the theoretical and technical conceptualization of activity and passivity. *Psychoanalytic Quarterly,* 37:173–198.

———— (1973), Action: Its place in psychoanalytic interpretation and theory. *The Annual of Psychoanalysis,* 1:169–196.

———— (1974), Talking to patients in psychotherapy. *Bulletin of the Menninger Clinic,* 38:503–515.

Schlesinger, H. (1969), Promises, promises: Making them set up a tension system. *Roche Report: Frontiers of Clinical Psychiatry,* 6:5–6.

Shapiro, A. (1971), Placebo effects in medicine, psychotherapy, and psychoanalysis. In *Handbook of Psychotherapy and Behavior Change,* by A. Bergin and S. Garfield. New York: John Wiley and Sons.

Shapiro, D. (1970), Motivation and action in psychoanalytic psychiatry. *Psychiatry*, 33:329–342.

Sharpe, E. (1959), *Dream Analysis*. London: Hogarth Press.

Silverberg, W. (1955), Acting out versus insight: A problem in psychoanalytic technique. *Psychoanalytic Quarterly*, 24:527–544.

Stone, L. (1954), The widening scope of indications for psychoanalysis. *Journal of the American Psychoanalytic Association*, 2:567–594.

———— (1961), *The Psychoanalytic Situation: An Examination of Its Development and Essential Nature*. New York: International Universities Press.

Strupp, H. (1973), Toward a reformulation of the psychotherapeutic influence. *International Journal of Psychiatry*, 11:263–365.

Wheelis, A. (1950), The place of action in personality change. *Psychiatry*, 13:135–148.

———— (1973), *How People Change*. New York: Harper & Row.

Winnicott, D. (1965), *The Maturational Processes and the Facilitating Environment: Studies in the Theory of Emotional Development*. New York: International Universities Press.

Chapter 20

Parkinson's Law
in Psychotherapy

STEPHEN A. APPELBAUM

A thirty-seven-year-old mother of two, an overweight ex-schoolteacher, had undertaken psychotherapy because of marital troubles, and now the treatment had come to the end. She was grateful to the therapist for the help he had given her, for being the one person in her life who had listened uncritically and understandingly to her, and she was tearfully unhappy at leaving him. At the same time, she recognized her anger at him for, among other things, allowing the treatment to end.

During therapy, the patient had learned about the central conflicts in her life: how she fought and stifled the identity of a striving, capable person because of the need to subjugate herself to her husband; how she bottled up her anger and renounced her desires because she feared that otherwise he would leave her. She recognized how such feelings and conflicts affected her relationship with her husband and children, and was able to see that this was a continuation of her past relationship with her mother. Mother, too, had done the patient's thinking, made her decisions, and controlled her life, something the patient had felt she needed at the time. Now she saw that she both needed and resented it, but was afraid of retaliation should mother learn how resentful she was. At times she wished her mother dead. She had experienced intensely in the treatment her terrified and lonely self. Her resistances came up mainly at times when she was about to feel the anger that, in fantasy, would result in such lonely terror. Eating had been one way of reassuring herself that she would never have to be entirely alone and without sustenance. In the course of working with this material she had given up a peculiar digestive symptom though she had not fully conquered the temptation to overeat. She was now able to set plans in motion to further her education in order to continue her career; and she could feel, despite occasional misgivings, that she had the right to take time and money from the

Reprinted with permission from the *International Journal of Psychoanalytic Psychotherapy*, 1975, Vol. 4, pp. 426–436.

family in order to do what was necessary for herself. She realized that her conflicts were not entirely resolved, but felt that her new awareness of them would help her not to give in to them as she continued to improve the quality of her life. In short, this patient and her therapist had ended their work feeling reasonably satisfied with a job seemingly well done.

This state of affairs at the end of a treatment is doubtless familiar to most psychotherapists, except for one thing. Agreed upon beforehand, the time of the treatment, from initial consultation to the last meeting, was nine hours. During the last hour, the patient said, "I had to work hard because I had so little time."

A thirteen-year-old patient in psychoanalysis, immediately after an ending date was agreed upon, said, "I have to say things now I can't put them off until tomorrow." And "I have to stop cutting off my nose to spite my face."

A woman had been treated for drinking and obsessional thoughts in a dynamically-oriented psychiatric hospital for six months without having involved herself psychologically. Several years later she returned with the same complaints for a one-week outpatient examination. Afterward, she reported to her husband, "I have gotten more from this one week than from my whole previous hospitalization." She did, indeed, surprise everyone with her ability to think psychologically and with other improved behaviors commensurate with her statement.

I suggest that these three patients were at least in part responding to Parkinson's Law, a social critic's droll statement of a profound observation: We shrink the time necessary to perform a task when little time is available, or expand the time work takes when more time is available (1957). According to Parkinson, the time needed to produce a result is subject to factors other than those inherent in the task itself.

If a patient goes to a surgeon he can rightfully expect the "procedure" to take a predictable amount of time, and be so informed. This prediction is based upon past experience with people much like the patient in question, and upon the implicit assumption that what will be done will be completed as quickly as the nature of the task allows. Any variations would be due only to the hasty or leisurely attitude of the practitioner, or unexpected complications with the patient.

None of these latter considerations apply very well to psychotherapy. Our diagnostic criteria are usually not fine enough to allow highly differentiated, accurate predictions of how long it will take any one person to solve his problem. The prescribed operations are abstract. Most important, the doer largely turns out not to be the practitioner and expert, the one who has a backlog of experience and precedent, but the patient. This is usually the patient's one and only "case," he flies at night, and responds to whatever buffeting and landmarks he encounters. Could it not be that one of these flying conditions is the amount of time scheduled for his trip, that patients unconsciously pace themselves according to their expectations of their time in psychotherapy just as people do with all other tasks?

A fixed time limit brings tautly into play influences inherent in beginnings, middles, and ends. The patients have almost a palpable sense of where in the process they are—the process has tonus (Phillips and Johnston, 1954). Some people start fast and slow up, others find it difficult to begin but gather momentum as treatment proceeds. Still others settle into what they experience as the real business in the middle, in contrast to those who get bored in the extended middle of things.

Endings, however, probably have the greatest psychological impact. Most people have noticed that when they are carrying something at the limit of their strength they often are able to carry it just to their destination; only when the destination is reached do they drop it. It is too much of a coincidence to think that the time and distance they have been carrying it corresponds exactly to the outer physical limit of their ability. Rather, it is more likely that the meaning of the ending of the task is decisive—for example, having proved one's self, relief, or anger at having had to work so hard. The perennial question, "If you had only a year to live, what would you do?" reflects an implicit awareness that a person's view of his life, his goals, and himself all change when the end is in sight.

A systematic clinical observation of last responses to psychological tests revealed that patients take advantage of the last response to offer a view of themselves which seems to have been held in abeyance during the long period of testing to that point (Appelbaum, 1961). Like the person carrying a weight almost too heavy for him, some of these test-takers seemed to have been unable to carry any further the defensive burden of screening those responses which indicated the extent of their difficulties. Others, like some patients in psychotherapy who offer important material only at the end of the hour, seemed to feel free to provide a view of what troubled them or of certain hidden strengths only when they knew that they would soon be out of the situation. Still others seemed to take the ending as a last chance to express themselves fully; it was now or never.

An understanding of endings requires that we consider the existential meaning of time, and that requires us to deal with death. The calendar doles out our lives. As the therapist, literally or figuratively, flips the calendar's pages, the patient, unconsciously at least, hopes that the therapist will never find the last page. Saying goodbye, surmounting loss, and bringing things to an inexorable conclusion are among the most difficult tasks we are asked to perform, as patients and as people. We fight these tasks as we fight the reality principle. We are quick to believe that all good things will come sooner or later, that the therapist has sunlit magic as mother did in the endless beginning before time was invented for us. This is as true of the procrastinator as it is of the counter-acting punctual person; of the independent, skeptical pessimist as it is of the clinging, believing optimist. As we are subject to the wish for endless mothering, so must we all come to terms with father's later rule-giving entry. Death is a male carrying a scythe (Lewin, 1952). This is the source of our "time horror" (Mann, 1973).

When we set the time and sound the existential echoes, separation and individuation become prominent, as noted by Mann (1973) and Langs (1974). Is such a bias artificial and diversionary? It seems not to be. Rather, separation and individuation, universally important developmental issues in themselves, become elaborated in the treatment according to each individual's central conflicts, defenses, and character.

Character often encapsulates content. The characterological way a patient reacts to the short time allotted, or to the imminence of ending, provides information whose interpretation is crucial.

A psychotically depressed woman in a sixteen-week psychotherapy reacted emotionally throughout that time to its stipulated length. She showed an inability to organize most of her thoughts temporally, with past events appearing as if they had just taken place, and present ones appearing to be from the past. One of this patient's central underlying difficulties was her inability to achieve liberation through mourning. The challenges began (so far as could be ascertained in this therapy) with the death of her father when she was fourteen, and included the death of her husband a decade previous to the treatment. She had become especially upset when some payments from his estate expired; this seemed to confront her with the reality of his death. Unable to recognize her anger toward these lost people, she could not mourn them well enough to allow the relationships to end. Her turning the anger against herself, instead, was the major focus of interpretations during the treatment, especially as linked to me and the ending which she so bitterly resisted. In the next to the last hour she remarked that she was confident that since I had not recommended drugs, then drugs could not be useful to her. Shortly afterward, she said that she liked me so much she could not be angry about my setting the time limit. I (again) said that she had great difficulty believing she could like me yet be angry and disagree with me, and that this is what made it difficult for her to come to terms with her losses. She said she had idealized her father in the same way that she had idealized her husband and me and, in the process, had denied her anger at him. She recalled, for example, that she resented his forcing her to take lessons on the piano and giving her the idea that she had to be good at it in order to have his love. She revealed that she had just thrown out her dead husband's letters, something she had wanted to do for many years but had felt too guilty to do.

A perennial question for psychotherapists is why patients fail to change even though they seem to have developed an understanding of those aspects of themselves which plausibly are preventing change. The explanation often given is that understanding in and of itself is insufficient, that conflicts must be resolved, and that material must be worked through. Another possibility, however, is that understanding does not result directly in change at all. For example, it may be an effect of change rather than a cause. As Allen Wheelis (1950, 1956) has pointed out, interspersed between understanding and changed behavior is the will to put the behavior into practice and the taking of the actions which operationally do bring about and consolidate change. This point is at least implicit in Roy Schafer's emphasis upon the patient as doer and intender—the often unwilling but decisive bearer of responsibility (Schafer, 1973). However, if the patient assumes that changes are going to take, for example, three years, even should he develop adequate understanding earlier, he may not realize that he has the option to employ will and take action then and there. Why should he, when change isn't supposed to come for a long time yet, and anyway (some patients feel) given the requisite amount of time, the treatment will do it for them? It makes more sense to employ will and action in order to bring about change when the expected time comes to do so. Thus, the self-fulfilling prophecy is indeed fulfilled—change comes at just about the time that it was assumed from the beginning it would. (It should be understood that "action" in this context need not refer solely to easily observed behavior. Action, or movement, can take place intrapsychically.)

Many therapists fear that instead of responding to a time limit with more information or faster movement, a patient will take advantage of the known end point to withhold himself and remain unchanged, aware that if he can just hold on long enough he will be free of challenges and tension. This could occur. Or he might change his behavior so as to convince himself and the therapist that no more work needs to be done, in treatment or out of treatment; and there would not be time for this "flight into health" to collapse of its own weight, which often happens in long-term open-ended treatment. As with any resistance, the effect of abusing the time limit depends upon whether the therapist can help the patient to learn about it and give it up. It may be that with less time available analysis of resistances would be more difficult. Or, it may be that with less time this task would go faster. While some resistances might be encouraged by realizing the finiteness of time, others might be alleviated.

In open-ended psychotherapy, the therapist has to deal with the resistance made possible by timelessness, the impression the patient may have that he need not bring up or work with certain material, or make changes on the basis of it at any particular point, since there is in effect no hurry. In such situations the therapist has to find ways of experientially reminding the patient that theirs is not an isolated activity, but part of life, and that life is passing by. With the end preordained, neither therapist nor patient can comfort himself with the feeling that there is always more time, that around some corner will appear the ultimately effective insights, memories, or feelings.

The clinical experience reported at the beginning of this paper was somewhat startling to me. To judge from the literature, it might well have been for many other analysts, many of whom do not do brief psychotherapy, with or without setting the end at the beginning.[1] But for several reasons there should have been no need for me to be startled at all. Through the years I have observed that the same inexorable and predictable patterns emerge in groups whether the groups meet for a few hours or a few years (Appelbaum, 1963, 1966, 1967). At the Menninger Foundation people come long distances for intensive outpatient examinations, which may last several days to two weeks; a local observation is that predictable beginnings, middles, and ends occur in these situations, and often a remarkable amount of change comes about during these brief examinations. Philip Holzman and I reported on a patient in long-term psychotherapy whose termination was set by external circumstances, and who then immediately changed in her use of the therapeutic process and in her behavior outside the treatment hours as well (1967). On the basis of his research on brief psychotherapy, Malan (1963) became favorably disposed to the idea of setting a time limit in advance.

Occupational characteristics, if not hazards, of being a psychoanalyst may contribute to surprise or disbelief as such a notion as Parkinson's Law being applied to psychological treatment. Such disbelief may stem in part from the analyst's theory and experience with the power of the unconscious, an unconscious which is so often unresponsive to commonsense ideas and homely considerations. Some psychoanalytic writings offer a conception of an unconscious which wends its inexorable way at its own pace, and which one is hard put to interfere with helpfully except in classical technical ways. The delivery of material to consciousness through couch-induced relaxation and letting thoughts come to mind in an atmosphere of evenly hovering attention are passive modes which are compatible with the unconscious taking all the time that it needs. By contrast many expensive years of treatment implies, if not forces, time-consuming perfectionism. Increasing preoccupation with deeper and earlier experiences stems naturally from such a contract and goal. Exceptions to standard conditions of analysis are labeled as parameters, a term which means, after all, departures from an agreed-upon classical system. The classical way of working is sometimes exalted even though it is inappropriate for many of the clinical problems most practitioners have to deal with. Therefore, analysts and analytically inclined psychotherapists may collude with the motives of the patient in extending treatment beyond the time it might otherwise take if a more pointed, problem-solving attitude were adopted, as instigated and dramatized by setting a time limit.

Malan (1963) found in his research group's cases that the willingness and ability of the patient to become deeply involved, matched by enthusiasm on the part of the therapist, were of crucial importance in bringing about a good result.

Hard work and enthusiasm are easier to sustain when the end is in sight, and thus are stimulated when the ending is agreed upon at the beginning of treatment. The longer the stipulated time, the less the effect, though even a distant end point may still be better than none at all, and it could serve to counter the apathy and routinization to which seemingly endless tasks are susceptible. I had originally recommended long-term psychotherapy to the patient reported upon in some detail at the beginning of this communication. But she insisted that she wanted to spend only a few hours talking with me. Once I agreed to this, she showed a high degree of willingness and energy in the work of psychotherapy. And despite the failure of my initial recommendation, I was enthusiastic about working with her, responding to her psychological-mindedness, and sharing her determination to see what could be accomplished in the short amount of time we allotted ourselves.

In addition to setting the brief time limit, I restricted "free" association in favor of attending to a focal conflict, which was selected on the basis of at least a beginning diagnostic understanding. (This understanding was facilitated by the patient's having filled out before the initial meeting a self-administered test procedure, which included semi-projective questions, her family constellation, and other life data [Appelbaum and Katz, 1975]. A full battery of individual tests would likely have been even more useful.) I worked in accordance with what Malan (1963) recommended on the basis of his findings. I offered interpretations not only earlier but somewhat more directly than I would have if the treatment had been undertaken without a stipulation as to the brief number of hours. I used the understanding of personality provided by psychoanalysis. The patient and I tied relationships from the past to the present especially from mother to husband, and to myself. We worked with the idealization that might have remained if the negative aspects of the transference had not been dealt with, especially her anger over termination, a task held by Malan (1963) to be necessary for a good result. There is nothing in brief psychotherapy or in using Parkinson's Law which in principle need contradict the essentials of psychoanalytic understanding. The basic tenets of the method and means of understanding remain, while allowing a range of technical decisions (Ramzy, 1961).

For those who take the analytic task to be the scientific one of observing as large a field as possible with the least observer influence on it, the Parkinson approach would smack of therapeutic rather than scientific zeal in that it would influence and diminish the field of observation. The unconscious is endless, however, and observations are always limited arbitrarily by termination. The *lack* of a specified ending also deletes something from the field of observation, namely the patient's reactions to an experience whose precise end is known in advance from the beginning. Rather than simply introducing a limiting variable by setting the end at the beginning, we exchange one limiting variable for another.

Options in the use of Parkinson's Law include (1) setting it in motion in the mind of the therapist only; (2) setting it in motion in the patient by stipulating the length of treatment to the patient at the beginning; or (3) setting it in motion by stipulating a termination date in the course of the treatment. The last, called in the literature "end-setting" when it is resorted to as a manipulation, is reported on by Freud (1955), Ferenczi (1955), Rank (1945), Orens (1955), and Dewald (1965, 1966).

How long a treatment would be responsive to Parkinson's Law? For some patients and some therapists there may be varying temporal points beyond which setting the end at the beginning would be irrelevant, harmful, or beneficial in varying ways and degrees. These are empirical and, in principle, researchable questions. On the face of it, invoking Parkinson's Law would seem most useful and appropriate with short-term psychotherapy. Over a short period of time, it could be expected to be best kept in mind and thus most effective, and would likely have the least damaging transference implications. As the length of time stipulated becomes longer, so would the implication that the therapist was harsh, arbitrary, or omnipotent in being able to predict and determine when an appropriate ending time would be. Such transference implications occur in short-term treatment as well, and are a major fulcrum for the treatment. However, since they are quickly brought into apposition with the patient's focal conflict and vigorously dealt with there, they are not the problem they would be in long-term psychotherapy where they might hamper the wide-ranging work.

As noted by Mann (1973) and experienced by me, the countertransference implications, also, are substantial. In addition to the general fear of innovation, short-term psychotherapy with the time limit set at the beginning inclines one toward a gnawing fear of having cheated the patient of the time he needs. Complaints by patient that they are still miserable and need more time are especially difficult to bear and analyze when the patients have had, in reality, a treatment which is brief in comparison with many of one's other patients. At such times the therapist may be inclined to fret that the gains may not last and that his reasons for going ahead and sticking with such a truncated schedule are suspect. Some of this is due to fantasy and fear, a result of the anxiety of separation which is shared by patient and therapist; some is due to the therapist's pride, conscientiousness, and sense of professional responsibility. Pragmatically, these feelings are easiest dealt with by selecting for such treatments only those patients who, for financial or other reasons, cannot have or will not agree to long-term psychotherapy.

Most people who do both kinds of treatment would probably agree that the gains from long-term psychotherapy are more extensive and durable. All other things being equal, I recommend extended treatment. But all things usually are not equal. Individual differences within the patient require that we guard against the twin dangers of recommending long-term psychotherapy to practically everybody who presents himself with a psychiatric problem, and of convincing ourselves that everybody can be optimally helped by the kind of brief psychotherapy described here.

Suppose, in two years, the patient who was reported at the beginning of this paper is doing much worse than when I last saw her? This could be taken as evidence that the nine hours either had no effect on her, or a deleterious one, giving her a little unworked-through insight which, if anything, made her sadder and more anxious and in greater conflict than she had been before. Such a line of reasoning depends, however, on the belief that all patients maintain their gains after having been treated by long-term psychotherapy. Test results from the Psychotherapy Research Project of the Menninger Foundation (Appelbaum, 1977) contradict this assumption. One-quarter of the patients considered at termination to have improved had taken a turn for the worse by the time they were examined two years later at follow-up. As far as I know, comparable figures for similar patients treated with brief psychotherapy are not available. I believe that my patient would have made more gains with more time. But I do not know of any formal research which would convincingly support this, and especially whether such added gains would be commensurate with the time added in long-term psychotherapy. Reports by Malan (1963), Mann (1973), Balint et al. (1972) do suggest that stable and substantial gains are realizable through brief treatment.

At the least, gains from brief psychotherapy with the time limit set at the beginning should outstrip what might be expected on the basis of a similar time segment undertaken without the benefit of the effects of Parkinson's Law.

ACKNOWLEDGMENT

I am grateful to Dr. Ann Appelbaum for her creative editing.

NOTES

1. Brief psychotherapy is defined in many ways in the literature, from one or two sessions to two years. Long-term psychotherapy is also subject to such arbitrary semantic usage and for many of the same reasons (Appelbaum and Katz, 1975).

REFERENCES

Appelbaum, S. (1961), The end of the test as a determinant of responses. *Bulletin of the Menninger Clinic*, 25:120–128.

——— (1963), The pleasure and reality principles in group process teaching. *British Journal of Medical Psychology*, 36:49–56.

———— (1966), The Kennedy assassination and the oedipal struggles of a training group. *Psychoanalytic Review*, 53:393–404.

———— (1967), The world in need of a leader: An application of group psychology to international relations. *British Journal of Medical Psychology*, 40:381–392.

———— (1977), *The Anatomy of Change*. New York: Plenum.

———— and Holzman, P. S. (1967), End-setting as a therapeutic event. *Psychiatry*, 30:276–282.

———— and Katz, J. (1975), Self-help with diagnosis (a self-administered semi-projective device). *Journal of Personality Assessment*, 39:349–359.

Balint, M., et al. (1972). *Focal Psychotherapy*. London: Tavistock Publication.

Dewald, P. A. (1965), Reactions to the forced termination of therapy. *Psychiatric Quarterly*, 39:102–126.

———— (1966), Forced termination of psychoanalysis. *Bulletin of the Menninger Clinic*, 30:98–110.

Ferenczi, S. (1955), *The Selected Papers of Sandor Ferenczi*. Edited by Michael Balint. New York: Basic Books.

Freud, S. (1955), From the history of an infantile neurosis. *Standard Ed.* 17:7–122. London: Hogarth.

Langs, R. (1974), *The Technique of Psychoanalytic Psychotherapy*. Vol. 2. New York: Jason Aronson, Inc.

Lewin, B. (1952), Phobic symptoms and dream interpretation. *Psychoanalytic Quarterly*, 21:295–322.

Malan, D. H. (1963), *A Study of Brief Psychotherapy*. London: Tavistock Publications.

Mann, J. (1973), *Time-Limited Psychotherapy*. Cambridge: Harvard University Press.

Orens, M. H. (1955), Setting a termination date—an impetus to analysis. *Journal of the American Psychoanalytic Association*, 3:651–665.

Parkinson, C. N. (1957), *Parkinson's Law*. Boston: Houghton Mifflin Company.

Phillips, E. L. and Johnston, M. S. H. (1954), Theoretical and clinical aspects of short-term parent-child psychotherapy. *Psychiatry*, 17:167–175.

Ramzy, I. (1961), The range and spirit of psycho-analytic technique. *International Journal of Psycho-Analysis*, 42:497–505.

Rank, O. (1945), *Will Therapy and Truth and Reality*. New York: Knopf.

Schafer, R. (1973), Action: Its place in psychoanalytic interpretation and theory. *The Annual of Psychoanalysis*, 1:159–196.

Wheelis, A. (1956), Will and psychoanalysis. *Journal of the American Psychoanalytic Association*, 4:285–303.

———— (1950), The place of action in personality change. *Psychiatry*, 13:135–148.

Chapter 21

Group Psychotherapy
for Borderline and
Narcissistic Patients

LEONARD HORWITZ

In the past few years, group psychotherapists have given increased attention to the treatment of borderline and narcissistic disorders, much as the mental health field has done generally during the past decade. Scientific articles, professional symposia, as well as special conferences are being devoted to this topic. This burgeoning interest may be understood mainly in terms of the difficulties these patients present to the therapist. For example, diagnostically, patients with borderline disorder are more puzzling and elusive than patients in any other diagnostic group (witness the number of research projects selecting just these patients as having multiple and divergent diagnoses in their records). And, once diagnosed, these patients are quite difficult to treat, making up a significant segment of therapists' treatment failures; they often pose severe countertransference problems based mainly on the weak and erratic alliance they form with the therapist.

   Small wonder, then, that the contributions of authors such as Kernberg, Kohut, and Masterson have aroused such interest. Each of these authors has applied aspects of object-relations theory to reach a better understanding of and more effective treatment strategies for borderline and narcissistic patients. In essence, they have either used Melanie Klein's theories of the paranoid-schizoid and depressive positions, or Mahler's formulations concerning the vicissitudes of separation-individuation or, as in the case of Kohut (1977), formulated a framework regarding the development of the nuclear cohesive self.

   I believe that the growing interest in understanding these new theoretical advances transcends the circumscribed area of specific treatment for this group of patients. Rather, the theories of early development (object-relations theory)

Reprinted with permission from the *Bulletin of the Menninger Clinic*, Vol. 44, No. 2, pp. 181–200, © 1980 by The Menninger Foundation.

represent a slowly growing but significant shift in the evolution of psychoanalytic theory as it applies to the diagnostic understanding and treatment of *all* patients, including well-functioning neurotic patients. Freud's early studies of hysteria led not only to enhanced understanding of the neuroses but to insights into normal and abnormal functioning generally. Similarly, the knowledge of the early phases of development, which has been so important in understanding borderline and narcissistic phenomena, is beginning to be applied to normal and neurotic functioning. Fairbairn (1952), writing in the 1930s and 1940s, was the first to introduce the notion that very early developmental fixations and conflicts (which he termed *schizoid*) left indelible marks upon the psyches of all people, and to a greater or lesser extent should be attended to in all psychotherapies. My own analytic work with well-functioning neurotic people has been enriched by knowledge of object-relations theory I learned in the context of treating patients with borderline disorder. I am now considerably more attentive than I used to be to problems relating to the development of the self stemming from early experiences in which the "true self" had to be submerged because of the patient's need to maintain a stable bond with a threatening or rejecting parent who was perceived as not tolerating the infant or child as an individual in his own right. To me, therefore, the popularity of borderline and narcissistic phenomena stems from the recognition in our field of a major advance in psychoanalytic theory via the incorporation of object-relations concepts.

Some Diagnostic Considerations

The diagnostic entity, borderline personality disorder, consists of a range of ego functioning which lacks the intactness of neurosis but is more organized and integrated than psychosis. Like the other superordinate categories of neurosis and psychosis, borderline functioning does not refer to a particular character organization; borderline patients come in different psychological sizes and shapes covering the entire spectrum of character types.

Grinker's (1968) well-known classification of borderline patients attempts to combine a characterological classification with one based on ego strength. Unfortunately, there are no classifications within the borderline syndrome clearly tied to treatment considerations. Burstein and Beale (1975) have suggested that the differences in treatment philosophy between Kernberg and Kohut may be understood in terms of the former working mainly with angry, belligerent patients while the latter focuses largely on more passive and compliant persons. Similarly, Masterson (1976) implies that an exploratory, reconstructive approach involving the confrontation of denial and interpretation of separation conflicts is usually most successful with mild borderline pathology as opposed to the need for a supportive approach with the more severely disturbed, pathologically organized, borderline patients. My belief is that increasing refinement in the diagnosis of varying degrees of ego organization and intactness of persons with borderline disorders will probably emerge as the most useful criterion in determining treatment strategies, whether individual or group.

In this paper, my major emphasis will be upon the group treatment of borderline patients paying particular attention to the narcissistic problems* such patients present. To do so I will present some generalizations concerning the usefulness of group treatment which apply to some but not all of these patients. My observations are based largely upon my experiences with eight patients I treated in group psychotherapy most of whom had had individual therapy either concomitantly or separately. Their treatment may best be characterized as analytic-expressive group psychotherapy (mainly with outpatients) utilizing a group-centered approach (Horwitz 1977a).

Adjunctive Supports

Kernberg (1975) recommends that borderline patients in individual psychotherapy often may need some kind of external structuring, whether it be the supportive interventions of a counselor to help with reality matters, or the more drastic intervention of hospitalization to control destructive behavior. The rationale for these measures is that the ego defects and weaknesses in these patients often make it necessary to provide special structuring in order to protect them and their treatment. If this recommendation is valid for individual treatment, it is even more so for a group approach where the possibilities for supportive interventions are more limited than in individual psychotherapy and where the experiences of frustration, particularly in the early phases of treatment, tend to be more pronounced.

The borderline patient tends to experience rather intense needs for time and attention, for magical solutions, for dramatic demonstrations of love, and is engaged in an incessant search for the good mother. Concomitantly, he or she has to cope with large doses of anger and frustration, feelings of being unloved and unlovable, not to speak of distorted paranoid perceptions of the attitudes of others. These instinctual, person-oriented needs, within a mental apparatus which is defective and handicapped, make it almost impossible for the usual outpatient analytic-expressive psychotherapy group to provide a "holding environment" which can keep internal pressures from spilling over into the patient's environment.

---

* Since I will be referring to narcissistic patients and problems, I should note that the designation "narcissistic character" refers to a type of defense organization which spans both the upper end of the borderline spectrum and the lower end of the neurotic range. Also, all borderline individuals show some degree of narcissistic functioning. Burstein and Beale (1975) have proposed a subtype of narcissistic character on the basis of classifying patients as "grandiose" versus "inadequate," which they see as two sides of the same coin. Basically, both types deal with fear and rage concerning frustrated dependency wishes, but take rather different stances around this conflict.

The major vehicle of the treatment should be one, and only one, expressive modality, whether group or individual, while the adjunctive treatment should be conceptualized as the structuring necessary to make this expressive treatment possible. Some authors (Stein 1964; Wong 1980) believe that concomitant group and individual psychotherapy is the ideal format for patients with borderline disorder, preferably with both roles being taken by the same therapist in order to minimize the problems of splitting and lack of communication. I would add that even where only one therapist is involved, one type of therapy is ideally an adjunct to the other.

Group therapists are familiar with their patients complaining, at some point in the therapeutic course, that individual psychotherapy is what they really need. These transference manifestations usually appear when the group is dealing with rivalry struggles and a patient experiences the need to be singled out as the therapist's favorite. Such expressions by patients need only to be interpreted, not acted on. However, in the case of borderline patients, these transference experiences may also express an important piece of reality. In my experience, the most common reason for treatment failure of borderline patients in group psychotherapy is the therapist's omission of adjunctive individual treatment.

INTEGRATION OF GOOD AND BAD EGO STATES

The main task in the psychotherapy of the borderline patient is to foster an integration of the split between the good and bad internalized self- and object-representations. Splitting is the major defense mechanism used by primitively organized patients to protect the good self- and object-representations from being invaded and contaminated by the bad ones. In Kleinian terms, splitting is an effort to defend the self against persecutory anxiety. The consequences of this defensive mechanism are weakened reality testing, identity diffusion, the failure to neutralize aggression, and the predominance of part- over whole-object relationships. Given the special difficulties borderline patients present and the burden they can often produce for a group, and given the fact that a modified psychoanalytic psychotherapy is often effective with such patients, what special advantages accrue from the use of group psychotherapy?

The therapist as an authority figure "looms less large" in groups as opposed to one-to-one relationships (Scheidlinger & Pyrke 1961); also, the intensity of emotional experiences, particularly negative transferences, often tends to be reduced in a group situation (Spotnitz 1957). But the major advantage of group over individual psychotherapy is that a group offers a more controlled therapeutic regression for many, if not most, borderline patients. Borderline individuals, unlike intact neurotic patients, typically begin their treatment with a marked potential for regressive reactions including paranoid distortions, destructive acting out, a vulnerability to severe losses of self-esteem, and a pronounced need for closeness combined with an equally pronounced fear of its consequences. The therapeutic task with such patients is not that of uncovering their pathological needs and fears or their primitive defensive organization, but of helping them experience and observe their own distorted perceptions and primitive defenses in a sufficiently muted quantity so that they can bring their ego capacities to bear on modulating and neutralizing their pathological reactions. Ideally, then, their transference reactions and characterological defenses can best be confronted, clarified, and interpreted in a therapeutic setting that moderates their regressive potentials.

In a previous paper (1977b), I discussed the phenomenon of transference dilution in groups which contributes to attenuating unwanted regressive reactions. Transference dilution may be understood in terms of several factors: (1) The patient may diffuse his transference reactions over multiple targets in the group, frequently from the therapist onto one or more peers. (2) A group provides the patient with opportunities for social and emotional distance, which the individual may find necessary at a given time. The reduced pressure to participate provides the patient with an opportunity to regulate the intensity of his emotional involvement. (3) A greater reality orientation is introduced in a group than in individual treatment by virtue of the group's stimulating a social interaction with a greater pull toward appropriate social responses. Transference dilution, however, may be offset by an opposing trend toward transference intensification which has been observed by Bion (1961) and other group-centered therapists. Affective stimulation resulting in contagion and resonance tends to enhance emotional responsiveness in group members. Also, competition and sibling rivalry may heighten feelings of frustration and aggression, and a group-centered orientation works particularly in the direction of therapeutic regression.

I believe that both vectors operate and that groups are capable of either intensifying or diluting the participant's emotional reactions depending on the patient and the context of the group. But most borderline patients, especially where a concomitant individual treatment relationship exists, tend to experience more muted reactions in a group setting than they do in an individual relationship. As mentioned earlier, the group—even a predominantly neurotic group—provides the disturbed patient with an opportunity to remain on the periphery of its emotional currents. Because of his narcissistic self-absorption and sense of uniqueness, the borderline patient may exclude himself from the common group tension. For example:

> One narcissistic young male patient consistently and for a long time took the attitude that the therapist's group-wide interpretations were not relevant to him. Haughtily and disdainfully, he let it be known that the others in the group might be so weak

as to be affected by the therapist's absence, but certainly he did not share their "shameful" dependency needs.

Another major buffer against intensification is the presence of concomitant individual treatment which encourages a channeling of transference needs into a potentially more gratifying relationship. As the patient's needs for dependency gratification or for exclusive attention get frustrated, he will tend to turn away from the group and divert his interest and attachment to his individual therapist. Ideally, such rechanneling will occur intermittently and temporarily and will be clarified and interpreted to the patient by one or both therapists. The following transferences are typical of patients with borderline disorder in a group setting and illustrate the thesis of controlled and diluted therapeutic regression.

Intense Primitive Wishes

Borderline patients typically make inordinate demands upon their therapists. They not only have fantasies of a magical cure (in addition to the fear that the whole experience will turn to ashes), but they expect their relief to be immediate and total. They are narcissistic and think of themselves as special persons; they have an attitude of entitlement—they expect to receive special privileges and a greater share of the therapist's time than all the other group members. Such needs are inevitably frustrated in an individual relationship but even more so in a group. More than any other factor, this situation provides the rationale for providing such patients with the gratification of an individual relationship. But the counterpoise to the patient's experience of frustration is the opportunity the group provides to begin appreciating the necessity to consider the presence and the rights of others. In an ideal group, borderline patients gradually will begin to appreciate the inappropriateness of their expectations and be able to tone down their rage at being frustrated. Of course, if they are unable or unwilling to tolerate frustration, they may angrily withdraw, act out, or even quit the group. But the opportunity to hear about the inner lives of their fellow patients in a way relatively unavailable to them prior to their group experience, contributes to their ability to see their fellow patients more as whole persons than as part objects whose presence only signifies the opportunity for exploitation and gratification. This positive therapeutic gain is best illustrated by the following example.

A female borderline patient made unusually good use of her three-year-long group experience, along with many months of hospitalization. At the end of her first year in the group she achieved her first important insight that she needed to learn that the world does not revolve around her alone. This awareness began to dawn on her as we tried to explore her tendency to sit silently in the group, expecting others to take the initiative in drawing her out, or even to know when she was distressed without being told. Much of her remaining group experiences consisted of successfully assimilating that important insight.

Erotization

An especially difficult kind of transference manifestation of some borderline patients is the tendency to erotize the relationship. Almost invariably such reactions are a genital expression of infantile needs to be nurtured, soothed, and comforted. The special difficulty presented by these reactions is the patient's tendency to project his or her instinctual wishes onto the therapist thereby acquiring a highly distorted view of the real relationship. In a dyad, as opposed to a group situation, the privacy of the setting not only stimulates such fantasies but in some instances contributes to the expectation that these wishes may indeed get gratified. For example,

A female patient, whom I treated individually for over a year before she terminated against advice, developed an intensely erotized relationship which she expected to be gratified. Because she considered her husband an inept lover and could not find sexual satisfaction with him, she expected the therapist to take care of such needs. Furthermore, she perceived the therapist as inviting her into a situation in which such fantasies were fostered and, like Eliza Doolittle, expected more than just words. Despite my interpretive efforts, the patient was unable to alter her expectations; her mounting frustration and anger led her to terminate the relationship.

Later, in a hospital setting, the patient started a three-year period of group psychotherapy with another therapist which was quite helpful to her. Her erotization of the transference continued in the group, but in a much more modulated form. During the first year of treatment, the group therapist wrote, "She makes it clear she would be only too glad to erotize the treatment situation and make the relationship with the therapist the end rather than a means. She makes no bones about this being difficult to do in the group and that this is a frustration for her. She makes veiled threats that she might be able to get her hospital doctor to yield to her entreaties and then she will have finished with me." In the course of a relatively long period of treatment, the patient was gradually able to experience less peremptory sexual demands and, when they did occur, she viewed them as embarrassing and depressing rather than as needs which should be fulfilled.

Overidealization and Devaluation

Splitting is the basis for the majority of transference reactions in borderline patients and the alternation between overidealization and devaluation is directly linked to these patients' oscillation between disparate ego states. A group provides a patient with an opportunity to correct these distortions and to limit the breadth of the pendulum-like oscillations. To the extent that such corrections occur, the patient's integrative capacities are strengthened.

Patients with borderline pathology typically view their therapists as all-powerful figures who are either their saviors or are callous, cold, and destructive. The presence of other patients in the group who have different perceptions frequently offers a corrective antidote. This factor is especially significant in a predominantly neurotic group where the group's collective capacity for reality testing is enhanced. In other words, the dyadic situation depends solely upon an already distorted-appearing therapist introducing reality clarifications, whereas the group situation provides multiple clarifying pressures.

Similar factors operate with regard to unrealistic perceptions of one's peers. Insofar as the other participants are able to be considerably more transparent and self-disclosing than the therapist, this additional information serves as a corrective factor attenuating the peer transference. For example,

> A male borderline patient with very strong tendencies to idealize others not only elevated the therapist to the status of "giant" but enviously viewed a seriously incapacitated woman in the group as competent and creative. As other members of the group, including this latter patient herself, shared their perceptions of her real handicaps, the borderline patient was able to tone down his overblown view of her capacities, a corrective strengthening experience.

Expression of Aggressive Impulses

A central problem for borderline patients is their difficulty in dealing with vast amounts of latent destructive energy because of excessive oral frustration. Furthermore, their inability to integrate good and bad internalized objects deprives them of the capacity to neutralize their hostility with quantities of libidinal impulses. The clinical picture these patients present consists either of markedly poor impulse control or immobilized passivity or, more usually, a fluctuation between these two extremes. In a group setting, expressions of disagreement, criticism, and anger, especially toward authority figures, are facilitated. Also, a group provides an "unfreezing" experience for the passive, inhibited patient by permitting him to identify himself vicariously with both aggressor and victim in hostile exchanges which can transpire in a group. Angry confrontations, attacks, and counterattacks occur without permanent damage to either party; eventually, the inhibited patient is able to express his anger toward other patients or the therapist. Several examples are offered in the literature (Greenbaum 1957) of borderline patients who were unable in dyadic relationships to make satisfactory progress because they were immobilized by their fear of hostility. When the patients were later placed in a group, their fears were gradually attenuated as they witnessed hostility being expressed toward the therapist without destructive results.

Vulnerable Self-esteem

Pines (1978) aptly compares the borderline patient with the hemophiliac person: as the latter's capacity for self-healing is defective, the former is ill equipped to deal with narcissistic injury: "they bleed at slight traumas that do not affect more robust characters . . . they are deficient in essential inner qualities for normal self-healing" (p.115). These hypersensitive reactions may be understood in terms of these patients' identity diffusion which deprives them of a stable, organized sense of self. Their views of themselves as loving and lovable persons are constantly being battered by feelings of deprivation, envy, ingratitude, and wishes to retaliate. Good feelings about themselves in relation to others are highly unstable.

Factors contributing to neutralizing these reactions consist of the predominance of positive responses which group patients usually receive from their peers for their contributions to the group, their efforts to improve, and their real achievements. Unless they become victims of scapegoating, which the therapist usually can control, most patients find the group experience a positive "holding environment," and a supportive refuge from the stresses of everyday life once they have become integrated into a cohesive group. Even more sustaining is the patient's experience of being a significant figure in the life of another person. Usually his presence is desired, his contributions are valued, and he undergoes the growth experience of being able to provide help to others. For example,

> A patient with severe borderline pathology showed minimal change over a period of several years of individual psychotherapy which started while he was hospitalized. He was referred for group treatment mainly because of the negative countertransference he elicited: his individual therapist alternated between feeling bored and frustrated by the patient's long-winded monologues and his failure to take initiative in his life. While the patient showed similar behavior in the group, the countertransference was attenuated and he found a safe, accepting refuge in the group mainly because the group therapist could maintain a more neutral attitude and did not convey too urgently that progress was necessary. Over a period of time the patient has been able to become increasingly self-sufficient, even though he is far from being an autonomously functioning individual.

Thus, for many borderline patients, the transference reactions cited above (which constitute a profound challenge for individual and group therapist alike) can be handled more effectively in a group than in an individual setting because the group provides a more controlled therapeutic regression. The actual presence of other persons besides the therapist introduces the significant factor of social reality which contributes to counteracting unrealistic expectations. Intense narcissistic expectations of entitlement and poorly controlled erotization of the transference often tend to get muted in a group situation. Another advantage of the group setting is that the contributions of the peer group neutralize the patient's reality distortions which impair his perceptions and functioning. Phenomena like overidealization or devaluation get dampened more readily in the group situation because of the patients' input. Further, the multiple identifications and behavioral models to which these patients are exposed facilitate new, improved behaviors such as appropriate expressions of anger and self-assertiveness. Finally, not only does the group provide the patient with the opportunity for greater detachment and low involvement when he needs it, but the group therapist likewise may retain greater neutrality and is often less prone to countertransference pulls. These favorable therapeutic influences contribute significantly to the major therapeutic task of integrating the split between the disparate good and bad self- and object-representations.

In most borderline patients, dilution of transference tends to dominate over intensification. In contrast to neurotic patients who are probably even more subject to intensification, most borderline individuals exploit those factors they need most, like dilution (Ethan 1978). It is still not possible to specify with definiteness which borderline patients are unable to tolerate a group experience. Probably the more disturbed, paranoid, and aggressive individuals who are prone to chaotic reactions and extreme degrees of polarization accompanied by poor frustration tolerance will fare worse in a group setting than in individual treatment. But many patients belonging to this syndrome will experience much benefit from a long-term group experience. Liff's (1978) observation that the all-important boundary regulation between self and other which is enhanced in groups is another way of conceptualizing the usefulness of group treatment for borderline and narcissistic problems.

REDUCING NARCISSISTIC AND ABRASIVE BEHAVIOR

In addition to reducing the split self- and object-representations, group treatment also seeks to control and reduce abrasive and narcissistic behavior. Such change may be less structural and intrapsychic than behavioral and interpersonal, but nevertheless it contributes immensely to improvements in patients' relationships. Unquestionably, a group provides a setting par excellence where patients can be made more aware of their inappropriate behavior.

In a group setting, the patient's egocentric, often repugnant, behavioral tendencies can be highlighted in the here-and-now. The patient's need to be special, his excessive demandingness, his view of the therapist as important only insofar as he gratifies the patient's needs, are all characteristics likely to go relatively unnoticed for a long time in individual therapy because in individual therapy the therapist gives the patient his undivided attention. In a group, not only is the patient unable to be always the center of attention, but he is even asked to listen to others and to respond to them in helpful ways. For example, one patient spoke with verve and enthusiasm when describing his own experiences, but became bored and often slept when the others began to speak (Horwitz 1977b). Such patients measure the amount of therapeutic help they get in the group by the amount of time the group focuses upon them. They object to being included in the therapist's group interventions since they view such comments as compromising their sense of specialness. Usually they attempt to monopolize the group's time and attention, and the therapist has the special task of protecting the group from being manipulated and exploited; at the same time, he must protect the offending patient from being scapegoated. But the major help these highly egocentric people receive usually comes from their peers whose confrontations (offered in a context of a basically helping attitude) enhance these patients' awareness of their abrasive behavior.

At the other end of the pole is the silent patient who often taxes the group's forebearance and the therapist's skills. Silence may communicate a variety of meanings and needs to be diagnosed and understood by the therapist. For instance, silence may convey an attitude of superiority, e.g., that one does not belong with this horde of inadequate characters or that others need the help more; another basis for silence is the self-absorption of the narcissistic character who has only a limited capacity for becoming engaged in matters preoccupying others and who, therefore, listens poorly or is unable to empathize with the pains or joys others experience. Frequently, silence is employed by a patient to call attention to himself, to test whether the group or the therapist will notice his nonparticipation. If he can uncover such narcissistic motivations, the therapist can help the patient become more allocentric and giving. A frequent comment made by successfully treated group patients is that they are now considerably more comfortable about participating in social groups, which is at least partly an effect of decreased narcissism.

Sometimes the major learning experience of a patient in a group setting consists of working through primitive envy and greed so that feelings of intense deprivation are no longer a primary theme in the patient's life. The group patient is implicitly asked to share the oral supplies available with his fellow participants. When he is able to overcome frustration and rage over these deprivations, he reaches a higher level of maturity, much as the infant must gradually give up the expectation of getting mother's breast whenever he wants it. Confrontation with his unreasonable demands and his anger at not being immediately gratified is potentially a most useful group experience. Put in another way, an intensive analytic long-term group experience provides the narcissistic patient with the opportunity to learn about his maladaptive infantile behavior and helps him to acquire new and more mature response patterns.

INTERNALIZATION OF NEW REPRESENTATIONS

The factors involved in the therapeutic task of integrating ego splits are mainly classical processes of transference interpretation, insight, and working through leading to conflict resolution. The reduction of narcissistic behavior involves something akin to social learning in which pathological behavior patterns become acknowledged as adaptive failures and are ultimately given up or reduced. Another curative process which may have special relevance to groups is best described as "internalization of new self- and object-representations."

The work of the Menninger Foundation Psychotherapy Research Project (a study of forty-two cases of individual psychotherapy and psychoanalysis) suggests the importance of internalization in intrapsychic and interpersonal change (Horwitz 1974). In individual treatment, the internalization process may consist of a patient introjecting the therapist's attitudes, ideals, and behavior patterns, while in group therapy the patient has the opportunity to see the therapist in a detached way. He witnesses the therapist engaging in a wide repertoire of behaviors and is able to assume the role of spectator while the therapist is either interacting with another patient or dealing with the group as a whole.

Sometimes patients discuss their impressions of the therapist's behavior and may report on their efforts to incorporate some aspect of the therapist into their ego ideal, as exemplified by the narcissistic man who became aware of his weak involvement in the lives of his family and reported on his effort to behave more like the therapist during the family's dinner hour. Or some patients might assume the role of therapist's assistant as one of their roles in the group. The term "therapist's assistant" generally has a pejorative connotation insofar as it is usually applied to those patients who use the role to resist other aspects of group participation such as self-disclosure and spontaneous interactions with peers. But if it does not become an exclusive role, it helps the patient give up his egocentrism. Thus, a narcissistic borderline woman had serious difficulty assuming a maternal role with her child and who struggled with a strong wish to give up her parental responsibilities developed a genuine interest in helping a younger female patient in the group who was clearly more handicapped and disorganized than herself. In part, it was a healthy identification with the therapist's helping role and her gratification from this experience that contributed to a marked improvement. The group not only fostered this identification, but encouraged its implementation within the group setting.

Another kind of internalization involves the acquisition of a new self- and object-representation by means of assimilating the gradually developing therapeutic alliance. Even though the major alliance is between the patient and the therapist, group therapy encourages several peer alliances, as well as an alliance to the group as a whole, which are capable of becoming internalized. As the patient progresses in therapy and develops a bond with the therapist, the expectation of being treated with respect and acceptance predominates over the fear of being manipulated for the therapist's benefit. This significant corrective experience becomes internalized in group treatment just as it does in individual therapy. In addition, the multiple relationships with one's peers—as they evolve into increased feelings of mutual respect, of misunderstanding and feeling understood, of efforts to empathize and help—are new kinds of relationships which borderline patients in particular are unable to experience prior to treatment. Thus, the alliance with both the therapist and one's peers is a potential curative factor in a group (Glatzer 1978).

CONTRAINDICATIONS FOR GROUP PSYCHOTHERAPY

As I have reminded the reader on a few occasions (and quietly reminded myself), any patient with borderline disorder is extremely difficult to treat whether in a group setting or in individual therapy. A paradox in all psychotherapy is that the very characteristics that make treatment necessary are also the ones that often lead to treatment failure. This paradox is even more pertinent to a group setting than to individual therapy because in group treatment the variables are more complex. Specifically, the success or failure of group treatment depends upon two major factors: the patient's ability to tolerate the frustrations and pressures of the group, and the group's ability to tolerate the demands of the patient.

Most therapy groups function best when they are composed predominantly of neurotic patients and contain only one or two borderline patients. Some of the latter's abrasive characteristics will inevitably produce friction and dissatisfaction. Monopolizing, lack of empathy, and the propensity for destructive acting out are characteristics that need treatment but may also place a heavy burden upon the whole psychotherapy group. Such patients because of their insensitivity, provocativeness, as well as their deviancy are usually prime targets for scapegoating. On the other hand, some of these individuals are capable of contributing to "loosening" group norms because of their tendency to think and act in unconventional ways. They also can help the work of the group because they can perceive unconscious motivations of behavior.

There is no precise set of indicators for selecting borderline patients suitable for group therapy. The main classification available (Grinker's [1968] four subtypes) does not seem to be particularly useful. It is clear, however, that the degree of borderline pathology should be a significant general consideration, insofar as the cases that are closer to neurotic functioning are more likely to possess ego strengths useful therapeutically.

Rigidity of defensive and behavioral patterns, particularly those which antagonize and alienate others, should be carefully scrutinized. The grandiose patient who needs to be smugly superior, contemptuous, and haughtily disdainful is unlikely to have a bright future in a group. Unless he also presents some redeeming qualities such as insight into and discomfort with his behavior, he would need considerable work in an individual setting before being considered for a group.

Borderline patients tend to show nonspecific ego weakness characterized by a low tolerance for anxiety and frustration. If the prospective patient does not have the capacity to tolerate minimal amounts of frustration without resorting to angry withdrawal or serious acting out, he is unlikely to have a successful group experience (one index of these characteristics may be a very erratic work record or a history of transitory relationships). The patient who easily finds his life situation ungratifying or intolerable and quickly moves on to greener pastures is likely to behave similarly in a group.

The greater the patient's proneness to disorganization of thinking, the less able he is to tolerate a group experience. The more prominent a paranoid potential, the more he will tend to be affected by the intensification process rather than the dilution process. Multiple stimuli in the group and the deep-seated fears of malevolent forces tend to make it difficult for a paranoid person to utilize the group's corrective features.

Matching the patient with a particular group primarily involves the dimension of deviancy. To what extent will a patient's characteristics, particularly his negative ones, make him stand out as odd, strange, and a potential object of ridicule? For example, the extremely schizoid patient whose language is stilted and cryptic, whose nonverbal mannerisms (like poor eye contact) are irritating, or whose attitudes are excessively puritanical and rigid will be seen as deviant. Also, a borderline patient's limited capacity to take on responsibility may make such a patient conspicuous when compared to the fuller life of his neurotic peers. Deviancy is usually the prime contributor to premature termination and is likely to be antitherapeutic for both patient and group (Yalom 1975).

There is a phenomenon in groups to which borderline and narcissistic patients are particularly susceptible which may best be described as "the six-month crisis." At about this time in the group process, patients begin to perceive with some accuracy what the eventual fate of their pathology is to be in the group. Their expectations of magical cure, the need to give up destructive passivity, the pressure on them to alter their grandiose stances toward others, all tend to come more sharply into focus as they observe the working of the group and how such issues are handled vis-à-vis other patients. Depending on their level of motivation as well as on their ego strength, they may opt to take their pathology and run, a crisis that often peaks around the six-month period.

THE ROLE OF INDIVIDUAL THERAPY

In a previous paper (1977b), I suggested that since individual psychotherapy might be more suitable for borderline patients dealing with integrating good and bad internalized representations than group treatment, concomitant individual treatment might be used as an adjunctive support of group treatment although many borderline patients might tend to use it as their primary treatment. But my main proposition at that time was that the core problem developed in a dyadic, mother-child relationship should ideally be resolved in a one-to-one setting. I also held that since borderline patients are fixated at the separation-individuation phase of development (most probably the rapprochement subphase), it would make theoretical sense to attempt a resolution of these problems in a crucible of a dyadic relationship.

Since then I have systematically examined several borderline patients who underwent both individual and group treatment—not as concomitant therapies but as separate ones—and have modified my original views somewhat. Since a group experience offers a more controlled therapeutic regression in which borderline patients can deal with their task of integration, I now suggest that a group psychotherapy experience would be the ideal *first* phase of treatment for most of these patients. I am not presenting group treatment as a preparation for individual treatment but rather as a coequal modality best suited to occur first. Concomitant individual therapy at this time would be used as an adjunctive support to help the patient tolerate his group experience. Transference dilution may assist the patient in dealing with his affective experiences and in working through his primitive defenses and conflicts.

Ideally, after a borderline patient has completed a reasonable termination of his group treatment, he should be prepared to deal with the intensity of a dyadic relationship and be able to move into intensive individual psychotherapy where the closeness of one-to-one therapy will activate and stimulate his core problems and thus permit a further working through of the underlying conflicts. My observations suggest that this pattern is a useful procedure. For example, the patient I described earlier in connection with erotization of the transference undertook a four-year course of individual treatment after terminating three years of group psychotherapy. The treatment notes indicate that intense erotization once again became a resistance but this time in a considerably more manageable manner. She viewed such wishes as ego alien and inappropriate, worked through her depressive feelings around having to give up her infantile strivings, and generally reacted more like a neurotic patient than a borderline patient. In my view, the opportunity to deal with these problems in the difficult, heated-up individual setting was a profitable experience.

Within the framework of these considerations, a number of individual variations are possible. One such variation has been suggested by Kosseff (1975) who proposed that following a period of individual psychotherapy, the patient should be transferred into a concomitant group psychotherapy with the same therapist. This experience could help the patient gain distance and "breathing space" in his struggle to separate from the individual therapist, i.e., the mother. But Kosseff also recommends that the eventual resolution of the patient's paranoid anxiety should ideally be done within the individual setting which most closely approximates the conflictual developmental situation, i.e., the mother-infant dyad. He exploits the special virtues of both individual and group psychotherapy, as I have tried to do in this paper.

SUMMARY

The consensus among group therapists is that most patients with borderline disorder need a concomitant individual relationship, preferably of a supportive nature, when treated in an outpatient analytic-expressive group. The major therapeutic task with these patients is to help them integrate disparate and contradictory internalized representations based on a predominant use of defensive splitting. Therapeutic groups assist in this task because of their transference dilution characteristics which permit a more controlled therapeutic regression than tends to occur in intensive individual psychotherapy. Group psychotherapy also gives these patients, as well as those with narcissistic disorders, an opportunity to reduce and control maladaptive abrasive behaviors. Internalization of new self- and object-representations based on the opportunity for multiple identifications in a group is also a significant curative factor. The suggestion is made that the ideal treatment for many of these patients would be a course of long-term group psychotherapy followed by an individual therapeutic experience to help the patient deal more effectively with the separation-individuation issues activated in a closer dyadic relationship.

REFERENCES

Bion, W. R.: *Experiences in Groups, and Other Papers*. New York: Basic Books, 1961.

Burstein, Esther & Beale, Estella: Group Psychotherapy: A Treatment of Choice for Narcissistic Disturbances? Unpublished paper presented to the American Group Psychotherapy Association, San Antonio, Texas, February, 1975.

Fairbairn, W. R. D.: *Psychoanalytic Studies of the Personality*. London: Tavistock Publications, 1952.

Glatzer, H. T.: The Working Alliance in Analytic Group Psychotherapy. *Int. J. Group Psychother.* 28(2):147–61, 1978.

Greenbaum, Henry: Combined Psychoanalytic Therapy with Negative Therapeutic Reactions. In *Schizophrenia in Psychoanalytic Office and Practice*, A. H. Rifkin, ed., pp. 56–65. New York: Grune & Stratton, 1957.

Grinker, R. R. *et al.: The Borderline Syndrome: A Behavioral Study of Ego-Functions*. New York: Basic Books, 1968.

Horwitz, Leonard: Group-Centered Interventions in Therapy Groups. *Comp. Group Studies* 2(3):311–31, 1971.

———: *Clinical Prediction in Psychotherapy*. New York: Jason Aronson, 1974.

———: A Group-Centered Approach to Group Psychotherapy. *Int. J. Group Psychother.* 27(4):423–39, 1977a.

———: Group Psychotherapy of the Borderline Patient. In *Borderline Personality Disorders: The Concept, the Syndrome, the Patient*, Peter Hartocollis, ed., pp. 339–422. New York: International Universities Press, 1977b.

Kernberg, O. F.: *Borderline Conditions and Pathological Narcissism*. New York: Jason Aronson, 1975.

Kohut, Heinz: *The Restoration of the Self*. New York: International Universities Press, 1977.

Kosseff, J. W.: The Leader Using Object-Relations Theory. In *The Leader in the Group*, Z. A. Liff, ed., pp. 212–42. New York: Jason Aronson, 1975.

Liff, Z. A.: Group Psychotherapy for the 1980s: Psychoanalysis of Pathological Boundary Structuring. *Group* 2(3):184–92, 1978.

Masterson, J. F.: *Psychotherapy of the Borderline Adult: A Developmental Approach*. New York: Brunner/Mazel, 1976.

Pines, Malcolm: Group Analytic Therapy of the Borderline Patient. *Group Analysis* 11(2):115–26, 1978.

Scheidlinger, Saul & Pyrke, Marjorie: Group Therapy of Women with Severe Dependency Problems. *Am. J. Orthopsychiatry* 31(4):776–85, 1961.

Spotnitz, Hyman: The Borderline Schizophrenic in Group Psychotherapy: The Importance of Individualization. *Int. J. Group Psychother.* 7(2):155–74, 1957.

Stein, Aaron, The Nature of Transference in Combined Therapy. *Int. J. Group Psychother.* 14(4):413–24, 1964.

Wong, Normund: Combined Group and Individual Treatment of Borderline and Narcissistic Patients: Heterogeneous versus Homogeneous Groups. *Int. J. Group Psychother. 30* (4): 389–404, 1980.

Yalom, I. D.: *The Theory and Practice of Group Psychotherapy*, Ed. 2. New York: Basic Books, 1975.

Chapter 22

Diagnosis and Prescription
for Psychotherapy

HERBERT J. SCHLESINGER

It is one of the paradoxes of psychiatry that our relatively sophisticated understanding of mental illnesses in terms of personality structure and conflicts between
unconscious motives and structures within the personality finds expression in a
relatively crude nomenclature that offers only a few widely-spaced categories to
capture and summarize our understanding of patients. That it does so poorly is
a source of continuing complaint. The model we have inherited from medicine
holds that rational treatment depends on accurate diagnosis. But, at best, our
diagnosis labels are only rough approximations of the state of affairs in the
patient and hardly satisfy the condition of accurate diagnosis that might permit
us to make an effective prescription for treatment. And, if diagnosis cannot guide
treatment, why diagnose at all?

There is a school of thought about psychotherapy that denies the necessity of
any sort of diagnosing as a preparation to treatment. I do not share this view,
but if our understanding of diagnosis were really to be so corrupted as to be
synonymous with diagnostic *labeling*, then I would have to agree about the
uselessness of diagnosing for guiding treatment. However, labeling is *not* diagnosis and, as I hope to demonstrate, the understanding of a patient derived
from his examination and history *can* provide a rational basis for guiding at least
the initiation of treatment.

We have many more or less sophisticated notions about the ways persons can
change or mature, can become relieved of symptoms or otherwise learn more
efficient and more humane ways of living. We explain these changes in terms
of theories of interpersonal relationships, of psychotherapeutic process, of learning theory and the like. It is ironic, however, that just as the final common path
of our subtle theories of personality may be a crude diagnostic label, a similar

Reprinted with permission from the *Bulletin of the Menninger Clinic*, 1969, Vol. 33, No. 5, pp.
269–278, © 1969 by The Menninger Foundation.

funneling may occur when prescribing psychological treatment. When we prescribe a course of treatment to accomplish such changes, we tend to resort to a nomenclature of treatment modalities that provides only a few widely-spaced categories of psychological treatment—psychoanalysis, expressive psychotherapy, supportive-expressive psychotherapy and supportive psychotherapy—and, in most settings, the choices range only between expressive and supportive psychotherapy.

Have we really nothing more to say to a psychotherapist-elect than that his efforts ought to be supportive or expressive? Are these really categories of treatment at all in the sense that psychoanalysis is supposed to be?* It is a waste of effort to examine a patient in depth only to have the range of therapeutics predefined by a two-fold classification. The time-honored terms, "supportive" and "expressive," do attempt a distinction that should be useful in describing or prescribing psychotherapy. But I believe they have come to be misapplied and, as used, no longer capture with any precision the distinctions they were coined to preserve.

One image evoked by "supportive psychotherapy" is of a therapist earnestly trying to talk with a patient about the details of everyday living, to suggest better ways of dealing with problems, to offer himself as someone to lean upon, but without specific ambitions to arrive at a point where the purpose of the treatment could be said to have been accomplished. He perhaps wishes to sustain a tentatively reconstituted schizophrenic patient in a marginal existence—a treatment in which "no movement is good movement." Like a good caricature, this image magnifies some part of the truth not beyond recognition and, even though it is a polar example of supportive psychotherapy, this prototype does exist and in large numbers.

For many patients such a concept of treatment is often entirely suitable—perhaps even exclusively suitable. My quarrel is not with the treatment I have sketched but with the name that is applied to it. It is called "supportive" because, I suppose, supporting the patient is its main purpose. But by arrogating the name "supportive" for a polar example of psychotherapy in which the purpose of supporting a patient is pursued in a particular way with particular techniques and with limited aspirations, we debase the term "supportive." We tend to obscure the fact that support is one of the essential purposes of all psychotherapy, and we use it to imply a specific *kind* of psychotherapy—which it is not.

It is, of course, characteristic of the concept "purpose" that it connotes an end achievable by more than one means. In psychotherapy the supportive purpose

---

* I shall exclude the category, psychoanalysis, from my discussion. While psychoanalysis as a treatment method encompasses a wide range of techniques, structural elements and styles of procedure, it is by and large distinguishable from other forms of psychotherapy and has a theory that attempts to explain the personal changes which it brings about.

can be implemented in a variety of ways: (1) by the therapist's accepting silence; (2) by the simple gesture of offering a Kleenex to a crying patient; (3) by a quizzical look conveying "You know better than that" to a quite disturbed patient who is tempted for the moment to accept as realistic an autistic notion; or (4) by a forthright so-called "reality interpretation." These few acts and many others all subserve a conservative or supportive purpose in treatment. It is true that the conservative purpose needs to be kept much more explicitly in the foreground of the therapist's attention in the treatment of certain patients, just as it is true that for others it hardly ever comes to the therapist's attention at all. I doubt, however, that in the latter instance it is also equally distant from the patient's awareness; those patients who impress us as likely candidates for expressive psychotherapy or psychoanalysis merely may be more fortunate than others in having the capacity to derive support from relationships with persons, institutions, things and ideals, including those that do not seem to offer such support in any explicit way. But support is there to be had by those who can make use of it, and it is probably true that those obtain support most successfully who do not seek it explicitly.

It would not be amiss on logical grounds to term that treatment "supportive" in which the psychotherapist must be ever mindful of the patient's need for support. But when used to denote a brand or type of psychotherapy this term has psychological pitfalls and may have unsought and even pernicious consequences. When "supportive" is used as a type-modifier of psychotherapy, some therapists understand that the term requires the *exclusive* use of certain explicit supportive techniques and prohibits the use of certain other techniques (notably content and even defense interpretations). The term suppresses the therapist's interest and alertness to (if not, indeed, rendering him fearful of) whole classes of content of the patient's communications not having explicit reference to the here and now of his experience. Supervisors of psychotherapy often hear a beginning psychotherapist report the painful gropings and musings of a patient who is struggling to master a painful conflict, and learn that the therapist is aware of at least some of the underlying meanings of the patient's difficulties. When the therapist is asked why he did not help the patient by interpreting the situation to him he answers, in the full confidence that it is an adequate response, "The patient is schizophrenic," or "The therapy is supportive." The prescription "supportive psychotherapy," like the label, "schizophrenia," has the potentiality for interfering with the proper treatment of a patient, limiting the achievements that the patient might make were he and his therapist unhampered by these restrictive designations.

But the term "supportive" has a place in the lexicon of psychotherapy even though not, in my opinion, as a category name. To use it as I have suggested, to denote one of the several interlocking purposes of all psychotherapy, suggests different connotations and imposes different requirements on the user. For instance, we would have to ask ourselves: In what sense (areas, instances, etc.) does this patient need support? More specifically, *what* in the patient needs support: (1) his sense of reality against the temptations of dereistic preoccupations, (2) his conscience against the temptations of corruption, (3) his frightened ego against the anxiety-inspired wish to banish all derivatives of a troublesome instinctual impulse or even against intense feelings of any kind? Or is it a fragile and remote impulse-derivative that needs support (*e.g.*, a tender, affectionate feeling against defenses that would stifle it), or perhaps it is the shaken patient who needs support against momentarily overwhelming outside pressures, or does his flagging motivation need support in order to continue treatment during a phase of uncomfortable resistance? Or is it the patient's self-esteem that needs support against the painful discovery of the infantile core of certain strivings?

The term "supportive" applies to each of these different situations though the manner in which the support would be offered, if indeed it would have to be explicitly offered by the psychotherapist at all, is likely to be quite different in each. In the phrase "supportive psychotherapy," "support" usually implies either support for the ego against the pressure of threatening impulses (*i.e.*, support for the testing of reality) or support against unbearable external pressures.* But even in these more restricted senses, no specific technical implications can be derived from the term "supportive." The support that is needed can be provided in many ways, depending upon the therapist, the patient and the context. Thus, one must not only ask "Support what?" but also "Support *how?*" And this question, like the first, cannot be answered without intimate knowledge of the patient, the therapist and the context.

When "supportive" is used in the sense of bolstering the patient's testing of reality against the pressures of instinct, the term is often linked with or even replaced by the term, "suppressive." This latter term, which is so rich in political connotations, is quite barren of specific technical psychotherapeutic implications. Like "supportive," "suppressive" characterizes all psychotherapy to some degree, though more euphonious, less tendentious terms may be used to describe the thinking and operations that could be arrayed under it. In brief, the whole issue of "dosing" interpretations so as not to force the patient's ego to cope with too much at any one time could be subsumed under this concept. Suppression is also accomplished by any expression of the therapist's interest in one rather than in another facet of a patient's communications.

For completeness' sake we must consider an additional question that a therapist should keep in mind about the term "supportive": Support *when?* What vicissitudes in the treatment, in the transference situation, in outside life circum-

---

* In this latter sense the term so dilutes the usual concept of psychotherapy that the task may be delegated to a less prestigeful person than a "doctor," and the process may be called "counseling."

stances, etc., increase or decrease the patient's need for support? Examples probably are not necessary here as they will come easily to your mind.

The therapist should also ask himself, When is support *un*necessary? After support, *then what*? This last is a misleading question, though it lends itself easily to apparently simple answers. The fallacy which this question contains is the implication that the terms supportive and expressive as applied to psychotherapy are antithetical. One is led to think that one prescribes and does *either* supportive psychotherapy *or* expressive psychotherapy (or psychoanalysis, *i.e., very* expressive psychotherapy). But can one straddle the issue with the category "supportive-expressive" therapy, thinking that perhaps the apparent antithesis is resolved by this composite form? While this hyphenated term would seem at first glance to be a hybrid that might combine the best features of two ideal parents, it is in fact a most unnatural and ungainly offspring. In one usage it is a changeling creature, now like one parent and again like the other, switching its guise as expedience dictates. In another usage it begins like the one parent, and at some inflection point becomes like the other.* The trouble with these fanciful metaphors is that, if we accept that there "ain't no such animal" as supportive psychotherapy, then our conceptual hybrid is left in the embarrassing position of being the offspring of only one parent whose existence, at this point, I hope you are beginning to doubt as well.

When one examines the logic of the supportive-expressive antithesis, then the terms appear obviously incoordinate. They refer to different areas of discourse (since the one refers to a therapist's *purpose* in psychotherapy while the other refers, if somewhat vaguely, to a *means* and *style* of doing psychotherapy) and can hardly be thought of as opposites or even as alternatives. A logical opposite to the term "expressive" might be "inexpressive," but I do not know of any therapist who would be willing to have his work so described. The term "suppressive," at least in some usages, seems conceptually coordinate with "expressive" and cannot be dismissed on *a priori* linguistic grounds. But when we consider that a psychotherapist may help a patient *suppress* something by encouraging the *expression* of something else, the clarity of the logical distinction is lost. Consequently, the term "suppressive" seems to me better thought of, like its kin "supportive," as a quite general part-purpose of all psychotherapy. Similarly "expressive," while really not of the same order, also characterizes all psychotherapy. A psychotherapy in which the patient is not helped to express something of the depth of himself would be quite unthinkable.

---

* I recognize that these situations do in fact arise in clinical practice, that these terms singly or in hybrid form do describe certain instances of psychotherapy. My objection, however, is to considering them as prototypes of treatment or as polar ideals, as examples to which all other instances of psychotherapy are supposed to conform in theory if not entirely in fact.

But you will insist that I am merely being perverse in hewing to the everyday senses of these terms while ignoring the technical connotations that they have long since acquired. They may be jargon, you will say, but they are useful jargon and convey to the initiated quite distinctive ideas that no other terms are now available to convey. I concede that in practice a poor tool may be better than none and that distinctions in the kind, style, method, etc. of psychotherapy need to be made—indeed made as precisely as they can be made. It is just for these reasons that I attack the current usage. For the terms we now use, I believe, obscure distinctions that ought to be made and supply only a pair of pseudo-categories which permit discrimination only between polar examples. As for the contention that they are nevertheless useful terms to the initiated, I would reply that it is just such initiated persons who should learn to be more discriminating in describing psychotherapy. The initiated have learned to supply their own private footnotes to fill the gaps in understanding that the category names leave. In short, it is just the "initiated" who have the least need for these misleading terms; they have ways to get around them and their obscurities.

The young psychotherapist who receives a treatment prescription of supportive psychotherapy for a patient will understand that he is not expected to work miracles and can be fairly certain that the patient is not suitable for psycho-analysis. With only this prescription to guide him, however, the therapist-to-be would not know if the patient is too sick to risk a more ambitious treatment or not sick enough to warrant the investment of more time (and possibly a better qualified psychotherapist). The tendencies of certain patients to judge their worth, and the esteem in which we hold their illnesses in terms of the number of hours per week we devote to them (and to a lesser extent, I believe, by whom), are matched by a quite similar if less openly verbalized set of values among therapists. But whatever index to socio-psychiatric status the terms may provide, they can hardly be defended on the grounds that they offer a succinct and accurate guide to a psychotherapist about what he should or should not do, or even to convey to a third party an adequate description of what was or was not done to or with a patient. Yet a psychotherapy prescription should certainly meet these minimal criteria.*

If we are to do away with "supportive" and "expressive" as defining adjectives, how then should psychotherapy be described and prescribed? I do not

---

* Perhaps the riddle of why psychotherapists have become used to uninformative treatment prescriptions is that, unlike the field of medicine in which the diagnostic function is in general more prestigeful than the therapeutic function, in psychiatry the therapeutic function is at present the more prestigeful. For example, a patient may be examined by a junior staff person whose prescription for treatment might be carried out by a therapist who possesses greater training and skill than the diagnostician. Perhaps the brevity and unspecificity of treatment prescriptions reflect this potential disparity of status and the justifiable feeling that a more detailed prescription might be considered presumptuous.

propose to banish these terms completely, but rather to use them more precisely in describing psychotherapy and to cease using them as if they described different *kinds* of psychotherapy.

It is unreasonable to expect that any word or brief descriptive phrase could convey the information and conclusions from the patient's psychological examination and history that should guide the treatment he is to be given. The usual sort of case summary or case abstract condenses the multiple overlapping points of view, historical and examinational, that have contributed to the understanding of the patient; but its primary purpose is to represent the several studies briefly but faithfully. It is not permitted the kind of selectivity and special emphasis that should characterize a treatment prescription. A treatment prescription should bear the same relationship to a case summary as a good map does to a guide book.

In the first place, a treatment prescription should serve as a guide in selecting a psychotherapist in terms of his level of skill, particular aptitudes and gender. In the second place, the prescription should serve to alert the psychotherapist-elect to the nature of the patient's problem in terms of the "language of control" (including likely pitfalls and sensitive areas, as well as his strengths and other factors that favor successful treatment) and help him to gauge the likely frequency of appointments that will be needed.

The following example of a treatment prescription for a hypothetical case has been divorced from the case summary that it should logically follow. Therefore, I must ask you to assume that the examination has established that the patient is moderately ill and severely incapacitated by his illness, and that psychotherapy is the treatment modality of choice. Rather than a prescription of techniques to be followed, this reformed psychotherapy prescription offers a precis of the case from the point of view of treatment, a hierarchy of treatment objectives supported by the findings of the examination, a rationale for an approach to the treatment that could assist the psychotherapist in choosing at least an initial treatment strategy, and an appraisal of the hazards as well as the favorable factors both within the patient and in his environment that could influence the progress of the treatment. The example is longer and more discursive than an actual one would need to be in order to make up for the absence of the supporting material that would normally be present.

PSYCHOTHERAPY PRESCRIPTION

1. *Objectives*: To help the patient resolve what he understands to be a conflict over whether to continue in a turbulent marriage and an uncomfortable job, a situation which appears to be merely the latest of repeated crises having the general form of a self-destructive and environment-manipulating attempt at

resolving an infantile conflict over autonomy versus dependency. While this problem has important pregenital roots, the most prominent obstacle to achieving a workable resolution at this time seems to be the patient's unsuccessful attempts to identify himself with his father whom he experiences as an unreasonable tyrant in whose value system the patient amounts to nothing. The patient's mother is an inconstant, alcoholic woman who attempts to be protective of the patient in relation to his father but who also behaves quite seductively to the patient and explicitly would like to keep him close to her. The patient's promiscuity and other misbehavior seem to amount to efforts at repudiating the unconscious attraction that his mother holds for him and to neutralize the father's implicit threat to him as a competitor. The patient seems capable of resolving the current aspects of this conflict on the basis of his glimmering awareness both of his father's actual weakness and dependence on the patient and that the patient's own value system has at least as much validity as his father's. The patient should be helped to express his deep-seated resentment and fear of his father and to understand the way in which he has allowed himself to be used as a pawn in their disturbed relationship. It seems likely that such a resolution could be favored if the patient would have an opportunity to identify himself transiently with a consistent and tolerant therapist in the course of working on his difficulties in current life terms.

2.   *Recommendations*:   The recommendation to attempt a resolution in current-life terms is based in part on the patient's intense investment in his current difficulties and the degree to which the present situation seems to recapitulate and contain much of the patient's pattern of difficulties of his infantile past. More important, there are contraindications to encouraging regression in the course of psychotherapy because of the ease of stimulating a latent homoerotic (passive feminine) attitude toward the father against which the patient is too weakly defended and in the face of which paranoid symptoms are a likely danger. The patient has already experienced episodes of acute panic in which flight, in the form of wild promiscuity, has been resorted to seemingly in an effort to avoid disintegration. It is expected that periods of hospitalization may be necessary in the course of outpatient psychotherapy when the temptation to flee from mounting anxiety becomes too great. In the hospital as well as out the patient should be encouraged to be active, to work at a job that taxes his abilities and be helped to perform at the highest level of which he is capable.

3.   *Selection of a Therapist*:   Attributes of the patient that should condition the selection of a therapist and may influence the course of treatment include the patient's analytic and creative intelligence with, paradoxically, a distrust of intellectualizing and his keen sensitivity to the least indication of insincerity in others, matched by a difficulty in trusting others. The patient loves and practices the outdoor life and has a broad romantic streak in his make-up, idealizing feats

of daring and mastery over the forces of nature. The patient has also demonstrated an ingrained sense of decency and fair play that stops somewhere short of application in his relations with women. This inconsistency in himself only vaguely disturbs the patient at present. Lastly, the patient has a fine sense of humor. A therapist-to-be will have to make an instantly good impression on the patient, and will have to be able to match wits with him, at least at the beginning of treatment. He will also have to be able to keep his equanimity and sense of humor in the face of the patient's almost certain efforts to test his sincerity and patience with misbehavior. Because of the patient's focal problem with his father and his feelings of contempt for women it seems likely that the initial course of treatment would go more smoothly if the therapist were male.

4. *Structural Elements*: At the close of the examination the patient and his family were advised that we recommend psychotherapy and that one-hour interviews two to three times per week for a period we estimate to be one to three years would be involved. They accepted these recommendations and the fee which was quoted to them. The patient is ready to begin treatment at any time. While his initial hostility to the idea that his troubles might have psychological roots within him has abated, he retains much skepticism about the potential helpfulness of psychotherapy.

SUMMARY

I have tried to show that the usual dichotomy, "supportive" versus "expressive," used in prescribing psychotherapy is inadequate and that a useful prescription must be much more explicit about what needs to be supported and when and why, and what needs expression and why. A thoroughgoing psychiatric examination can yield information that is indispensable in deciding upon a program of psychotherapy, if the information is properly organized in the form of a prescription.

Chapter 23

The Use of the Psychological
Test Report in Setting
the Focus of Psychotherapy

ROWE L. MORTIMER AND WILLIAM H. SMITH

Assume for a moment that a patient of yours is speaking. "He was really putting me down with his superior-looking helpfulness. The more he hovered over me the dumber I got. It was like my mother used to treat me, like I was retarded or something and needed her to do everything. Then, when he turned his back on me, it was just too much. If I had stayed around, I'd have hit him for sure, so I ran out of there. I needed to pass his course to graduate, but there was no sense going back there anymore after what I did." Which theme or issue would you pick from that wide array of possible themes? Would you take up with him his vulnerability to feeling degraded? Would you address the transference issue of how others who offer help are experienced as hovering and depreciating? Would you point to how threatened he is by his dependency wishes (feeling degraded by his wish to be helped), his style of defending against his anger by taking flight, or the degree of pessimism which was illustrated by the patient's judging the situation to be unredeemable? Any one of the themes could be picked as the central issue to be worked with, depending on your understanding of the patient.

Within any theory of personality organization and treatment there are a number of theoretical constructs with which one may arrange and order the information generated in therapy hours. Within the context of their theory, psychotherapists select what to attend to in accordance with their assumptions about the treatment needs of the patient. Such selection occurs not only in psychodynamic treatments but in behavior modification as well. Thus, Klein, Dittman, and Parloff (1969) were able to write, upon observing the work of Wolpe and Lazarus, that these clinicians were working from a conceptual framework by which they selected

Reprinted with permission from the *Journal of Personality Assessment*, Vol. 47, No. 2, pp. 134–138, © 1983 by the Society for Personality Assessment, Inc.

what they defined as the "basic problem." Shevrin and Shectman (1973), in describing the process of psychiatric evaluations, made a strong case that selection of the wrong presenting problem in the diagnostic process generates a faulty array of data about the patient.

Researchers in the Menninger Foundation's Psychotherapy Research Project created a diagnostic statement for each patient in the project under the title "Core Neurotic Conflict" (Wallerstein and Robbins, 1956). When the psychotherapies were described clinically, however, it was apparent that some of the therapists focused on the core neurotic conflicts of the patients while others focused on patterns of defense and still others focused on overt behaviors and their consequences—aiming at what appeared to be relatively superficial or modest changes (Horwitz, 1974).

The psychotherapist has three alternatives. He can choose the central issue to which others are subordinated, although related; he can choose an issue which, although true in some respects, is not actually central or emotionally relevant to the patient; or he can try to hit all the bases and leave the patient feeling confused and poorly understood. We would like to describe three cases which demonstrate the value of well-written psychological test reports in helping the therapist determine the appropriate focus for treatment. All three patients were hospitalized during the initial stages of psychotherapy. The psychotherapies with patients II and III were quite expressive and could not have been accomplished without the emotionally supportive and action-limiting effects of hospitalization. The test batteries from which the reports were written were modeled after the test battery studied by Rapaport, Gill, and Schafer (1968).

CASE I: FOCUS ON EGO DEFICITS

The patient had been admitted to the hospital with a diagnosis of chronic schizophrenia. After years of intense, stormy treatment during which she had frequently seemed invested only in making a crazy sham of her own life and the lives of others, she had carved out something of a life for herself. She had been out of the hospital for three years and had been happily married for two of those. Despite her investment in her marriage, in her training as a teacher, and in decorating her home, she had collapsed into an acute psychotic state which was marked by considerable bizarreness, abrupt shifts into suicidal hopelessness, and a fear that she would be abandoned by her husband. When she was sufficiently remitted from the most acute psychotic state, testing was requested.

The examining psychologist stated firmly that the central problem was a set of specific ego deficits consistent with a central nervous system impairment. The deficits had three major effects: They set limits on what she could do intellectually, they created difficulty with affect modulation which caused a need for motoric release of tension at times of affect arousal, and they contributed to states of overwhelmed confusion at times when she would try to attend to several things at once. She would then deride herself mercilessly for the confusion, pushing herself into depression and eventually giving herself over to psychotic thinking and bizarre actions.

The psychotherapist, who had been hearing the material presented in the therapy hours as representing a fear of individuation, took a new direction from the test report. He began hearing the content of therapy hours in terms of the patient's response to cognitive limitations. With the permission that this form of selective attention by the therapist offered, the patient was able to explore her difficulties with spatial designs and patterns. She identified her memory deficits and developed ways of working around them. Most important, she could explore what occurred when she had, as she put it, "too much on her mind."

As a result of this new focus, the following changes occurred. She became more forgiving of her limitations and saw them as specific deficits rather than as indications of a generalized inadequacy. For example, she could understand her difficulties in teachers' training as due to spatial and abstraction difficulties, and not as an indictment of her ability to offer love to children. She became freer to avoid stressful tasks and to provide crutches for herself. Also, she became able to forecast and prevent the overloaded states of mind which had triggered previous decompensations. She did this simply by cutting back on the number of tasks and concerns with which she could deal at critical times and by self-consciously giving herself breathers in which she would pull back from her efforts to handle multiple problems.

The content of the therapy continued to be rich and varied. The therapist's attitude toward the material, however, had been beneficially redirected by the test report. By maintaining some focus on assessing with her how she was dealing with the array of events in her life and by supporting her efforts to take only one issue at a time, the therapist assisted the patient to develop successful and stable patterns of coping which, in turn, led to considerably enhanced self-esteem. A planned termination was carried out successfully, and the patient has not required hospitalization again in the four years since last discharged.

CASE II: FOCUS ON AN IMPULSE-DEFENSE CONFIGURATION

The patient, a young woman, chose hospital treatment as an alternative to a jail sentence for possession of heroin. Drug use was clearly in keeping with her image of herself as a devil-may-care free spirit, a person of the streets.

She was tested as part of her initial hospital evaluation. The psychological test report indicated she was as smooth, capable, and intelligent as she had appeared interpersonally. Structured and unstructured tasks alike were performed easily and with dispatch. The test report noted a "get it done quickly and move on" style and an intricate layering of defenses against the conscious experiences of anxiety, depression, and anger which prompted her to avoidant action. The defenses against feelings were seen as rigid and pervasive. A prediction was made from the tests that the patient's use of avoidant action would remain a central issue in treatment for some time, only to give way eventually to a study of the layering of other defenses against feelings.

In fact, the patient's propensity to act quickly (often skillfully and apparently appropriately) in order to avoid feelings was never let out of sight during the four-year therapy. The therapist, guided by the test report, developed the following strategies: First, he watched carefully for the feeling-avoidant aspect of any action (even those actions which were effective and healthy-looking). Frequently this necessitated the therapist's pointing out the pathological aspects of such positive-looking actions as getting a job, enrolling in college, and tapering off Methadone. Second, he kept alert to situations in the patient's life which ought to stir feelings in order to predict her avoidant actions to her in advance and to demonstrate the inner states which had prompted the action. And third, late in the therapy, when the therapist and patient were working together on the recognition and acceptance of her dependency wishes, the therapist kept tracing the defensive pattern: The dependency wish prompted a wish to avoid the feelings associated with dependency, and an urge to act to avoid the feelings.

It was one of those therapies which could have gone astray in any of several directions. The therapist could have worked on her becoming a productive member of society and could have fostered her educational and occupational efforts. This would have seemed quite successful in the short-run, since she could have set off in the apparent direction of achieving goals the day she entered treatment. However, such an effort would have collapsed into flight, drug abuse, and perhaps disappointment and anger on the part of the therapist once the patient was faced with even signal levels of the defended-against feelings. The therapist could have worked with her on a variety of important beliefs she had about herself and others and on the genetic development of these attitudes. It would have been easy work for her. She could have spun out impressive, dynamically sophisticated accounts of how she got to be this way, while at the same time neither facing nor changing the pattern of denial and flight.

Following termination of psychotherapy, the patient had approximately four years of very successful adjustment. She married, had a child, and found work that she enjoyed and found meaningful. More recently, she lapsed into drug use, for which she quickly sought help again in her present community.

CASE III: FOCUS ON A TRANSFERENCE PARADIGM
OR PERHAPS A CORE NEUROTIC CONFLICT

The patient had become increasingly depressed and anxious during a two-year course of expressive psychotherapy. He was referred for hospitalization combined with psychotherapy because of his inability to use outpatient treatment and his potential for suicide. The question posed to the examining psychologist was: "What has caused this bright, often hard-working young man to spoil his treatment?"

The examining psychologist pointed to a variety of ego deficits which were consistent with a diagnosis of borderline personality organization, and also to the patient's rigid defenses against emotion. In explaining the failure of the earlier therapy, however, he did not point to ego deficits nor to the patient's defensive structure, but rather to the difficulty the patient had, and could continue having, in accepting help. The test report used a quotation from one of the patient's Thematic Apperception Test stories to describe the patient's near-conscious experience of this difficulty: "He must find the strength from within himself. Outside help just disturbs his concentration." Even more important was the examiner's portrayal in the test report of two intrapsychic forces which left the patient unwilling and, for all practical purposes, unable to take in the help of another. First, the patient harbored primitive anxieties about being invaded by a frightening, overpowering treater. These fantasies were captured in the fear of homosexual penetration and at a still more primitive level in the fear of being totally invaded and taken over. Second, the patient was vulnerable, whenever he was not completely competent, in charge, and in need of no help, to feeling like "an outrageously grotesque and angry infant who is deprived, malnourished, orally needful, and filled with guilt."

The test report portrayed the patient's dilemma about using psychotherapy in dramatic terms. If the therapist was capable, strong, and effective, he then also was experienced as having sufficient power to invade the patient and take over. This loss of selfhood and autonomy would be terrifying to the patient. On the other hand, if the therapist's help was needed or found useful, then the patient was transformed from the competent ideal self he tried to maintain into the grotesque infant he feared himself to be.

Based on the test report, the therapeutic strategy included two key elements. First, don't invest too much in helping the patient to change and do not try to be incisive or effective with him. In short, stay back and give him room. Second, assume at the outset that the exploration of his conflicts about taking in help constitute the principal focus of the whole therapy. Over time the patient was able to unfold the important facets of this central problem. After some initial depreciation of the therapist for failing to produce the brilliant, effective interpretations he had expected, the patient was able to explore his own harsh intolerance of any imperfection or needs in himself. Gradually, he was able to allow himself occasional mediocrity and occasional (though rare) minor failures. He then became unhappy with the therapist, believing that since the therapist was not invested in perfecting him that the therapist was not invested in him. Gradually he was able to observe his own ways of turning away the help he wanted and from that was able to begin exploring his fear of homosexual penetration by the therapist-powerful father and his fear of invasion and takeover by the therapist-engulfing helpful mother. Once those fears were conscious, he was able to explore his intense wish to be guided, nurtured, and guaranteed a successful life and was able to recognize that it was this wish which had activated the core fear that he would lose his selfhood and autonomy. His increased freedom to accept from others became manifest in his schoolwork because he could learn easily when others' knowledge was not experienced as an intruding, overpowering force. He was also able to develop a relationship with a girlfriend on whom he could depend for support when he needed it.

We need not speculate on what would have happened had the patient's fear of invasion and the wish behind it not been kept as the focus of therapy: prior to the successful therapy, the patient already had two therapeutic failures. Although the second failure occurred after the testing was done, the therapist was apparently not mindful of the test report.* The first therapy was done by a skilled interpreter of unconscious process who, in the process of interpreting, became frighteningly knowing and powerful in the eyes of the patient, thus helping generate the panic and depression which brought the patient to the hospital. The second therapist provided the patient with considerable amounts of encouragement and support. The patient liked the second therapist, but saw himself as moving in the direction of the intolerably needy infant he feared himself to be and so terminated the therapy. Following this discharge, the patient has reported a very successful life for several years now. He has resumed his education and is pursuing advanced professional training.

As psychotherapists, we have become convinced that an unfocused or inaccurately focused treatment may be a considerable disservice to the patient. At the same time we recognize how easy it is for therapists to be swept along by the ongoing process of a therapy and how easy it is to lose sight of a central theme, especially when the treatment is a lengthy one. The test report is a useful tool to help establish a central focus initially and to regain it when the report is reviewed.

As diagnosticians, we feel a responsibility for helping therapists and other treaters to appropriately focus their treatment efforts. Although it is easier to write a test report which sets no priorities, we have sufficient diagnostic and conceptual tools for determining the critical issue to be addressed in treatment for many of the patients we test. In order to use these tools we need to be willing to assess the relative importance of a given set of ego functions, a given pattern of defenses, or a given transference paradigm with reference to its pervasiveness and significance in the life of the patient. When we determine the relative

---

* For a further elaboration of errors which occur as a result of ignoring the psychological test report, see Appelbaum (1977), Chapter 8.

centrality of the different facets which the patient presents to us in testing, we are able to help psychotherapists determine where to focus their efforts and attention.

REFERENCES

Appelbaum, S. A. *The anatomy of change*. New York: Plenum, 1977.

Horwitz, L. *Clinical prediction in psychotherapy*. New York: Aronson, 1974.

Klein, M. H., Dittman, A. T., & Parloff, M. B. Behavior therapy: Observations and reflections. *Journal of Consulting and Clinical Psychology*, 1969, *33*, 259–266.

Rapaport, D., Gill, M., & Schafer, R. In R. R. Holt (Ed.), *Diagnostic psychological testing*. New York: International Universities Press, 1968. (Originally published 1945.)

Shevrin, H. & Shectman, F. The diagnostic process in psychiatric evaluations. *Bulletin of The Menninger Clinic*, 1973, *37*, 451–494.

Wallerstein, R. S. & Robbins, L. L. The psychotherapy research project of the Menninger Foundation: Rationale, method, and sample use IV concepts. *Bulletin of The Menninger Clinic*, 1956, *20*, 239–262.

Epilogue

One of our colleagues, Dr. Lisa Lewis, drew our attention to a portion of Tolstoy's *Resurrection*:

> It is one of the most common and generally accepted superstitions to attribute some particular leading quality to every man—to say of him that he is kind, wicked, wise, foolish, energetic, or dull. This is wrong. We may say of a man that he is more frequently kind than cruel, wise than foolish, energetic than apathetic, or vice versa—but it could never be true to say of one man that he is kind or wise, and of another that he is wicked or foolish. Yet this is our method of classifying mankind, and a very false method it is. Men are like rivers. The water is alike in all of them; but every river is narrow in some places and wide in others; here swift and there sluggish, here clear and there turbid; cold in winter and warm in summer. The same may be said of men. Every man bears within himself the germs of every human quality, displaying all in turn; and a man can often seem unlike himself— yet he still remains the same man.

What Tolstoy teaches is what we have sought to demonstrate with this collection of papers: That an understanding of people must go beyond the general and address the individual in all the manifold shifting states and conditions which characterize and particularize a person's life and troubles, if understanding is to meaningfully precede treatment.

Menninger et al. (1963) are unequivocal in their view on this matter:

> We, the authors, vigorously oppose the view that treatment, other than first aid, should proceed before or without diagnosis. On the contrary, we feel that diagnosis is today more important than ever. The very fact that psychiatric designations have become so meaningless by conflicting usage makes it more rather than less necessary that we approach the specific problem of illness with a cautious, careful scrutiny and appraisal that has characterized the best medical science since the early days. It is still necessary to know in advance, to plan as logically as we can, what kind of interference with a human life we propose to make. (p.6)

Another colleague, Dr. Irwin Rosen, reviewed our selection of papers and wrote the following note about them:

371

While they demonstrate not only the importance of recognizing and respecting the uniqueness and complexity of the individual patient, they do not flinch from suggesting that diagnostic categories (labels to some) do provide ways of bringing past clinical experience to current problems with which they are conceptually and theoretically linked. The plea here is not against diagnostic categories but for their optimal use.

Indeed, we do not wish to imply that an emphasis on exquisite sensitivity to the individual comes at the expense of classificatory schemata which allow understanding to be meaningfully ordered and hence comprehensible. In fact, is not such classifying a necessary (though not sufficient) part of diagnostic understanding?

> A clinician does not have to forego attention to an individual's uniqueness simply because he identifies some characteristics that the individual shares in common with other people and which suggest some diagnostic classification. How an individual is like other people and how he is different from them are complementary bits of information that the clinician can and should use together in his efforts to understand and help his patients. It furthermore cannot be overlooked that the price of disavowing classification can be very steep. As soon as similarities between people as expressed in classificatory labels are dispensed with, cumulative clinical wisdom becomes impossible. (Weiner, 1972, p. 538)

Our point is that such classifying should be a beginning point, not an end one. The 1980s have ushered in a new classification of mental disturbance (Spitzer and Williams, 1980). Such a schema can serve as a beginning framework with which to locate the individual, analogous to Holt's view that ". . . diagnoses are not addresses of buildings into which people may be put, but landmarks with respect to which people may be located" (1968, p. 14).

Doctor Rosen also noted that this volume could be castigated because it does not address psychopharmacological and other burgeoning medical-biological approaches to diagnosis and treatment. However, he was quick to add, "I believe that such critics will have missed the essential point of this anthology which is not to posit one treatment approach against another but is rather to urge that *any* therapeutic endeavor be based upon a thorough psychological understanding of what is wrong with (and right with) the patient."

In short, what these papers illustrate is not so much a particular technique of diagnostic practice and treatment but an overarching orientation to the process of diagnosing and treating. Yet, as we end, we confess that the "elusive connection" of our title still is less than firmly made. This collection demonstrates how worthwhile is that search. And so we hope this book challenges the reader to extend and refine the quest for the elusive connection.

REFERENCES

Holt, R. Editor's foreword. In *Diagnostic psychological testing* by D. Rapaport, M. Gill & R. Schafer. Rev. ed. R. Holt (Ed.). New York: International Universities Press, 1968.

Menninger, K., Mayman, M., & Pruyser, P. *The vital balance.* New York: Viking Press, 1963.

Spitzer, R. & Williams, J. Classification of mental disorders and DSM-III. In H. Kaplan, A. Freedman, & B. Sadock (Eds.), *Comprehensive textbook of psychiatry.* 3rd ed. Baltimore: Williams and Wilkins, 1980. (Chapter 14.1, pp. 1035–1072.)

Weiner, I. Does psychodiagnosis have a future? *Journal of Personality Assessment,* 1972, *36,* 534–546.

Index

Action, in psychotherapy, 313-317
Activity therapy, analysis of, 275-282
  prescribing, 264-274
Admission procedures, psychiatric hospital, 243-263
Affect, cognition vs., 304-306
Alliance, diagnostic, 36, 224-226
  group psychotherapy and therapeutic, 349-350
  testing, 92, 102
  see also Diagnostic partnership
Assessment, communicating results of diagnostic, 191-208

Beginnings, psychology of, 251-261
Behavior modification, 21-23, 34
  psychoanalysis and, 285-298
Borderline personality disorder, 338-354

Case examples:
  admission procedures, 249-251, 252-254
  borderline patients in group psychotherapy, 342-346
  diagnostic process, 45-50
  diagnostic team practice, 71-82
  diagnostic understanding, 186-189, 222-223
  early memories, 128-130
  ego states, 151-155
  idealization of insight, 306
  insight as defense, 317-318
  masochism, 117-120
  milieu therapy, 268-272
  negative reaction to insight, 309
  psychiatric evaluation, 24, 39, 45-50
  psychological testing & treatment outcome, 210-216, 226-227, 364-370
  relationship factors in psychotherapy, 311
  resistance to treatment recommendation, 44
  schizophrenic thought organization, object relations and Rorschach test responses, 162-170
  tester-patient interaction, 97-99
  time-limited psychotherapy, 328-329, 331
Casework, diagnosis in, 75-77
Change, insight and psychotherapeutic, 299-327
Character formation, early memories and, 122-140
Character organization, diagnostic triangle of, 40-43
Chess, analysis of, 275-282
Children, early memories of, 124-126
Classification, diagnosis and nosological, 27-29
  language of psychiatric, 58-59
  see also Labeling
Collaboration, diagnostic, 10-13, 69-82
Communication, in chess, 277
  by consulting psychologist, 220-229
  defensive, 198
  of diagnostic assessment results, 185-208
  in hospital admissions procedure, 255-261
  privileged, 230-236
  of test report in psychotherapy, 209-219

Confidentiality, of psychological test
    reports, 230-236
Consultant, psychiatric team, 79-82
Consultation, boundaries between treatment
    and, 227-228
  relationships in diagnostic, 193-199,
    220-229

Deficit, in schizophrenic thinking, 157-
  159
Dehumanization, of hospital admission pro-
    cedures, 245-251
  in medical diagnosis, 5-6
Determinism, psychic, 33-34
Devaluation and overidealization, by border-
    line patients, 344-345
Deviations, in psychoanalytic techniques,
    318-324
Diagnosis, controversial issues in, 19-32
  decision making in, 7-10
  unreliability of, 28-29
Diagnostic assessment, communicating
    results of, 191-208
Diagnostic language, pitfalls in, 61-65
Diagnostic partnership, 9-13, 224
Diagnostic process, abuse of, 24-25
  humanistic values of, 5-17
  language pitfalls in, 55-68
  in psychiatric evaluations, 18-54
  team concept in, 69-82
Diagnostic testing, early memories as a form
    of, 122-140
  interpersonal context of, 87-106
  of masochistic character disorder, 107-
    121
  psychoanalytic study of self-organization
    with, 141-156
  schizophrenic thought organization, object
    relations and, 157-179
  see also Psychological testing
Diagnostic understanding, communication
    of, 185-236
  and treatment implications, 237-370
Dreams, memories and, 122-123

Early memories, 122-140, 145-154
Education, milieu therapy as, 268-269
Ego psychology, psychoanalytic, 141-156
Ego-strengthening activities, 269-271
Encounter groups, diagnosis and, 19-23

psychoanalysis and, 285-298
End setting, in psychotherapy, 328-337
Environment, therapeutic aspects of
    hospital, 264-274
Erotization, of relationships by borderline
    patients, 344
Evaluation, diagnostic process in
    psychiatric, 18-54
  of masochistic character disorders, 107-
    121
Evolution, of psychoanalytic theory, 301-
    304, 318-324, 338-339

Fantasies, early memories as, 123 124, 127-
    128

Group psychotherapy, for borderline and
    narcissistic patients, 338-354

History, writing of, 124-125
History-taking, diagnosis and, 20-21, 36,
    41, 43-45, 48
Holding environment, therapy groups as,
    346
Hospitals, see Psychiatric hospitals
Humanism, in medicine, 5-17
Humanistic values, in diagnosis, 5-17

Idealization and devaluation, by borderline
    patients, 344-345
Insight, therapeutic change and, 299-327
Intellectual processes, in chess, 279-280
Intellectualism, in diagnosis, 19-21
  in psychoanalysis, 304-305
Interactions, in diagnostic testing interview,
    87-106
  milieu therapy and therapeutic, 271-
    272
  patient-examiner, 224-226
  patient-hospital staff, 251-263
  patient-interviewer, 36, 45-50
Interdisciplinary differences, 195-196
Interdisciplinary teamwork, diagnostic
    partnership and, 10-13, 69-82
Internalization, in group psychotherapy,
    349-350
Interpersonal relationships, insight and,
    309-311
Interpersonal themes, in early memories,
    131-136, 147-151